ANGLO–FRENCH R
THE LATE EIGHTEENTH CEN

This work, intended to commemorate the centenary of the *Entente Cordiale* in 2004, examines aspects of Anglo–French relations since the late eighteenth century, when both Britain and France were pre-eminent great powers at war with one another, through to the post-Second World War period when both had become rival second class powers in face of American and Soviet dominance. The chapters in this book examine and illuminate the nature of the Anglo–French relationship at certain periods during the last two hundred years, both in peacetime and in war, and include political, economic, diplomatic, military and strategic considerations and influences. While the impact of Anglo–French relations is centred essentially on the European context, other areas are also considered including the Middle East, Africa and the North Atlantic. The elements of conflict, rivalry and cooperation in Anglo–French relations are also highlighted whether in peace or war.

This book was previously published as a special issue of *Diplomacy and Statecraft*.

Glyn Stone is Professor of International History at The University of the West of England, Bristol.

T. G. Otte is Senior Lecturer in Diplomatic History at the University of East Anglia.

ANGLO–FRENCH RELATIONS SINCE THE LATE EIGHTEENTH CENTURY

Edited by Glyn Stone and T. G. Otte

Routledge
Taylor & Francis Group

LONDON AND NEW YORK

First published 2008
by Routledge
2 Park Square, Milton Park, Abingdon, Oxon, OX14 4RN

Simultaneously published in the USA and Canada
by Routledge
270 Madison Avenue, New York, NY 10016

Routledge is an imprint of the Taylor & Francis Group,
an informa business

Transferred to Digital Printing 2009

© 2008 Glyn Stone and T. G. Otte

Typeset in Times by RefineCatch Ltd, Bungay, Suffolk NR35 1EF

British Library Cataloguing in Publication Data
A catalogue record for this book is available from the British Library

Library of Congress Cataloguing in Publication Data
A catalog record has been requested

ISBN 10: 0-415-39578-X (hbk)
ISBN 10: 0-415-49500-8 (pbk)

ISBN 13: 978-0-415-39578-6 (hbk)
ISBN 13: 978-0-415-49500-4 (pbk)

Publisher's Note
The publisher has gone to great lengths to ensure the quality of this reprint
but points out that some imperfections in the original may be apparent.

CONTENTS

INTRODUCTION: THE *ENTENTE CORDIALE* AND THE SEA SERPENT

Philip Bell

Serge Sazonov, the Russian foreign minister before the Great War, once said of the Triple Entente between Britain, France and Russia that its existence "was no better authenticated than that of a sea serpent". In this centenary year, I am tempted to transfer this remark to the Entente Cordiale. Sightings of this creature are frequently reported. Photographs show Queen Elizabeth II in conversation with President Jacques Chirac. Prime Minister Tony Blair has addressed President Chirac on TV as "Jacques," which sounds terribly cordial. The royal Mint has struck coins bearing the inscription "Entente Cordiale 1904–2004," and depicting a strange double-headed figure made up of Britannia and Marianne. And yet a nagging doubt persists: is there really solid evidence that the *Entente Cordiale* exists?

In one respect we must accept at once that the existence of the Entente is indeed better authenticated than that of the sea serpent. In this very building (The National Archives) we can hold in our hands certain documents signed on 8 April 1904: a convention respecting Newfoundland and West and Central Africa; a declaration respecting Egypt and Morocco; secret articles attached to this declaration; and a declaration concerning Siam, Madagascar and the New Hebrides—this last document being firmly hand-written in a good round script. These documents embodied a number of colonial deals, reached according to the methods of the old diplomacy. The British were to have a free hand in Egypt, which they had occupied since 1882 but where they had been constantly harassed by French obstruction, and the French were to have a free hand in Morocco, which they intended to occupy at some stage in the future. The agreements also defined boundaries between French and British colonies in West Africa, allotted spheres of influence in Siam, agreed on a condominium in the New Hebrides, and settled disputes over fishing rights off Newfoundland. All these matters had been discussed in strict

This was originally delivered as the keynote lecture at the Entente Centenary Conference in June 2004.

secrecy, and with little regard to the wishes of the peoples concerned, or of the existing rulers of Morocco, Egypt or Siam.

These agreements also marked a move in European politics. Foreign minister Théophile Delcassé intended that they should lead on to an alliance with Britain, to strengthen the French position against Germany. The British did not intend to go down that road, and Lord Lansdowne was not prepared to incur the formal obligations of an alliance with France. But during the very next year, 1905, Lansdowne himself proposed close consultation with the French, directed against Germany. His successor as foreign secretary, Sir Edward Grey, made the entente with France the basis of his policy. Secret military staff conversations worked out detailed arrangements to send a British expeditionary force to France in the event of war with Germany, and naval talks agreed that the French fleet should hold the western Mediterranean while the Royal Navy concentrated on the North Sea. The possibility of war against Germany on the side of France was well in sight, though by no means certain.

The Entente was thus in its origins and early years a colonial deal and a combination against Germany. Of these two aspects not a shred remains. The British and French empires have vanished almost completely, and with them the imperial cast of mind which was still strong in 1904. The under secretary at the Foreign Office, introducing the debate on the Anglo–French agreement in the House of Commons spoke of "the inevitable dissolution of ancient barbarisms when brought into contact with the march of Western civilisation"—which is not a sentiment we hear very often nowadays. The secret diplomacy which produced the agreements is also remembered with distaste, and was supposedly abandoned, as early as 1919, in favour of open covenants openly arrived at. (It is true that neither imperialism nor secret diplomacy has entirely vanished from the face of the earth, but we must let that pass.) The colonial deal between Britain and France is a thing of the past, and remembered only to be deplored.

As for Britain and France combining against Germany, such an association is now inconceivable. The boot is on the other foot. Under the terms of the Franco–German Treaty of Paris of 1963 the French and Germans hold summit meetings twice a year, and in practice meet more frequently than that. In April 1969 President Charles de Gaulle, in the month of his resignation, told Maurice Schumann, the one-time broadcaster for *France Libre*, that no French foreign policy could be conceived which was not founded on "the irreversibility of Franco-German reconciliation." Less formally, he remarked on another occasion: "Europe is Germany and ourselves. Les autres, c 'est les légumes." (At the time, the vegetables were Italy and the Benelux countries.) Giscard d'Estaing, in his seven years as president, held the prescribed 14 summit meetings with the West German Chancellor, plus another 10 less formal meetings. Later, President

François Mitterrand and Chancellor Helmut Kohl always had breakfast together at summit meetings of the EEC, to plan out the day's work. Jacques Attali once observed with delight that they agreed to nominate Jacques Delors as the next president of the European Commission without even mentioning his name—"A masterpiece of dialogue between two allies who had no need to go into details to understand one another." This close Franco–German relationship deserves some emphasis, because Britain usually finds itself outside this magic circle. We are sometimes told that one prime minister or another has joined the club, but it never quite comes off. An article in *The Economist* on the centenary of the Entente stated simply that "France and Germany are enmeshed in a way that would be unthinkable for the French and British." The British must get used to the Franco–German couple.

The two main characteristics of the Entente of 1904, the colonial deals and anti-German combination, have vanished. The Entente of a hundred years ago no longer exists. What about the Entente today? On big foreign policy issues, Britain and France have been in opposition. When the Americans attacked the Taliban regime in Afghanistan at the end of 2001, Britain joined in with substantial forces, while France remained no more than a cautious and limited participant. In 2003 Britain took a large part in the American invasion and subsequent occupation of Iraq, while France opposed the war and followed a separate diplomatic line at the United Nations. This difference in policy continues to this day, and has at times been accompanied by personal friction between foreign ministers and between Prime Minister Blair and President Chirac. The triangular relationship between Britain, France and the United States, which has never been easy, is going through a particularly difficult phase. (Incidentally, it was with a real *frisson* that I read in Paul Cambon's letters the comment he made in August 1904 as ambassador at London that the British "never lose an opportunity to humiliate themselves before the Americans." A hundred years later a Frenchman might well say *Plus ça change.*

The issue of European integration provides another bone of contention. In 1999 Blair wrote in a foreword to a pamphlet on *Britain and France: Partners for the Millenium* that the two countries were "committed partners in the European Union." He forebore to add that they differ markedly in the nature and degree of their commitment. Even with a prime minister who is in principle in favour of joining the eurozone, the British government has not yet put the question to a referendum. Britain and France are uneasy partners at best.

The military aspect of Franco–British relations is in better shape. There is a considerable degree of cooperation between the armed services of the two countries. Since 1997 the chiefs of staff and their deputies have met twice a year. The military staffs hold annual talks; the navies join in various exercises; a joint Air Group was set up in 1998. And while the staff talks before 1914 were kept secret, the existence of current military contacts is published for all to see on the Ministry of Defence website. The two countries have been willing to cooperate, up to a point, in setting up a European Rapid Reaction Force, an idea agreed upon at a Franco-British summit meeting at St. Malo in December 1998, though in practice the rate of progress has been far from rapid. It has become something of a commonplace to say that the organization of Europe for military purposes cannot be envisaged except in terms of Franco–British cooperation, which is probably true. The trouble is that such cooperation is much less impor-tant than it once was. The British and French staffs work closely together, but the forces they can deploy are small in number and power compared to those of the United States. A close military cooperation which might have been immensely valuable before 1939 is now of only marginal significance.

Outside high politics and military affairs, there is the remarkable phenomenon that people are crossing the Channel in vast numbers. In the year 2000 there were nearly 12 million visits from the United Kingdom to France, and 3 million in the opposite direction — a striking statistic which shows, or perhaps only confirms, that the British are keener to travel to France than the other way about. Many of the British visits were simply day trips to Calais to buy drink, but there were (and are) many British people who are buying property in France, whether as holiday homes or permanent residences; and the new British property-owners come from a far wider range of society than those who lived in Nice or Cannes before 1914, "when the Riviera was ours." In the other direction, Britain has lit-tle appeal to French holiday home buyers. (I am still waiting for some French equivalent of Peter Mayle, who will write a best-seller about the delights of a year in Yorkshire.) But the French are coming to work in Britain in increasing numbers, and the Eurostar has made London an attractive posting for employees of French companies.

How much these movements of people, and the changing attitudes that go with them, affect relations between the two countries is doubtful. By getting along together, living and working in one another's countries, and through many daily contacts, the British and French peoples are probably closer together now than at any other period, when links were mainly between elites; yet this leaves the political problems largely untouched.

Nothing remains of the Entente of 1904, with its colonial deals and anti-German motives. At present, relations between the British and French governments display a good deal of friction, only partly tempered (if at all) by the mingling of their peoples. What about the century that lies between? There would be little point in going through a hundred years of Franco-British relations, even at a good round trot; and in any case there are many papers to follow. But no-one will dispute that there have been ups and downs! Rather strangely, aspects of the two World Wars figure on the plus side. On state visits, when the leaders of the two countries set out to emphasize what unites them, speech-writers turn repeatedly towards wartime experiences. During the royal visit to France by George VI in 1938, the French radio broadcast an "Ode à l' Angleterre" in honour of the British war dead—"Soldats anglais couchés dessous une croix blanche/Héros de la Bassée et vainqueurs de Vimy." In 1992, during another royal visit to France, the French premier, Pierre Bérégovoy, made a moving speech about the young men of both countries who died for liberty and were not forgotten. In April 2004, president Chirac's speech at the state banquet during the Queen's visit to Paris referred to Britain protecting the flame of French resistance during the years of Nazi occupation; and the Queen conferred a decoration on an 89-year old British woman who had been an accomplished saboteur with the Resistance. The sentiments are doubtless real, and the honour certainly well deserved, but such memories fade with time, and comradeship in the World Wars is a wasting asset for the Entente.

The low points in Franco–British relations have been numerous, and sometimes virtually continuous. The Great War had its fair share of disputes between the Allies, and so did the Paris Peace Conference. Between the wars each country felt that the other was letting it down, often with much truth—the British made a separate naval agreement with Germany in 1935 without even informing the French; while during the Ethiopian crisis of 1935–6 the French denied support to Britain at crucial points. Michael Dockrill has devoted a book to *British Official Perceptions of France, 1936–1940*, which were sometimes comical, sometimes tragical, but rarely amicable! During the Second World War, relations between Prime Minister Winston Churchill and de Gaulle were often explosive, and one of their quarrels, on 4 June 1944, two days before D Day, left an enduring scar on relations between their two countries. De Gaulle understood Churchill to say that, in the event of disagreement between the United States and France, Britain would always choose the former, and that whenever there was a choice between Europe and "le grand large," Britain would choose "le grand large." This was not exactly what Churchill said, and certainly did not represent the essence of his thinking; but de Gaulle's impression of the occasion never faded. He was to recall it nearly 20 years later, when preparing to reject Britain's first application to join the EEC. President Chirac, who likes to think of himself as de Gaulle's heir, used the term "le grand large" earlier this year. The general picture was confirmed after the failure of the Suez expedition in 1956, when the British decided that never again must they act without American support or against American wishes, while the French were reinforced in their commitment to Europe.

There is no need to go on. The picture is distinctly bleak. The original bases for the Entente in 1904 have disappeared. Present relations between the British and French governments are badly strained. On the whole, the intervening hundred years have witnessed more disagreement than harmony between the two countries. Yet here we are, in the centenary year of the Entente, which is being marked in both countries by politicians, the media, and after our own fashion by historians. The substance of the *Entente Cordiale* appears threadbare, and yet the phrase is in constant use. Why is this? What accounts for the longevity of the phrase, and what sort of essence lies behind it? Are we looking for a sea serpent which we are not likely to find, or for a living creature which we can describe from observation? Let me look at how the two countries have seen one another at certain crucial points.

It is worth starting at the beginning, because from the start the agreements of April 1904 were not solely a matter of power politics, but were regarded in Britain as having a special character which transcended their workaday details. Sir Henry Campbell-Bannerman, the leader of the Liberal Party, described the agreement as "a great instrument for bringing together two neighbouring nations and two old rivals . . . and for promoting friendship and cooperation between the two nations of Europe most identified with progress and freedom." Arthur Balfour, the Conservative prime minister, wound up the debate in the Commons by claiming that "this great instrument will be looked back upon as the beginning of a new and happier era in our international relations." The Entente was thus launched on a wave of cross-party goodwill. By February 1914 the MPs who moved and seconded the Address at the opening of Parliament were only too happy, among the bitter strife over Home Rule, to find a non-controversial subject by welcoming the forthcoming visit by King George V and Queen Mary to France. One of the speakers referred to the cordial relations between the two countries, "which nature and temperament seem at once to mark out and to bring together as the vigilant parents of freedom and of justice." The visit itself marked the tenth anniversary of the Entente, and president Raymond Poincaré spoke of "the considered wishes of two powerful nations, equally attached to peace, equally passionately devoted to progress, equally accustomed to the ways of liberty. . . . After a long rivalry . . . France and Britain have learned to have affection for each other, to think alike and to unite their efforts." These words doubtless sound like platitudes and wishful thinking; but even in wishful thinking, it is well worth noting what people were wishing for.

Let us jump to 1944, the 40th year of the Entente. We remember it as the year of the great quarrel between Churchill and de Gaulle, which I have already mentioned. But it was also the year of a recovery of friendship. On the French side, Jacques Debu-Bridel, one of the earliest *résistants*, visited London in the autumn of 1944 and set down his impressions in a book, *Carthage n'est pas détruite*. He admired the voluntary discipline and civic spirit of the British people, and he found a sense of unity between Britain and France which sprang from a shared civilisation—or rather, "une seule et meme civilisation," which is more emphatic. At the same time, Pierre Bourdan was writing a much longer and more profound book on Britain and its people, *Perplexités et grandeur de Il 'Angleterre*. Bourdan was deeply impressed by the immense strength which Britain drew from its tradition and continuity, at that time almost unique in Europe, where almost every other country had suffered defeat, occupation or revolution. Yet he found that the British could also adapt their traditions, as they had succeeded in doing during the trials of war. He too was impressed by the common civilisation which bound Britain and France together. He wrote in his *carnets* when embarking for Normandy with General Philippe Leclerc's famous Second Armoured Division that he was leaving one of the last bastions of a civilisation "which was also our own." Now, no-one would claim that these two writers represented France, but even so they wrote for a substantial French readership, and they stood in a line of French writers who had interpreted Britain to their fellow-countrymen with a keen yet critical admiration—André Siegfried and Jacques Bardoux are obvious examples.

On the British side, there were a number of ardent Francophiles who had felt utterly bereft when France was defeated and occupied in 1940, but had never lost faith. Alexander Werth wrote in 1942 that "The future of Europe needs . . . a France whose creative genius will once again shine across the world after the years of twilight and darkness." After the Liberation, Raymond Mortimer, the literary editor of the *New Statesman*, devoted all his space in one issue to a discussion of the first non-clandestine number of *Les Lettres françaises*, while *Time and Tide* once gave up its books pages entirely to the publications of *Les Editions du Minuit*. It is striking that the editors concerned took it for granted that their readers would be happy with these arrangements. In October 1944 Charles Morgan (now, I think, a forgotten name, but then a literary star) visited Paris and heard his "Ode to France" declaimed at the *Comédie Française* in the presence of de Gaulle himself, and wrote to a friend "An Englishman can't ask much more of life." Incidentally (or not so incidentally), this glow of admiration for French culture came at the same time as British popular opinion was grumbling that the French in Normandy seemed to have plenty to eat, and that the autumn Paris fashion shows demonstrated an incurable frivolity.

These views across the Channel were in a broad sense characteristic of their time—which is I think now long past. A French elite admired British stability and civic virtue; a British elite admired French culture, and especially literature. Both were conscious of belonging to a common civilisation, which had just had a very close call. Both elites were, almost by definition, far removed from the concerns of most people, French and British, who were simply trying to live from day to day among the stresses of war, and for whom a country across the Channel might well have been on another planet.

Fast forward ten years, and we arrive at 1954 and the 50th anniversary of the *Entente Cordiale*, which was widely marked in both countries. The French National Assembly sent a message of goodwill to the House of Commons where Anthony Eden, Clement Attlee, Clement Davies and Jenny Lee all spoke warmly of the Entente; so cross-party support was strongly maintained. The Queen and the President of the Republic exchanged messages, and so did the two prime ministers, Joseph Laniel and Churchill, and the two foreign ministers, Georges Bidault and Eden. These formal courtesies are worth emphasizing, because they showed that the Entente had a high profile in politics and in the public mind. The tone of comments in the press, which were plentiful, looked back to wartime comradeship; made good resolutions to forge a new entente; and offered mixed speculations about the future. In Paris there was a widespread hope that the British would restrain the Americans from rash actions—a long article in *Combat* argued that Britain was the best guarantor of peace, because the British would not let the Americans drag them (and others) into an ideological crusade. *The Times* judged that the Entente faced a serious difficulty on the question of the extent to which Britain could or would be "continentally involved"; while the French journalist "Perti-nax," writing in the *Telegraph*, wondered whether the roots of the Entente were being severed because France had embarked on an experiment in the fusion of sovereignty in the Coal and Steel Community, to which the British were obsessively opposed. These proved farsighted comments. In our own day, the British government, far from restraining the Americans, has joined them in a sort of ideological crusade in Iraq; while the question of the degree of British involvement with the continent has never been fully settled.

By the time the 90th anniversary of the Entente was reached in 1994 it was plain that doubts and troubles had accumulated. *The Times*, in a lead-ing article, felt obliged to point out that "France is, in fact, the friend, ally and partner of Great Britain, and not her enemy"—something which could no longer be taken for granted, but had to be said. *Le Monde* marked the occasion with a long article, noting that in recent years England had succumbed to her old temptation of isolation from Europe, while France had achieved reconciliation with Germany; the two coun-tries had thus turned away from one another, and the Entente seemed no more than a golden but fleeting moment of friendship. A former editor of

Le Monde, André Fontaine, contributed a long article to *The Economist*, observing that the two countries were each in its own way insular—Britain because it was geographically an island, France because of an insular cast of mind. Each was acutely conscious of its individuality, and "To affirm one's singularity is, by definition, to cultivate one's differences." Among those differences, Fontaine seized particularly upon language, which created crucial barriers of resentment on the French side and incomprehension on the British. The French were anxious, even desperate, to protect the standing and influence of their language, an attitude which the British regarded with an indifference which only exasperated the French further. Charles Bremner, the long-serving *Times* correspondent in Paris, took up the same point: "French civilisation is being drowned by its ancestral Anglophone rival," and French civilisation was afraid of Anglo-Saxon (meaning mostly American) cultural supremacy. Europe was still a point of conflict. Fontaine appealed to the French and British to stop wrangling about Europe, and instead to "try to settle on a common answer to this question of what Europe should become." This was unlikely. Since the Second World War, the French had thrown themselves into building a Europe created in their own image; most of the French political establishment believed that Britain did not really want to take part in this new Europe, which would have to be achieved against British opposition.

Things did not seem much changed by the opening of the Channel Tunnel. This was the end of an old story—one historian of the Tunnel counted no fewer than 138 projects for a fixed link, whether tunnel or bridge, since the first in 1802; and the fate of these projects had formed a barometer of the state of relations between the two countries. When the deed was finally accomplished, the French press with almost one voice proclaimed that England was no longer an island. The British newspapers tended to agree, but were not sure whether they welcomed the new state of affairs. Anyway, what did the tunnel signify? The *Guardian* brought out a special joint edition with *Libération*, in which the *Guardian's* editor predicted that in the future the date of the Tunnel's opening would be engraved on peoples' memories, while that of the Normandy landings would become merely an obscure anniversary. (I wonder whether the date, 6 May 1994, is indeed engraved on our memories?) François Bédarida, on the other hand, doubted whether the Tunnel would have much effect on attitudes on either side of the Channel. Rivalries between the two countries were the legacy of history and a part of national identity. Metaphorically, he wrote, the train of prejudice was still on the rails, and it was unlikely that the TGV would actually displace it. This has proved very near the mark. The Tunnel has become prosaic. For two centuries a dream for some and a nightmare for others, it has proved to be merely a slightly unusual stretch of railway line.

So we return to the present day. What is the best that politicians and the press now find to say about relations between Britain and France? In 2003 Blair and Chirac declared at Le Touquet that "There is more that unites us than divides us"; though they did not say exactly what. Jack Straw, then foreign secretary, asserted that our countries share the values of democracy, human rights and the rule of law, which they aspire to extend across the globe. Dominique de Villepin, who until recently was the French foreign minister and is now prime minister, has assured us that in Franco–British relations "the search for agreement and the habit of dialogue are firmly entrenched," and that we are able to surmount differences thanks to the friendship that unites us and the values we share. The *Guardian* claimed in a leading article (5 April 2004) that the Entente embodied the principle that disputes between states are better settled by diplomacy than by war, and that Britain and France are nations with shared problems, interests and values.

It is pretty thin stuff. Is there anything of more substance? The *Guardian* has again got together with *Libération* to produce a special supplement for the centenary. One article claimed that Chirac and Blair had developed "a surprising rapport," but spent most of its space describing their disagreements and personal quarrels, and ended by quoting an unenthusiastic Downing Street official as saying that "We are two countries who are condemned to live together." There was a long article by Peter Mayle, telling us that he finds France a wonderful place to live in; and two pages of exchange articles by cultural critics, which to my mind shed little light on a common culture. The *Independent* also produced a special supplement, including a long article on the middle-class English invasion of Normandy; a much shorter article on two French families living in London, where they found the prices high and the people cold; and (believe it or not) an interview with Peter Mayle. And yet, as I began by saying, there has been no lack of visits and meetings, and positive showers of compliments.

Are we left with the sea serpent? Perhaps so. It has always seemed to me that people *want* to believe in the Loch Ness monster, and it is apparently the case that various people *want* to believe in the *Entente Cordiale*; which raises the question of why they wish to do so. There is another question: what is the entente that people want to believe in? And here I must change the analogy. We are not looking at the sea serpent, but at Proteus, Neptune's herdsman who could change his shape at will. The name *Entente Cordiale* has remained unchanged for a hundred years—the index to *The Times* introduced a special heading for it in January 1905. This represents a remarkable triumph for the power of a name, of which any public relations man would be proud—as far as I know, the phrase goes back to King Louis Philippe in 1844, though there are other contenders. What's in a name? Rather a lot. To give someone or something a name is an act of powerful symbolism—strong magic, even. The attraction of the name *Entente Cordiale* seems irresistible, and it seems that there is still some adhesive quality at work. But the meaning attached to the name has changed repeatedly. Even in this brief survey, we have observed: in 1904, imperialism, power politics and common values; in 1944, cultural admiration and a common civilisation; in 1954, wartime memories tempered by unease about European integration; in 1994, fading wartime memories plus hopes pinned to the Channel Tunnel; and in 2004 common values plus British property-owners in the Dordogne. All these different aspects have been subsumed under the heading of *Entente Cordiale*, which is used to signify Franco–British relations in their better moments and seen in their best light. The name will doubtless be with us for some time yet, and it signifies something more than a mythical sea-serpent; but what it represents is a Protean figure, a shape-shifter, hard to get hold of.

What do we expect of an entente between states? We may put it like this: a similar political and cultural outlook; compatible (not necessarily identical) interests; and a broad confidence in one another. Britain and France still share a common civilisation, and have a marked similarity of political and cultural outlook, and much shared history, even if it is a story of conflict as much as harmony. But how far are their interests compatible, on the important issues of European integration and relations with the United States? How much confidence do they have in one another, and how much doubt or plain antagonism arises between them? The answers, it seems to me, are not encouraging. There remains some foundation for an entente, but it is a slender basis for the superstructure which is sometimes placed upon it.

TALLEYRAND AND ENGLAND, 1792–1838: A REINTERPRETATION

Alan Sked

Talleyrand has always had a very good press in the English-speaking world. John Holland Rose in his biography of Napoleon wrote of him that "he was destined to achieve the greatest reputation of the age."[1] Sir Charles Petrie called him "the shrewdest brain in Europe."[2] Herbert Fisher described him as "the shrewdest head in the French Empire."[3] According to Sir Henry Bulwer: "In this [National] Assembly, M. de Talleyrand was the most conspicuous figure after Mirabeau, as he was hereafter in the Empire the most conspicuous personage after Napoleon."[4] The Duke of Wellington famously defended him in the House of Lords after an attack on him by Castlereagh's half-brother in 1831 with the words: "no man could have conducted himself with more firmness and ability with regard to his own country, or with more uprightness and honour in all his communications with the ministers of other countries, than the Prince de Talleyrand."[5] Talleyrand was especially touched by this, as he told Lord Alvanley the next day that Wellington had been "the only public man in the world who had ever said a good word for him."[6] The American historian Crane Brinton in the preface to his study of *The Lives of Talleyrand* was disarmingly frank about his approach: "I should warn the reader that I have come to like Talleyrand and to think very highly of him. I shall not mind very much if I am accused of trying to whitewash the old double-dealer . . . I do not think I like him *because* he was—at times—a liar and a thief; nor to be quite honest, *in spite of* his being—at times—a liar and a thief. His thieving is to me pretty much unimportant in a man who did so much that I regard as useful in the world."[7]

Talleyrand's fascination can be attributed to many things, especially his wit, his style, his nonchalance, his epigrams—perhaps even his policies. The common image of him is that of a living waxworks model standing absolutely still before ending a conversation with either a devastating piece of sarcasm or a pointed *bon mot*. In Rose's words: "his gaze, intellectual yet composed, blenched not when he uttered a scathing criticism or a diplomatic lie: his deep penetrating voice gave force to all his words and the curl of his lip or the scornful lifting of his eyebrows sometimes disconcerted an opponent more than his biting sarcasm. In brief, this disinherited noble, this unfrocked priest, this disenchanted Liberal, was the complete expression of the inimitable society of the old regime, when quickened intellectually by Voltaire and dulled by the Terror."[8] The French historian, Albert Sorel, although he called Talleyrand "the least romantic of men," wrote much the same: "Talleyrand was an incomparable conversationalist. He had a quick and ready reply. He excelled at summarising a situation in a phrase, a thought in a word. Grand seigneur, philosophe, prelate at court, diplomat, he had refined through culture and constant use these two qualities he possessed to such a high degree: the taste that makes a writer and the tact that makes a statesman."[9] Curiously, however, despite Sorel's famous praise for Talleyrand's literary style, Talleyrand's main critics were the giants of French literature: Chateaubriand, Victor Hugo and St. Beuve.[10]

This is not to say that he had no other critics. In fact, he had many and most were famous Frenchmen. Carnot said of him: "He brings with him all the vices of the old regime, without having been able to acquire any of the virtues of the new one. He has no fixed principles; he changes them as he does his linen, and takes them according to the wind of the day—a philosopher, when philosophy is the mode; a republican now, because that is necessary in order to become anything. Tomorrow he will declare for absolute monarchy, if he can make anything out of it. I don't want him at any price."[11] Mirabeau called him "this vile, base trickster,"[12] and wrote: "It is dirt and money that he wants. For money he would sell his soul—and he would be right for he would be trading muck for gold."[13] Chénier, who summoned him back from exile wrote: "This limp-foot, without respect for his bishopric, is like a sponge which sucks up every liquid into which it is dropped, but unlike the sponge, gives nothing back. Here he is recalled from exile yesterday, and proposing prescriptions for tomorrow. If the Directory wants blood, look out for your head—Maurice will not refuse it."[14] Chateaubriand said: "When Monsieur Talleyrand is not conspiring, he is making corrupt bargains."[15] Gouverneur Morris, who had represented America in Paris, said: "This man appears to me polished, cold, tricky, ambitious and bad."[16] Morris was probably completely right about Talleyrand.

Recently, however, after years of neglect, the French have been reassessing Talleyrand and in February 2004, for example, a huge international conference was held at the Palais du Luxembourg, under the auspices of the French Foreign Minister, to celebrate the 250th anniversary of his birth. Its title was *Talleyrand, Prince des Négociateurs.*[17] This author was invited to talk on Talleyrand and Metternich and rather disgraced himself by arguing that Talleyrand, far from being a prince among negotiators, had resigned twice as foreign minister, once under the Directory and once under Napoleon, because no one listened to what he had to say. Talleyrand was also corrupt, a traitor who, for hundreds of thousands of francs, had sold the French army's order of battle in Spain and Germany to Austria immediately before war broke out with that country in 1809, a traitor who had conspired with Alexander I of Russia to defeat Napoleon's diplomatic aims at Erfurt, and who had offered to sell Alexander the French war plans for one and a half million francs.[18] All of this was simply ignored in Paris and Professor Tulard, the president of the conference and France's leading expert on Napoleon, while agreeing in his introductory lecture that Talleyrand had committed treason, merely brushed this aside as "cynicism." Talleyrand's true admirers would argue in any case, that his actions should be interpreted as those of a statesman whose true policy was to bring peace to Europe, with or without Napoleon, establish a just equilibrium between the powers and base future peace on Anglo–French cooperation. If this meant betraying Napoleonic France, so what? Peace and Europe were higher causes. And in an age of "good Europeans," why should anyone disagree, especially if Britain were to benefit?

The most powerful statement of this case in my opinion was put forward in Oxford by the former French foreign minister Maurice Schumann in the Zaharoff lecture for 1976–7, entitled *Talleyrand, Prophet of the Entente Cordiale.* Schumann quoted Michelet who had written after meeting Talleyrand in 1831: "England is the world's ideal for him; he is so English it makes us tremble."[19] The French historian Émile Dard, believed that the greatest intellectual influence on Talleyrand had been Voltaire and that as a youth Talleyrand had inherited Voltaire's anglophilia.[20] Certainly by the 1780s Talleyrand seems to have accepted the free trade ideals of Adam Smith and after 1786 he became a supporter of the commercial treaty of that year between England and France. Yet Schumann argues that "a good understanding between England and France" as part of a general European equilibrium became the central plank of Talleyrand's diplomacy and diplomatic ideals from 1792 until his death: "He did indeed have an unchanging doctrine. He never modified it and he never deviated from it. When forced by circumstances, he provisionally gave up following it, but he neither renounced it nor forgot it. His philosophy was often held in check, but he never changed that philosophy."[21]

Four texts, according to Schumann, the first and last almost forty years apart, but all of them almost unchanging in content, provide evidence for this assertion. The first is Talleyrand's famous memorandum written in London on 25 November 1792 to the new French Republic and preserved by Danton, which advocated that France should surrender all her annexations, particularly Belgium, in order to maintain British neutrality. "All territorial extensions are but the cruel games of political madness," stated Talleyrand.[22] Then in August 1797, as foreign minister of the Directory, he commented on the annexation of Belgium to France by the Treaty of Campo Formio in the following terms: "The quarrel which is momentarily stilled by the discomfiture of the vanquished is not of a kind to be definitely concluded by arms, so long as hatred persists. . . . What is a peace treaty? It is a treaty which in settling all matters of dissension, ensures not only that war gives way to peace but that hatred gives way to friendship."[23] It was therefore essential to settle all matters of dissension by making peace with Britain. Again on 17 October 1805 after Austria's capitulation at Ulm, Talleyrand sent Napoleon a memorandum inviting Napoleon "to stretch out a hand to the vanquished" and begging him to spare Austria, since otherwise the Russians "as masters of Hungary" would become "all-powerful in Europe."[24] Finally, on 27 November 1830, as French ambassador in London he argued in his first despatch to Paris that "France must be on good terms with a few powers. . . . Our links of kinship will henceforth be formed by the progress of civilisation. . . . This leads us naturally to consider England as the power with whom it is convenient for us to maintain the closest relations. . . . England is the only power which, like ourselves, sincerely wishes for peace. . . . It is with England that France should seek to act."[25]

This constantly adhered-to "philosophy" that Schumann discerned throughout Talleyrand's career was based, he argued, on two ideas, one economic and one ideological. The first was based on the fact that Talleyrand had become, like Mirabeau, a supporter of the 1786 free-trade treaty with England that had been inspired by Quesnay and Dupont de Nemours. Pallain, editor of his correspondence from England in 1792, confirms this: Talleyrand, along with Mirabeau, Dupont de Nemours, Panchaud etc., belonged a group of disciples "devoted to a new science, 'economics,' decided partisans of peace and the improvement of human life, for whom the great thing was to assure above everything the commercial and industrial development of France and for whom it was a commonplace to say that peace between England and France commanded the peace of Europe."[26] Hence Talleyrand's report of 25 November 1792 had set out the thesis that a great industrial revolution had begun in Europe with England and France playing first and second roles respectively. The French revolution had accelerated this process in France by abolishing internal customs barriers and corporations thus benefiting free trade and free labour. The question was would England and France become rivals or would they cooperate? Talleyrand seemed to think that they could carve up the world between them (with France controlling the Mediterranean).[27]

Talleyrand also had his ideological reasons. Unlike Mirabeau, in June 1790 he had supported Robespierre's proposal that the Constituent Assembly should declare France's frontiers to be "eternal" and that there should be a "renunciation of conquests"—both proposals being overwhelmingly defeated when put to the vote. Moreover, he always said that Britain and France should adhere to "common principles"—"reasonably liberal principles" in order to "draw the bonds linking the two countries even closer."[28] In a letter dated 2 July 1799 he stated: "It is in the nature of a free state to desire that other peoples be called to enjoy a good which, once it has spread wider, promises to Europe and to the world the extinction of a large part of the disputes which ravage it. To take away the liberty of other nations with undisguised force is the surest way to make it an object of hatred and to prevent its triumph."[29] However, for most of his career, as Schumann conceded, Talleyrand was simply in no position to dictate such a policy. In his own words, he had to make a "very great sacrifice" and consent to be "the publisher responsible for other people's works."[30]

None the less, Talleyrand did from time to time make his views known publicly as Schumann records. In March 1798, for example, he told one of the Directors, Rewbell: "While the Directorate cries war against England, I cry for peace . . . because of the measures taken against neutral nations, all Europe's trade has been put in England's possession. People get angry when I talk like this and they do not want to be enlightened."[31] In February 1800 Napoleon wrote to George III saying "Does this war, which for eight years has been ravaging the four quarters of the globe, have to go on forever? Is there no way of coming to an understanding?"[32] Schumann says that the words were really those of Talleyrand. Certainly, on 4 February 1805, Talleyrand informed the Senate that Napoleon had again written to George III declaring that for France the matter of colonies was a secondary one. But still there was no peace. There were peace negotiations in 1806 but they again failed. By this time Talleyrand's desire for peace with England was an open secret. Metternich wrote: "M. de Talleyrand would like to retire from affairs, but he makes it a point of honour first to succeed in concluding peace with England."[33] Savary, then

French Minister of Police, wrote: "There is nothing he would not have given to achieve the conclusion of peace with England. He would say this to anyone who would listen."[34] Talleyrand's diplomacy at the Congress of Vienna, his correspondence with Louis XVIII in which he talked of the need for reconciliation and cooperation with England, and the mutual defence treaty signed on 3 January 1815 with England and Austria, again seemed to prove the tenacity of his ideas. Finally, when he came to London between 1830 and 1834 he agreed with Louis Philippe that a revolutionary war between England and France would be a disaster, so that his policy became one of preventing French intervention in Belgium if possible, preventing the Eastern powers from forcing Belgium to remain under Dutch rule, and associating England with a guarantee of Belgian neutrality and inviolability. He would love to have capped his work with the signing of a treaty of mutual defence between Britain and France. He even got the Duc de Broglie, to include in his instructions, which in fact he had drawn up himself, the following sentence: "I take it as a fact that if France were to become the victim of gratuitous and unprovoked aggression, England would involuntarily and instinctively defend France and espouse her cause."[35] And this consideration would lead other powers to "restrain from any impulsive desire for expansion."[36] Palmerston, however, was only to offer a Quadruple Alliance over Spain and Portugal. Still, there were to be no more wars between the two countries in the future and according to Schumann, "Talleyrand was without doubt the only one to foresee this change, which was of lasting and general importance, because he had persistently willed it to occur."[37] In Schumann's eyes, therefore, Talleyrand "had founded the Entente Cordiale."[38]

Schumann's views have been given such a generous account here, partly because they are so relevant to a discussion of Anglo–French relations in general, and partly because the case he makes out may in fact be irresistible. On the other hand, there are causes for doubt. For example, what was Talleyrand doing writing letters to the French government in November 1792 when he had assured the British foreign secretary that he was here only in a private capacity as a private individual? Why was he thrown out of the country in January 1794 at 24 hours' notice despite letters to the prime minister and foreign secretary seeking an explanation and stating that he had been innocent of any hostile thought or deed? Why did he receive no answer? Again, if he was such a good European, what exactly was his vision of a European equilibrium? Was it not simply one which left France as the dominant power? And, finally, what exactly was his policy in 1830–1834? Talleyrand's reputation for dishonesty, corruption,[39] and treason[40]— all of it very well-documented—makes one extremely hesitant to take him at his word.[41]

Talleyrand came to England in 1792 to carry out the policy of Mirabeau, who had died the previous year, of concluding a defensive alliance with England. Mirabeau had believed that the British people were basically pro-French and that the British government which needed the support of public opinion would be forced to agree to this. Pitt, however, would only agree to neutrality, although his government was very strongly neutral.[42] Talleyrand was not ambassador—that officially was the job of Chauvelin—but Talleyrand told the director-general of the French foreign ministry that he himself wrote "the greatest part" of the ambassador's despatches.[43] He also wrote to France that since he was very closely watched and was accused of being too closely connected with the opposition—Fox, Sheridan, Grey, Priestly, Paine, Horn Took—he had to take great care lest any pretext whatever should be used to frustrate his diplomatic aims (i.e., turning neutrality into an alliance) and did so by reasoning with radical journalists and by attempting to persuade the National Assembly to distinguish between friends and foes and not to stir up trouble in the territories of friendly states.[44] In any case, after returning from France in September 1792, he informed the British government that he had returned "*sans caractère ni mission*,"[45] and would reside in Britain merely as a private person. His exact words to Lord Grenville, the Foreign Secretary, were: "I am desirous that you should know that I have at this time *absolutely no kind of mission in England* and that I have come here solely for the purpose of seeking repose and the enjoyment of liberty in the midst of true friends"[46]—although he added that he would be happy at any time to inform the British government of the true state of affairs in France after the events of 10 August 1792.

This, however, was only one side of the story. Barrère who met Talleyrand at Danton's office in Paris in September while Talleyrand was waiting to receive his passport, wrote in his memoirs that Talleyrand had told him: "I am leaving for London this morning on a mission for the executive."[47] The French historian, Dr. Robinet, who examined Danton's diplomacy in 1792–94 concluded that "It seems clear to us that thereafter (i.e., after September 1792) Talleyrand had to be, in England, the agent of the agreement between *le conventionnel* [the revolutionaries in France] and the British revolutionary party."[48] According to Robinet, Danton's policy was to use the Whigs to bring about a republic in England. On 14 March 1793 he told the Convention "if France moves, the republicans in England will give you their hand and the world will be free."[49] Robinet also produces evidence that Talleyrand was mixed up from London in the negotiations between Lord Auckland and Dumouriez in Belgium.[50] Finally, after the fall of Robespierre, when the Convention was asked to give permission to Talleyrand to return to France, Chénier, the deputy who proposed this, said that Talleyrand's passport in 1792 had borne the words "*allant à Londres par nos orders*" ("going to London on our orders"),[51] in other words Talleyrand *had been* on an official mission, something which, after he resigned as foreign minister of the Directory in 1797, Talleyrand himself confirmed in a pamphlet stating: "I was sent to London on 7 September 1792 by the executive government. My passport, delivered to me my the provisional council, is signed by its six members, Lebrun, Servan, Clavière, Roland, Monge. It was in these terms: "*Laissez-passer Ch. Maurice Talleyrand, allant à Londres par nos orders.*" Thus I was authorised to quit France and to remain out of it until my orders were revoked, which they never were."[52]

But what were his orders? Chénier in his speech to the Convention had also referred to Talleyrand's peace-loving memorandum of 25 November 1792, so that his admirers have always been able to argue that he was still trying to reconcile England and France. But what of Robinet's accusations that he was in England to stir up revolution? These are always overlooked in the literature on Anglo–French relations in this period. Which fact is extremely curious since Whitelaw Reid, the U.S. Minister in Paris, who in 1891 contributed the introduction to the official English edition of Talleyrand's memoirs, included the following passage:

> Talleyrand evidently cherished bitter memories of his expulsion from England by Pitt but he finds it well to pass the subject with the slightest possible mention. *Nor does he refer at all to the strange letters he had previously sent his Government, reporting that England was practically on the verge of a revolution like that in France, analysing the inadequate military resources at hand to meet it, and proposing a plan for a French invasion and capture of Ireland.* Eight days, he said, were sufficient to land 60,000 men at twenty or thirty different points. As a matter of prudence, they might perhaps go in the character of *émigrés*, so as to avoid arousing the suspicions of the government.[53]

Reid even quotes from a letter of Talleyrand to Lebrun dated 10 October 1792, months before war broke out between France and England:

> Once masters of the principal ports, once with the English fleet in our power, we can easily bring from France such reinforcements as are needed; and besides, as the march of our troops will have been preceded by a proclamation in the name of the sovereign people of France, addressed to the sovereign people of Great Britain and Ireland, as their faithful allies, no doubt this country will be thrown into a revolution more prompt and more happy than that of 1688. The elements for a republic are riper in England than they were in France

four years ago, and it may take fewer weeks to accomplish this great and salutary change, than we spent years.[54]

So much for the Entente Cordiale!

Reid unfortunately gives no source for these letters, although they must be regarded as genuine, given that they are quoted in the official introduction to Talleyrand's official memoirs. This author's researches at The National Archives and the British Library into Cabinet papers, personal papers, and Foreign Office papers have revealed no evidence that the British government was aware of them. Nor do the works of the latest experts on Anglo–French relations covering the period 1792–94 seem aware of any activity on the part of Talleyrand; indeed, they do not even refer to Reid at all. This is true of recent books by Jeremy Black,[55] Marianne Eliott,[56] R.B. McDowell,[57] Jennifer Mori,[58] John Clarke,[59] Robin Reilly,[60] Peter Jupp[61] and Michael Fry.[62] And several of these authors claim to have used the French foreign ministry files as well. Enquiries by this author to the French archives have so far met with only a negative response. Indeed, there is only one source that indicates any real suspicion of Talleyrand in the active subversion of England and Ireland and that is the correspondence of George III. The king on 1 May 1792 wrote to Pitt:

> I received last night the enclosed paper from the Duke of Gloucester; it is drawn up by the same pen from which intelligence was sent on Saturday from the same channel by Lord Sydney to Mr. Dundas. It deserves the attention of the administration and it seems highly worthy of enquiry whether any large sum of money has been provided for France from Ireland and what Irishmen are connected with the French emissaries in this country. I desire Mr. Pitt will in my name give the paper this day to Mr. Dundas, that he may have the matter attended to and I should think it might easily be traced whether Mons. de Périgord has been secretly at London the last week and whether he returned to Dover and has publicly returned within these two days.[63]

In fact, the British government was much less concerned about the French threat than the king. Dundas himself, the Home Secretary and the man in charge of British intelligence, called in 1792 for a reduction in "the military establishment maintained for the general defence of the Empire" and only about £8,500 was spent on the secret service in 1792 compared with £127,000 in 1793.[64] Moreover, according to Michael Fry, Dundas's biographer, "the government's main clandestine activity had been in talks with Charles de Talleyrand," to keep Britain neutral![65] When Talleyrand was kicked out of Britain in 1794, Dundas even offered to allow him to stay in his house at Wimbledon until his ship was ready to sail, but Talleyrand, already on board, refused the offer of hospitality saying he "never wanted to set foot on English soil again!"

Talleyrand was expelled from England at 24 hours' notice under the Aliens Act of December 1792 which compelled foreigners to register their presence in Britain and to give security for their good behaviour. According to Huskisson, whose good French made him the first head of the Aliens Office, Dundas had described the aims of the Act as "to show every respect to all foreigners whose conduct in this country had not given rise to any suspicion and especially to save the ladies the trouble of appearing at the public offices."[66] Talleyrand on 1 January 1793, according to Foreign Office papers, filed a statement under the Act stating his good intentions.[67] He accompanied this with a private letter to the foreign secretary, again affirming that he was a private citizen who only wished to "lead a life most obscure, most peaceful and most alien to any kind of public concerns and solely to occupy myself with personal affairs." He confirmed that he "was no longer charged with any mission on behalf of France and had completely broken all relations with M. Chauvelin."[68] Why then was the Act used against him in January 1794? Once again, on 29 January 1794, he wrote to Lord Grenville, the foreign secretary in the following terms: "I defy anyone at all to prove a sole fact against me, either in word or deed or writings. I demand to know what I am accused of, without even demanding to know the names of my accusers. I consent to be entirely convinced if there remains even the slightest doubt or the slightest suspicion after I shall have been heard by a minister of the king or by whatever person he should wish to designate to me."[69] But there was no reply and Talleyrand had to leave for America. Why in any case had he been allowed to remain in England until 1794 if his letters to France since his return to London in September 1792 had been so compromising? When did the British government become aware of his activities?[70] Why was he finally expelled?[71] These questions have all still to find a definitive answer. But on that answer depends the final verdict regarding Talleyrand's true feelings towards England.

With regard to Talleyrand's activities as foreign minister of Napoleon, two points need to be made: first, he was in no position to dictate events. Only Napoleon made decisions of any weight concerning foreign policy.[72] He did not delegate. Talleyrand's eventual reaction was to commit high treason, although this also failed since the Austrians, to whom he gave the French military plans were too incompetent militarily to benefit from them.[73] Was Talleyrand's treason committed for the benefit of England and Europe's balance of power? Hardly. His "dream plan" of 1805 was predicated on a France enjoying very generous natural frontiers, including the Rhineland, to which he had become devoted, a reduced Prussia, an Austria shorn of her German and Italian territories and removed to the Black Sea, and a Russia expelled to Asia.[74] In short, he wanted France to dominate Europe. He never really gave up this idea either. Hence he opposed the limited territorial reductions and other penalties of the Second Treaty of Paris,[75] and on his death bed in 1838 expressed his hope to the Duchess of Dino that the King of Prussia's embroilment in the Cologne church dispute would enable France to regain the Rhineland.[76]

What about his actions at the Congress of Vienna? It is true that some historians have argued that he ended French isolation by forcing himself on the British and Austrians over the Polish-Saxon dispute and thereafter dominated the Congress with his doctrine of legitimacy. But this is sheer myth. As Metternich was all too well aware, powers which had recognised Napoleon as Emperor of the French, and his relatives as monarchs in Spain, Holland, Italy and Germany were in no position to uphold such a cause.[77] Besides, many small states were simply negotiated out of existence in 1815, while others were transferred, merged, or split up. The Polish-Saxon settlement was merely a repeat of the Polish partitions of the eighteenth century. Everyone at the time recognised the peace settlement as a deal done by the great powers at the expense of the lesser ones. Its great achievement was indeed to establish a balance of power which lasted until the 1860s. Paul Schroeder's reinterpretation of the period is simply wrong.[78]

Talleyrand had little influence at the Congress.[79] He had no part in deciding the details of the first Treaty of Paris and he was in no position to dominate the Congress. Far from imposing himself on England by taking advantage of the Saxon–Polish dispute, Talleyrand was used by Castlereagh to resolve the dispute once Hardenberg had threatened war. Given Talleyrand's previous outspoken support for Saxony in the name of legitimacy, there was no other course he could have taken. In any case, the British had not been impressed by Talleyrand.[80] Previously they had complained that he had spent too much time disputing "particular points of influence."[81] They then complained to Louis XVIII in Paris about him and the French king agreed that his minister had "acted foolishly" and had misrepresented Castlereagh in his reports.[82] When Talleyrand proved difficult over Italian affairs, Louis XVIII settled matters with the Austrians behind Talleyrand's back.[83] In any case, the British and Austrians knew of Talleyrand's treason and therefore could have blackmailed him at any time. The end result was Gentz's famous epithet referring to "the nullity of the French plenipotentiaries in all the negotiations" at the Congress.[84] Again, after the defeat of Napoleon at Waterloo, Talleyrand would not accept the terms of the Second Treaty of Paris. When Castlereagh tried to coax him with the words that he should become a "minister of Europe," he said that he preferred "only to be minister of France."[85] Louis XVIII, whom he accused in frustration of not understanding legitimacy, was glad to dismiss him.[86]

Back in London between 1830 and 1834, Talleyrand again attempted to win a defensive alliance with Britain. In point of fact, France had wanted to hold the conference on Belgium in Paris but this had been rejected by Wellington. Talleyrand's contribution to the diplomacy of the Belgian affair has been quite positively evaluated. According to Major John Hall, "Talleyrand as was his invariable practise [sic] in these disputes between France and England, left no stone unturned to dissuade his government from embarking upon a course of conduct inevitably designed to revive the old rivalry between the two countries."[87] But Talleyrand was not always kept informed of French diplomatic moves in Belgium by Sébastiani, the French foreign minister, and besides there were times when he thought that Belgium might have to be partitioned.[88]

All of this meant that Palmerston did not trust him. Palmerston, who spoke fluent French and had visited Paris in 1829 had come home convinced that the French liberals were all expansionists and wanted the natural frontiers. At one point Lord Granville wrote to Lord Holland: "I think with you that Palmerston's Foreign politicks are essentially good and liberal, but he is constantly apprehensive, not of being duped, but of being thought to be duped by Talleyrand and the French government."[89] Palmerston believed that alliances were not popular in England, but that if France were attacked unjustly, England "would beyond a doubt be found upon her side."[90] Yet he also talked of the partition of Belgium as Talleyrand's "favourite object."[91] In 1830 he had written when he first arrived at the Foreign Office that he was most anxious "to be well with France" and felt "strongly how much a cordial good understanding and close friendship between England and France must contribute to secure the peace of the world and to confirm the liberties and promote the happiness of nations."[92] However, such good will had been undermined by the constant appearance of ill-faith on the part of the French and "the spirit of aggression and the ardent thirst of aggrandisement which was betrayed, instead of being concealed by the underhand intrigues and double diplomacy which was intended to veil them, proved to us that those who thus had been courting our alliance only meant to make us the instrument of their own ambition."[93] Had Talleyrand been a saint, which clearly he was not—the only Supreme Being he had ever admitted to worshipping was, notoriously, Madame de Flahaut—he would still have been unable to win an alliance from Palmerston. In the end he settled in 1834 for France becoming a full member of a Quadruple Alliance with Britain, Spain and Portugal, which, despite its propaganda value as the liberal answer to the Holy Alliance, was, like the Holy Alliance itself, not of any real significance.

To conclude, there is indeed a case, perhaps a strong one, for calling Talleyrand the founder of the Entente Cordiale. But like the Entente itself, it is based on ideals rather than realities. Talleyrand drifted across the Channel many times but always in a fog and that cross-channel fog, historically speaking, is probably the best symbol I can think of for the Entente Cordiale. Should that fog one day disperse, it may well leave Talleyrand looking rather exposed and lacking in substance.

NOTES

1. John Holland Rose, *The Life of Napoleon, Including New Materials from the British Official Records* (2 vols., London: George Bell and Sons, 1902) vol. 1, p. 164.
2. Sir Charles Petrie, *When Britain Saved Europe: the Tale and the Moral* (London, Eyre and Spottiswoode, 1941), p. 202.
3. H.A.L. Fisher, *Studies in Napoleonic Statesmanship: Germany* (New York, Haskell House, repr.1968), p. 108.
4. Sir Henry Lytton Bulwer, *Historical Characters: Talleyrand, Mackintosh, Cobbett, Canning* (London: Richard Bentley, 1870), p. 78.
5. *The Times* report of Wellington's speech and other contributions to the debate of 29 September 1831 in the House of Lords is reprinted in Talleyrand's memoirs, see Duc de Broglie (Ed.), *Memoirs of the Prince de Talleyrand* (5 vols., London and Sydney: Griffin, Farran, Okeden, and Welsh, 1891–2) vol. 4, pp. 208–209.
6. Major John Hall, *England and the Orleans Monarchy* (London: Smith Elder, 1912), p. 86.
7. Crane Brinton, *The Lives of Talleyrand* (New York: W. W. Norton, 1963), p. x.
8. Rose, *Life of Napoleon*, p. 165.
9. Albert Sorel, "Talleyrand au Congrès de Vienne" in *Essais d'Histoire et de Critique* (Paris: Plon-Nourrit, 4th ed., 1919), p. 57.
10. Particularly St. Beuve, whose essays on Talleyrand in Vol. 12 of his *Nouveaux Lundis*, in Brinton's view, "fixed Talleyrand's evil reputation in the mind of a cultivated people." See Brinton, *Talleyrand*, p. 306.
11. Quoted by the U.S. newspaper magnate and politician, then U.S. Minister to France, Whitelaw Reid, in his neglected but extremely important official introduction to the English edition of Talleyrand's memoirs edited by de Broglie (Ed.), *Memoirs of Talleyrand*, vol. 1, pp. xxxviii–xxxix.
12. Ibid., p. xxxix.
13. Ibid.
14. Ibid.
15. Ibid. "Quand Monsieur Talleyrand ne conspire pas, il traffique."
16. Ibid.
17. The most recent biography in French of Talleyrand, Emmanuel de Waresquiel's *Talleyrand, le Prince Immobile* (Paris: Fayard, 2003) takes an even-handed view of him, although it could be more critical. His motto in life is given in his words to Vautrin (p. 15): "*Il n'y a pas de loi, il n'y a que des circonstances.*"
18. Alan Sked, *Metternich and Talleyrand*, unpublished conference paper.

19. Robert Schumann, *Talleyrand: Prophet of the Entente Cordiale* (London: OUP, 1967), p. 4.
20. Émile Dard, *Talleyrand and Napoleon* (London: Philip Allen, 1937), pp. 15–16.
21. Schumann, *Talleyrand*, p. 6.
22. Ibid., p. 7.
23. Ibid., p. 7.
24. Ibid., p. 8.
25. Ibid., p. 8.
26. G. Pallain (Ed.), *La Mission de Talleyrand à Londres en 1792* (Paris: Plon-Nourrit, 1889), pp. xi–xii.
27. Schumann, *Talleyrand*, pp. 9–11.
28. Ibid., p. 13.
29. Ibid., pp. 13–14.
30. Ibid., p. 15.
31. Ibid., p. 17.
32. Ibid., p. 17.
33. Ibid., p. 18.
34. Ibid., pp. 18–19.
35. Ibid., p. 20.
36. Ibid., p. 20.
37. Ibid., p. 22.
38. Ibid., p. 22.
39. For the list of bribes (almost 15 million francs!) taken by Talleyrand in the three year period 1797–99, listed by the future French foreign minister, Louis Bastide, in his 1838 biography of his predecessor, see Whitelaw Reid's introduction to Talleyrand's memoirs, p. xlviii. Talleyrand's exemplar may well have been Danton, see Norman Hampson, *Danton* (London: Duckworth, 1978), but for further evidence of Talleyrand's love for bribes see Fisher, *Napoleonic Statesmanship*, pp. 61–62 and 117. On the whole issue of *douceurs* for diplomats, see M.S. Anderson, *The Rise of Modern Diplomacy, 1450–1919* (London: Longman, 1993), pp. 49–52 and 126.
40. For his treasonous relations with Austria and Russia, see Manfred Botzenhart, *Metternichs Pariser Botschafterzeit* (Münster: Aschendorff, 1967).
41. For a fuller discussion of all these points, see below. It should be noted, however, that in his memoirs, Talleyrand brushes quickly over the period, stating: "My mornings were spent in penning down my impressions of the previous day, and when, on my return from America, my friends forwarded to me all the notes taken during the time I resided in England, I was extremely surprised to notice that they could be of no service to me for the work I am now writing. It would now be impossible for me to relate the events of this period, I do not recollect them; their connecting link is lost for me," Broglie (Ed.), *Memoirs of Talleyrand*, vol.1, p. 171. How very convenient!
42. In the one interview he had with Pitt, the latter devoted merely a few words to recall the six weeks he had spent with Talleyrand and his uncle, the Archbishop of Reims, in 1783. Talleyrand was bitterly insulted. See G. Lacour-Gayet, *Talleyrand, 1754–1838* (3 vols., Paris: Payot, 1930) vol.1, p. 65. On Pitt and neutrality only, see Pallain (Ed.), *La Mission de Talleyrand*, pp. xx–xxi.

43. Ibid., pp. 330–331. Talleyrand to Louis XVI, London, 28 March 1792, states that Chauvelin's title of ambassador "ne sera exactement qu'un prête-nom." Another letter of the same date to the Director-General of the French Foreign Ministry, Guillaume de Bonne-Carrière, stated that he, Talleyrand, had edited a despatch of Chauvelin's "with great care" and that he always wrote "the greatest part" of such despatches.

44. Ibid., pp. 325–328.

45. Ibid., pp. xxvi–xxvii.

46. Bulwer, *Historical Characters*, pp. 159–60, Talleyrand to Grenville, London, 18 September 1792.

47. "avec une mission du Pouvoir executif," as quoted in Dr. Robinet, *Danton Émigré: Recherches Sur La Dipomatie de la République (An 1er-1793)* (Paris: H. Le Soudier, 1887), p. 13.

48. Ibid., p. 12.

49. Ibid., p. 92.

50. Ibid., pp. 269–70.

51. Bulwer, *Historical Characters*, pp. 171–172, quotes Chénier's speech of 18 Fructidor to the French National Convention, in which the deputy quotes from a memoir found in Danton's papers, which points out that Danton had granted Talleyrand a passport on which these words were written.

52. Ibid., pp. 187–190. The pamphlet quoted was entitled *Éclaircissements donnés par le citoyen Talleyrand à ses concitoyens.*

53. Introduction by Reid to Broglie (Ed.), *Memoirs of Talleyrand*, vol. 1, p. lii (author's emphasis).

54. Ibid.

55. Jeremy Black, *British Foreign Policy in an Age of Revolutions, 1783–1793* (Cambridge: Cambridge University Press, 1994). This discusses Talleyrand's 1792 missions and mentions fears regarding the Alien Act but has nothing to say on Talleyrand's expulsion. Black has seen the relevant French archives.

56. Marianne Elliott, *Partners in Revolution: the United Irishmen and France* (New Haven, CT, and London: Yale University Press, 1982). According to p. 52, fn. 6, she has examined Lebrun's correspondence with England in 1792, but she has nothing to say about Talleyrand during that year.

57. R. B. McDowell, *Ireland in the Age of Imperialism and Revolution, 1760–1801* (Oxford: Clarendon Press, 1991). This does not mention Talleyrand.

58. Jennifer Mori, *William Pitt and the French Revolution* (Edinburgh: Keele University Press, 1997). Nothing on Talleyrand, but points out (p. 101) that Pitt was very sanguine about the French revolution to begin with, telling Burke: "Never fear, Mr. Burke: depend upon it we shall go on as we are until the Day of Judgement." Dundas seemed equally sanguine. (See p. 120).

59. John Clarke, *British Diplomacy and Foreign Policy, 1782–1865. The National Interest* (London: Routledge, 1989). This does not mention Talleyrand at all.

60. Robin Reilly, *Pitt the Younger, 1759–1806* (London: Chapman and Hall, 1978). Contains nothing on Talleyrand's position.

61. Peter Jupp, *Lord Grenville, 1754–1834* (Oxford: Clarendon Press, 1985). Acccording to p. 146, fn. 87, Grenville referred to the "ignorance and absurdity" of Chauvelin's mission. According to p. 146, Grenville's policy "consisted

of stating the government's determination to remain neutral in terms that were uninformative as to its general views on the continental situation and in a manner that in French eyes was cool and at times offensive. Talleyrand, for example, was met with a wall of silence on the grounds that he was an unaccredited representative." As for Chauvelin, "Grenville took every opportunity to lecture him on the finer points of diplomatic etiquette." However, there is no discussion of Talleyrand's enforced departure or reasons for it.

62. Michael Fry, *The Dundas Despotism* (Edinburgh: Edinburgh University Press, 1993). Nothing on Talleyrand. According to Fry (p. 189), the government's attitude in 1792 "remained one of faintly irresponsible optimism."

63. A. Aspinall (Ed.), *The Later Correspondence of George III* (Cambridge: Cambridge University Press, 1962) vol. 1, *December 1783–January 1793*, p. 591, King to Pitt, 1 May, 1792.

64. Fry, *Dundas Despotism*, p. 189.

65. Ibid.

66. Lewis Melville (Ed.), *The Huskisson Papers* (London: Constable, 1931), p. 18.

67. The National Archives (Public Record Office) [hereafter TNA (PRO)], Foreign Office Papers [hereafter FO] 27/41, Declaration of M. de Talleyrand, 1 January, 1793.

68. TNA (PRO), FO 27/41, Talleyrand to Grenville (no.3), 1 January 1793.

69. TNA (PRO) FO 27/43, Talleyrand to anon.[presumably Grenville], 29 January 1794. There is a second, longer letter of protest of 30 January in which he keeps addressing "My Lord" and insists he has done nothing. By this time Chauvelin had been ordered out of the country by an Order in Council dated 24 January 1793 demanding that "he do depart this realm on or before the 1st day of February next," TNA (PRO) FO 27/41.

70. Before his expulsion (see previous footnote) Chauvelin had written to Grenville on 17 January 1793 urgently demanding a meeting in which he hoped to secure guarantees "que l'on respect mes couriers et le secret des lettres que j'envoye et que je reçois." He said he was willing to show Grenville his letters of credence once again and protested that the terms of the Alien Act should not be applied to him or his staff. Clearly, however, he knew that the British authorities had intercepted very compromising correspondence. Talleyrand, no doubt, was equally compromised. See TNA (PRO), FO 27/41. Chauvelin had had previous experience of Britain retaining compromising (perhaps even intercepted) correspondence. Pitt, for example, had written to Grenville on 18 August 1792 in the following terms: "There is nothing new since I wrote to you except Chauvelin coming to me with much Agitation to beg that his Note might be returned to Him and never mentioned. It seemed important to refuse his request which he urged on the grounds that it might injure the king if the contents transpired, which proceeded I believe as much from fear for himself," see British Library, Add. Mss. 58906, Dropmore Papers, fol. 134.

71. Presumably on account of activities such as those exposed by Reid. But why did the authorities wait till January 1794 to expel him for espionage undertaken in October 1792? Maybe Talleyrand's activities only came to light later. Just before he was told to leave, there is a tantalising correspondence between Pitt and Grenville in the Dropmore Papers. On 24 December 1793, Pitt wrote to

Grenville from Wimbledon: "Painful as the whole subject is, it is one on which it is much better to converse than to write, and I therefore wish much for an early opportunity of seeing you, when I must tell you without reserve all that I think and feel." That conversation was postponed, for on Christmas Day 1793 Pitt wrote to Grenville: "But whatever is the end of the present Embarrassment, there are one or two points connected with it which it will be a satisfaction to talk over at leisure." Did any of this correspondence between the prime minister and foreign secretary have anything to do with Talleyrand, who in January 1794 was told to quit the country? British Library, Add. Mss. 58906, Dropmore Papers, fol. 134.

72. See Dard, *Talleyrand and Napoleon.*
73. See Botzenhart, *Metternichs Pariser Botschafterzeit.*
74. On the whole subject of Talleyrand's plans in 1805, see Kurt von Raumer, "Politiker des Masses?: Talleyrand's Strassburger Friedensplan (17 Oktober 1805)," *Historische Zeitschrift,* vol. 193 (1961), pp. 286–368.
75. See below.
76. See Dard, *Talleyrand and Napoleon,* p. xvi. Talleyrand on his return from America became a firm supporter of France's natural frontiers.
77. The best book on Metternich and the Congress in English remains Henry Kissinger's *A World Restored. Metternich, Castlereagh and the Problems of Peace, 1802–1822* (London: Phoenix, 1957).
78. For a critique of Schroeder, see Alan Sked, "The European State System in the Modern World" in Attila Pók (Ed.), *The Fabric of Modern Europe: Studies in Social and Diplomatic History. Essays in Honour of Éva Haraszti Taylor on the Occasion of her 75th. Birthday* (Nottingham: Astra Press, 1999), pp. 21–37.
79. There is no space here to list books representing the huge international historiography on the Congress. Talleyrand's self-serving memoirs are contradicted by those of Metternich and by the documents published in C. K. Webster (Ed.), *British Diplomacy, 1813–1815. Select Documents Dealing with the Reconstruction of Europe* (London: G. Bell, 1921). The best account of the diplomacy of the Congress is Douglas Dakin, "The Congress of Vienna, 1814–1815 and its Antecedents" in Alan Sked (Ed.), *Europe's Balance of Power 1815–1848* (London: Macmillan, 1979), pp. 14–33.
80. See for example, Castlereagh to Liverpool, 9 October, 1814: "unfortunately the manner in which Prince Talleyrand has conducted himself here, rather excited apprehension in both the Austrian and Prussian ministers, than inspired them with any confidence in his views," or in another letter to Liverpool on the same day: "I had a long interview with him, in which I took the liberty of representing to him without reserve the errors into which he appeared to me to have fallen since his arrival here. . . . I could not disguise from him the general impression resulting from his demeanour had been to excite distrust and alarm with respect to the views of France; and that the effect of this had been to deprive him of his just and natural influence for the purposes of moderating excessive pretensions, while it united all to preserve the general system," Webster (Ed.), *British Diplomacy,* pp. 202 and 204.
81. Castlereagh to Wellington, 25 October 1814: "M. Talleyrand appears to me . . . more content upon particular points of influence than upon the general balance

to be established, and his efforts upon the Neapolitan and Saxon questions are frequently made at the expense of the more important question of Poland, without essentially serving either of these interests upon which he is most intent," ibid., pp. 217–218.

82. Wellington to Castlereagh, Paris, 5 November 1814, and Wellington to Castlereagh, Paris, 7 November, 1814, ibid., pp. 227–8 and p. 229.
83. For Talleyrand's outmanoeuvring by Louis XVIII and Metternich, see Heinrich, Ritter von Srbik, *Metternich: Der Staatsman und der Mensch* (2 vols., Munich: Wissenschaftliche Buchgesellschaft, 1957) vol. 1, pp. 214–21.
84. Memoir by Friedrich Gentz, 12 February 1815, on the Congress of Vienna. This began famously with the words "the real purpose of the Congress was to divide amongst the conquerors the spoils taken from the vanquished." All other phrases, he stated, were merely "uttered to tranquillise the people, and give an air of dignity and grandeur to this solemn assembly." Regarding France, Gentz wrote that previous agreements among the victorious powers, fear of being seen to be ganging up with France, not to mention the lack of credibility of any French military threats, undermined her diplomacy totally. The French government longed for peace: the outbreak of war would see France risk another revolution and invasion. Louis XVIII could simply never contemplate that, see Prince Richard Metternich (Ed.), *Memoirs of Prince Metternich* (5 vols., London: Richard Bentley, 1880) vol. 2, pp. 553 and 560.
85. De Broglie (Ed.), *Memoirs of Talleyrand*, vol. 3, p. 203.
86. Ibid., pp. 202–203.
87. Hall, *England and the Orleans Monarchy*, p. 79.
88. For the diplomacy of the Belgian settlement see both ibid., chapters 3 and 4, and Kenneth Bourne, *Palmerston: The Early Years, 1784–1841* (London: Allen Lane, 1982), chapter 8.
89. Bourne, ibid., p. 350.
90. Ibid.
91. Ibid.
92. Ibid.
93. Ibid.

CASTLEREAGH AND FRANCE

John Charmley

Although all nineteenth century British Foreign Secretaries had France as one of their major concerns, only Castlereagh had to cope with the reality of France as an enemy. His major task from 1812 until 1814 was to create a coalition capable of defeating Napoleon; this was succeeded by the urgent need to negotiate a peace settlement which would provide a framework within which the great Powers could live; and finally, it fell to him to try to maintain that settlement.

The first thing to be emphasised is the personal nature of Castlereagh's foreign policy; for once it is not just historian's shorthand to call it "Castlereagh's foreign policy." The Prime Minister, Lord Liverpool, was not one to keep a pedigree dog and to bark himself; he trusted his Foreign Secretary, as did most of his colleagues; and at least in the first two phases, this was a crucial element in Castlereagh's diplomacy. Since C. K. Webster's magisterial studies historians have treated Castlereagh with more respect than they used to, but he still has to find his place in the tradition of British Foreign Secretaries; as it is he appears to have neither predecessors nor progeny. Historians have been anxious to stress that he was not the arch-reactionary portrayed by Byron and Shelley, and they have tended to follow Webster in creating a Castlereagh fit for a more liberal age; for this there appears to be little proof.

Castlereagh would not have thrived in modern politics; he lacked both charisma and vision. Of all his successors, he resembled most the fifth Marquess of Lansdowne. He was a technician, repairing the machinery of British diplomacy and making it run well, Castlereagh eschewed the broad sun-lit uplands occupied by his immediate successor, George Canning. To those, like Talleyrand, who aspired to a broader view of diplomacy, Castlereagh appeared to be a narrow and insular figure, lacking even in the most fundamental requirement of the diplomatist—a knowledge of geography.[1] Before we take this too tragically, we might also recall that Talleyrand also accused him of a want of principle—a subject on which he might be taken to have been something of an expert. In fact Castlereagh's diplomacy was an exercise in three-dimensional geography. He knew enough about Europe to know how a balance of power might be constructed, and enough about the House of Commons to know how a settlement which secured it might be defended. Central to this cartographic exercise as the fate of France.

It was precisely Castlereagh's want of vision and charisma that fitted him for the task that lay before him in 1812. His European opposite numbers had had a sufficiency of both characteristics in the form of Napoleon, and a surfeit of them in the form of Tsar Alexander I. Because Castlereagh was calm and workmanlike, Metternich, the crucial figure in the reconstruction of Europe, identified him as a man with whom business could be done; and since the key to a successful settlement lay in Britain finding a reliable European partner, this alignment of temperament became the foundation for the settlement of 1815. Metternich boasted of being a man of "prose" rather than of "poetry"; he found a soul-mate in Castlereagh. Because of the pace with which events moved during 1814, it would have been impossible to have implemented any blueprint for the future of Europe, so the fact that Castlereagh did not have one was an advantage. But the absence of a blueprint should not be taken as evidence of a want of ideas. Castlereagh knew where he was trying to get to, but like any good driver, he was less concerned about what route he took than about achieving the object of his journey.

In the first phase his policy was easily described. As he told the British ambassador in St. Petersburg, General Lord Cathcart: "Whatever scheme of policy can most immediately combine the greatest number of powers and the greatest military force against France . . . before she can recruit her armies and recover her ascendancy, is that which we must naturally desire most to promote."[2] But this was the means to a greater end: France had to be brought back within the boundaries she had occupied in the eighteenth century; having willed this end, Castlereagh was unfussy about the means. His Europe was that of the late eighteenth century, and a strong France was essential in order to maintain the balance of power; not having had the advantage of reading the works of Professor Schroeder, Castlereagh actually believed that there could be a balance of power.[3]

We get some sight of this in 1814 at the height of his dispute over the fate of Saxony and Poland. As he told Wellington on 29 October: "the difference in principle between M. Talleyrand and me is chiefly that I wish to direct my main efforts to secure an equilibrium in Europe; to which object, as far as principle may permit, I wish to make all local points subordinate. M. Talleyrand appears to me, on the contrary, more intent upon particular points of influence than upon the general balance to be established; and his efforts upon the Neapolitan and Saxon questions are frequently made at the expense of the more important question of Poland, without essentially serving either of those interests upon which he is most intent."[4] Castlereagh saw in Talleyrand's elevation of detail, an inability to distinguish between the particular and the general—and he was always more concerned with the latter. But then Talleyrand was trying to exploit the disputes over Saxony and Poland in order to recover France's diplomatic position, whilst Castlereagh was trying to prevent it from destroying the foundations of the grand alliance.

In achieving an "equilibrium of Europe" the position of France was, and remained, vital, so a good deal of Castlereagh's mind was given over to it; but as in any calculation of equilibriums, it was necessary to bear in mind the other parts of the machinery of the balance of power. Thus France served a number of purposes for Castlereagh over the decade from 1812. In the first instance she was the cause of the disequilibrium and therefore needed to be reduced to her proper size; this made him ultimately the enemy of Napoleon and the ally of Talleyrand; not that the latter showed much appreciation. In this phase Castlereagh was not only the enemy of Napoleonic megalomania, but also of those who wanted to be revenged upon France. He recognised that Europe needed a strong France, and was prepared to deal with any regime, even a Bonapartist one, that would accept an end to the ambitions born of revolution and Empire. The second purpose France served for Castlereagh required her to be a Great Power. When he told Alexander I that "it depends exclusively upon the temper in which your Imperial Majesty shall meet the questions which more immediately concern your own Empire, whether the present Congress shall prove a blessing to mankind or only exhibit a scene of discordant intrigue and a lawless scramble for power," Castlereagh touched upon the main reason Europe needed a strong France. Restoring France to her proper dimensions would not remove the danger of European disequilibrium. The way in which Alexander behaved at the start of the Congress of Vienna, particularly over the issue of Poland, showed the potential Russia possessed to fill the place vacated by Napoleon. Just as Castlereagh could not be sure in 1813 and early 1814 that Metternich would not cut a deal with Napoleon, so too was he unsure whether he would cut one with Alexander; the Prussians, as they showed at Vienna, would always come to heel at the Tsar's command. In such a Europe, a strong and independent France was a necessity to Britain. These attitudes were not common: the predominant feeling in the British Cabinet was that France should be severely punished for her sins; a feeling that grew stronger after Napoleon's return from Elba and the Hundred Days. But Castlereagh, with the invaluable support of Wellington, stood his ground.

As early as November 1813, Castlereagh recognised that "peace with Buonaparte on any terms will be far from popular" and that "this nation is likely to view with disfavour any peace that does not confine France strictly within her ancient limits."[5] In order to accommodate Metternich and the Tsar, he was willing to run the risk of making peace with the Corsican ogre—but not even for them would he make a peace that did not "confine" France. He did not want, as some did, to undo the work of Louis XIV, but he had a shrewd eye for the bigger picture. As he told Aberdeen on 13 November, the "destruction of th[e] arsenal [of Antwerp] is essential to our safety. To leave it in the hands of France is little short of imposing upon Great Britain the charge of a perpetual war establishment." Castlereagh was willing to let others see whether Napoleon could be brought to agree on terms, but he did not trust him and doubted whether it would be wise to let others act as though he was trustworthy; but in late 1813 and early 1814 the British Foreign Minister was not in the driving seat and it was necessary to appear to be willing to treat with Napoleon; but even at this stage he deprecated any premature declaration of the terms the allied powers might insist on.

His concern with the fate of Antwerp, and his distrust of Napoleon, explain Castlereagh's anxiety at Aberdeen's acceptance of the proposals drawn up by Metternich at Frankfurt in November 1813, which defined France's "natural frontiers" as including most of the old Austrian Netherlands; that he had also made no objection to terms which seemed to infringe upon Britain's Maritime Rights was a further cause for concern. Fortunately, and not for the last time, Napoleon's intransigence prevented him from capitalising upon the potential for dissention amongst his opponents. For all Professor Schroeder's faith in the wisdom which the Allied statesmen had acquired by the bitter experience of a quarter of a century of warfare, there seems little sign of it in the period up to the Congress of Vienna. Metternich would have been quite happy to have come to a deal with the father of the next (half-Habsburg) Emperor of France, especially if it provided a counter-weight to the Polish ambitions of the unaccountable Alexander; the Tsar himself wished to be arbiter of Europe and looked upon Britain's colonial conquests as bargaining counters in his own ambitious schemes; there was plenty of room for manoeuvre here for someone less inflexible than Napoleon; at several points between Frankfurt and Chaumont tactical acceptance of some of the Allied demands would have sown dissension in their ranks; but Napoleon would never compromise.

However, at least until Chaumont itself, Castlereagh's thinking on France, and thus on the future of Europe, was dominated by the thought that it would be Napoleon who would be governing post-war France.

Castlereagh was not prepared to accept a "Continental" peace of the sort outlined in the Frankfurt proposals. He wanted an alliance because "whilst Bonaparte shall continue to rule France, perhaps even while the system itself, which he has matured, shall continue to give impulse to the military resources of that great Empire, the only safety for other Powers of Europe is to impose upon the ambitious propensities of France that constraint in time of peace, to which alone they will owe the concessions, which may by war be extracted from the enemy."[6] Only a general alliance could ensure the equilibrium of Europe, and only a settlement which kept Belgium out of French hands would be acceptable to British interests. As seen earlier, an alliance was necessary because a France governed by a Bonaparte could not be trusted to keep within its "ancient" frontiers. It was, of course, possible that restoring the "ancient" family represented by the bulky form of Monsieur would produce a France that could do this, but Castlereagh did not wish to prejudge the will of the French people, nor yet do anything that would identify the Bourbons too firmly with France's enemies.[7] The best that could be done at this juncture was the alliance signed at Chaumont in March, when the allies not only bound themselves to make no separate peace with Bonaparte but also to protect Europe against every attempt which France might make "to infringe the order of things" resulting from any peace settlement. To achieve this Castlereagh pledged more than £5 million in subsidy to Britain's allies; again, little sign here of the wisdom of experience.

A Napoleonic France threatened the equilibrium of Europe because it would only stay within its proper territorial limits if forced to by a Grand Alliance; but a Bourbon France, content to stay within those limits, could be an aid to British diplomacy. As late as the signing of the Quadruple alliance of November 1815 France still appeared to Castlereagh as a potential threat: "I feel strong persuasion," he told Liverpool, "that nothing can keep France quiet and within bounds but the strong hand of European power." We can see in the territorial parts of the Vienna settlement the extent to which the geography of Europe was shaped by the need to provide France with the international equivalent of warders: thus on her north-western boundary temptation was removed by the union of the Austrian Netherlands to Holland; across the Rhine a watch was kept by Prussia, whilst Germany itself was reorganised into a Confederation under Austrian leadership; Austria again provided security against French expansionism by the role she took in the Italian peninsula, whilst Piedmont's power to provide a buffer was increased by the gains she made at the settlement.

In the summer of 1814 Talleyrand initiated a series of diplomatic overtures to Castlereagh designed to convince him that France could be a useful partner. Wellington, whose views on this, as on much else, were eminently sensible, saw a considerable advantage in Britain and France understanding each other—provided nothing was done that ran counter to the Quadruple Alliance; he was alive to the possibility that Talleyrand might wish to profit from the obvious dissention within the Allied ranks over Poland. For Castlereagh, Talleyrand, handled correctly could be a useful ally—which may, of course, help to explain the largely hostile picture of the former he presented in his memoirs. Talleyrand accused Castlereagh of wanting to isolate France[8] and criticised his "utter ignorance" of the "simplest matters of continental geography"[9] and his want of principles which did not, he told Louis XVIII "appear to be his forte."[10] He did not, he wrote on 24 November 1814, want to accuse Castlereagh of "having propagated the prejudices which we have to combat" but did so all the same. In his view the English Foreign Secretary lacked the power "of judging to what extent times had changed."[11] He concluded that Castlereagh lacked that "spirit of decision that it would be so necessary for him to possess" and that much of his vacillation was produced by "the spectre of parliament that ever haunts him."[12] If a descent to such personal criticisms is typical of the Frenchman, it is equally so of the British statesman that he refrained from personalities.

Castlereagh understood Talleyrand's motives, but thought his technique deficient. Castlereagh's mind was dominated by the need to reconstruct Europe in a way that would bring an end to the warfare that had dominated the previous quarter of a century. He was in a unique position. No other British politician cared for much beyond making peace and going home; foreign politics was not a British forte, and parliament wanted an end to the expense engendered by war; most of his colleagues would have been more than happy to have left the details about the future of Poland to those with a direct interest in them. Where Castlereagh differed from his peers was his conviction that Britain's interests demanded a continental settlement that was stable. Demanding no territorial compensation for his own country, Castlereagh sought to moderate the demands of others—which included those of the French. The proposals of the Marquis d'Osmond for an "augmentation of a million of subjects" including most of the Austrian Netherlands met with peremptory refusal from Castlereagh, who told Talleyrand in May that "if he wishes peace to last" this "false notion of Flanders being necessary to France" would have to be dropped.[13] It was, but it did not endear the British Foreign Secretary to Talleyrand, even though the wily old statesman had suspected that the British would prove obstinate. Castlereagh ensured that before the Congress met the British had achieved their one territorial aim—the incorporation

of the Low Countries with Holland. On the colonial question, where Talleyrand again dug in his heels, Castlereagh had to remind him how much
the Bourbon regime owed to British help. Castlereagh himself cared little
for colonies, taking the view that "our reputation on the Continent as a
feature of strength, power and confidence is of more moment to us than
acquisitions thus made," but he recognised the need to satisfy the
demands of the Commons.[14]

It was, however, easier for Castlereagh to get his way over the peace
with France than on the general question of reconstruction; as everyone,
including Talleyrand, recognised, all the victorious Powers could agree
on France's frontiers—they could not do so on the broader questions at
stake at Paris and in Vienna—which, of course, gave Talleyrand the
chance to pay such signal service to his country.

The question which caused most vexation was the fate of Saxony and
Poland. Talleyrand, who strongly approved of Castlereagh's opposition to
the Tsar's plans for Poland, was baffled by his willingness to go along
with Prussian demands for large parts of Saxony, which he put down to a
desire to conciliate parliament.[15] In this he was incorrect. It would be little
exaggeration to say that no other English politician cared a whit for Saxony or Poland, and had Castlereagh courted easy popularity he would
have allowed the Continental Powers to have decided the fate of these far-
away places without troubling himself with the details; as it was, he got
no thanks and much criticism, even from close colleagues, by interfering.
It was natural for Talleyrand to resent what appeared to be a British
attempt to aggrandise Prussia in order to restrain France, but the British
statesman's eyes were fixed on a canvass wider than that of France alone.
His aim, as he told Liverpool in November, was the establishment of a
"just equilibrium in Europe."[16] It would be impossible to "find a satisfactory system of balance in Europe unless Prussia could be induced to take a
part." If Prussia were satisfied over Saxony, it might work with Austria,
Britain, Holland and the minor German states to create an "intermediary
system between Russia and France." It was, of course, possible to leave
Prussia disappointed, but that would mean she would lean towards Russia,
which in turn would mean that in order to restrain the latter, Britain and
Austria would have needed French help. This, in turn, would "render Holland
and the Low Countries dependent upon France for their support, instead
of having Prussia and the Northern States of Germany as their natural pro-
tectors." In the event of a war this risked "exposing all the recent cessions
by France to re-occupation by French armies." It was. He told Liverpool
on 25 October 1814, this weighty consideration which had induced him to
take the opinion that, "however pure the intentions of the King of France
were," Britain "ought not to risk so much upon French connexion." It
was, he concluded, "wiser to preserve, as far as possible, the good will of

France, whilst we laboured to unite Germany for its own preservation against Russia."[17] When one understands Castlereagh's reasoning, it becomes easier to explain the irritation of Talleyrand; it is unlikely that the French statesman read the situation in a different way to his British counterpart.

The position which Talleyrand professed to find incomprehensible was dictated by the logic of Castlereagh's ultimate objectives. A "just equilibrium" meant strengthening the centre of Europe against the east and the west, and this meant, in turn, the creation of a strong Prussia allied to Austria. The resentment felt by Talleyrand towards Castlereagh resembled that of a suitor to a rival, since both men courted the same object—a stable European balance of power. Had Castlereagh followed the line of his colleagues on the questions of Poland and Saxony, it would have fallen to France to have acted as mediator between the Austrians and the Russians in order to create a just equilibrium, which would have secured in a swift and decisive fashion the Frenchman's aim of re-establishing France as a Great Power. The ambiguity of Alexander's policy and the fears this aroused gave Talleyrand and Louis XVIII the opportunity of achieving their goal for France; Castlereagh's refusal to lead a British withdrawal from intervention helped to deny that opportunity. In that sense the Frenchman's acerbity is understandable.

The acidic nature of Talleyrand's comments in his memoirs should not distract us from the central fact that the Vienna Congress saw the formation of an informal Anglo–French partnership. If Alexander's aims appeared ambiguous at the start of the Congress, by November he had made one of them crystal clear: Russia held Poland and would continue to do so and would therefore do what she wanted with it; this, Alexander told Castlereagh was what Russia was owed for her sacrifices.[18] With the Prussians firmly aligned with the Russians, Castlereagh was convinced that Europe was within sight of war unless Britain intervened. It is a tribute to his sense of the equilibrium of Europe that he went beyond the insularity of his colleagues, who could not quite see what a quarrel in a far away country of peoples about whom they knew nothing had to do with Britain. They were even more alarmed at his suggestion that Britain might join with France in a species of armed mediation. Seeing the reluctance of his colleagues, Castlereagh responded evasively to Talleyrand's suggestion of 23 December 1814 that an alliance should be formed against Russia and Prussia by France, Britain and Austria—but four days later he acknowledged that in the face of Russian intransigence there seemed no alternative. If war broke out, he told Liverpool, Britain was bound to become involved in it, and a French alliance would preserve the Vienna frontiers as well as saving Austria "and consequently the Continent." Fortunately, Castlereagh's brinkmanship worked, but the episode is significant in showing the way towards the role that France would play in the final stages of Castlereagh's diplomacy.

At Vienna, Castlereagh was able to use his links with Talleyrand and Metternich to ensure the sort of peace settlement he had wanted. Those who had wanted a vengeful peace were disappointed, but Castlereagh correctly divined that any such settlement would be little more than an extended armistice. The same reasoning dictated his line in 1818 and Aix-la-Chapelle, where he was happy to see France restored to her position; in many senses the Congress marked the culmination of Castlereagh's policy towards France. The problem for Castlereagh in the ensuing period would not be with France, but rather with Russia—which is another story altogether.

NOTES

1. Duc de Broglie (Ed.), *Memoirs of the Prince Talleyrand* (5 vols., London, 1891) vol. ii, p. 15.
2. C. V. Stewart, 3rd Marquess of Londonderry (Ed.), *The Correspondence, Despatches and other papers of Viscount Castlereagh, Second Marquess of Londonderry* (12 vols., London, 1850–53) [hereafter *CC* followed by volume number], Castlereagh to Cathcart, 15 January 1813, vol. viii, p. 304.
3. See P. W. Schroeder, "Did the Vienna System Rest upon a Balance of Power," *American Historical Review* xcvii (1992), pp.683–706, and *The Transformation of European Politics, 1763–1848* (Oxford, 1994), pp. 575–82.
4. *CC* ii, pp. 173–174
5. Ibid., ix, pp. 73–75, Castlereagh to Aberdeen, 13 November 1813.
6. C. K. Webster, *British Diplomacy, 1813–1815: Select Documents Dealing with the Reconstruction of Europe* (London, 1921) [hereafter *BD*], Castlereagh to Cathcart, 18 December 1813, p. 56.
7. *CC* ix, Castlereagh to Liverpool, 31 December 1813, pp. 130–132.
8. Broglie(ed.), *Memoirs of Talleyrand* ii, p. 278
9. Ibid., iii, p. 15.
10. Ibid., ii, p. 261.
11. Ibid., p. 339.
12. Ibid., p. 223.
13. *BD*, p. 185.
14. Ibid., pp. 217–8.
15. Broglie (ed.), *Memoirs of Talleyrand* ii, pp. 255 and 261.
16. *BD*, p. 232.
17. Ibid., pp. 218–9.
18. H. Kissinger, *A World Restored: Metternich, Castlereagh, and the Problems of Peace* (Boston, MA, repr. 1968), p. 154.

PALMERSTON AND ANGLO–FRENCH RELATIONS, 1846–1865

David Brown

Domestically the mid-Victorian years in Britain might have been an "age of equipoise," a period of stability and absence of great alarms, but during this same period Britain's relationship with its neighbour and erstwhile rival, France, hovered uneasily between *entente* and *mésentente*. While many in Britain abhorred the political and social unrest of 1848 and viewed the Second Republic with wariness, British foreign policy sought to foster a good understanding with the new regime. The Second Empire, after 1851, seemed to many the very worst neighbour Britain could hope to have, yet Palmerston saw good reason to welcome it, even if he did lose his post as foreign secretary as a result. Renewed war scares in the 1850s were not enough to jeopardize a valuable military alliance against Russia

For permission to use copyright material I am grateful to the Trustees of the Broadlands Archives (Palmerston Papers, Hartley Library, University of Southampton), to the Société civile du Val-Richer (Guizot Papers, Archives Nationales, Paris), and to the Controller of Her Majesty's Stationery Office (Crown copyright material).

in the East and though Italian unification and the French annexation of Savoy and Nice would put a strain on Anglo–French relations in 1859 and 1860, the need for an Old World balance, of sorts, against the continued rise of the New in America, as well as cold calculations of commercial interest were enough to keep matters *cordiale*. In pursuing a foreign policy generally sympathetic to France, Palmerston twice lost office as a result of perceived deference to French demands, in 1851 and 1858, and yet it was Palmerston, the avowedly "most English minister," whose foreign policy was increasingly identified with values and characteristics that were anything but aligned with France, in which the notion of a developing "Britishness," forged in terms of being, it might be said, "not France," perhaps had some currency.[1]

I

It is usually maintained that Lord Aberdeen, as foreign secretary under Peel (1841–46) and his counter-part in France, François Guizot, successfully carved out an *entente cordiale* in the early 1840s, and that, as one early writer on this subject observed, "France and Britain might have sailed out on to the calm seas of enduring friendship if Palmerston had not come back to office in 1846 to take the wheel out of Aberdeen's patient hands, and wreck the *Entente Cordiale* with his heavy handed helmsmanship."[2] Certainly Palmerston did little to dispel the myth of a close relationship between Britain and France under Aberdeen, though in Palmerston's eyes this was not something to applaud: it was anything but a compliment he intended when he observed in 1846 that for the previous five years Aberdeen had been guilty of "making himself under secretary to Guizot."[3]

Yet this is too much of a distillation of a complicated relationship. Aberdeen, though well disposed towards France, was by no means a puppet of the French government. Exasperated, he would complain that the French "go to work in such a roundabout way that it is difficult for them to inspire confidence." Only his faith in the "veracity of M. Guizot," it seems, preserved his confidence in the possibility of a good understanding between the two countries.[4] Aberdeen's belief that Guizot offered the best hope of a peaceful policy was often put to the test: in the Near East, in Morocco, in Africa, over rights of search of merchant shipping in the pursuit of the suppression of slavery; and notably in 1844 as tensions in, among other places, Tahiti, raised the spectre of war.[5] Greece, for example, in 1843–44 became the scene for a significant test of the durability, even existence, of an *entente cordiale*. Divergent views over Greece, exacerbated by the actions of the British and French representatives at Athens, Sir Edmund Lyons and Théobold Piscatory, led Britain and

France to collide in their attempts to secure an ascendancy for the "English" and "French" parties within a Greek government destabilized by revolution. As tensions between the two countries (or more specifically between Lyons and Piscatory) grew, only renewed fears of an augmentation of Russian influence and the threat to constitutional government in Greece were sufficient to prevent a significant breach. Guizot may have claimed that "*en Grèce, l'entente cordiale a décidément passé de nous à nos agens*," but the episode had only underlined the fact that ultimately it was realpolitik considerations that had prevented a clash.[6]

Yet peace was maintained and with it the notion of an *entente cordiale*— a notion, a myth, arguably, more than a solid understanding, at best an understanding resting on the "personal friendship and mutual confidence of Aberdeen and Guizot."[7] If it was a myth, it was a powerful one, however. Guizot, for example, insisted: "*Nous faisons ensemble depuis trois ans, my dear lord Aberdeen, de la bonne, honnête, et grande politique. J'ai la confiance qu'elle réussira, et que nos deux pays en recueilleront les fruits ; mais quoiqu'il arrive, cette politique là aura ma reconnaissance, car je lui devrai votre amitié.*"[8] It was, indeed, an alliance underpinned by a progressive spirit; as Guizot commented in another letter to Aberdeen: "*Plus je vis, plus je m'affirme dans la conviction que notre politique est la seule bonne, la seule qui assure au monde, non seulement les biens de la paix, mais le bien, encore plus rare, du progrès de la moralité et de la justice dans les rapports de peuples.*"[9] A saddened Guizot could scarcely believe that such a fruitful relationship could come to an end, declaring himself "*bien triste*" at such a prospect in November 1845.[10] Sir Robert Peel, the prime minister, also recognized the concord:

> By means of reciprocal Confidence, of views and purity of Intentions (I may add without arrogance after the Receipt of your kind note) by means of a reciprocal Esteem and private Regard, we have succeeded in elevating the Tone and spirit of the two Nations, have taught them to regard something higher than paltry jealousies and hostile Rivalries, and to estimate the full value of that moral and social Influence, which cordial Relations between England and France give to each for every good and beneficent Purpose.[11]

Yet, as even Aberdeen himself observed, just two months prior to Peel's eulogy, such was the fickle nature of diplomacy that even "a policy of friendship and confidence has been converted into a policy of hostility and distrust."[12]

So far as Aberdeen and Guizot had fashioned an *entente*, then, it seemed particularly, and acutely, apparent primarily in retrospect, particularly once Palmerston had returned to the Foreign Office, bringing with him, supposedly, the Francophobe baggage that had made his relations with Francophile Foxite Whigs, keen to foster a liberal alliance, so difficult in the 1830s.[13] And yet Palmerston had, during the 1830s and early 1840s, frequently found cause to adopt or to urge a friendly policy towards France,[14] and had himself described Guizot in 1841 as "the oldest and dearest friend I may have in the world," and declared his most ardent wish "to maintain the closest possible union between France & England."[15] If he had been guilty of occasionally "dousing the *rapprochement* with cold water,"[16] as in, for example, the late 1830s over the Mehmet Ali question when Palmerston had been receptive to the idea of British cooperation with Russia and in 1840 even undermining a French-brokered Turco–Egyptian settlement of that issue, nonetheless, Palmerston had implicitly recognized the importance of a good understanding with France when, in seeking to restore publicly his reputation abroad he had undertaken a bridge-building visit to Paris during Easter 1846, where, apparently, *ce terrible Lord Palmerston* had become *ce cher Lord Palmerston*.[17]

Palmerston, however, was nothing if not a pragmatist. His charm offensive in Paris had been an attempt to sugar the pill of his return to the Foreign Office, designed to reassure Whigs at home as well as the French "by ocular Demonstration that I have not cloven Feet & a Tail," and to disabuse them of the notion that he "hate[d] France & love[d] war," and remind them that he had "maintained Peace through Ten years of unexampled Difficulty, and that the constant accusation made against me by the Tories when I was in, & they were out, was that I was far too partial to France, and that I leant unduly to an alliance with her, & neglected too much the other Three Powers."[18]

Not all Whigs were convinced; nor, significantly, it seems were many in France. As Guizot reported, "*Il a répété, à tout le monde, qu'il était, autant que personne, ami de la paix, de la France, partisan de l'entente cordiale, et bien décidé a la continuer s'il lui arrivait de revenir au pouvoir*," but, still, "*depuis quelques jours, autour de l'opposition et jusque dans son sein, on commence à dire que c'est trop de fête, et que probablement lord Palmerston n'est pas lui-même si changé qu'on doive changer si complètement envers lui, de sentimens [sic] et d'attitude*."[19] Meanwhile, Cobden, himself no friend of Palmerston, while touring Europe, met Louis Philippe, King of the French, in August 1846 and noted in his diary: "He [Louis Philippe] was not very complimentary to Lord Palmerston, applying to him a French maxim which may be turned into the English phrase 'if you bray a fool in a mortar he will remain a fool still.'"[20] However, while Palmerston did not share Aberdeen's confidence in the pacific outlook of the French governments with which he would work, frequently his balance-book approach to foreign policy directed Palmerston to a pro-French position by default.

II

Between 1846 and 1848 Anglo–French relations worsened. Any lingering hopes for the preservation of some sort of an *entente* were finally quashed as Palmerston sought above all else to steal a march on France in the Iberian peninsula—allowing diplomatic disagreements between Britain and France over the "Spanish marriages" question where both parties sought to gain influence in the peninsula and check the ambitions of the other—to dominate all other issues; surprising in one sense, as Roger Bullen observed, given the many other "pressing problems elsewhere in Europe which were of common concern to both powers."[21] Indeed, it was only the revolutionary movements that spread through so much of continental Europe in 1848 that ended this diplomatic impasse.

From 1848, talk in Britain was less concerned with ideas of an *entente cordiale* that was grounded in some sense of a common political heritage; rather attention turned to a more pragmatic assessment of Britain's material interests and this in turn generated a more consistent and long-lasting harmonious relationship.

Initially, another revolution in France was greeted in Britain with some concern. Palmerston tried to keep an open mind and remain optimistic that Lamartine was strong enough to resist aggressive, bellicose tendencies within the new government, but he also counselled caution: "It must be owned that the prospect of a republic in France is far from agreeable; for such a Government would naturally be more likely to place peace in danger than a monarchy would be," he noted in February 1848, adding, "But we must deal with things as they are, and not as we would wish to have them."[22] In the event, it seemed, things were not too far removed from how the British would wish to have them. Louis Napoleon's ascendancy by the end of the year seemed to reassure many members of Russell's Whig ministry that the new government in France was at least made up of moderates, mindful of the interests of private property, of order and of the rule of law; moreover, a benevolent attitude towards the Second Republic seemed to Palmerston the best way of ensuring Britain's commercial interest by avoiding any further disruption of the continent by intervention in French affairs. And if the revolutionary movements of 1848 in France might have been fuelling unrest in Britain and Ireland, this was as nothing compared to the prevailing sense that the revolution in France tended only to confirm a widespread feeling among Britain's ruling elite, having avoided the social turmoil endured by much of continental Europe, of a certain politico-cultural superiority.[23]

Confidence in the Second Republic was not exclusively an elite view: significantly in an era of growing extra-parliamentary influence, even on foreign policy-making, it is perhaps interesting to note that beyond

Westminster, too, there was a sense that the new government would pursue a more pacific, conciliatory course.[24] France, then, under Louis Napoleon, was a power Britain could work with: cooperation seemed to promise (relative) stability while hostile commentators could content themselves to some extent with thinking that 1848 had revealed France to be a weaker, junior, partner to Britain on the international stage.

For a while, therefore, all seemed well. A few war scares aside, and a persistent concern with national defence to rebuff any French invasions, relations between the two countries proceeded along relatively smooth lines: as one commentator has put it, once it became clear that the French navy was not about to sail up the Thames, "the panic dissipated."[25] Predictably, perhaps, this was not to last. In December 1851, famously on the anniversary of Austerlitz, Louis Napoleon seized power in a *coup d'état* by way ultimately of promoting himself from President to Emperor.

The British public was highly alarmed. So too were many within government when it became known that Napoleon had told Lord Cowley that "he was determined not to fall as Louis-Philippe had done by an extra-pacific policy; that he knew well that the instincts of France were military and domineering, and that he resolved to gratify them."[26] Yet Palmerston adopted a rather less hysterical point of view. He had welcomed the prospect of an enlargement of Napoleon's power as early as 1848 as a bulwark against a resurrection of Bourbon influence,[27] and in 1851, as he would tell his brother-in-law, it seemed that:

> the course of events during the preceding period since the meeting of the assembly had placed the assembly & the President in such a state of antagonism that a conflict between them had obviously become inevitable and that it probably was true as asserted, that if the President had not dissolved the Assembly the Assembly would have tried to arrest him, & that it seemed to me to be better for France & for the tranquillity of Europe that the President should prevail over the Assembly than the Assembly over the President because the success of the Assembly who had no good candidate to offer for the government of France would probably lead to civil war.[28]

Palmerston was dismissed from the Foreign Office following his supposed breach of etiquette in apparently officially endorsing Napoleon's *coup*, but in fact his fall occasioned no substantial change in the view of the British government, although his resignation was, officially, a source of regret to the French government and to Napoleon himself.[29] Russell, the prime minister, had been at pains to reassure the French government that Palmerston's dismissal would result in no change in the policy or sentiment of the British government towards France. In an interview with Walewski, reported to Palmerston by Peter Borthwick of the *Morning Post*, Russell is said to have "expressed himself in language *precisely similar in every respect* to that which had been originally held by your Lordship and the terms in which Walewski has conveyed the explanations of Lord John to his govt are to the full as warm as those in which he reported his first conversation with you."[30]

Yet it was clear that the British government's policy—concerned with maintaining European peace and commercial prosperity—was not wholly in accord with public opinion—which held to notions of Britain's prestige and perceived national honour. As one of Palmerston's critics asked of what he saw as a hasty fraternization with Louis Napoleon: "are these the fitting achievements and habits of the Protestant, English, and Liberal statesman *par excellence* [i.e., Palmerston]?"[31] Palmerston's supporters preferred to see his dismissal as the product of European intrigues, and Palmerston himself was not above suggesting that his removal from office was in part the result of "a weak Truckling to the hostile Intrigues of the Orleans Family, Austria, Russia, Saxony & Bavaria & in some Degree also the present Prussian Govt . . . ."[32] And it was thanks to this impression, that the "most English," "People's" minister had been sacrificed to continental despotism, that Palmerston could get away with approving of an unpopular *coup* in Paris. Yet this episode reveals an important tension in Palmerston's foreign policy towards France. Whereas popular Russophobia, for example, dovetailed nicely with a general sense that Russia was something of a threat to Britain's interests and strategic security, with regard to France, the issue was not so clear cut. Palmerstonian foreign policy had somehow, rhetorically at least, to accommodate a widespread fear of French military ambitions at Britain's expense and a popular Francophobia which underpinned many Britons' sense of English- or British-ness,[33] whilst also, in diplomatic terms, serve commercial, balance of power and strategic interests that frequently demanded close co-operation and alliance with France.

III

Traditionally France was a potential rival and enemy to British interests. With technological advances in steam navigation, fears of a "steam bridge" across the Channel able to transport rapidly the French army to the English coast were neither uncommon nor without foundation. The threat was not consistent, but fears of French invasion informed debates about British defence planning throughout the later 1840s and 1850s.[34] There could be no doubt, for example, that plans for the development of the port of Cherbourg, monitored closely in Britain, could have no other object than to check British naval mastery.[35] In a period of economic depression and financial retrenchment in France, British ministers drew pessimistic conclusions from the intelligence that a sum of £272,000 had apparently been earmarked for "works of defence" for Cherbourg in 1851.[36] In fact French naval expenditure between 1846 and 1853 fell by approximately 16%, amid protestations from Paris that France had no such hostile intentions in view.[37] But, Britain's international power and prestige rested on the maintenance of naval supremacy and any potential challenge to this inevitably assumed a high profile in political considerations.

While invasion panics remained a feature of British politics in the early 1850s, however, such considerations were secondary to the need to establish an alliance with France in 1854 for the purposes of resisting threatened Russian expansionism into the Ottoman empire: Aberdeen reflected that the French alliance established in this year was "the renewal of *our entente.*"[38] The omens for this renewal of cordial relations were positive: "*je dis nous parce que je ne sépare pas l'intérêt de la France de celui de l'Angleterre,*"[39] insisted Napoleon in a letter to Palmerston (who although home secretary maintained a prominent international profile) about the arrangements for his "*Armée d'Orient*" while a few months later, having secured his accession to the premiership, Palmerston enthused to the French emperor: "*L'alliance qui unit si heureusement la France et l'Angleterre et promet des Résultats si avantageux pour toute l'Europe, prend son origine dans la Loyauté, la Franchise, et la sagacité de votre Majesté, et votre Majesté pourra toujours Compter sur la Loyauté et la Franchise du Gouvernement Anglais*".[40] Yet this was an alliance forged in adversity; a negative rather than positive impetus to act together. There was a certain duplicity in Palmerston's stated desire in June 1854 to make sure that neither France nor Britain "lose caste in the world" by concluding "the war with only a small Result."[41] For while his plans for a re-drafting of the map of Europe—producing a Cabinet memorandum "on the measures to be adopted against Russia"—sought to strike a "heavy blow" at Russia's naval power and territorial possessions,[42] his interest in the international stock of France was in fact very limited. He took no pleasure in seeing Sebastopol fall in September 1855 to forces in which the French outnumbered the British and would have preferred to fight on for a more decisive *British* victory. Clearly Palmerston feared losing caste in the world, and at home, by concluding with not just a "small result," but also with a French one.

As a decisive conclusion to a war, the Peace of Paris (1856) was hardly a triumph. The Eastern question was certainly not answered, but neither had an Anglo–French military alliance, it seemed, laid the groundwork for a more enduring understanding or *entente*. Palmerston felt that France had been far too weak and too Russian in its approach to the negotiations.[43] Victoria and Albert might have enjoyed the fruits of a cordial relationship between France and Britain when visiting Paris in 1855 at the height of the two powers' co-operation, but soon could themselves be found retailing fears of French militarism. By 1858, although remaining well-disposed towards Napoleon personally, Victoria was alarmed by French naval expansion which called for redoubled British efforts to maintain a military superiority over France (and other European rivals), a matter on which, she feared by early 1859, Britain's "very existence may be said to depend."[44]

This supposed vulnerability harked back to concerns about Britain's status in the face of resurrected French naval ambitions. British national identity may or may not have been "forged" by reference to France; Britain's sense of itself as a major international power most certainly was. The renewed *entente* of 1854 was clearly of short duration and by 1858 France again seemed to be positioning itself as a rival to Britain; and furthermore, French policy seemed designed not just to achieve parity with Britain but actively to subjugate Britain to the French political will. Napoleon's plans in the aftermath of the Crimean war for a re-drafted map of Europe, in which borders were shifted eastwards allowing France to appropriate much of Belgium, Savoy, and the Rhineland, while creating loose federal structures in Italy and Germany where France would be able to exercise indirect influence if not control, would be underpinned by a dramatically reinvigorated French naval capability. The threat to Britain was clear but made far more explicit in 1860 when the French ambassador told the British government bluntly that if British support for the French over unification of the Danubian Principalities were not forthcoming, then British dockyards, and thus by extension British power, would be destroyed.[45] The full import of the redevelopment of Cherbourg was now impressed on Britain as both countries embarked on an arms race, which had no fixed point of real antagonism, by way of mutual self-definition and in order to lay claim to international relevance. Palmerston, particularly once returned to office in 1859, played up the Anglo–French rivalry to justify high levels of defence expenditure in the face of loud demands for retrenchment and greater economy (not least from the chancellor of the exchequer, William Gladstone). Only by neutralising, or countering, the French challenge, it was argued, could Britain regain an independent voice in international affairs, a significant matter, it was maintained, as France sought to extend its influence in Italy at this time.[46]

Anglo–French relations cooled in other regards too. In January 1858 Felice Orsini, an Italian nationalist, tried to assassinate Napoleon in Paris using bombs which had been made in Britain, and according to a plan apparently hatched by refugees in London. Against the back-drop of a naval arms race, this threatened to force a significant breach between the two powers and Orsini's attempt on the Emperor's life sparked one of the most serious diplomatic incidents between the two countries in this period. Palmerston would for the second time lose office due to a dispute about France, this time seeing his government fall to a parliamentary defeat when, at the insistence of the French, he agreed to introduce a Conspiracy to Murder Bill in February 1858. Palmerston, and most of his cabinet, judged maintaining close relations with France more important ultimately than considerations of national pride; as Palmerston put it in a circular memorandum to colleagues, "it is no slight evil that England should fall into Dishonor in the opinion of all the nations of Europe; and it is a greater evil that the animosity which still rankles in the Breast of every Frenchman against England in Consequence of our naval & military Triumphs over France in the War ended in 1815 should meet with a plausible and avowable Cause which all Europe will admit to be just."[47] It did not help, however, that Francophobic sentiments were being whipped up outside as well as inside parliament at just this moment as rumours circulated suggesting that a legacy of 10,000 francs from the will of Napoleon Bonaparte had since 1851 been paid to reward the actions of a French soldier, Cantillon, who had attempted to assassinate Wellington back in 1818.[48] The timing, from Palmerston's point-of-view, was unfortunate. Lord Cowley, Britain's ambassador in Paris, and Napoleon together smoothed ruffled feathers, and Disraeli, back in office briefly until Palmerston returned in 1859, talked of an *entente cordiale* again in parliament, yet the dominant mood remained suspicion. Renewed war scares and further tension over Italy suggest relations were still not close. Palmerston, indeed, back in government as prime minister again after 1859, seemed in many respects determined to heighten tensions between the two countries. As Sir John Trelawny observed from the backbenches in 1860 when proposals for strengthening Britain's coastal fortifications were under review, "It was remarkable that Palmerston threw off all diplomatic reserve & plainly indicated where danger lies—viz, in France." It was felt Palmerston's increasingly belligerent tone towards France, warning of naval threats, critical of Italian intervention, may well be taken in France "as a menace."[49] Palmerston, however, was reacting to perceived French aggression: as he had recorded in his diary in March 1860, there had been a "scene" at the Tuileries in which Napoleon had publicly chastised the British ambassador, Lord Cowley, over Britain's policy towards the projected annexation of Savoy and had declared that "it was impossible to maintain friendly Relations with England."[50]

Yet there was no war between Britain and France and relations even at this critical juncture were not so unequivocally hostile as narratives of a naval race might imply. Palmerston, the gun-boat diplomat and populist minister, need not have looked too far for popular backing for a show-down with France: as Lord Aberdeen remarked:

> Notwithstanding the amicable settlement of the differences connected with the Conspiracy Bill, and the concessions made by the French Government, a sore feeling remains, and the Emperor has become universally unpopular. People here regard the state of France with much alarm. It is difficult to believe that the present state of suspicion and severity should endure; but the consequence of any crisis can only I fear be such at present as to lead to the most gloomy apprehensions.[51]

Nonetheless, Palmerston insisted throughout, whatever he might have said in the Commons about naval and military rivalries, that "in spite of conflicting interests which might place England at variance . . . with France and the United States, the ties of commercial interest are too strong to be broken."[52] Palmerston's faith in free trade might be traced back to his university education in Edinburgh at the very beginning of the nineteenth century, and it was a principle he held to; indeed, at just this time he even went so far as to tell the Russian ambassador that if it was the aim of any country "to secure a good understanding with England, they ought to liberalize their commercial system."[53] The Commercial Treaty between Britain and France brokered by Richard Cobden in 1860 was fundamental to preserving good relations between the two countries. It was, however, a political prescription and not an economic one. The tariff reductions agreed in 1860 pre-empted any conflict, and set the stage for a period of harmonious relations, but both countries soon found the agreement less useful than hoped for, and it was abandoned in the 1880s.[54] Palmerston had reservations about the apparent imbalances within this agreement for mutual tariff reductions at the time and wondered how he might sell the idea to parliament and the British public, but he suppressed his doubts on the basis that a commercial agreement would off-set other potentially damaging areas of disagreement.

Hence Palmerston's reluctant acquiescence in French annexation of Savoy and Nice in 1860. France, of course, had claimed Savoy and Nice as a reward from Piedmont-Sardinia in return for support in the war with Austria the previous year. Yet, for all the reported fears that this was the harbinger of further French expansionism, it is reported by Lord Malmesbury that Palmerston not only knew of Napoleon's intention to claim these territories as reward for French intervention as early as November 1858 but that he "entered into the plan completely."[55] Indeed, Palmerston insisted in a speech to parliament that French conduct in Italy only confirmed Napoleon's much earlier stated intention to preserve peace, not wage war in Europe: "I do not hold," Palmerston insisted in the Commons, "that . . . what took place in Italy last year . . . was any departure from that principle . . . France undertook a noble enterprise . . . freeing Italy from foreign domination—aye . . . French domination included. . . ."[56]

Palmerston may have had his reservations about France under Napoleon, but he was more worried about what or who might follow the Empire or the Emperor. Thus his defence building concerns were against future threats more than present dangers. Fears of a naval challenge from France—it was feared by 1859–60 that the French navy might actually exceed the British in both size an sophistication[57]—were part of a much broader concern about Britain's ebbing world power. There was certainly considerable alarm in Britain in the late 1850s and early 1860s over a potential conflict with France, causing Tennyson to issue his famous call to "Riflemen, form!" in *The Times*,[58] and even the Queen was drawn to complain angrily in May 1860:

> Really it is too bad! *No* country, no human being would ever dream of *disturbing* or *attacking* France; every one would be glad to see her prosperous; but *she* must needs disturb every quarter of the Globe and try to make mischief and set every one by the ears; and, of course, it will end some day in a *regular crusade* against *the universal disturber of the world!* It is really monstrous![59]

Yet projected naval and military threats need not be taken at face value. If Palmerstonian foreign policy was about anything it was about pragmatic checks and balances. His insistence on Britain having "no eternal allies" and "no perpetual enemies," only interests that "are eternal and perpetual" has become a platitude, but Palmerston did see this as an important foundation for his politics. As he reminded Clarendon in 1859, "Governments and nations are less influenced by resentment for former antagonism or by gratitude for former services than by considerations of present or prospective interest."[60]

France, and specifically France under Napoleon III, was a known quantity. Commercial ties and common security concerns (notably containment of Russia) were enough to underpin a common bond in a changing world. Palmerston might not have liked the balance of power in Europe at all times, but it was more familiar and broadly manageable than the unknown ramifications of a growing American world role as civil war upset the *status quo* in America, where Britain had important economic interests too, of course. There was perhaps reason to see a benefit in a cordial understanding with Britain's close neighbour across the Channel, therefore, not just to avoid war there: as Palmerston put it in 1865, clearly with concerns about the possible spread of American democracy to Europe if Europe seemed weak, a goodwill visit to Britain by the French navy had several benefits, including: "a most wholesome effect in Yankee land, where they [demonstrations of friendship between Britain and France] will be taken as indications of a closer union than in fact . . . exists, and . . . will thus tend to disincline the Yankees from aggression on us."[61] In a period of instability in north America, Palmerston was keen to convey this impression that "the Yankees will be all the less likely to give trouble in Canada or Mexico."[62] It may have been that this over-arching concern of maintaining an *entente* ultimately distracted Britain, and France, from the only slightly longer-term challenge of Prussia,[63] but nonetheless Anglo–French harmony seemed the best guarantor of international relevance and influence in both countries.

IV

British foreign policy towards France and Anglo–French relations in the age of Palmerston might defy neat categorisation, but it is not perhaps quite as reckless or even schizophrenic as it might have appeared at times. It is necessary to understand something of Palmerston's position and priorities to make sense of it. He saw benefits, certainly, in a sense of antagonism (the popular perception of that was as, if not more, useful as an actual rivalry). It served his interest as the supposedly most patriotic minister who would defend British, perhaps more accurately English, values against illiberalism and unconstitutionalism and he was no doubt happy enough that his naval defence building and fears of French invasion complemented a popular suspicion of France. It mattered not that the electorate of France under Napoleon was the largest in Europe; Palmerston played on stereotypes and not always accurate accounts. But this was not to be pushed too far and remained a largely rhetorical device rather than an unalterable instrument of policy: there were too many hard, practical considerations that demanded Anglo–French cooperation. There may have been a party political aspect to all this as well. As Trelawny commented in 1861, it was largely foreign affairs that kept Palmerston's ministry in power: the "Govt is mainly sustained by their foreign policy," he wrote, "& the great apprehensions most men now have of the effect of change at this moment. America, France, Italy, Poland, Hungary— danger everywhere. Who is to open the ball in this dance of death?"[64] Who indeed, but to Palmerston it seemed taking France as a partner made the dance floor a slightly safer place.

Salisbury's criticism of Palmerston's foreign policy, that he failed to keep France on side (indeed even exacerbated Anglo–French hostilities) and simultaneously failed to harmonize Anglo–Russian relations (or neutralize Russia through a durable Anglo–French alliance) has been echoed in some recent work on Palmerston.[65] But the charge is taken from a too simplistic reading of that policy. Palmerston did not revive the *entente cordiale*; he did not abandon his suspicion of France, and he happily, on occasion, used fear of France to justify his defence arrangements and even his claims to represent the true interests of England (or Britain) by exploiting a popular prejudice towards France and the French. But Palmerston's approach to Anglo–French relations in the period between the 1840s and 1860s, so far as it displayed any consistencies, demonstrated a clear commitment to sustaining so far as possible commercial ties and strategic alliances (especially directed against Russia) to preserve the balance of power, even when those considerations conflicted with his own instincts to align British foreign policy against rather than alongside France.

For all the building of forts, or follies, in the early 1860s and a supposedly deteriorating relationship between the two countries, Anglo–French relations in the era of Palmerston and Louis Napoleon, if not quite amounting to an *entente cordiale*, were at least grounded in a mutual appreciation of the benefits of a common accord. And even if they lacked the romanticized trappings of a liberal alliance forged from common cultural ties as looked to in the 1830s, or the personal warmth of a meeting between Aberdeen and Guizot in the early- to mid-1840s, Anglo–French relations between 1846 and 1865, whether in spite of or because of Palmerston, were perhaps no less conducive to peace and prosperity than they had been in the 15 years or so before 1846. It was not mere sentimental hyperbole, therefore, that caused the French government to lament on the occasion of Palmerston's death in 1865 that:

> *Pour nous, Monsieur, nous avons eu dans plusieurs circonstances importantes, l'occasion d'apprécier les hautes qualités dont Lord Palmerston était doué, et nous aimerons toujours à nous rappeler combien il a contribué à l'établissement des rapports de confiance et d'amitié qui, dès les commencements du Second Empire, ont existé entre la France et l'Angleterre.*
>
> *Lord Palmerston a été le premier, au mois de Décembre 1851, à reconnaître le caractère des courageuses résolutions que la situation de la France a inspirées à Sa Majesté. Il en a loyalement accepté les conséquences, en se plaçant au dessus des ressentiments du passé, avec une liberté de jugement d'autant plus digne d'éloges, qu'au début de sa carrière, il avait été mêlé aux anciennes luttes; il a usé de son influence pour faire comprendre à ses concitoyens les services rendus à la cause de l'ordre en Europe par les évènements accomplis en France.*[66]

NOTES

1. On Britishness defined by reference to "Other(s)" (principally a Catholic France), see L. Colley, *Britons: Forging the Nation, 1707–1837* (New Haven and London: Yale University Press, 1996); but as a counterpoint see also, e.g., L. Brockliss and

D. Eastwood (Eds.), *A Union of Multiple Identities: The British Isles, c.1750–1850* (Manchester: Manchester University Press, 1997) and K. Robbins, *Great Britain: Ideas, Institutions and the Idea of Britishness* (Harlow: Longman, 1998).

2. A. B. Cunningham, "Peel, Aberdeen and the *Entente Cordiale,*" *Bulletin of the Institute of Historical Research* xxx (1957), p. 191.
3. Palmerston to Russell, 8 Dec. 1846, Russell Papers, The National Archives (Public Record Office) [hereafter TNA (PRO)], Gifts and Deposits, PRO 30/22,/5F, fols. 96–97.
4. Aberdeen to Lieven, 19 Oct. 1841, quoted in Cunningham, "Peel, Aberdeen and the *Entente Cordiale,*" p. 191.
5. Ibid., esp. pp. 194, 200–01.
6. For a fuller discussion of this episode see D. McLean, "The Greek revolution and the Anglo-French entente 1843–4," *English Historical Review* xcvi, 378 (1981). McLean attributes Lyons' antipathy towards Anglo–French cooperation to his connections with Palmerston: "He [Lyons] was one of Palmerston's protégés and Aberdeen always found it rather difficult to convey the message of Anglo-French *entente* to him," (p. 125).
7. R. Bullen, *Palmerston, Guizot and the Collapse of the Entente Cordiale* (London: Athlone Press, 1974), p. 335.
8. Guizot to Aberdeen, 12 Jan. 1845 (copy), Papiers Guizot, Archives Nationales, Paris, 42 AP 211/114 [163 MI 51].
9. Guizot to Aberdeen, 3 June 1845 (copy), ibid., 42 AP 211/116 [163 MI 51].
10. Guizot to Aberdeen, 13 Nov. 1845 (copy), ibid., 42 AP 211/122 [163 MI 51].
11. Sir Robert Peel to Guizot, 18 Dec. 1845, ibid., 42 AP 221/1 [163 MI 55].
12. Aberdeen, Sept. 1845, quoted in Cunningham, "Peel, Aberdeen and the *Entente Cordiale,*" p. 204.
13. See, for example, L. Mitchell, *Holland House* (London: Duckworth, 1980), pp. 11–38, 146–72, 269–301; idem, *Lord Melbourne, 1779–1848* (Oxford: Oxford University Press, 1997), p.156. On the Francophilia of English Whigs in this period, which extended to admiration of French sartorial, literary, cultural and architectural tastes, see R. Eagles, "Beguiled by France? The English Aristocracy, 1748–1848," in Brockliss and Eastwood (Eds.), *Multiple Identities.*
14. As Palmerston had insisted in a letter to his brother in 1836, for example, however hard Russia and Austria might try, nothing would undermine the alliance between Britain and France, Palmerston to Sir William Temple, 5 Mar. 1836, Palmerston Papers, Southampton University Library, GC/TE/243.
15. Palmerston to H. L. Bulwer, 17 Aug. 1841, (copy) [letter forwarded to Guizot by Bulwer, 19 Aug. 1841], Papiers Guizot, 42 AP 223/7 [163 MI 55].
16. R. Golicz, "Napoleon III, Lord Palmerston and the Entente Cordiale," *History Today* v, 12 (2000), p. 11.
17. E. Ashley, *The Life and Correspondence of Henry John Temple, Viscount Palmerston* (2 vols., London, 1879) i, p. 499.
18. Palmerston to Sir William Temple, 10 Apr. 1846, Palmerston Papers, GC/TE/314.
19. Guizot to Aberdeen, 28 Apr. 1846 (copy), Papiers Guizot, 42 AP 211/124 [163 MI 51].
20. M. Taylor (Ed.), *The European Diaries of Richard Cobden, 1846–1849* (Aldershot, 1994), p. 44 [6 Aug. 1846].

21. Bullen, *Palmerston, Guizot and the Collapse of the Entente Cordiale*, p. 336.
22. Palmerston to Lord Westmorland (Minister in Berlin), 29 Feb. 1848, in
    K. Bourne, *The Foreign Policy of Victorian England, 1830–1902* (Oxford: Oxford
    University Press, 1970), p. 291.
23. Fabrice Bensimon, *Les Britanniques face à la révolution française de 1848* (Paris:
    L'Harmattan, 2000), p. 399: "*A travers ce qu'expriment les notables victoriens sur
    la révolution française de 1848, nous voyons l'Angleterre à laquelle ils aspirent:
    libérale, loyale, dominante, sûre d'elle, fière de ses traditions et respectueuse de ses
    clivages sociaux, avec ses classes laborieuses et ses élites éclairées.*"
24. R. Postgate and A. Vallance (Eds.), *Those Foreigners. The English People's Opin-
    ion on Foreign Affairs as reflected in their Newspapers since Waterloo* (London:
    Harrap, 1937), esp. pp. 61–2. See, for example, the quoted extract from *Britannia*,
    11 Mar. 1848, a popular Tory, patriotic, title: "We must acknowledge that
    there is some retribution in all this, for the irreconcilable bitterness and saucy
    scorn with which everything English has been treated by everything French for
    the last half-dozen years. There was not a Minister in the Cabinet who did not
    contemplate a war with England with as much *sang-froid* and as much satisfac-
    tion as he contemplated a Cabinet dinner; nor a *militaire*, from the field-mar-
    shal down to the drummer, who did not regard an invasion, as in their own
    phrase, a *promenade d'armes*, which, after walking over some hundred thou-
    sand of our volunteers between Dover and London, should seat themselves
    comfortably in Buckingham Palace, pen in hand, dismembering the Empire.
    Those visions, however, we presume have been pretty well put to flight; and,
    England having not the slightest passion for either cutting the throats or plun-
    dering the goods of its neighbours, it is to be hoped that the French, being
    taught be experience, will learn better thoughts of us, and that all will be quiet,
    at least for a time."
25. Golicz, "Napoleon III, Lord Palmerston and the Entente Cordiale," p. 12.
26. Quoted in D. Newsome, *The Victorian World Picture: Perceptions and Introspec-
    tions in an Age of Change* (London: John Murray, 1997), p. 102.
27. Palmerston to Sir William Temple, 9 Dec. 1848, Palmerston Papers, GC/
    TE/322: "People seem still to think that Louis Napoleon will be President.
    That will not at first or for a certain Time make any material Change in the
    Foreign Policy of France; but in the long Run, and indeed before next sum-
    mer is over it will have some very sensible effect. I should not be sorry if it
    ended in Louis Napoleon being made Emperor, & thus ridding us of both
    Branches of the Bourbons; but the adherents of that Family certainly imag-
    ine that they will be able to get rid of Louis Nap and set up a Bourbon in his
    stead. . . ."
28. Palmerston to Laurence Sulivan, 26 Dec. 1851, in K. Bourne (Ed.), *The Letters
    of the Third Viscount Palmerston to Laurence and Elizabeth Sulivan, 1804–1863*
    (London: Royal Historical Society, 1979), pp. 298–9.
29. A. Lefèvre, "La chute de Palmerston (1851): la part de responsabilité
    française," *Revue d'histoire Diplomatique* lxxxiv (1970), p. 94; Count Alexandre
    Walewski to Palmerston, 26 Dec. 1851, Palmerston Papers, GC/WA/13.
30. Palmertson Papers, GMC/47/1–2, Peter Borthwick to Palmerston, 27 Dec. 1851.
    For a fuller consideration of the domestic impact and consequences of this episode

in Britain, see D. Brown, *Palmerston and the Politics of Foreign Policy, 1846–55* (Manchester, 2002), pp. 119–29 and D. Brown, "The Power of Public Opinion: Palmerston and the Crisis of Dec. 1851," *Parliamentary History* xx, 3 (2001).

31. W. Wilks, *Palmerston in Three Epochs: a Comparison of Facts with Opinions* (London: Wm Freeman, 1854), p. 57.

32. Palmerston Papers, GC/TE/341/3: Palmerston to Sir William Temple, 22 Jan. 1852.

33. See Brown, *Palmerston and the Politics of Foreign Policy*, esp. pp. 34–5, 39, 40–2, 118–9. Cf. Colley, *Britons*.

34. M.S. Partridge, "The Russell Cabinet and National Defence, 1846–1852," *History* lxxii (1987), pp. 231–250. Palmerston spoke of a "steam bridge" in a speech to the House of Commons on 30 July 1845, ibid., p. 232.

35. The following extracts from a report by M. le Général Randon, Ministre de Guerre on the importance of Cherbourg in the event of war with Britain were extracted from the *Moniteur* of 2 Mar. 1851 and circulated among ministers in Britain: "*Depuis plus d'un demi-siècle, le Département de la Marine travaille avec persévérance à la création de ce vaste établissement, qui, par sa position géographique à trente lieues de l'Angleterre, par les ressources qu'il offrira à la navigation, en paix comme en guerre, et par les sacrifices mêmes que le pays s'est déjà imposés, afin de tirer parti des avantages naturels de son site, peut être à bon droit, aujourd'hui, considéré comme le point militaire le plus important de nos cotes. . . . Cherbourg est donc parfaitement propre au rassemblement d'une flotte; c'est le seul point qui, en cas de guerre, nous donne le moyen de tenir en échec une Puissance voisine et rivale, pour laquelle il deviendra de plus en plus un objet d'envie, et qui, sans aucun doute, tâchera de le détruire si l'occasion s'en présente. . . . En seconde lieu, aujourd'hui que l'enceinte du port militaire est sur le point d'être terminée, il n'est pas douteux qu'une attaque par terre ne soit infiniment moins probable qu'une attaque par mer . . .,*" Palmerston Papers, MM/FR/21.

36. Memorandum on the Defence of Cherbourg, [c. Mar.] 1851, (Copy, in Palmerston's hand but author not identified, possibly Sir John Burgoyne), ibid., MM/FR/23/enc.1 (1–2).

37. Crédits accordés au Ministère de la Marine (in francs)—1846: 140,247,101; 1847: 158,093,515; 1848: 153,615,777; 1849: 128,137,418; 1852: 117,215,804; 1853: 117,181,001. See R. Edwards to Palmerston, 29 Nov. 1852, Palmerston Papers, MM/FR/25 and MM/FR/25/enc.1.

38. Aberdeen to Guizot, 14 May 1854, Papiers Guizot, 42 AP 211/51 [163 MI 51].

39. Napoleon III to Palmerston, 16 Dec. 1854, Palmerston Papers, GC/NA/96.

40. Palmerston to Napoleon III, 8 Feb. 1855 (copy), ibid., GC/NA/100.

41. Broadlands Papers, CAB/65, memorandum by Palmerston "on the measures to be adopted against Russia," 15 June 1854.

42. See Broadlands Papers, CAB/65–79, and also M.E. Chamberlain, *Lord Palmerston* (Cardiff: University of Wales Press, 1987), pp. 94–6, for a discussion of these cabinet papers.

43. Palmerston to Walewsky, 10 Sept. 1856 (copy), Palmerston Papers, GC/WA/24.

44. Queen Victoria to Derby, Jan. 1859, quoted in Newsome, *Victorian World Picture*, pp. 109–10.

45. A. D. Lambert, "Politics, Technology and Policy-Making, 1859–1865: Palmerston, Gladstone and the Management of the Ironclad Naval Race," *The Northern Mariner* viii, 3 (1998), p. 10.
46. Ibid., pp. 13–14.
47. Memorandum by Palmerston on Conspiracy to Murder, 23 Jan. 1858, Palmerston Papers, CAB/89. For cabinet members' comments see ibid., CAB/90–101.
48. See *Cantillon's Legacy; when was it paid, and who paid it? Speech of William Stirling, MP for Perthshire, in asking the above question in the House of Commons on the 12th Feb.,1858; with the reply of Viscount Palmerston, KG, First Lord of the Treasury, &c. together with official documents from the "Moniteur," and other sources, relating to that legacy* (London, 1858).
49. *The Parliamentary Diaries of Sir John Trelawny, 1858–1865*, (Ed.), T. A. Jenkins (London:Royal Historical Society, 1990), pp. 141 (23 July 1860), and 146 (24 Aug. 1860).
50. Palmerston's diary, 6 Mar. 1860, Palmerston Papers, D/20.
51. Aberdeen to Guizot, 19 Mar. 1858, Papiers Guizot, 42 AP 211/69 [163 MI 51].
52. Palmerston to Clarendon, 18 May 1858, quoted in E. D. Steele, *Palmerston and Liberalism, 1855–1865* (Cambridge: Cambridge University Press, 1991), p. 246.
53. Palmerston to Clarendon, 18 May 1858, quoted in ibid., p. 249.
54. P. T. Marsh, "The End of the Anglo-French Commercial Alliance, 1860–1894," in P. Chassaigne and M. Dockrill (Eds.), *Anglo-French Relations 1898–1998: From Fashoda to Jospin* (Basingstoke: Palgrave Macmillan, 2002), pp. 34–43.
55. Malmesbury's account (from his unpublished diary) quoted from and discussed in Steele, *Palmerston and Liberalism*, pp. 267–8.
56. Palmerston in House of Commons, 13 Mar. 1860, quoted in ibid., p. 267.
57. C. J. Bartlett, *Defence and Diplomacy: Britain and the Great Powers, 1815–1914* (Manchester: Manchester University Press, 1993), pp. 64–5.
58. Alfred, Lord Tennyson, *The War*. This call for volunteers was published in *The Times*, 9 May 1860.
59. Queen Victoria to the King of the Belgians, 8 May 1860, in A. C. Benson, and Viscount Esher (Eds.), *The Letters of Queen Victoria: A Selection from Her Majesty' Correspondence between the Years 1837 and 1861* (3 vols., London: John Murray, repr. 1908) iii, p. 399.
60. Palmerston to Clarendon, 4 Nov. 1859, quoted in Steele, *Palmerston and Liberalism*, p. 249.
61. Palmerston to Somerset, 27 Aug. 1865, quoted in Steele, *Palmerston and Liberalism*, p. 254.
62. Quoted in Lambert, "Politics, Technology and Policy-Making," p. 28.
63. Ibid., p. 30.
64. *Trelawny Diaries*, p. 188 (22 July 1861).
65. J. Charmley, "Palmerston: 'Artful Old Dodger' or 'Babe of Grace'?," in T. G. Otte (Ed.), *The Makers of British Foreign Policy from Pitt to Thatcher* (Basingstoke: Palgrave Macmillan, 2002), pp. 93–94.
66. M. Drouyn de Lhuys to Baron Baude, Chargé d'affaires de France à Londres, 20 Oct. 1865, communicated 23 Oct. 1865 (copy), Palmerston Papers, BR22(ii)/22/2.

FROM "WAR-IN-SIGHT" TO NEARLY WAR: ANGLO–FRENCH RELATIONS IN THE AGE OF HIGH IMPERIALISM, 1875–1898

T. G. Otte

Shortly after the conclusion of the Anglo–French convention and declarations of 8 April 1904 a pen portrait of Britain's ambassador at Paris, Sir Edmund Monson, appeared in the *Pall Mall Magazine*. Its author commented: "The *entente cordiale* is a reality, established and perpetuated by the Anglo-French treaty. Long before so happy a consummation, there were influences at work to change the misunderstandings and misrepresentations between the two peoples into something akin to good feeling."[1] This was very much a case of painting the recent past in colours that suited present tastes and needs.

1904 has cast a long shadow across the twentieth century. As Maurice Vaïsse and Robert Frank noted recently, "the *entente cordiale* has largely overtaken, in historical importance, the event itself." Thus, a recent French foreign minister celebrated that, on the basis of common values, "*le coq et le lion choisissent finallement de s'entendre*"; but the very notion of the *entente* has tended to obscure important façets of a more complex history.[2] Before 1900, Anglo-French relations at state-level, as Philip Bell observed in his magisterial survey of cross-Channel relations in the first half of the twentieth century, "were . . . close but complicated. The attitudes which the two peoples held towards one another were also deep-rooted and ambiguous."[3]

Ambiguity characterised Anglo–French relations in the realm of international diplomacy and in terms of public opinion. It was, after all, a French writer who first coined the *mal mot* of the "*perfide Albion*," and Léon Gambetta, the great Republican statesman, referred to her as "*l'égotiste Angleterre*." Successive occupants of the embassy in the Rue du Faubourg St. Honoré complained of the "scoundrelly press of Paris."[4] Jules Lecesne, newpaper proprietor and deputy of the *extrème gauche*, confided to *The Times* correspondent at Paris that "England was a treacherous friend and the French would never forget the conduct of the perfidious government of the hypocritical Prime Minister, Mr. William Gladstone, and he hissed out the 'William' as if it were a word of abuse."[5] French journals invariably railed against the evil machinations of British diplomacy lubricated by the wealth of the City of London, revelled in anti-British cartoons of dubious taste, or delved into the peccadilloes (real and mostly imagined) of members of the British Royal family. All of this had the effect of leaving the French public, as Monson resignedly commented in 1900, "educated in hostility of England."[6]

Across the Channel such sentiments were heartily reciprocated. Anglo–Saxon, Protestant suspicions of Catholic France and her disparate traditions of monarchical absolutism, religious obscurantism, revolutionary republicanism and Bonapartist demagoguery were common. French political instability suggested fickleness as the dominant national characteristic. Even a Francophile like Sir Charles Dilke felt compelled to complain that French ministers "behave like children; they do not understand politics and shuffle around in the dark." Many of them, moreover, were "obscurantists" beholden to clerical interests. Besides, it was widely agreed that the "Great Republic," as Lord Rosebery sneered, was "a centre of corruption," both political and moral.[7] Francophilia, moreover, did not translate into an absence of suspicion and mistrust.[8]

A posting to Paris remained highly desirable for budding British diplomatists. The French capital, F.O. Adams, chargé d'affaires there in the mid-1870s, noted, was "for us diplomats at least, the very pleasantest place in the world. . . . Life is so easy, with a certain amount of occupation the days pass so pleasantly that one has not time to be so miserable or to desire more."[9] Edwin Egerton, embassy secretary in the late 1880s, conceded that politically "Paris is no great centre"; but it remained a good staging post *en route* to more important, though less glittering, posts, such as St. Petersburg or Berlin. Besides it was close to home, as Henry Howard, then a junior clerk at the Foreign Office noted in the early 1880s: "those fellows at the Paris Embassy are always coming over to London on some excuse or another; hardly a week passes without seeing one of them over here."[10]

Ambiguity also extended to state level. For Britain, France was a troublesome overseas competitor; but she was also an important part of the continental equilibrium.[11] It was with France that Britain concluded a free-trade treaty in 1860, thereby laying the foundations of a series of free-trading arrangements with most continental countries. Occasional trade disputes notwithstanding, Anglo–French commercial relations were characterised by "a conciliatory spirit" until France withdrew from the free trade treaty network in 1890.[12]

The complexity and ambiguity of Anglo–French relations are well illustrated by the period of the last quarter of the nineteenth century. The choice of dates may appear arbitrary. But it is not without reason, for the two dates define a discrete period in relations between France and Britain. It is a period defined by two major international crises, the "War-in-Sight" crisis of 1875 and the Fashoda stand-off in 1898. Both events also illustrate another characteristic feature of cross-Channel relations: the tension between core European security calculations and extra-European imperial and strategic interests. France had to deal with two problems. In Europe, the antagonism with Germany, with the "lost provinces" of Alsace and Lorraine at its core, seemed irremovable. Beyond Europe lay Britain and her empire. Paris and London were in frequent dispute over such diverse matters as fishing rights along the Great Bank of Newfoundland, strips of sand in West Africa, control over the headwaters of the Nile or the Mekong valley in Siam. The dynamic between these conflicting interests and concerns shaped Franco–British relations in this period.

I

In the history of nineteenth century Great Power politics 1875 marked a crucial *caesura*. The Franco–German war scare, the beginning of the Great Eastern crisis, and Britain's acquisition of the majority of the Suez Canal shares were to influence relations between the Great Powers for the next quarter of a century and longer. The crisis in the West was the result of the machinations of the German chancellor, Prince Otto von Bismarck. From the autumn of 1873 onwards international politics had become more fluid again, following France's fulfillment of her reparations obligations to Germany and the final evacuation of German troops from northern France. To ensure permanent French weakness Bismarck sought to isolate France by combining with the two other Eastern Powers, Russia and Austria-Hungary, in the 1873 *Dreikaiserbund*. However, these attempts were in danger of being undermined in the autumn of the following year by the efforts of Prince Aleksandr Mikhailovich Gorchakov, the Russian chancellor, to bring about a rapprochement with France, as had been the aim of Russian diplomacy in the years between the Crimean War and the Polish uprising of 1863. An attempt to win over Gorchakov to the idea of a closer Russo–German combination having failed in early 1875, Bismarck decided to pressurize France.[13]

The ratification of a new French army law, which stipulated a substantial increase in the size of France's armed forces in war-time, provided the needed pretext. An inspired article in the *Berliner Post* on 8 April 1875, entitled "Is War in Sight?," raised the spectre of renewed Franco–German conflict.[14] A fortnight later, the French ambassador at Berlin, Elie visconte Gontaut-Biron, was told that, unless France's armaments programme were abandoned, Berlin felt justified in considering a preventive war.[15] Bismarck's rationale was simple enough, though the crisis that followed was a bluff that got out of hand. Four years after the end of hostilities the French army was no match for Germany. France would have to yield to German pressure, and would so be relegated permanently to the second flight of Powers. Bismarck's apparent desire to fasten a quarrel upon France triggered a flurry of diplomatic activity in the chancelleries of Europe. The French foreign minister, Louis-Charles duc Décazes, used the growing war panic to launch a diplomatic and press counter-offensive. He urged London and St. Petersburg to support France, or else accept the further growth of German power.[16]

Décazes's appeal met with a mixed reception in Britain. The ambassador at Berlin, Lord Odo Russell, acknowledged Bismarck's "sensational policy," but doubted that he sought renewed war. Berlin's assumption, he reasoned, was that "the warning given by the press of Berlin will be sufficient to convince the French Government that they will better desist from organizing their army in a manner that must be looked upon as a threat to Germany."[17] If Russell did not believe in a war, the Queen, and to some extent Prime Minister Benjamin Disraeli and his Foreign Secretary, the Earl of Derby, did. The Queen, more jingoistic than many of her subjects, was "eager to do something."[18] Disraeli, anxious in equal measure to please the Queen and to play a major role in European diplomacy, did little to restrain the indignant monarch. He wished "to encourage confidence and goodwill on the part of France towards England," without giving the impression of "a special and separate understanding as would arouse the jealousy of Bismarck."[19] Disraeli suspected the German chancellor of "playing the game of the old Bonaparte."[20] Were France to submit to German bullying, and so be reduced to the rank of a minor Power, it would remove the option of future diplomatic cooperation with Paris, and so narrow the room of manouevre of British diplomacy.

Disraeli could not move without Derby, one of the unjustly underrated Victorian Foreign Secretaries. Although he shared Disraeli's concerns about Bismarck's presumed Napoleonic ambitions, he was also aware of the constraints placed upon Britain. As he commented on Décazes's appeal for Russia and Britain to put a stop to German pretensions, "easier said than done."[21] Russell's repeated assurances that war was not imminent made some impression on him. Any active step, then, ran the risk of escalating the situation. Derby was also concerned about the stability of the French state. Following the upheavals of 1870–1, France was "a country whose traditions have been violently broken through." Any major foreign crisis was likely to result in further domestic turmoil and international unrest.[22]

Between them, Disraeli and Derby blocked "the Great Lady" and her ideas of drastic unilateral diplomatic action. The key to the situation lay in Berlin, and Bismarck's fear of Russian interference. Derby pinned his hopes on "*la salutaire influence*" that Russia could bring to bear upon the German chancellor, as he impressed upon the French chargé d'affaires, Charles Gavard.[23] Tsar Alexander II's long-arranged visit to Berlin on 10 May, Derby calculated, provided a diplomatic opening: "It cannot be in the interest of Russia to have France destroyed and Germany omnipotent." Russian intervention was the most effective means of restraining Germany: "Bismarck would hardly undertake to fight Russia and France combined. I see little other prospect of averting mischief."[24]

Prime Minister and Foreign Secretary pursued a two-pronged approach. The Tsar was encouraged, through Royal channels, to use "*votre grande influence*" to maintain peace and to dissipate "the profound alarm" in Europe caused by Bismarck's language.[25] At the same time, Derby obtained Cabinet approval for Russell to support Russian mediation efforts at Berlin. Anglo–Russian cooperation—the first such combination since the Crimean War—came as an unpleasant surprise to the German chancellor, and he was forced to disengage.[26]

The "War-in-Sight" crisis was significant on a number of counts. British intervention in the war-scare was motivated principally by general balance-of-power calculations. Privately, Derby scoffed at Décazes's later attempts "to make it appear in the eyes of Europe that we have taken the side of France . . . , instead of simply intervening to keep the peace, as is the fact."[27] The outcome of the crisis circumscribed Germany's freedom of manoeuvre, but confirmed her position as the "semi-hegemon" of Europe. The joint intervention by Russia and Britain, moreover, revealed how flimsy the ideological sticking plaster of the 1873 *Dreikaiserbund* already was. Finally, the crisis did not determine the future course of Anglo-German relations. Derby, in fact, stressed in July 1875 that there was no fundamental difference of interests between the two Powers.[28] For his part, Bismarck now encouraged renewed overseas expansion, a new phase in international politics initiated by Disraeli's purchase of the majority of the Suez Canal shares in November 1875.

All of this had a profound impact on Anglo–French relations. Their focus now shifted to the Eastern Mediterranean. Britain's *de facto* control over the Suez maritime defile created a new strategic logic. It bolted together the hitherto separate, British–European and the Anglo–Indian blocs of the Empire. The strategic line of communication with the Canal and India transformed the Mediterranean into a "great strategic corridor" for the British Empire. Although Britain claimed some seniority of interest in Egypt, London and Paris acted together. During the Russo–Turkish war of 1877–8 and at the Berlin congress, diplomatic cooperation with France as well as Austria and Germany ensured Russian isolation.[29]

Anglo–French cooperation came at a price. Britain's acquisition of Cyprus in June 1878 made it necessary to compensate France. Following the Berlin congress French diplomacy became more active: "*au recueillement succède la politique d'opportunisme*," oscillating between "*la politique de revanche et la politique d'abdication*."[30] Already at Berlin, the new Foreign Secretary, Lord Salisbury, and William Henry Waddington, the French chief delegate, had come to some form of private understanding. Britain was an Asiatic Power, Waddington, the son of an English claret merchant, product of Rugby, and Cambridge rowing blue, explained. France was a Mediterranean Power, and needed a free hand in the region. Salisbury encouraged France to seize Tunis: "Do what you like there. [. . .] You will be obliged to take it; you cannot leave Carthage in the hands of the barbarians." He similarly disclaimed any British interest in Syria, whilst in Egypt the two countries would cooperate.[31] Although Salisbury denied having made a formal offer, he had undoubtedly proceeded rashly, and was forced formally to confirm that France would have a free hand in Tunis. This acknowledgement, followed in 1879 by the removal of Britain's consul at Tunis, amounted to a virtual recognition of French predominance along this stretch of the north African coast.[32] Britain's Egyptian pretensions and the need to keep open the French diplomatic option made this an acceptable sacrifice.

To counteract French ambitions in the region Salisbury also encouraged Italian designs on Tunis. Italy's exposed coastline forced her to align with the strongest naval power in the Mediterranean. Italo–French competition in Tunis, then, made impossible a rapprochement between the weakened Great Power France and the Italian bit-player on the international stage. Both would be dependent on Britain; and, in turn, this helped to safeguard Britain's strategic corridor in the Mediterranean. It also gave additional leverage over France in Egypt as well as rendering impracticable Italian irredentist ambitions against Austria-Hungary, thus reinforcing the Habsburg bulwark against Russia in the Balkans.[33]

Egypt remained the main focus of Anglo–French relations. Salisbury was able to fend off Waddington's demands for a convention to extend the 1876 dual control regime over Egypt's messy finances to some form of outright political control. He realised that Egyptian affairs might take a turn for the worse, "and it may suit us at some future period to push ahead." Any binding agreement with Paris would be an impediment.[34] Ironically, attempts by the Khedive Ismaïl Pasha in 1879 to rid himself of the dual control led to his deposition and the strengthening of the Anglo-French regime. Cooperation with France was intended to be temporary. Having agreed with Waddington to exclude other Powers from Egypt, the main task of British diplomacy in Egypt now was to contain French influence there.[35]

The seeds of future Anglo–French discord had been sown. Irritation between London and Paris grew from 1881 onwards. The attempts of Charles de Freyçinet's government to strengthen France's grip on Tunis and the unsatisfactory progress of commercial talks created an 'uncomfortable' situation, as Viscount Lyons, the long-serving ambassador at Paris observed.[36] Matters came to a head when the new Khedive, the less obstreperous but ineffectual Tewfik Pasha, lost control to Colonel Ahmed Arabi's nationalist-panislamist movement, which was secretly financed by French agents.

Initially, Prime Minister William Ewart Gladstone and his Foreign Secretary, the Earl of Granville, were anxious to maintain Anglo–French unity of action; but cooperation with France was undermined by mutual suspicions and the instability of successive French governments. Gladstone's preference for a collective solution under the auspices of a revived European concert, combined with his own peculiar brand of legalism, made British diplomacy pursue a European mandate for intervention by Turkey as the suzerain overlord of Egypt.[37] While the ambassadorial conference sat at Constantinople, the course of events in Egypt forced the Gladstone-Granville duo to act unilaterally. From the outset of the crisis, Granville had been adamant that "anarchy, or some attack on the Canal" would trigger British intervention.[38] In June 1882, both eventualities seemed to materialize. British diplomatists at Cairo had consistently urged intervention. Now caught between riots in Alexandria and the safety of the Canal on the one side, and the prospect of a split in his Cabinet on the other, Gladstone was propelled towards a military solution, and his concert ideas and legal notions went overboard.[39] With French politics gripped by one of the periodic ministerial crises, a bilateral intervention was no longer practicable. Gladstone's pious hope that the naval bombardment of the Alexandria forts on 12 July "would somehow overthrow Arabi" was misplaced, and a full-scale military operation became necessary.[40] After Sir Garnet Wolseley's routing of Arabi's forces at Tel-el-Kebir in September Gladstone's administration found itself the improbable, sole master of Egypt; a circumstance which was underlined by Granville's unilateral dismantling in October of the dual control regime without any formal compensation for France.[41]

Britain had drifted into the occupation of Egypt; and, once established on the Nile, it proved difficult to withdraw from there. The occupation of Egypt had significant European repercussions: it alienated France; and, until 1904, Egypt was to remain a festering sore in Anglo–French relations. Egypt, "*le patrimoine de la France*," had been snatched from her, as Gambetta declared emphatically at the time.[42] Attempts by Granville, and later by Salisbury in 1887, to negotiate a settlement of the Egyptian question came to nothing.[43] Britain's acquisition of Egypt in a fit of somnambulism shattered general Anglo–French cooperation. From the outset, Paris opposed sole British control at Cairo. Encouraged by Bismarck, French diplomacy under Jules Ferry sought means of pressurising Britain, most notably on the lower Niger and elsewhere in sub-Saharan West Africa.[44] Thus, by stumbling into the occupation of Egypt, the Liberal administration had triggered the final phase of the partition of Africa.

The rising Anglo–French antagonism complicated Britain's international position. For as long as Paris remained unreconciled to British control of Egypt, the option of cooperation with France, which Salisbury had been at pains to retain, was no longer practicable politics. Tensions with France, and the continued uncertainty of Britain's hold over Egypt this implied, translated into greater dependence on the goodwill of Germany. Egypt was Gladstone's *damnosa hereditas*. As Salisbury noted in 1887, the estrangement from France had cost Britain "a pack of bothers in various parts of the world."[45] French hostility and the enforced leaning towards Berlin narrowed Britain's diplomatic freedom of manoeuvre, and left her vulnerable to Berlin's attempts at what "in a humbler walk of life would be called *chantage*."[46] Sir William Harcourt, Gladstone's last chancellor of the exchequer, drew a similar conclusion: "[Egypt] makes us what we ought not to be, a continental Power—for Egypt is *politically* part of Europe, and involves us in all the *tracasseries* of continental politics."[47]

Anglo–French tensions were not confined to the Mediterranean and sub-Saharan Africa. In Southeast Asia France steadily pursued a policy of "*pénétration pacifique*," in the hope that Burma would eventually pass under her formal protection. In London the advance of French commercial and political ambitions in the region was perceived to be a threat to India. The India Secretary, Lord Randolph Churchill, demanded "prompt and decided measures" to safeguard "the paramount interests of India in the Indo-Chinese peninsula."[48] Waddington, ambassador in London since 1883, suggested negotiations on a division of the region into spheres of influence. Salisbury's counter-proposal, a form of negative bargain, binding both parties not to acquire Siamese territory, fell still-born.[49] The conclusion of a Franco–Burmese treaty and King Theebaw's confiscation, encouraged by France, of the property of a British trading company, triggered a British invasion, followed in January 1886 by the formal annexation of Burma. The annexation necessitated various political adjustments with France in relation to her Indochinese possessions.[50]

Egypt and Burma further soured Anglo–French relations. "For the present," Salisbury concluded in early 1887, "the enemy is France."[51] Not only was French public opinion gripped by rampant anglophobia, French domestic politics were also convulsed by an anti-parliamentary crisis, fuelled by Ferry's colonial setbacks and bribery scandals involving President Jules Grévy's innermost circle. A symptom of the malaise of republican institutions was the rise of General Georges Boulanger. Based on the cult of the army and a curious amalgam of republicanism and hyper-nationalist sentiments, *boulangerisme* briefly established itself as a proper political movement, with strong following especially in Paris. Boulanger's vociferous advocacy of aggressive *revanchisme* against Germany and a bullish colonial policy against Britain threatened to draw France and Russia closer together. Salisbury regarded the Boulanger phenomenon as a danger to European peace.[52] When Bismarck used Boulanger's armament programme as a pretext for yet another war scare in 1886–7, Salisbury inspired an article in a friendly newspaper in February 1887, strongly intimating that Britain would allow Germany to violate Belgian neutrality in the event of a continental war.[53] Continued squabbles with France over Egypt, Southeast Asia and more recently the New Hebrides necessitated a leaning towards the German-led Triple Alliance. "It is very difficult," Salisbury complained to Lyons, "to prevent oneself from wishing for another Franco-German war to put a stop to this incessant vexation."[54]

Just as 1875 marked a turning point in Great Power relations, so did 1886–7. The Austro–Russian dispute over Bulgaria expedited the collapse of the renewed *Dreikaiserbund*. Franco–Italian differences over North Africa extended the room for manoeuvre for British diplomacy. It also helped to strengthen Britain's ties with the Triple Alliance Powers in the shape of the Mediterranean *entente* with Italy and Austria-Hungary. The first agreement of February 1887 provided for unspecified Anglo–Italian cooperation against France along the southern shores of the Mediterranean. This fell somewhat short of the original Italian idea of a full alliance. Still, the rise of *boulangerisme* and the spectre of a Franco–Russian rapprochement justified the limited commitment to Italy. It was, Salisbury ratiocinated, the most efficacious means of reducing "the fearful risk, and cost" inherent in diplomatic isolation.[55] Austria's swift adherence to the agreement in March lent greater significance to it. The Mediterranean triplice was aimed at upholding the regional status quo. Significantly the realigment with Rome and Vienna did not incur specific obligations on London's part. The combination of the three Mediterranean Powers improved Britain's position *vis-à-vis* France, though Germany's Egyptian leverage remained unaltered.[56]

The mismatch between diplomatic cooperation with the Ballhausplatz and the Quirinale and Britain's weakening naval position in the Mediterranean undermined the credibility of British foreign policy. The Mediterranean remained Britain's "Achilles heel." This was underlined when, in early 1888, the Admiralty was thrown into a blue funk following reports of extraordinary preparations at France's main naval base at Toulon.[57] The farçical naval scare of 1888, and the growing realization that British naval intelligence was less than *au fait* with recent changes in the French naval programme and in battleship design created a new momentum in British strategic policy.[58] Salisbury, who also chaired the Cabinet's defence committee, was actuated by a strong sense of the inadequacy of Britain's preparations against a surprise French attack on the south coast. German military intelligence, made available through the London embassy, consular estimates of the available French shipping tonnage in French channel ports, and the continued flowering of *boulangerisme* made this a not unrealistic prospect: "Our stake is so great that full precautions must be taken against even a distant possibility." To deter potential French aggression Salisbury devised the 1889 Naval Defence Act, which laid down the "Two-Power-Standard" as the guiding principle of British security policy. The Act also signalled the acceleration of the ongoing international arms race.[59]

Still, Britain's naval position in the Mediterranean slowly deteriorated. In 1889–90 the Admiralty concluded that any attempt to defend the Turkish Straits against a Russian descent on Constantinople might endanger the security of the British Isles, if France were also hostile. As Lord George Hamilton, the First Lord of the Admiralty observed, such an eventuality would place Britain at a "great strategical disadvantage." Only about a third of Britain's navy was stationed in the Eastern Mediterranean, he warned,

> and a French Fleet superior to it is on the line of its communications. The naval supremacy of England in the Channel might be endangered and the dispersion of force necessitated by a large operation at the extreme end of the Levant . . . greatly reduces the force available for a concentrated attack or defence elsewhere. Moreover, the presence of a great French Fleet at Toulon with nothing between it and the squadron at Brest and Cherbourg would give to France a strategical position of overwhelming importance.[60]

Throughout the late 1880s and 1890s Britain was engaged in a naval arms race with France and Russia, which was more intense than the later

Anglo–German naval race, and entailed greater strategic risks for Britain's naval mastery.[61] It also very nearly tore apart Gladstone's last administration in 1893. The continuous growth of the French navy in the Mediterranean, and the concomitant growth of French political influence in countries like Greece, was countered by an augmentation of the Mediterranean squadron and a reorganization of the navy in Home Waters. Yet, already in 1892, the Admiralty had to concede that this force was "not equivalent to the total aggregate French force in commission and reserve."[62] Worse, Earl Spencer, the First Lord of the Admiralty, argued that Russia "cannot be ignored and she is building a great deal notwithstanding financial difficulties: . . . France is doing a great deal in the same way and is spending as much or more than we are in new construction." By 1896, he warned, the Franco–Russian combination would "by then have more ships and we shall only be about equal to them in power."[63]

The high-profile visits of a French squadron to Cronstadt in 1892 and the Russian fleet to Toulon in 1893 were strong indications of the emerging Franco–Russian alliance.[64] In British naval circles it was well known that Admiral Fournier, the French chief of staff in the mid-1890s, was a strong advocate of a "vigorous offensive" in the event of a Franco-British war. The combination of the Royal Navy's Channel and Mediterranean squadrons was sufficient only to cope with the French naval forces at Toulon. A Russo–French naval combination operating in the Mediterranean, it was feared, had the potential to threaten Egypt and disrupt the route to India. Until 1904–5, therefore, "the chessboard of the Western Mediterranean" remained the focus of British war planning.[65] Moreover, with the Franco–Russian dual alliance a reality since 1894, France now increasingly acted as the "jackal of Russia."[66] In China, very much the focus of Great Power attention in the late 1890s, the French minister Auguste Gérard and his Russian colleague Mikhail Nikolaevich Giers were known as "the Siamese twins," acting jointly on all occasions.[67]

The combination of Britain's weakening naval position in the Mediterranean, the Sultan's declining power over the Ottoman dominions, and Salisbury's failure to extricate Britain from Egypt provided an incentive now to tighten British control there. British diplomatic strategy thus came to revolve around Cairo as its pivot rather than Constantinople. The growing importance of Egypt brought Eastern Africa, and more especially the upper reaches of the Nile valley, into sharper focus. In 1884, after Gordon's disastrous Khartoum expedition, Britain had abandoned the Sudan; and East Africa south of Egypt remained an international power vacuum. But this state of affairs could not last. "Whatever Power holds the Upper Nile Valley must, by the mere force of its geographical position, dominate Egypt," the Earl of Cromer, the long-serving imperial pro-consul at Cairo, warned.[68]

The Anglo–French agreement of 5 August 1890 bought off the French threat to the Nile region with concessions in West Africa and the Western Sudan.[69] Similar agreements with Germany, Italy and, later in 1894, Rosebery's Anglo–Congolese agreement served the same purpose. The West African agreement with France offered a glimpse of future possibilities. Yet, any rapprochement with France ran the risk of Italy leaving the Triple Alliance and the subsequent regrouping of the Powers: "Italy & France together, England say neutral, Germany, Austria & Russia together, Russia receiving rights over Constantinople, Austria taking over the rest of the Turkish Empire as far as Salonica."[70] A good understanding with France was not worth such risks.

The 1890s were characterised by efforts to arrive at negotiated regional settlements with France, without involving a major redirection of British foreign policy. Talks on the delimitation of colonial boundaries in West Africa, however, were fraught with problems and so made only slow progress. If Granville and Lyons had found the French "difficult to deal with" in the 1880s, their successors did not fare any better a decade later. Following Rosebery's return to the Foreign Office relations with France deteriorated sharply. "The mistrust between the two foreign ministries . . . is greater than even in Lord Salisbury's time," Prince Münster, Germany's anglophile ambassador at Paris reported.[71]

Two factors contributed to the decline in Anglo–French relations. The Heligoland–Zanzibar agreement with Germany in July 1890 had heightened French and Russian fears that Britain would join the Triple Alliance. Salisbury had, thus, bequeathed a difficult situation to Rosebery. The Anglo–German African treaty kept Germany out of the Upper Nile Valley; but, at the same time, it facilitated the rapprochement between Paris and St. Petersburg that would result in the Franco–Russian alliance of 1894. The conduct of official relations between Downing Street and the Quai d'Orsay, moreover was made almost impossible by Rosebery's and Waddington's mutual antipathy, which bordered on barely concealed hatred. It was something of a farce in high places: "Waddington has returned and with him I fear *Atra Cura*! I cannot divest myself of the idea when he enters the room that he is a Churchwarden come round for a subscription. . . . [H]e brings nothing, but generally tries to take something away: and always with the unctuous air of Arthur Kinnaird [a Director of Barclays Bank] reproving a customer for an overdraft."[72] When Waddington sought to commence negotiations over Egypt in direct talks with Gladstone, but behind the Foreign Secretary's back, Rosebery erupted with fury. The ambassador, he warned Gladstone, had "now rendered the transaction of business almost, if not quite impossible so far as I am concerned"; and he inisted that all questions of foreign policy be treated through his department.[73] At their next meeting, instead of greeting Waddington with a formal handshake, Rosebery extended only two fingers to express his displeasure. As an old Rugbian, the ambassador can have been under no illusions about Rosebery's two-digit diplomatic salute. Indeed, by May 1893, the Quai d'Orsay had been persuaded to recall its ambassador from London.[74]

The strained relations between the two men were symptomatic of the deeper malaise in Anglo-French relations. At the Quai, Lord Dufferin complained, French ministers frequently took refuge in "impudent quibbles" when negotiations reached a delicate stage.[75] The chief West African negotiator at the Paris embassy, Constantine Phipps, found himself frequently frustrated by French negotiating behaviour: "I am always averse if possible to sending in formal notes to such argumentative people as the French when they may embark us in a paper controversy."[76] In the late 1890s, the tensions with France over West Africa became wound up in the now more strained relations between London and Berlin. Any concessions to France in Africa, Salisbury noted, were "irritating to Germany; and that irritation may be inconvenient if at the time or a short time afterwards an opportunity should occur for giving practical expression to it."[77] Frustration was mutual. As the French foreign minister Gabriel Hanotaux noted, in the course of negotiations, British diplomats were apt to proceed *"non sans une certaine hauteur."* For their parts, Dufferin and Rosebery's successor as Foreign Secretary, the Earl of Kimberley, acknowledged Hanotaux's professed despire for *"une bonne entente avec l'Angleterre,"* but remained sceptical about his ability to deliver an acceptable agreement.[78]

West Africa apart, negotiations for the settlement of regional disputes frequently ended in failure. Given the importance of the Mediterranean sea-line of communication, the future of Morocco was a constant concern for ministers. In the wake of the gradual internal collapse of the Moorish kingdom, the country's future became a more acute international problem.[79] It presented British diplomacy with an awkward dilemma. Much of Morocco had no intrinsic strategic value for Britain; not so, however, the coastline opposite Gibraltar which guarded the Western entrance to the Mediterranean. To keep it out of the hands of another European Power, Tangier's neutrality had to be preserved. Yet, to broach the matter formally with the Quai d'Orsay ran the risk of encouraging further French encroachment upon Morocco from the East, before the question could be settled.[80] There was also the risk of a squabble between Italy and Spain, which might force Britain to take sides, so reducing the value of the Mediterranean agreements with these two minor regional Powers. An Anglo-French arrangement, in the shape of a "negative bargain," pledging both parties to abstain from acquiring Moorish territory, was briefly discussed in 1894, but proved unacceptable. It "remained one of the might-have-beens" of nineteenth century diplomatic history.[81] Britain's policy of maintaining Moroccan independence against France by promoting internal reforms under the Sultan's authority only reached the end of its life span with the collapse of the Sultan's rule at the end of 1902.[82]

In the course of the 1890s a new pattern emerged in Anglo–French relations. Whenever negotiations reached a dead-end, both sides were ready to employ more drastic measures. In Southeast Asia the initiative lay with France. A French ultimatum and subsequent seizure of Siamese territory in 1893 led to a stand-off between British and French gunboats in Bangkok harbour. A British foray into the Upper Mekong Valley in May 1895 threatened to rekindle that crisis.[83] Kimberley found "the French . . . so slippery and so anxious to trip us up [in Siam] whenever they can, that I almost despair of ever arriving at a good understanding with them."[84] Siam was of little intrinsic value to Britain, had it not been for the country's geographical position as a "buffer" between India and French Indochina, as Maurice de Bunsen, chargé d'affaires at Bangkok, summarized bluntly: "It is of course our game to keep them [viz. the Siamese] going as a buffer state, but the French who are always nagging at them in the hope of getting another slice, make it a very difficult task." French encroachments on Siam and expansion into southern China threatened to "lead us into an Eastern frontier question."[85]

The combination of conciliation and firmness led to the Anglo–French convention of 15 January 1896, which conceded certain rights to France in the Mekong valley, but otherwise pledged both sides to strict non-interference there, thus neutralising Siam as a source of future tensions. It also annulled French trading advantages in southern China, and so helped to stop further French efforts to carve out a protectorate over the Yunnan and Kwantung provinces. Finally, the Anglo–French compromise gave Paris a stake in the status quo in the Far East, thereby removing whatever incentive French statesmen might have had to support Russia's forward policy in Asia. Appeasing French designs in the Mekong Valley, then, had the pleasing effect of weakening the cohesion of the *Franco–Russe* in Asia.[86]

Following the compromise over Southern China and Siam, the focus of attention shifted once more to East Africa. Rosebery and Salisbury kept a weather eye on developments there. In 1893, Rosebery blocked French attempts to re-open talks on Egypt, much against Gladstone's inclination. The Prime Minister had hoped to use the Egyptian question to improve Anglo–French relations.[87] For Rosebery, diplomatic considerations apart, there was the additional danger of British and French expeditions stumbling into each other in contested areas in the interior of Africa. In March 1895, Sir Edward Grey, then Kimberley's Parliamentary Under-Secretary, delivered a strongly worded warning to France not to advance into Britain's sphere of interest in the Upper Nile Valley. Grey's "bellicose attack on France" caused a stir in European diplomacy.[88] Although the affair blew over soon, it highlighted the strategic importance of the Sudan for both countries.[89]

The sharpest crisis arose in the autumn of 1898, centred on Fashoda on the White Nile. The *de facto* collapse of Britain's traditional policy at Constantinople had further enhanced the strategic importance of Egypt. When the Italian campaign in Abyssinia was routed at Adowa in March 1896, Salisbury responded by sending Kitchener's Egyptian army into the Sudan, ostensibly to alleviate the pressure on Italy.[90] In reality, he hoped to contain French designs in East Africa; for, as Captain Jean-Baptiste Marchand's expedition edged its way towards the headwaters of the Nile, the continued existence of the Sudanese power vacuum became a source of growing concern. While Salisbury appreciated Hanotaux's "quaint . . . olive branch[es]" in Egyptian matters, he was nevertheless anxious to prevent France from filling that vacuum.[91] By September 1898, Kitchener had brought most of the Sudan under his control; shortly afterwards his Anglo–Egyptian steamroller confronted the French peanut in the shape of Marchand's handful of men still capable of fighting.[92] In the eyes of foreign diplomats, the stand-off at Fashoda had brought Britain and France to the brink of war in October 1898.[93]

Théophile Delcassé, the new French foreign minister, was well aware that the Nile Valley was not worth the bones of a single French zouave. The French naval staff considered that the navy was in no position to sustain a war against Britain. With St. Petersburg preoccupied with Far Eastern affairs, moreover, no support was to be expected from that quarter. The domestic position of the French government was also fragile. France's best course, therefore, was to find a face-saving exit route. The evacuation of Fashoda, semi-official papers in Paris commented, was entirely *"conciliable avec l'honneur national."*[94] Delcassé's problem was that Salisbury offered no such route. The Foreign Secretary was adamant "that the valley of the Nile had belonged, and still belonged, to Egypt." Following Kitchener's victory over the Mahdist army at Omdurman that title had been restored: "There was no pretence therefore for the contention that the region was open to the enterprises or the occupation of a third power."[95] France had no alternative but to back down.

Fashoda left a deep scar in France on the French national psyche, one that would re-emerge as part of the collective memory of the nationalist Right after the defeat of 1940. Yet, it was the purgative necessary before Anglo–French relations could improve. Significant sections of the *parti colonial* now abandoned the previous policy of confronting Britain in Egypt in favour of one of compensation in Morocco. Fashoda made possible French recognition of Britain's predominance in the Upper Nile Valley already in the Anglo–French agreement of 21 March 1899, in return for minimal British concessions in the Darfur region of Western Sudan.[96]

Ambiguity, a combination of conciliation and firmness, had marked British policy towards France in the last quarter of the nineteenth century. The Anglo–French agreements concerning Southeast Asia and the Nile Valley of 1896 and 1899 laid the foundations of the 1904 *Entente*. In some respects, that agreement was little more than a formal tidying up of remaining, mildly contentious issues. Changes in the wider international context, however, meant that this tidying-up was to have ramifications beyond relations between London and Paris.

NOTES

1. C. Dawbarn, "Sir Edmund Monson: Our Ambassador to the French Republic," *Pall Mall Magazine* xxxiii (1904), p. 318.
2. M. Vaïsse and R. Frank, "Introduction: L'entente cordiale," *Relations internationales*, no. 117 (2004), p. 3; D. de Villepin, "Avant-propos," M. Vaïsse (on behalf of Ministère des Affaires Étrangères) (Ed.), *L'Entente Cordiale de Fachoda à la Grande Guerre* (Paris: Éditions complexes, 2004), p. 9.
3. P. M. H. Bell, *France and Britain, 1900–1940: Entente and Estrangement* (London: Longmans, 1996), p. 2.
4. Dufferin and Ava to Gladstone (private), 17 Jan. 1894, Gladstone Mss, British Library, Add.Mss. 44151; cf. S.J. Reid (Ed.), *The Memoirs of Sir Edward Blount, KCB* (London: Longmans, 1902), pp. 279–85.
5. Sir T. Barclay, *Thirty Years: Anglo-French Reminiscences, 1876–1906* (Boston, MA: Houghton Mifflin, 1914), pp. 36–37.
6. Monson to Salisbury (private), 7 Sept. 1900, Salisbury Mss, Hatfield House, 3M/A/118/59.
7. Quotes from Herbert von Bismarck to Prince Bismarck (private), 3 Sept. 1882, J. Lepsius et al. (Eds.), *Die Grosse Politik der Europäischen Politik, 1871–1914* (40 vols., Berlin: Deutsche Verlagsanstalt für Politik und Geschichte, 1924 et seq.) iv, no. 730 [hereafter *GP*]; and Rosebery to Cromer (private), 22 Apr. 1895, Cromer Mss, The National Archives (Public Record Office) [hereafter TNA (PRO)], Foreign Office Papers [hereafter FO] 633/7.
8. Harcourt to Kimberley, 2 July 1894, Harcourt Mss, Bodleian Library, Oxford, Ms. Harcourt dep. 51. For an instructive case study, cf. R. Tombs, "'Lesser Breeds without the Law': The British Establishment and the Dreyfus Affair, 1894–1899", *Historical Journal* xli, 2 (1998), pp. 495–510.
9. Adams to Russell (private), 12 Jan. 1874 [*recte* 1875], Ampthill Mss, TNA (PRO), FO 918/13.
10. Quotes from Egerton to De Bunsen (private), n.d. [but before Apr. 1886], De Bunsen Mss, Bodleian Library, box 14; and Howard diary, 10 Jan. 1881, Howard-von Reccum Mss, Library of Congress, Washington, DC, box 1; cf.

E.T.S. Dugdale, *Maurice de Bunsen: Diplomat and Friend* (London: John Murray, 1934), p. 66.

11. Lyons to Russell, 7 May 1872, and *vice versa*, 14 Mar. 1873, Ampthill Mss, FO 913/52.

12. Kennedy to Fergusson, 20 Dec. 1886, Fergusson Mss, TNA (PRO), FO 800/26; cf. P.T. Marsh, *Bargaining on Europe: Britain and the First Common Market, 1860–1892* (New Haven, CT: Yale University Press, 1999), pp. 23–28 and 129–47.

13. Faverney to Décazes (no. 17), 25 Mar. 1875, Ministère des Affaires Étrangères (Ed.), *Documents Diplomatiques Français, 1871–1914*, first ser. (1871–1900) (14 vols., Paris: Imprimerie Nationale, 1929) i, no. 373 [hereafter *DDF* (1) i]; Loftus to Derby (no. 87, confidential), 16 Mar. 1875, FO 65/908. For the background, J. Stone, "The Radowitz Mission: A Study in Bismarckian Foreign Policy," *Militärgeschichtliche Mitteilungen* li, 1 (1992), pp. 47–71.

14. Bismarck to Hohenlohe, 26 Feb. 1875, *GP* i, no. 155. Another consideration was the *Kulturkampf* church question, cf. Morier to Derby (no. 30), 21 April 1875, TNA (PRO), FO 244/287.

15. Gontaut-Biron to Décazes (no. 28, *confidentielle*), 21 Apr. 1875, *DDF* (1) i, no. 395; Lyons to Derby (no. 329, confidential), 23 Apr. 1875, FO 27/2107; A. Mitchell, *The German Influence in France after 1870: The Formation of the French Republic* (Chapel Hill: University of North Carolina Press, 1979), pp. 124–30.

16. Décazes circular to London, St. Petersburg, Vienna, The Hague, Holy See and Rome (no. 46, *confidentielle*), 29 Apr. 1875, *DDF* (1) i, no. 399; Adams to Derby (no. 339, most confidential), 26 Apr. 1875, FO 27/2107.

17. Russell to Derby (no. 184, confidential), 27 April 1875, FO 64/826; cf. W. Taffs, *Ambassador to Bismarck: Lord Odo Russell, First Baron Ampthill* (London: Frederick Muller, 1938), p. 87; K. Urbach, *Bismarck's Favourite Englishman: Lord Odo Russell's Mission to Berlin* (London: I.B. Tauris, 1999), pp. 138–9.

18. Derby diary, 7 May 1875, J.R. Vincent (Ed.), *A Selection from the Diaries of Edward Henry Stanley, 15th Earl of Derby (1826–1893) between September 1869 and March 1878* (London: Royal Historical Society, 1994), p. 215 [hereafter *DD*].

19. Lyons to Adams, 21 Apr. 1875, Lord Newton, *Lord Lyons: A Record of British Diplomacy* (2 vols., London: Edward Arnold, 1913) ii, p. 73.

20. Disraeli to Lady Chesterfield, 5 May 1875, Marquess of Zetland (Ed.), *The Letters of Disraeli to Lady Bradford and Lady Chesterfield* (2 vols., London: Ernest Benn, 1929) i, pp. 236–37.

21. Derby diary, 26 and 28 Apr. 1875, *DD*, pp. 211–2; Queen Victoria's journal, 6 May 1875, G.E. Buckle (Ed.), *The Letters of Queen Victoria*, 2nd ser. (3 vols., London: John Murray, 1926) ii, p. 391 [hereafter *LQV* (2) ii].

22. Derby to Lytton (private), 15 Oct. 1874, Lytton Mss, Hertfordshire Record Office, Hertford, D/Ek.030/16; to Disraeli (private), 18 Apr. 1875, Disraeli Mss, Bodleian Library, dep. Hughenden 112/2.

23. Gavard to Décazes (no. 51), 2 May 1875, *DDF* (1) i, no. 400; also Corry [Disraeli's Private Secretary] to Derby, [9 May 1875], Hughenden Mss, dep. 112/2.

24. Derby to Russell, 3 May 1875, Newton, *Lyons* ii, p. 75; Disraeli to Derby, 6 May 1875, W. F. Monypenny and G. E. Buckle, *The Life of Benjamin Disraeli, Earl of Beaconsfield* (6 vols., London: John Murray, 1910–20) v, p. 422.

25. Queen Victoria to Tsar Alexander II, 10 May 1875, *LQV* (2) ii, p. 396. Derby and Disraeli knew that the Queen's letter would not arrive in time "to do either good or harm," Derby to Disraeli (private), 10 May 1875, Disraeli Mss, dep. Hughenden 112/2.

26. Derby diary, 8 May 1875, *DD*, p. 216; tel. Gontaut-Biron to Décazes (no no.), 11 May 1875, *DDF* (1) i, no. 416; cf. Taffs, *Odo Russell*, pp. 97–8.

27. Derby diary, 20 May 1875, *DD*, p. 218; Adams to Derby (no. 388), 12 May 1875, FO 27/2108.

28. A. F. Pribram, *England and the International of the European Great Powers, 1871–1914* (Oxford: Clarendon, 1931), p. 10.

29. W. N. Medlicott, *The Congress of Berlin and After: A Diplomatic History of the Near Eastern Settlement, 1878–1880* (London: Frank Cass, 2nd ed. 1963), pp. 137–47. For the "strategic corridor," cf. J. Darwin, "Imperialism and the Victorians: The Dynamics of Territorial Expansion," *English Historical Review* cxii, 3 (1997), p. 622.

30. Hanotaux's characterisation, as quoted in L.-P. Deschanel, *Histoire de la politique extérerieure de la France* (Paris: Payot, 1936), p. 260.

31. Waddington to d'Harcourt, 21 Mar. 1878, *DDF* (1) ii, no. 330; Salisbury to Waddington, 6 July 1878 (copy), Tenterden Mss, TNA (PRO), FO 363/4; A. Marsden, *British Diplomacy in Tunis, 1875–1902: A Case Study in Mediterranean Politics* (Edinburgh: Scottish Academic Press, 1971), pp. 53–9.

32. Salisbury to Lyons (no. 493), 7 Aug. 1878, FO 27/2300; d'Harcourt to Waddington (no. 720, 24 July 1878, and reply (*trés confidentiel*), 25 July 1878, *DDF* (1) ii, nos. 324–25.

33. T. G. Otte, "'Floating Downstream': Lord Salisbury and British Foreign Policy, 1878–1902," idem (ed.) *The Makers of British Foreign Policy: from Pitt to Thatcher* (Basingstoke and New York: Palgrave, 2002), pp. 106–7.

34. Salisbury to Beaconsfield (private), 5 Sept. 1878, Disraeli Mss, dep. Hughenden 92/3. For a discussion of the financial control regime, cf. R. Owen, *The Middle East in the World Economy, 1800–1914* (London: I.B. Tauris, 1993), pp. 130–35.

35. Salisbury to Vivian, 3 May 1878, Lady G. Cecil, *Life of Robert Cecil, Third Marquis of Salisbury* (4 vols., London: Hodder & Stoughton, 1921–32) ii, p. 330; cf. P. M. Holt, *Egypt and the Fertile Crescent, 1516–1922: A Political History* (Ithaca, NY: Cornell University Press, 1975 (pb)), pp. 207–10.

36. Lyons to Granville (private), 15 Mar. 1881, Granville Mss, TNA (PRO), PRO 30/29/171; Marsh, *Bargaining on Europe*, pp. 140–44.

37. Lyons to Granville (private and confidential), 19 Jan. 1882, Granville Mss, PRO 30/29/172; Gladstone to Granville, 28 May and 21 June 1882, A. Ramm (Ed.), *The Political Correspondence of Mr Gladstone and Lord Granville, 1876–1886* (2 vols., Oxford: Clarendon, 1962) i, nos. 716 and 728; H. C. G. Matthew, *Gladstone, 1875–1898* (Oxford: Clarendon, 1995), pp. 130–35.

38. Granville to Lyons, 7 Nov. 1881, Lord E. Fitzmaurice, *Life of Granville George Leveson-Gower, Second Earl Granville, KG, 1815–1891* (2 vols., London: Longmans, 1905) ii, p. 252; E.D. Steele, "Britain and Egypt, 1882–1914: The

Containment of Islamic Nationalism," in K.M. Wilson (Ed.), *Imperialism and Nationalism in the Middle East: The Anglo-Egyptian Experience, 1882–1982* (London: Mansell, 1983), pp. 3–5.

39. Memo. Hartington, 18 June 1882, Granville Mss, PRO 30/29/132; Malet to Granville (private), 4 Apr., 2 and 16 May 1882, ibid., PRO 30/29/160; cf. A. Schölch, "The 'Men on the Spot' and the English Occupation of Egypt in 1882," *Historical Journal* xix, 4 (1976), pp. 773–74.

40. Gladstone to Queen Victoria, 3 July 1882, TNA (PRO), Cabinet Papers [hereafter CAB] 41/16/33; cf. M.J. Williams, "The Egyptian Campaign of 1882," B. J. Bond (ed.), *Victorian Military Campaigns* (London: Donovan, repr. 1994), pp. 241–78.

41. Granville to Lyons (no. 1198, confidential), 23 Oct. 1882, FO 27/2557; Duclerc to Tissot (*privé*), 28 Oct. 1882, *DDF* (1) iv, no. 551. Berlin was informed of this before Paris, cf. Herbert von Bismarck to Prince Bismarck, 22 Oct. 1882, *GP* iv, no. 731.

42. As quoted in P. Deschanel, *Gambetta* (Paris: Hachette, 1920), p. 281.

43. Granville to Lyons (private), 12 Mar. 1884, Granville Mss, PRO 30/29/204; cf. M.P. Hornik, "The Special Mission of Sir Henry Drummond-Wolff to Constantinople, 1885–7," *English Historical Review* v, 4 (1940), pp. 600–7.

44. Duclerc to Tissot, 4 Jan. 1883, *DDF* (1) iv, no. 594; Ferry to Waddington, 13 Nov. 1883, F. Waddington, 'Lettres inédites de Jules Ferry à W.H. Waddington', *Revue d'Histoire Diplomatique* li, 2 (1937), pp. 308–9; C.W. Newbury and A. S. Kanya-Forstner, "French Politics and the Origins of the Scramble for West Africa," *Journal of African History* x, 2 (1969), p. 269.

45. Salisbury to Malet (private), 23 Feb. 1887, Malet Mss, TNA (PRO), FO 343/2.

46. Salisbury to Wolff, 23 Feb. 1887, Cecil, *Life of Salisbury* iv, p. 41. French diplomats arrived at a similar view, Courcel to Ferry (*confidentiel*), 4 Jan. 1885, *DDF* (1) v, no. 507.

47. Harcourt to Gladstone, 8 Sept. 1891, A. G. Gardiner, *The Life of Sir William Harcourt* (2 vols., London: Constable, 1923) ii, p. 129.

48. Churchill to Salisbury, 28 Aug. 1885, W. S. Churchill, *Lord Randolph Churchill* (London: Odhams, s.a. [c. 1951]), p. 398.

49. Salisbury to Walsham (no. 781A), 28 Sept. 1885, FO 27/2727.

50. Dufferin to Churchill, 19 Oct. 1885, Sir A. Lyall, *The Life of the Marquis of Dufferin and Ava* (2 vols., London: John Murray, 1905) ii, pp. 119–20; A.T.Q. Stewart, *The Pagoda War: Lord Dufferin and the Fall of the Kingdom of Ava, 1885–1886* (London: Faber, 1972), pp. 72–81.

51. Salisbury to Paget (private), 9 Feb. 1887, Paget Mss, British Library, Add.Mss. 51229; to White (private), 10 Aug. 1887, White Mss, TNA (PRO), FO 364/8.

52. Lytton to Salisbury (private), 28 Jan. and 5 Mar. 1889, Lytton Mss, D/Ek.O39; cf. F. Goguel, *La politique des parties sous la IIIe république* (Paris: Édition du Seuil, 5th ed. s.a. [1957]), pp. 61–65; D.B. Ralston, *The Army and the Republic: The Place of the Military in the Political Evolution of France, 1871–1914* (Cambridge, MA: MIT Press, 1967), pp. 171–73.

53. *The Standard* 4 Feb. 1887. The financial markets at Paris and Berlin were gripped by a war panic, tel. Herbette to Flourens (no. 97, *très confidentiel*), 25 Jan. 1887, *DDF* (1) vi, no. 508.

54. Salisbury to Lyons, 5 Feb. 1887, Newton, *Lyons* ii, p. 386.
55. Salisbury to Queen Victoria, 10 Feb. 1887, CAB 41/20/31; C.J. Lowe, *Salisbury and the Mediterranean, 1886–1896* (London: Routledge & Kegan Paul, 1965), pp. 16–17.
56. Salisbury to Paget (no. 39, secret), 26 Feb. 1887, FO 7/1113; Lumley to Salisbury (no. 80, secret), 15 Mar. 1887, FO 45/574.
57. Pauncefote to Admiralty (secret), 3 Feb. 1888, TNA (PRO), Admiralty Papers [hereafter ADM] 1/6932; tel. Waddington to Flourens (no. 49, *très confidentiel*), 6 Mar. 1888, *DDF* (1) vii, no. 69; cf. A. J. Marder, *The Anatomy of British Sea Power: A History of British Naval Policy in the Pre-Dreadnought Era, 1880–1905* (London, repr. Frank Cass 1964), pp. 126–9.
58. It transpired that the Germans were better informed than the Royal Navy, min. Morgan, 20 May 1888, on Capt. Domville [Naval Attaché at Paris] to Lytton (no. 50), 17 May 1888, ADM 1/6933.
59. Mema. Salisbury, "French Invasion," 29 June and 6 Nov. 1888, CAB 37/21/18 and 22/32; cf. J.T. Sumida, *In Defence of Naval Superiority: Finance, Technology and British Naval Policy, 1889–1914* (London: Routledge, 1991), pp. 13–17.
60. Memo. Hamilton, 10 June 1890, ADM 121/75; cf. T.A. Brassey, *The Naval Annual* (Portsmouth: Griffin, 1890), pp. 114–19.
61. Memo. Lt.-Col. Slade, 29 Jan. 1889, FO 45/623; H. Le Masson, "La politique navale française de 1870 à 1914," idem, *Propos Maritime* (Paris: Éditions Maritimes et d'Outre Mer, 1970), pp. 197–213.
62. Memo. Hamilton, "English and French Fleets in the Mediterranean" (confidential), Jan. 1892, ADM 121/75; Rosebery to Gladstone, 9 Sept. 1892, Gladstone Mss, British Library, Add.Mss. 44289.
63. Spencer to Rosebery, 26 May 1893, Rosebery Mss, National Library of Scotland, Edinburgh, 10062; memo. Spencer, "Navy Estimates, 1894–5," 13 Dec. 1893, CAB 37/34/59; cf. P. Stansky, *Ambitions and Strategies: The Struggle for the Leadership of the Liberal Party in the 1890s* (Oxford: Clarendon, 1964), pp. 19–25.
64. Howard to Salisbury (no. 200), 3 Aug. 1891, FO 65/1399. Still useful, W.L. Langer, *The Franco-Russian Alliance, 1890–1894* (New York: Octagon, repr. 1977), pp. 184–89 and 348–49.
65. Quotes from memo. Fisher, "Strategic Position of the Mediterranean Fleet in War," 1 Nov. 1899, ADM 121/75; and memo. Selborne, "The Navy Estimates and the Chancellor of the Exchequer's memorandum on the growth of expenditure" (confidential), 16 Nov. 1901, CAB 37/59/118.
66. Currie to O'Conor (private), 15 Apr. [1896], O'Conor Mss, Churchill College Archive Centre, Cambridge, OCON 6/1/7.
67. V. Chirol, *Fifty Years in a Changing World* (London: Jonathan Cape, 1927), p. 118.
68. Cromer to Salisbury (no. 405, secret), 15 Dec. 1889, FO 78/4243.
69. Waddington to Ribot, 1 Aug. 1890, *DDF* (1) viii, no. 136; A.S. Kanya-Forstner, "French African Policy and the Anglo-French Agreement of 5 August 1890," *Historical Journal* xii, 4 (1969), pp. 628–50.
70. Salisbury to Currie, 18 Aug. 1892 (copy), Rosebery Mss, 10132. The letter was meant for Rosebery's consumption, Currie to Rosebery, 18 Aug. 1892, ibid.

71. Münster to Caprivi (no. 235), 12 Oct. 1892, *GP* viii, no. 1743.
72. Rosebery to Gladstone (confidential), 19 Oct. 1892, Gladstone Mss, Add.Mss. 44290. On the Rosebery–Waddington relationship cf. J.R. James, *Rosebery: A biography of Archibald Philip, Fifth Earl of Rosebery* (London: Weidenfeld & Nicolson, 1964), pp. 272–73.
73. Rosebery to Gladstone (confidential), 4 and 7 Nov. 1892, Gladstone Mss, ibid.; also West diary, 4 Nov. 1892, H. G. Hutchinson (Ed.), *Private Diaries of the Rt. Hon. Sir Algernon West, GCB* (London: John Murray, 1922), p. 75.
74. Rosebery to Queen Victoria, 23 Dec. 1892, *LQV* (3) ii, pp. 192–93.
75. Dufferin to Kimberley (private), 15 Feb. 1895, Kimberley Mss, Bodleian Library, Ms.Eng.c.4402.
76. Phipps to Kimberley (private), 27 Nov. 1894, ibid., Ms.Eng.c. 4401. Hanotaux returned the compliment, Hanotaux to Decrais (no. 132), 17 Aug. 1894, *DDF* (1) xi, no. 218.
77. Salisbury to Monson (private), 12 Feb. 1897, Monson Mss, Bodleian Library, Ms.Eng.hist.c.594.
78. Quotes from G. Hanotaux, *Fachoda* (Paris: Ernest Flammarion, 1899), p. 85; Dufferin to Kimberley (private), 26 June 1895, Kimberley Mss, Ms.Eng.c.4401.
79. Waddington to Ribot, 23 Dec. 1891 and 22 Jan. 1892, *DDF* (1) ix, nos. 113 and 176; cf. the reflections of Walter Harris, *The Times* correspondent at Tangier, idem, *Morocco That Was* (London: Eland Press, repr. 1983), pp. 65–69; and M. Aflalo, *The Truth about Morocco: An Indictment of the Policy of the British Foreign Office with regard to the Anglo-French Agreement* (London: Bodley Head, 1904), pp. 41–53.
80. Salisbury to Dufferin (no. 81, confidential), 17 Apr. 1891, and memo. Oakes, "Memorandum respecting the Agreement of 1887 between Italy and Spain for the maintenance of the status quo in the Mediterranean," 18 Apr. 1891, both FO 181/703.
81. Memo. Ridgeway, "Report on Morocco," 10 July 1894, FO 99/304; Ridgeway to Rosebery (private), 4 June 1893, Rosebery Mss, 10133. Further details can be gleaned from A. J. P. Taylor, *Rumours of War* (London: Hamish Hamilton, 1952), pp. 134–7.
82. Tel. Kimberley to Wolff (private), 5 Jan. 1895, Kimberley Mss, Ms.Eng.c. 4400; Nicolson to Sanderson (private), 14 Oct. 1895, Nicolson Mss, TNA (PRO), PRO 30/81/11.
83. Chapman [Director of Military intelligence] to Rosebery (private and confidential), 10 Aug. 1893, Rosebery Mss, 10133; Courcel to Hanotaux (no 99), 30 Mar. 1895, *DDF* (1) xi, no. 421; and tel. (no. 111), 20 May 1895, ibid. (1) xii, no. 13.
84. Kimberley to De Bunsen (private), 17 Sept. 1894, De Bunsen Mss, Bodleian Library, Oxford, box 14.
85. Quotes from De Bunsen to Fane, 9 Aug. 1896, Fane Mss, Wiltshire Record Office, Trowbridge, Acc. 1976; and Reay [Governor Bombay] to Elgin [Viceroy] (private), 29 June 1895, Elgin Mss, British Library Oriental and India Office Collection, Mss.Eur.F.84/25.
86. Memo. Curzon, "Siam, France, and China," 13 Aug. 1895, Curzon Mss, British Library Oriental and India Office Collection, Mss.Eur.F112/3. For the text of

the convention cf. *DDF* (1) xii, no. 272; cf. also J.D. Hargeaves, "Entente Manquée: Anglo-French Relations, 1895–6," *Historical Journal* xi, 1 (1953), pp. 65–92.

87. Rosebery to Gladstone, 22 May 1893, Gladstone Mss, Add.Mss. 44290; cf. memo. Gladstone, n.d. [Apr. 1893], and min. Rosebery, 20 Apr. 1893, Rosebery Mss, 10133; cf. D.R. Brooks, "Gladstone's Fourth Ministry, 1892–1894: Policies and Personalities" (Ph.D. thesis, Cambridge, 1975), fo. 209.

88. Harcourt to Kimberley, 29 Mar. 1895, Kimberley Mss, Ms.Eng.c.4378; Grey to Rosebery, 30 Mar. 1895, Rosebery Mss, 10021; cf. G. Martel, *Imperial Diplomacy: Rosebery and the Failure of Foreign Policy* (Kingston and Montreal: McGill, 1986), pp. 236–41.

89. Tels. Courcel to Hanotaux (no. 32) and reply (no. 36), both 2 Apr. 1895, *DDF* (1) xi, nos. 423–24.

90. Ferrero to Visconti-Venosta (no. 620/265), 6 Nov. 1896, Ministero degli Afferi Esteri (ed.), *I Documenti Diplomatici Italiani*, 3rd ser (1896–1907) (7 of 11 vols., Roma: Istituto Poligrafico e Zecco dello Stato, 1953–2000) i, no. 274 [hereafter *DDI* (3) i].

91. Salisbury to Sanderson (private), 2 Nov. 1896, Sanderson Mss, TNA (PRO), FO 800/1; Grey to Rosebery, 14 Nov. 1897, Rosebery Mss, 10028; cf. G.N. Sanderson, *England, Europe and the Upper Nile, 1882–1899* (Edinburgh: Edinburgh University Press, 1965), pp. 314–19.

92. Delcassé to Trouillot (*très urgent*), 7 Sept. 1898, and Geoffray to Delcassé (no. 471), 7 Sept. 1898, *DDF* (1) xiv, nos. 329–30.

93. De Renzis to Canevaro (no. 357), 7 Nov. 1898, *DDI* (2) iii, no. 106.

94. As quoted in P. M. de la Gorce, *La République et son Armée* (Paris: Fayard, 1963), p. 95; C. Andrew, *Théophile Delcassé and the Making of the Entente Cordiale: A Reappraisal of French Foreign Policy, 1898–1905* (London: Macmillan, 1968), pp. 98–102; R. Glenn Brown, *Fashoda Reconsidered: The Impact of Domestic Politics on French Policy in Africa* (Baltimore, MD, 1969), 104–5.

95. Salisbury to Monson (no. 393), 12 Oct. 1898, FO 27/3409; tel. Courcel to Delcassé (no. 196), 13 Oct. 1898, *DDF* (1) xiv, no. 433. For detailed discussions cf. D. Bates, *The Fashoda Incident of 1898: Encounter on the Nile* (Oxford: Oxford University Press, 1984), pp. 151–68; J. A. S. Grenville, *Lord Salisbury and Foreign Policy: The Close of the Nineteenth Century* (London: Athlone Press, rev. ed. 1970), pp. 218–34.

96. For the text cf. Cambon to Delcassé (no. 61), 21 Mar. 1899, *DDF* (1) xv, no. 122; J. J. Cooke, *New French Imperialism, 1880–1910: The Third Republic and Colonial Expansion* (Newton Abbott: David & Charles, 1973), pp. 95–97.

CLEMENCEAU'S CONTACTS WITH ENGLAND

David R. Watson

Georges Clemenceau must be the most Anglophile prime minister ever to have held office in France, in spite of the fact that his defence of French interests in the peace negotiations at the end of the First World War produced conflict with David Lloyd George and the British delegation at least as hard-fought as that with President Wilson. He was one of the very few important political figures in the France of his day to be fluent in English: no other French politician came anywhere near his level of contact with and knowledge of British society and politics. By 1919 these contacts went back more than fifty years: they included intimate personal relationships, as well as intellectual and political aspects: their exploration is important for analysis of Anglo-French relations over this period, and for a full understanding of Clemenceau himself.

Clemenceau's Anglophilia was well known in his lifetime: in fact it was notorious. The English connection played a big part in his electoral defeat of 1893, which seemed to have ended his political career, after a campaign in which he was followed by jeering crowds, drowning his attempts to speak with cries of "Aoh yes, aoh yes." Posters were distributed showing him on stage as a dancer, juggling with four bags of money

I wish to thank three French friends for their assistance, André and Marcel Wormser, who facilitated consultation of Clemenceau's letters to Violet Maxse, at the Musée Clemenceau, and loaned me photocopies of them, and Serge Cottereau for allowing me to quote from his conference paper "les remonstrances d'un anglophile," and for sharing his unparalleled knowledge of the contacts between Clemenceau and the Maxse family. I am also grateful to the staff of the West Sussex Records Office for their help in consultation of the Maxse papers.

labelled "livres sterling." In the prompter's box a stereotyped Jewish figure representing Cornelius Herz conducted the performance: the title given to this caricature was "*le pas du commandité*," implying that Clemenceau was a puppet controlled by Herz, acting for the British government.[1] This campaign was orchestrated by the Boulangistes who had previously attempted to prove that he was in the pay of the British secret service by crude forgeries, the Norton letters.[2] Although the absurdity of these documents, when read out in the Chamber of Deputies, completely discredited Clemenceau's attackers, Millevoye and Déroulède, there were those who believed that this simply showed the supreme cunning of the governing republican party. Just as the Toreador's red cloak distracted the bull from the target it should have charged, the Norton letters distracted attention from real evidence of the British money that accounted for Clemenceau's Anglophilia.[3] This evidence was never found, although in a sense it was there, as will be shown later in this paper. It was provided not by the British government, but by Admiral Frederick A. Maxse, Clemenceau's closest friend of any nationality. Although it would be absurd to think that Maxse's financial support accounted for Clemenceau's pro-English attitude, it would have been highly embarassing for him if hard evidence had emerged about the substantial loan at this time. We have hints that rumours did circulate during these years, but nothing precise could be proved. This important matter will be discussed in more detail later.

Before beginning an account of Clemenceau's long involvement with English intellectual and political life, reference ought to be made to an article by Robert Hanks which has the merit of opening up academic discussion on this topic.[4] Although Hanks has discovered and utilised much valuable material, his use of it is to some extent out of focus, and this has led to a final judgement on the significance of Clemenceau's English contacts which is misleading. Hanks's view is that these English contacts were marginal and eccentric figures, and that they gave him a deep-rooted mistrust of the English governing class, a mistrust that led to serious errors in his negotiations with the leaders of that class in 1919. To arrive at this view he lists Frederic Harrison, Henry M. Hyndman, and the Maxse family, as Clemenceau's main English friends and he makes Positivism an important element in their mutual sympathy.[5] Joseph Chamberlain, the most important English political figure to have contact with Clemenceau is mentioned only in passing. On this basis Hanks thinks that Clemenceau's contacts were eccentric, extreme Radicals, out of touch with the main strands of British political society. It is true that the positivist Harrison and the Marxist stockbroker Hyndman were marginal figures in British political and intellectual life. But it would be far from correct to call them Clemenceau's friends; his contacts with them were brief and incidental.

Hyndman, it is true, wrote a eulogistic biography when Clemenceau was at the peak of his fame as Père-la-Victoire, and exaggerated these earlier contacts in his own autobiography, but there is little evidence that the two had ever been close.[6] Certainly Clemenceau did not look to Hyndman in 1917–19 for insights into British politics although he found time to meet Hyndman during his brief visit to London in December 1918. It was only Hyndman's volteface at the outbreak of war, when the dogmatic leader of the Social Democratic Federation turned into a superpatriot, that brought him close to Clemenceau. Clemenceau had been happy to publish Hyndman's denunciation of E.D. Morel, and other leftwing opponents of British participation in the war, in his newspaper. But over the previous thirty years their views had been very different, and they had in reality had little contact. Hyndman's biography of Clemenceau is full of errors that show he had little knowledge of his early life. Hanks himself admits that Harrison's admiration for Clemenceau was a one way street and that the latter's knowledge of Harrison and English Positivism was negligible.[7]

A better assessment of the English dimension in Clemenceau's life needs to be centred on the Maxse family, whose importance over more than fifty years is of a completely different order to his ephemeral contacts with such as Harrison and Hyndman. In addition some mention needs to be made of his youthful translation of John Stuart Mill into French, and of his contacts with Joseph Chamberlain and John Morley resulting from his friendship with Maxse. The main point is that the Maxse family connection, far from taking Clemenceau into a bizarre fringe of British society, eventually provided him with close contacts in the ruling elite. Although Maxse in his early political career was an extreme Radical, that *rara avis* an English republican, he was also a rich landowner and a member of an aristocratic family. Like his friend Chamberlain the Home Rule crisis of 1886 saw him take the Unionist road from Radicalism to patriotic — one could even say jingoist—Conservatism. In 1893 he bought a moribund monthly magazine, the *National Review*, in order to install his son Leo as editor. Leo Maxse, also a close friend to Clemenceau after his father's death in 1900, made the *National Review* the voice of Right-wing Unionism and Edwardian Imperialism. His sister Violet married Lord Edward Cecil, a younger son of the Prime Minister Lord Salisbury, and then had a close relationship with Alfred Milner, whom she eventually married after the death of her first husband. When her daughter married in 1921, the King and Queen were guests, and Lady Elizabeth Bowes Lyon, future Queen and Queen Mother, was a bridesmaid.[8] One could not get any closer to the centre of British high society. Admiral Maxse's children, Leo, Violet and Olive were among the closest friends that Clemenceau ever had. He had much less contact with the eldest son,

Ivor, a professional soldier. After seeing Violet as an additional daughter he fell in love with her in spite of their difference in age, and was bitterly disappointed when she chose Milner, also much older, although thirteen years younger than he was.[9]

Clemenceau's English contacts began in August 1865, when, accompanied by his father, he crossed the channel to meet Herbert Spencer and John Stuart Mill, before continuing his journey to the United States. Mentioned in all standard accounts, the evidence for his visits to these two eminent men of letters is his own reminiscences recorded by Jean Martet more than sixty years later.[10] Nothing of significance is known about the meeting with Spencer, and sources on him have nothing about Clemenceau.[11] Clemenceau's library includes several of Spencer's works, in American editions, published in 1865–68 and acquired no doubt during his stay in the United States at that time. Many years later he referred to Spencer's ideas in some of his socio-political essays, but there is no evidence of further direct contact.[12] More is known about Clemenceau's relations with John Stuart Mill, then at the height of his fame as a philosopher and social scientist who was also involved in practical politics: he was elected MP for the popular constituency of Westminster on 12 July 1865, just before meeting Clemenceau. It has frequently been stated that Clemenceau was introduced to Mill by his father, who had been in contact with him for many years.[13] There is no sign of this in the extensive published collection of Mill's letters, and it seems improbable, as Mill's French contacts were much less left-wing than Clemenceau *père*. The precise reason for the meeting was because Clemenceau had agreed to translate a short book by Mill on Auguste Comte and Positivism. In my view that was arranged by Littré who was approached by Mill on the subject in March 1865: Mill sent him a copy on 11 May 1865 *"pour le traducteur."*[14] The editors of Mill's letters add a footnote stating that Littré did not, as requested, arrange for the translation, and that it was given to Clemenceau after the two had met in the spring of 1865. This is not correct: the meeting was in England, and must have been in August, and Clemenceau told Martet that it was already agreed that he should do the translation before he met Mill: it was part of a bargain by which the French publisher Bailliere would produce a new edition of his medical thesis in return.[15] Littré probably passed on Mill's request to his friend Robin, Clemenceau's professor and patron, who saw him as the ideal candidate for this task. Although Clemenceau had not yet acquired a full command of English, his four years stay in America and the hard work involved in translating Mill meant that he emerged with a good knowledge of the language. Clemenceau's library retains a copy of Mill's s book on Comte, dedicated to him and referring to their meeting, while he in turn sent Mill a dedicated copy of his thesis *De la Génération des Eléments Anatomiques*.[16]

There was to be no further contact with Mill, who died in 1872. Clemenceau's command of the English language must, however, have been improved by his marriage to an eighteen year old American girl, who at first had little French. One letter has survived that he wrote to her when besieged in Paris in the autumn of 1870, in idiomatic English. Mary Plummer is an almost invisible figure in accounts of Clemenceau's life, in spite of having lived with him for nearly twenty two years, and being the mother of three children. His American wife did not mean that Clemenceau retained a serious interest in the USA. He never visited the United States between 1869 and 1922; there are no signs of her presence in his visits to England, nor mention of her in what we know of his English contacts. After their divorce in 1892 she disappears completely, although she lived on in Paris until 1923.

The central figure of Clemenceau's contacts with England after 1870 was Admiral Maxse, to whom he was introduced by Louis Blanc in 1872. Blanc, a republican who had played a leading role in the 1848 revolution remained a political emigré in London until the fall of the Second Empire, thus acquiring many contacts in British left-wing circles. On his return to France he became the leader of the extreme non-revolutionary republicans, that is of the faction joined by Clemenceau. Maxse's sympathy for France in the Franco–Prussian war and his attitude towards the Paris Commune brought the two men together; Maxse spent a good deal of his time in France, being as Francophile as Clemenceau was Anglophile. Most of his other close English contacts were acquired through Maxse and his children with whom he remained intimate after Maxse's death: he called them his English family. It was through Maxse that he met Joseph Chamberlain, and John, later Viscount, Morley, as well as Hyndman.

Maxse, the younger son of a rich landowning family, entered the navy aged fourteen in 1846. He served on land in the Crimean War, an experience which filled him with contempt for aristocratic bungling and made him a political radical. It also made him a Francophile, presumably in reaction to his aristocratic and aged superior officers who could not stop referring to their French allies as the enemy. In 1860 he reacted to the anti-French scare of that year by publishing, anonymously, a pamphlet entitled "A word for truth concerning our attitude to France by an English seaman." He had already published a novel *Robert Mornay* under the pseudonym of Max Ferrer, and was in touch with the writer George Meredith, who remained a lifelong friend, taking him as the real-life model for the hero of his novel *Beauchamp's Career*. Meredith told him that his pamphlet was "too emotional, too pro-French, and critical of England."[17] He did not again go to sea, and began to devote himself to writing and to radical politics, retiring from the Navy in 1867. This meant going on to half pay and still allowed him to be eventually promoted to admiral by seniority. Thus he was never in a real sense an admiral but he seems to have been proud of and to have used the title. Maxse was unusual because he supported France throughout the Franco-Prussian War: the great majority of British opinion was much more sympathetic to Prussia and only a few wavered even after they heard of the annexation of Alsace-Lorraine. The main exceptions to this anti-French stance were to be found among the tiny group of English disciples of Comte's Positivism, among whom Frederick Harrison is the most important.[18] Maxse adopted exactly the same position as Clemenceau towards the Paris Commune: that is, without in any way supporting the Commune, he was horrified by the ruthless massacre and the arbitrary verdicts of the courts martial which followed the suppression.[19] Maxse was in Paris during and after the suppression of the Commune and discussed it in a pamphlet, *The Causes of Social Revolt*, published in 1873. Maxse's eyewitness account was used by Harrison for his article on the Commune in the *Fortnightly Review*. On 30 May 1871 Maxse had written to Harrison asking him to protest about the severe repressive measures, but Harrison had refused, saying that the Thiers government should be supported as it was establishing a Republic. An indication of the future difficulties Maxse would have in presenting Clemenceau to English opinion-formers is that Harrison found that his English audience confused Positivism, Communism, and the Commune.

For at least ten years after 1867 Maxse played a prominent role in British Radical politics, several times standing as a parliamentary candidate, though he was never elected. Nevertheless he was a leading figure in many political organisations, the Land Tenure Reform Association, the National Education League, and the Electoral Reform Association among others. He had plans to set up a newspaper for working men or alternatively to take over one that already existed, *The Beehive*. Probably the most important of his activities was his leading role in the National Education League, which brought him into contact with Joseph Chamberlain. Formed to oppose taxpayers' money going to Church of England schools, this organisation was mainly supported by Nonconformists. Maxse, however, argued from an atheist position against all religious content in public education. In this as in other matters he came to be seen as too extreme for practical politics. However he remained for many years in close contact with Chamberlain and provided Clemenceau with contacts with him as also with Morley.

Although Clemenceau was not a member of the French Assembly between 1871 and 1875, he was seen as an up-and-coming figure in the republican party, and Maxse introduced him at this time to several English Radicals, notably Joseph Chamberlain and John Morley. Sir Charles Dilke has also been mentioned, but no trace of contact between them could be found, except for a brief reference to a meeting when Dilke was in Paris in November 1881, negotiating with the French government about commercial matters.[20] In 1875 Maxse introduced Clemenceau to Chamberlain and Morley on a joint visit to Paris, and this trio continued to have relatively frequent contacts with him until 1893, either in Paris or in London. Morley's memoirs recall a visit to Paris, no doubt in the 1880s, when Clemenceau and Chamberlain talked for hours and found that they shared many political goals. He continues, "A dream came before his [Chamberlain's] vision as we sauntered down the boulevard, a dream of practical co-operation with Clemenceau in the common interest of European democracy. Alas, like the dreams of the international socialists, such visions had far too little common basis against divergent tongues, race, tradition, economic interest, spiritual faith. . . ."[21]

Clemenceau's foreign contacts really developed from 1883 onwards. As well as the English contacts discussed here, he had equally close contacts in Austria-Hungary, with the journalist Moritz Szeps and his family. One of Szeps's daughters was to marry his brother Paul.[22] In my view Clemenceau's seeking of these foreign contacts was related to the death of Léon Gambetta on the last day of 1882. Gambetta, until his early and unexpected death, the leader of the republican party, felt that it was important to establish such contacts to show that the leaders of the French Republic could play their part in a Europe still overwhelmingly monarchical and aristocratic. Gambetta himself had established such contacts, and had left his lower-middle class image behind. With his death Clemenceau saw himself as the future leader of the republican party who would need to play a role on the European stage. Not himself an aristocrat, but every inch a gentleman, he could move on equal terms in cosmopolitan and aristocratic society in several countries. He looked down on his rival as republican leader, Jules Ferry, as a parochial figure, not a man of the world, who had allowed himself to be manipulated by Prince Bismarck, the German chancellor. As a result France occupied a subordinate place in a diplomatic system dominated by the German Empire. When he came to power he wanted something very different. Even at this stage, not yet having held ministerial office, a young man in a hurry, he wanted to establish the personal and political links that would be useful if his ambitions came to fruition.

Already in January 1883 he met Gladstone on holiday in Cannes. Gladstone, staying with aristocratic friends at the Château Scott, met Clemenceau along with the comte de Paris, the claimant to the French throne, and the Duke of Argyll. This situation epitomises Clemenceau's life style at the time. This extreme-left republican, deputy for a proletarian Paris constituency, spokesman for the working class, was nevertheless to be found mixing in the most opulent circles. Gladstone found him "decidedly pleasing"; he wrote to Lord Granville that their conversation "was mainly on Egypt, about which he spoke in a temperate and reasonable manner". Reports of this conversation appeared in the French press and then in the *Daily News* in London, where attention was paid not to Clemenceau's views on Egypt, but to Gladstone's on Ireland. He said that "he wished to make the humblest Irishman feel that he is a self-governing agency." Clemenceau was very sympathetic to Gladstone's Irish policy and is reported to have said in 1886 that he was "*tout bonnement l' homme politique le plus épatant des temps modernes.*" Nevertheless, he allowed his friend Maxse to publish articles in *La Justice* violently opposing Home Rule in 1887.[23] Maxse had separated from his wife in 1877, and thereafter spent much time in Paris; he had a *pied-à-terre* there, for some time in the same street as Clemenceau's flat. By the 1890s the two friends also developed the habit of taking the waters together at Carlsbad every summer.

The years 1883–4 were the high point of Clemenceau's English connections in the earlier part of his life. In 1883, he was elected as a foreign member of the Cobden Club, causing the resignation of several members under the misapprehension that he was a revolutionary socialist who had supported the Paris Commune.[24] The next year, 1884, Maxse arranged a visit to London by Clemenceau that is well documented. French police informers reported back to Paris that Clemenceau was staying with his friend Maxse, described as an ardent democrat and socialist, and that he was being entertained at several of the best London clubs: he also dined with the foreign minister Lord Granville and at the French embassy. Mrs. Humphrey Ward's memoirs tell of a dinner chez Maxse with Clemenceau and Chamberlain present. *The Life of Canon Barnett* offers a glimpse of a day Clemenceau spent in Whitechapel visiting schools, hospitals, the workhouse and Toynbee Hall of which the canon was the warden. This was part of an enquiry into social conditions in England and into the working of the English poor law.[25] There is other evidence of Clemenceau's contacts with Joseph Chamberlain at this time. They met in Paris in 1885 and in 1887 at a country house party for the Ascot races. In July 1891 Maxse arranged a meeting with Chamberlain at which Clemenceau advocated a settlement of issues in dispute between France and England, much along the lines of the subsequent Entente.[26]

Another fact emerges from the Maxse family papers. In 1886 Maxse had loaned 100,000 francs (c. £4,000) to Clemenceau, a very substantial sum at that time. Maxse wrote to Clemeceau on 7 December 1888:

> I want to speak to you on one matter, or would rather write on it to avoid talking to you about anything so disagreeable. God knows I would not add to any of your troubles if I could help it, but I have had some rather serious losses this autumn . . . I am obliged most reluctantly to

turn to you and ask whether you can repay the 100,000 francs. I have not said a word on the subject, as you know, for two years and I have asked for no security. If you are in difficulties I will not press, but I hope you will give me some prospect.[27]

Nothing was repaid then, and only a quarter of the total two years later, as emerges from a letter from the admiral to his son Ivor, on 11 August 1892. The Maxse papers do not reveal whether the money was ever repaid. This did not affect the cordial relations between the two men. Maxse was rich enough to be philosophical about it. It would be ludicrous to suggest that Clemenceau's pro-English line was a product of the loan, but it would have been very embarrassing for him if it had ever been made public. As well as the Norton letters and the successful smear campaign that led to his electoral defeat in 1893, there are other traces of the rumours circulating in Paris about Clemenceau's English money. Léon Daudet reports on a dinner in London, with Maxse, Balfour, Henry James and Morley, at which the question was discussed. While Daudet is not in general to be relied on, he claims to have been present on this occasion, which gives it some credence. The most extreme version of the charge that Clemenceau was throughout in the pay of the British government is to be found in the writings of the journalist, Ernest Judet. It is interesting that it has recently been proved, as was long suspected, that Judet was in the pay of the German government for many years.[28]

1893 marks the end of the first period of Clemenceau's contacts with British politics. His own political career seemed to have ended and Maxse himself had become marginalised in British politics. His opposition to Irish Home Rule had taken him from the left to the right of the political scene. This also applied to his friend Chamberlain, although not to Morley who remained a leading figure in the Liberal party. Maxse gradually abandoned direct political activity. However, in 1893 he bought a moribund monthly magazine, the *National Review*, in order to install his son Leo as its editor. It proved to be a success, surviving until 1960, its period of greatest influence being down to 1918, as the voice of right wing Unionism and Imperialism. Admiral Maxse himself died in 1900 from typhoid contracted in South Africa, but Clemenceau remained close to his children Leo and Violet. Leo's role as editor of the *National Review* gave him contacts with a new generation of British political figures. The evolution of the political views of the Maxse family meant that these contacts were not of the radical left but of the right, something that mirrored Clemenceau's own political evolution. Contact with Morley continued intermittently. Violet Maxse describes a dinner party she gave early in her married life, in 1898. Her father, Clemenceau and Morley were the only guests. She tells us that they disputed over the outcome of the ideals they had shared twenty years before, with Clemenceau admitting their failure while Morley was reluctant to do so, although Morley's recollections suggest opposite stances. Clemenceau was sarcastic about Morley's opposition to British entry into the war, writing to Violet on 7 August 1914 *"Tout le monde me dit que Morley a été ignoble contre nous. J' expliquerais cela par son gâtisme."* Nevertheless they met again in 1919, according to Morley on good terms.[29]

Clemenceau's political eclipse lasted barely five years. From 1898 his role in the Dreyfus Affair brought him back onto the political stage. In addition to the immense number of articles which he wrote on the Affair, he found time to comment on international affairs, primarily in the weekly *Le Bloc*, entirely written by him. Like most French commentators he was critical of British foreign policy, both at the time of the Fashoda crisis, and during the South African war. A long letter to Admiral Maxse, of October 1899, when he had just heard that Lord Edward Cecil was besieged in Mafeking, brings this out. After referring to the divergence of their views on the war, he continues:

> *C'est affreux pour Violette. Mon coeur saigne avec le sien, avec le vôtre, avec celui d'Olive . . . Qu'est -ce que la politique dans tout cela? Je suis avec ceux que j'aime et il n'y a rien au dela . . . Il faut que vous sâchiez que je ne puis pas, pour des causes de vaine politique, séparer ma cause de la vôtre. Je l'ai senti dès que j'ai appris le malheur dont était menacée notre chère Violette. Je ne peux pas songer à autre chose et je voudrais que tous les Boers fussent au fond de la mer . . . .[30]*

His English friends Chamberlain and the Maxse family were, of course, among the most ardent supporters of the South African war. This neither clouded his friendship with them, nor limited his criticism of British policy. In fact the war brought tragedy for the Maxse family. Ivor Maxse and Violet's husband Lord Edward Cecil were involved as professional soldiers. Although they survived the war unscathed, other consequences were tragic. Violet, like many officers' wives and high society ladies went out to Cape Town with her husband. While he was besieged in Mafeking she began her relationship with Milner which led soon afterwards to the effective breakdown of her marriage, although they never divorced.[31] Whether because of this or from a wish to see the war at close quarters, Admiral Maxse also went to South Africa, where he contracted typhoid, from which he died on his return to England. Clemenceau's letters to the bereaved family show the intensity of his friendship with the admiral: those to Violet in particular show his developing emotional involvement with her. In April 1901 he stayed with her for about ten to fourteen days at her house in Park Street, Mayfair.[32]

Soon after Clemenceau's return to mainstream politics, with his election as senator in April 1902, he resumed contact, through the Maxse family, with important British political figures. Austen Chamberlain wrote to his father Joseph on 19 December 1902:

> On Tuesday I dined with Leo Maxse to meet Clemenceau. The other guests were Edward Grey, Clinton Dawkins and Rowland Blennerhassett. Clemenceau looked younger and better than when I last saw him, and talked with wonderful verve and freshness. He is now a senator and according to Maxse (who says he is not blinded by friendship—he hears the same thing on all sides) his position has marvellously improved. The colonial party have given up, for the time being at least, the policy of *embêter les anglais* and have expressed to Clemenceau a wish for his cooperation and assistance. Clemenceau himself wishes to draw closer to England, not relinquishing the Russian alliance, but giving one hand to Russia and the other to England. . . . The great danger of the future is Pan-Germanism. . . . There was a time when France and England were in rivalry for the world. Now that is settled. England is doing a great work for liberty and civilisation . . . Therefore Clemenceau feels no jealousy of it . . . *Mais . . . Il viendra un moment òu l'Angleterre aura le besoin de causer avec la France.*[33]

In spite of his support for a *rapprochement* with England, Clemenceau had no part in the negotiation which produced the *Entente Cordiale*, as he was still out of office. But just before he returned to office as minister of the interior in Sarrien's government in March 1906, he visited London in December 1905, at the moment of the transition from a Conservative to a Liberal government. As well as seeing his Maxse friends, he met Morley although a meeting with Sir Edward Grey proved to be impossible.[34]

A more personal matter can be mentioned at this point. As has been stated above, Clemenceau confessed that he had fallen in love with Violet Maxse, after the failure of her marriage to Lord Edward Cecil, but that she had preferred Lord Milner. Although the letters that she presented to the Musée Clemenceau reveal virtually nothing, there is a letter of 29 October 1905 that must refer to this matter, Clemenceau wrote to "*ma chère enfant*": "*J'ai été tres content de voir Lord Milner avec qui j'ai causé au fond pendant plus d'une heure. J'ai taché de lui faire comprendre òu nous en étions et il m'a dit très clairement òu vous en étiez. Des deux parts il ne pouvait y avoir que des avantages à connaître la vérité.*" Although enigmatic, this letter must refer to some resolution of the personal situation between Violet, Clemenceau and Milner. After this date, although their correspondence continued, Clemenceau's letters to Violet are less intimate than they had been in the previous six years, when they had been drawn together by their common grief at the death of the admiral, and he had known of her estrangement from her husband.[35]

After 1906, Clemenceau occupied an eminent position among European statesmen: he had many contacts with leading English political figures, as well as in other European countries. His meetings with Lloyd George, and King Edward VII at Carlsbad are well known, and have been well explored by Duroselle.[36] It could no longer be a matter of personal friendship, but of the many contacts involved in inter-State relationships. Nevertheless alongside such networking it is clear that Clemenceau, through his Maxse contacts, retained close and intimate relationships with English people that were of a different order from the mere political. Although, in some eyes Leo Maxse's *National Review* might seem to have led him to an extreme right-wing fringe of British politics, after 1914 this group came back into the centre of the political stage.[37] The war brought personal tragedy immediately to Violet Maxse, and through her, to Clemenceau. Her son George, aged eighteen and just out of Sandhurst, was reported missing in September 1914. In spite of his other preoccupations Clemenceau devoted much effort in the attempt to find out about his fate. George was eventually proved to have been killed.

Nothing could better symbolise the conjunction of Clemenceau's personal and political relationships than the dramatic meeting at Doullens in March 1918. At this great crisis, when the German army had broken through the allied front, and seemed to be on the point of dividing the British and French armies, Clemenceau met Milner as British plenipotentiary to agree on the appointment of Foch as supreme allied commander, a decision that has been seen as vital to the avoidance of allied defeat. Not only was this decision taken by Clemenceau and Violet Maxse's lover, but the general in command of the British XVIII corps that had broken was her brother, Ivor Maxse, eldest son of his old friend.[38]

But Clemenceau could draw a firm line between personal relationships and national political interests. He had made the point in letters to the Maxses during the South African war, when he criticised the British position in his newspaper articles, but in his private letters of sympathy to his friends, said that he wished the Boers were at the bottom of the sea. If he fought so hard in the peace negotiations to reconcile French demands with the preservation of the alliance with Britain it was because he was convinced that the French national interest demanded it: he also believed that Britain needed an alliance with France in her own national interest. Problems between Britain and France in 1919 and afterwards were no doubt inherent in the respective situations of the two countries whose wartime alliance had been made against a German threat to both, which seemed to have been removed. Insofar as personalities came into it, it was Lloyd George, hardly a member of the traditional English governing class, who mattered. Clemenceau certainly disliked and distrusted Lloyd George, and had been amazed by his ignorance on first meeting him in 1908.[39] But by 1919 he recognised his immense achievement in leading Britain through the last two years of the war, and any personal antipathy was not allowed to impede their bargaining. No doubt, having to deal with Woodrow Wilson as well made Lloyd George seem more reasonable. The topic of the peace negotiations is too vast to be entered into here, but it can be stated that as historians continue to reassess the treaties Clemenceau's achievement emerges more and more clearly. He won a settlement that not only provided for essential French interests but one which, if it had been adhered to in the following years, could have given stability and peace to Europe as a whole.[40] Clemenceau could rightly feel that he had been double-crossed by the tricky Welshman, on the vital matter of the promised treaty of guarantee, as well as on several other less important questions where Lloyd George had made promises to him which were not kept. But however much he was to be disappointed by developments after he left office in January 1920, there can be no doubt about his skill in playing a weak hand in the 1919 negotiations. One factor in this was certainly that he alone of the three key figures was fluent in both English and French: another was the intimate knowledge of British politics and society that he had built up during fifty years.

NOTES

1. This caricature appeared in *Le Petit Journal, Supplément illustré* (19 Aug. 1893). On the 1893 election, see D.R.Watson, *Georges Clemenceau, A Political Biography* (London: Eyre Methuen, 1974), pp. 127–130, and J.-B. Duroselle, *Clemenceau* (Paris: Fayard, 1988), pp. 281–306.
2. The Norton letters are discussed in all accounts: the most recent treatment is by Bertrand Joly, *Déroulède, L'inventeur du nationalisme français* (Paris: Perven, 1998), pp.191–94, and *Dictionnaire Biographique et Géographique du Nationalisme Français* (Paris: Honoré Champion, 2005), pp. 284–5, article on Millevoye.
3. This is the interpretation given in Maurice Barres' novel *Leurs Figures*, and was also that of Edmond de Goncourt who noted on 22 June 1893 "*le triomphe insolent de Clemenceau, sortant de ces accusations fausses, mais vraies au fond, indemne, pur, insoupçonnable,*" Edmond et Jules de Goncourt, *Journal* (Paris; Bouquins, 1989) p. 840.
4. Robert K. Hanks, "Georges Clemenceau and the English," *Historical Journal* xlv, 1 (2002), pp. 53–77.
5. Hanks states that "Positivism was also one of the initial building blocks in Clemenceau's relationship with Maxse," ibid., p.61. However Morley, who was much involved with the English Positivists, states that Maxse was not a Positivist, John, Viscount Morley, *Recollections* (2 vols., London: Macmillan, 1917) i, pp. 45–6.Clemenceau himself, although he did in his student days call himself a

Positivist, was not a strict follower of Comte, as the English Positivists were. Like his professor, Robin, he was one of the dissidents who followed Littré. For an attempt to assess Clemenceau's Positivism, see D. R. Watson, "A note on Clemenceau, Comte, and Positivism," *Historical Journal* xiv, 2 (1971), pp. 201–4.

6. H. M. Hyndman, *Clemenceau, the Man and his Time* (London: Grant Richards, 1919) and *Record of a Adventurous Life* (London: Macmillan, 1911) include remarkable errors about Clemenceau.

7. Hanks, "Georges Clemenceau and the English," p. 58.

8. Hugh and Mirabel Cecil, *Imperial Marriage: an Edwardian War and Peace* (London: John Murray, 2002), p. 299; Terence O'Brien, *Viscount Milner of St. James and Cape Town, 1854–1925* (London: Constable, 1979), p. 363.

9. Duroselle, *Clemenceau*, p. 376.

10. Jean Martet, *M. Clemenceau, peint par lui-même* (Paris: Albin Michel, 1929), pp. 208–9.

11. D. Duncan, *Life and Letters of Herbert Spencer* (London: Methuen, 1908); Herbert Spencer, *An Autobiography* (2 vols., London: Williams and Norgate, 1904).

12. Sylvie Brodziak, "Clemenceau et la culture anglo-saxonne," unpublished conference paper, 2004.

13. Duroselle, *Clemenceau*, p. 69.

14. Mill was himself in France, mainly at Avignon, until the end of June 1865. Clemenceau and his father crossed to England on 25 July. He was in New York by 21 August, and thus must have left England no later than 14 August. The meeting with Mill was probably in the last week of July, as Mill spent 2–8 August in Cornwall. Mill's movements can be detailed from his published letters: John Stuart Mill, *Collected Works*, vol. xvi *Letters 1865–1868* (Toronto: University of Toronto Press, 1972); Martet, *Clemenceau*, pp. 221–5, reprints a letter from his friend, Gustave Jourdan to Clemenceau, in reply to one from the latter, in New York, dated 21 August: "*Votre père m'a conté en détail, et, ma foi, très gaiment, votre entrevue avec Stuart Mill.*"

15. Martet, *Clemenceau*, p. 191.

16. Clemenceau's library has remained in his last home, now the Musée Clemenceau, 8 rue Franklin, Paris. Its contents have been discussed in Sylvie Brodziak, *Clemenceau Ecrivain* (Ph.D. thesis, Université de Cergy-Pontoise, 2001) i, pp. 103–4. Hyndman noted that Mill's copy of Clemenceau's thesis had found its way to the London library; it is still there, with its dedication.

17. There has been no study of F. A. Maxse, in spite of the fact that he was a most significant figure in English radicalism. He is mentioned in passing in Royden Harrison, *Before the Socialists: Studies in Labour and Politics, 1861–1881* (London: Routledge and Kegan Paul, 1965), p. 243, and in S. Maccoby, *English Radicalism, 1853–1886* (London: Allen and Unwin, 1938), p. 200. He figures on several occasions in J. L. Garvin (continued Julian Amery), *Life of Joseph Chamberlain* (5 vols., London: Macmillan, 1932–1969), and in studies of his children, Cecil, *Imperial Marriage*, J. A. Hutcheson, *Leopold Maxse and the National Review 1893–1914* (London, 1989) and John Baynes, *Far from a Donkey: The life of General Sir Ivor Maxse* (London: Brassey's, 1995). Material in the Maxse family papers in the West Sussex Record Office, Chichester, includes

several letters from Clemenceau: others, including letters from him to Violet and Olive Maxse are in the Musée Clemenceau.

18. Martha S. Vogeler, *Frederic Harrison: Vocation of a Positivist* (Oxford: Clarendon Press, 1982) p. 102.

19. F. A. Maxse, *The Causes of Social Revolt* (London, 1873) and *The Suppression of the Commune, being a translation of "La Semaine de Mai," by Camille Pelletan, with preface, appendix and notes by vice-admiral Maxse* (London, 1883).

20. David Nicholls, *The Lost Prime Minister: A Life of Sir Charles Dilke* (London: Hambledon Press, 1995), p. 98. Dilke wrote that he had met Clemenceau and found him to be "an inferior Randolph Churchill." In 1906 Dilke wrote to him on behalf of the Congo Reform Association, asking him to put pressure on King Leopold, without success, ibid., p. 307.

21. Morley, *Recollections* i, pp. 161–2. Morley does not give a precise date for this meeting, but Chamberlain in a letter to Potter of October 1883 states that he and Morley had talked with Clemenceau for several hours. A copy of this letter in the Musée Clemenceau was published in G. Wormser, *La République de Clemenceau* (Paris: Presses Universitaires de France, 1961) pp. 489–490. Chamberlain also wrote to Maxse, 14 October 1883, about this meeting: "We had a long and interesting talk with Clemenceau. I think highly of his capacity, and generally approve his programme. But he has a terribly difficult team to drive," Maxse Mss 206. See also Garvin, *Chamberlain* i, p. 500, n.1, recounting an interview with Morley in 1923.

22. Watson, *Clemenceau*, pp. 91 and 137.

23. John Morley, *Life of William Ewart Gladstone* (3 vols., London: Macmillan, 1903), p. 103; Stephen Gwynn and Gertrude M. Tuckwell, *The Life of the Right Honorable Sir Charles W. Dilke, Bt.* (London: John Murray, 1917); Christine d'Haussy, "Gladstone et la France," *Franco-British Studies* xxxii (Spring 2003), p. 15.

24. Clemenceau's election to the Cobden Club caused much discussion in the press, and is mentioned in A. W. Paul, *History of Modern England* (4 vols., London: Macmillan, 1905) iv, p. 311. Maxse wrote to *The Times*, indignantly attacking those who resigned for their ignorance of Clemenceau's real views: "No true disciple of Cobden can object to him on political grounds," ibid. (21 June 1883).

25. Préfecture de Police, Paris, BA 93, report of 19 février, 1884. Mrs Humphrey Ward [i.e. Mary A. Ward], *A Writer's Recollections* (London: Collins 1918) p. 221; *Canon Barnett, His Life, Work and Friends by His Wife* (2 vols., London: John Murray, 1918) ii, p. 45; Duroselle, *Clemenceau*, p. 198; Watson, *Clemenceau*, p. 88.

26. Chamberlain to Maxse, 3 January 1885, Maxse Mss 206, and 25 April 1885, complaining about French hostility to Britain: "It is all very well for French statesmen to talk privately about their friendly sentiments. In public their conduct is lache. . . . They have deserted the most friendly English government that ever held office"; also Chamberlain to Clemenceau, 5 June 1885, in Wormser, *Clemenceau*, p. 491. For the Ascot country house party, W. T. W. [Quin], Earl of Dunraven, *Past Times and Pastimes* (2 vols., London,1922) i, p. 259. For the 1891 meeting between Clemenceau and Chamberlain, see C. H. D. Howard (eds.), *J. Chamberlain: A Political Memoir, 1880–1892* (London: Batchworth Press, 1953), pp. 295–7, and Watson, *Clemenceau*, p. 122.

27. Maxse Mss 147.
28. Leon Daudet, *La Vie Orageuse de Clemenceau* (Paris: Albin Michel, 1938), pp. 103–4; Ernest Judet, *Le Véritable Clemenceau* (Berne: F. Wyss, 1919); Duroselle, *Clemenceau*, p. 281, proof of Judet being in German pay.
29. Viscountess Milner, *My Picture Gallery 1886–1901* (London: John Murray, 1951), p. 116. Clemenceau's letter to Violet Maxse, Musée Clemenceau; John H Morgan, *John Viscount Morley: An Appreciation and Some Reminiscences* (London: John Murray, 1924), p. 91.
30. Clemenceau to F.A. Maxse, Musée Clemenceau. Clemenceau's articles on this topic have been analysed by Serge Cottereau, "Les remonstrances d'un anglophile, 1877–1902," unpublished conference paper.
31. Cecil, *Imperial Marriage*, pp. 106–177.
32. Viscountess Milner, *My Picture Gallery*, p. 242.
33. This letter is published in Garvin and Amery, *Life of Joseph Chamberlain* v, p. 137.
34. Clemenceau's articles have been analysed by Serge Cottereau, "Clemenceau journaliste et l'Entente Cordiale," in L. Bonnard (ed.), *France—Angleterre, un siècle d'Entente Cordiale, 1904–2004: Deux Nations, un seul but?* (Paris, L'Harnattan, 2004), pp. 47–65; Clemenceau to Leo Maxse, 1 October, 6, 11 and 18 December 1905, Maxse Mss 453; Clemenceau to Lady Edward Cecil, 29 October 1905, Musée Clemenceau.
35. Clemenceau to Lady Edward Cecil, 29 October 1905, Musée Clemenceau.
36. Duroselle, *Clemenceau*, pp. 774–800; Watson, *Clemenceau*, pp. 225–26.
37. Hutcheson, *Maxse and the National Review*, passim; A. J. A. Morris, *The Scaremongers: Advocacy of War and Rearmament, 1896–1914* (London: Routledge and Kegan Paul, 1984) has many unsympathetic references to *the National Review*, its author's bias being revealed in his subtitle. Leo Maxse did not advocate war, but rearmament to prevent war. A selection of his articles was reprinted in Leo J. Maxse, *Germany on the Brain, or the Obsession of a Crank: Gleanings from the National Review, 1899–1914* (London: the National Review Office, 1915). An example of the hatred felt towards Leo Maxse by liberals is a letter from Lytton Strachey to his sister, complaining about meeting him at a house party, "a mere spider in mind and body," Michael Holroyd, *Lytton Strachey* (London: Heinemann, 1994), p. 297.
38. Hanks, "Clemenceau and the English," p. 65.
39. Watson, *Clemenceau*, p. 226, fn. 126, quoting Clemenceau's letter to Pichon, 21 August 1908. On 1 September 1908 he wrote to Leo Maxse about Lloyd George's ignorance, Maxse Mss 458.
40. For example, Michael Dockrill and John Fisher (Eds.), *The Paris Peace Conference 1919, Peace without Victors?* (Basingstoke: Palgrave, 2001); David Stevenson, *1914–1918, The History of the First World War* (London: Allen Lane, 2004); Zara Steiner, *The Lights that Failed, European International History, 1919–1933*. (Oxford: Oxford University Press, 2005).

THE ANGLO–FRENCH VICTORY ON THE SOMME

William Philpott

The 1916 Somme offensive, 141 days of hard attritional slogging over the slopes of an insignificant range of small hills in Picardy, is generally judged to epitomise the "futility and slaughter" which is shorthand for military operations on the western front in the First World War. The casualties speak for themselves: approximately 420,000 British and 205,000 French, and at least 400,000, arguably as many as 680,000 German, depending on accounting system.[1] Why were over 1 million men killed or wounded in a small area of ground of no strategic significance?[2] There was little to show for this blood-letting materially, and its impact on morale and fighting capacity, although hotly debated subsequently,[3] was unquantifiable. Ergo, being such an unprecedented happening, the Somme has lost its context, ceasing to be an episode—the central episode—in the longer military continuum of the First World War in which allied French and British armies took on and defeated their German opponent in a lengthy war of attrition. It has become an event apart, and is so much studied and argued over that arguably today the Somme has become as much a cultural phenomenon as a military action. However, placing the battle in its proper place in the wartime continuum helps in an understanding of its true nature and impact, shorn of it subsequent notoriety and iconography.

The allied commanders and armies judged at the time that they had won a victory—it was their enemies after all who subsequently pulled back their line to new defensive positions and began putting out peace feelers—albeit a hard-won and indecisive one. It would take two further years of fighting before their military superiority was conclusively demonstrated. Nevertheless, it is appropriate to consider why they reached this judgement, and how this battle fitted into their broader strategy.

The battle of the Somme took six months to plan and organise, and lasted for four-and-a-half months; not a battle as might be traditionally identified, more a season's campaigning.[4] It was a triumph of Anglo-French cooperation, despite inevitable frictions; and of allied military force, yet this is all but forgotten in the consuming British obsession with 1 July 1916 and the supposed "lost generation". The French army, despite their effort and sacrifice alongside the British throughout the battle, get barely a paragraph in English language histories of the battle,[5] and their German adversaries get little more.[6] By ignoring the French role in the genesis and conduct of the battle in particular, the all important context is lost, for the Somme was a battle that was part of an agreed allied strategy (including contributions by the Russian and Italians), a strategy formulated and managed by General Joseph Joffre, France's commander-in-chief.

Awareness of this fact leads to the first important question which needs to be addressed. Why was the battle of the Somme fought? Studies of the battle tend to answer this question superficially if at all,[7] in order to get on to the more important issue of how it was fought. The second question that needs to be addressed is, with what result? In answering these questions it is posited here that the battle of the Somme, for all its horror and death, clearly fitted into a broader Anglo–French strategy for winning the war on the western front, which we would now characterise as a strategy of attrition. Notwithstanding the negative associations of that strategic concept, much of it derived from this battle itself,[8] and its prequel and sequel, Verdun and Passchendaele, attrition represented one means to win a war which pitted whole societies against each other. Possibly it represented the only means when the whole product of science and industry were being brought to the battlefield, thereby imposing a new dynamic of machine-age war on the combatants. And it worked, slowly but surely, if brutally. The Germans had a word for it—*Materialschlacht*—and it was this new form of fighting, unrelenting and material-intensive, which the allies imposed on their enemy on the Somme. In doing so, this battle marked the beginning of the end, as was recognised at the time, for Germany's attempt to impose her hegemony in Europe. After the Somme the German army, for all its tactical and operational skill, could not compete at this new form of industrial battle, which the allies were able to intensify in subsequent engagements. While today one may find it hard to condone such a sacrifice of life, on both sides, contemporaries formed a different judgement of the "clash of empires" on the Somme. Above all, this was an Anglo–French victory: it was the two allied armies fighting side-by-side and hand-in-hand which imposed this strategic reverse on their common foe. Although the German Army would fight on for two more years, it would be at a continual disadvantage in industrial war.[9] Unexpected political developments, particularly the collapse of Russia in 1917, granted her army a reprieve, but this was only temporary; allied material superiority and improved fighting methods would tell in the end.

I

On 6 December representatives of all the allied armies met at General Joffre's headquarters at Chantilly to decide the strategy for the 1916 campaign. Joffre had two objectives at the meeting, to secure proper coordination between all the allied fronts, and to ensure that all the allies accepted French strategic direction for the coming year. Since the principal allies were underrepresented—Britain by her soon to be sacked commander-in-chief, Sir John French, and her stop-gap Chief of The Imperial General Staff, Sir Archibald Murray, and Russia by her military attaché in France, General Gilinski—Joffre's objectives were easily achievable. The conference agreed to undertake co-ordinated attacks on all the allied fronts, in an attempt to overstretch the Central Powers who previously had been able to take advantage of their interior lines to check unsynchronized offensives on the individual allied fronts. When and where the attacks were to take place was to be decided later, although all the allied armies were supposed to be ready to attack in the spring, to seize the initiative from the enemy.[10]

From this conference onwards the British and French were committed to a coalition, offensive strategy in 1916, designed to bring about to "the destruction of the German and Austrian armies." Yet the form which the offensive was to take was still to be negotiated. Significantly, the Chantilly conference had recognised that before the German army could finally be defeated, an attritional campaign would have to be waged. Only after the German army's fighting capacity had been worn down could a decisive attack break the stalemated front in France.[11] Attrition had always figured in allied strategic planning: from the moment the front stabilised "bean counters" on the allied military staffs had totted up the available manpower and fighting formations of the belligerents. As early as January 1915 it was accepted that allied superiority in manpower and productive capacity would eventually prove decisive: they could put more divisions in the field and sustain them longer than the Central Powers. But it would be a slow process, for Russian manpower would need to be equipped, while British manpower would need to be mobilized. In the long game, the allies had the advantage, although in the short-term Germany seemed to have the upper hand. As the French general staff acknowledged, even after a year of hard fighting, current statistical analyses suggested that the wearing down of the German army would take time, and that "the decisive moment of the war may still be far off."[12]

Moreover, France had a particular problem. She was invaded, and considerations of national cohesion and morale obliged her to fight a war of liberation. The consequence, a series of costly manpower-intensive offensives in 1915, had not done much for her morale, although they had contributed to the attrition of the enemy. But, and this is generally overlooked in the hitherto limited analyses of the French army's military development, these attacks had taught France's commanders and soldiers valuable lessons on how to fight on the modern industrial battlefield, which were to bear fruit in 1916. However, they had also had the effect of reducing France's own fighting capacity. If her army was to see things through to the climax of the war, Joffre judged that it was essential that France's allies—in particular those with greater manpower reserves, Great Britain and Italy—were to take a greater share in the fighting. In particular, he hoped that they would carry out the attritional phase of the coming allied offensive.[13]

Thus the "Allied General Offensive," as the press were to call it, was conceived at the end of 1915. The Anglo–French element was to be the battle of the Somme. Why then was the Somme sector chosen for this operation? Over-simplified analysis suggests that as the junction of the two armies on their common front this was the obvious point of attack. Attacking here would allow better coordination and a longer front of attack. In reality, the choice of the Somme front was a hard fought compromise; the outline agreement on the battle reached in February 1916 forced Sir Douglas Haig, the new British commander-in-chief, to give way on the place of attack, and Joffre to concede on the method of attack.[14]

Both Joffre and Haig had concluded from their 1915 experiences that a wider front was key to breaking through the enemy's defensive positions. Previous attacks had been blunted by counter-attacks and artillery fire from the flanks, and so the offensive front must be as long as possible, and at least 25 miles long. Both also recognised the need for what Haig called a "wearing out attack" (*bataille de usure* was the equivalent French term) before the main offensive, which would draw in the enemy's strategic reserves which otherwise could be brought up to plug any breach in the line. Joffre wanted the British to fight the attritional battle in the north, before the French broke through on a wide front south of the Somme. Haig wanted the British to fight the main battle in Flanders. Eventually Joffre agreed to forego the British attritional battle. Instead the British army was to capture the Thiepval Ridge, north of the Somme, and establish themselves on the Bapaume-Péronne road, in a supporting offensive which would facilitate the French crossing of the river Somme once Péronne was outflanked.[15] This made tactical sense when the battle was conceived in February 1916. The British would have 25 divisions to capture the ridge, and the French 40 to break through further south.[16]

Unfortunately for the allies, their enemy had other ideas. One of the principles of the December 1915 agreement was that the allies would be ready to attack early in the spring, to prevent the enemy taking the initiative. But it was the Russians, still short of guns and munitions, who forced a delay until the summer even before the Anglo–French plan had been settled. Then, in the last week of February, the German army attacked the French at Verdun, in an attritional offensive of its own. This immediately altered the strategic landscape. While on the one hand the defence of Verdun would require the French to do the attritional phase of the joint offensive themselves, the longer it went on, the more it would alter the ambitious Anglo–French plans for the Somme offensive. Immediately Haig had to give up ten divisions to relieve French divisions for Verdun, shrinking his own force for the battle: better that he concluded than a premature offensive on the British front to relieve pressure on the French.[17] Secondly, the French contribution shrank steadily as their divisions were ground down in the "Meuse mill," from 40 division in February, to 30 in May, and by June to a mere 11 for the first phase of the attack.[18] The British contribution was to be 17 infantry divisions, so altogether the allies initially committed only 43-percent of the forces envisaged four months earlier.[19] Inevitably the nature of the operation changed. It is generally noted that the armies' roles were reversed. Now the French astride the river were to "support" the larger British attack against the main ridge. It is generally overlooked that this shrinkage fundamentally changed the nature of the combined offensive. As the French *Official History* makes clear, Joffre and his battle commander, General Ferdinand Foch, scaled down their objectives from the strategic to the tactical, and rather than try to break the German front rapidly in a massive battle, decided to proceed methodically, in proportion to the means now available, in a prolonged offensive with the intention of "battering the enemy, and pushing him as deeply as possible out of the ground he had conquered."[20] Although in his heart Joffre still hoped that such a method might produce the decisive strategic victory which France desperately needed,[21] he was well aware that it might not. Foch certainly doubted it, and had earlier tried to persuade Joffre to postpone the offensive till 1917.[22] Joffre himself authorised a massive new armaments programme for the coming year on 30 May 1916,[23] a month before the Somme offensive opened, a clear indication that he was preparing for the worst. The attack at least would take pressure off his hard-pressed army at Verdun, and bring support to the Russian and Italian offensives which were already underway, even if it might not immediately end the war.

Haig was well aware of the changed nature of the offensive; just before it began he cautioned the Prime Minister that it would be a battle of, in Foch's words, *"durée prolongée."*[24] Since the subsidiary British offensive had become the main offensive its operational rationale—to support a French crossing of the river—was nullified. However, as long as the French planned to attack, the British, having both a formal and moral obligation, had to attack alongside them. Unfortunately, Haig seems to have forgotten this new rationale in his plan for the first assault. It is this plan, and its supposedly calamitous failure on 1 July, which has ever since clouded understanding of the battle. Certainly the plan was over-ambitious for the means at Haig's disposal, and the methodical steps proposed by his field commander, General Henry Rawlinson, would have served the allies" purpose better. Haig seems however, once the French took the junior role, to have confused the tactical objectives of his early supporting operation—to seize the ridge and get astride the Bapaume-Péronne road to turn the river line—with the strategic objective of Joffre's initial plan—to break the German front decisively and defeat the German army in the field.[25] However much subsequent generations criticise and deplore Haig's decision to try to "push the cavalry through" to Bapaume, this thrust is understandable in the context of the operational planning which had taken place in earlier months. Nor was it simply a late rush of blood to the head on Haig's part. On the basis of intelligence reports on the weakness of German forces opposite his front of attack, and the limited number of German divisions in reserve on the western front, Haig judged that the attrition of the German army at Verdun had weakened it enough for such a bold thrust to have a real chance of success.[26] It was a rational professional judgement, even if flawed in retrospect. Thus the seeds were sown for the Somme of popular memory: Britain's "greatest military disaster" on 1 July 1916.

II

If the Somme was not, Haig's hopes notwithstanding, to be the decisive thrust for military victory envisaged at the turn of the year, should it still have gone ahead, and what was to be expected from it? Foch, in overall charge of the Anglo–French attack, certainly believed, after his 1915 experiences, that the allied armies needed to wait till 1917 when they had the necessary superiority in weapons and munitions for the new matériel intensive warfare which was emerging on the western front.[27] Moreover, Haig himself had argued for a delay at least until mid-August, when he believed his raw New Army divisions would be adequately trained for the attack.[28] On the other hand, the Anglo–French armies were beholden to their allies. In early June Brusilov's offensive on the Eastern Front had made spectacular progress against the Austrian army. In the south the Italians were heavily engaged in the Trentino and preparing their sixth attack on the Isonzo river. The western allies could not abandon their offensive without serious international repercussions. If the Russians reached Vienna without their allies attacking then they would dictate the future of Europe. If they failed to reach Vienna without the allies attacking, of course their allies would be blamed.

Strategic considerations closer to home also needed to be taken into account. One of the arguments frequently employed at the time was for an offensive to relieve pressure on the French army at Verdun, either combined or by the British army alone. Certainly this was a central factor in French government discussions and Anglo–French negotiations. Haig explicitly told the British government in May that the objective of the coming offensive was to "*dégager Verdun*," and they sanctioned the offensive on these grounds, as much as because it had been agreed between the allied commanders-in-chief in the winter, a military decision on which they had always tried to hedge their bets.[29] Whether Verdun would have fallen is a moot point,[30] but it is more certain that French morale was crumbling after four months of sapping defensive attrition. It was necessary, and it perhaps has not been emphasised, for the French army to resume the offensive for morale purposes—both military and civilian—and not to leave things to their allies.[31] It would be better to use their last reserves for a counter-attack, Joffre always contended, than to feed them into the mincing machine (which would have to be the case if the attack was delayed until August).

In this strategic and international context, the interminable discussion of the problems of operational planning and the failures at tactical obsession with just so-much barking up the wrong tree. Whatever the ins-and-outs of Haig's initial plan of attack, by June 1916 the Somme was no longer conceived simply as a massive breakthrough offensive, designed to quickly restore open warfare and inflict a decisive victory (although this possibility was not ruled out), but as a slow, steady advance designed to put sustained pressure on the German army, under which it might eventually crack. The enemy's men were to be killed, his matériel destroyed, and his will to fight broken: "our primary objective is to destroy the enemy's armies," Joffre informed his commanders in his final instruction.[32] The message did not go unheeded. As Haig's director of intelligence, John Charteris, noted on the eve of battle: "We are fighting primarily to wear down the German armies and the German nation, to interfere with their plans, gain some valuable position and generally to prepare for the great decisive offensive which must come sooner or later, if not this year or even next year . . . it will be slow and costly."[33] In such a scenario, to obsess about the presence or otherwise of cavalrymen in the streets of Bapaume, or anywhere else for that matter, is to reduce the greatest clash of arms the world had yet seen, the General Allied Offensive of which the Somme was a principal part, to an argument over minutiae.

III

Having established the context and nature of the Anglo–French offensive which began on 1 July 1916 and was to last until the middle of November, it is possible to assess its conduct and achievements against the parameters established by its directors in the months leading up to the battle, rather than against those supposed by superficial engagement with the planning process, or imposed with short-sight or hindsight.

It is popular knowledge, to the point of cliché, how badly things went for the British army on the first morning of the battle. But even so, 1 July 1916, while a reverse, was certainly not a defeat. Looking along the whole 16 mile Anglo–French front of attack, the offensive was partially (perhaps even largely) successful: indeed of the eight army corps which attacked,[34] three failed, one was partially successful, and four (three of them French) gained their objectives relatively easily. On the northern sector of the British front between Serre and La Boiselle very little progress was made by the three attacking corps. Where gains were made, such as the 36th (Ulster) Division's penetration north of Thiepval, these could not be held against strong German counter-attacks. From Fricourt westwards, the results were much better. By the end of the day the British XV and XIII Corps had captured their first objectives, the former with difficulty, the latter with greater ease. The French on their left had given the Germans a real surprise, one all-but forgotten in British accounts of the battle. The main French assault force, XX and I Colonial Corps (the elite "storm-troop" formations of the French army), took all their objectives with moderate losses, and on the extreme south the XXXV Corps, while not as overwhelming as their neighbours, effectively completed their mission of establishing a flank guard for the main attack.

So even at the very start there was clear, if not complete, tactical success, more than enough to justify the prolongation of the offensive. The French army's new firepower-intensive tactics, refined since their costly attacks in 1915, were paying dividends. These tactics, using massive and carefully targeted artillery barrages to subdue the strong-points in the enemy's defences, before these were rushed by small, heavily-armed and well led infantry squads—the prototype of what came to be known as "storm-troop" tactics—allowed them to fall rapidly on a demoralised enemy. The light French casualties,[35] and large haul of prisoners taken in the first attack on the French front, indicate that by this point in the war they had found the correct tactical principle—summed up in their adage "the artillery conquers, the infantry occupies"—although this method imposed a certain slowness on the advance, which was always to be kept within the effective range of the supporting artillery. This was very different from the imprecise artillery methods and the linear infantry tactics adopted by the less experienced British 1 July 1916.[36] As Foch told Lloyd George when he enquired why the French did so much better than the British army, "our divisions were green soldiers, and his were veterans."[37]

The French certainly were very pleased with their initial achievements. It was just what they needed after the moral-sapping defensive of Verdun, to be back on the offensive and once again liberating occupied national soil. As Lieutenant-General Henry Wilson noted when he visited Foch's headquarters: "Foch was. . . . well pleased with his attack. . . . It is the finest attack performance of the war. . . . Result is a very high moral tone in his men."[38] However, what the French also had to cope with was inefficient allies who had to be nurse-maided through subsequent operations.

Of course Haig had warned Joffre of the British Army's unpreparedness, but his army's reverse obliged a rapid rethink of the combined operation. Nevertheless, it should be acknowledged that when the allied commanders met on 3 July to review the effects of the first step and decide how to proceed their glass was half full, and they were thinking of how to exploit success, not redeem failure. South of the river the French Colonials had followed up their first-day victory by capturing the enemy's second defensive position, and the way was open for a relatively easy advance to the river line at Péronne. Of course the French could not exploit their success and push on across the river while the high ground to the north remained in German hands. North of the river, the battle had to be rethought, and refought. The plan for 1 July had envisaged breaking the German second position on the northern sector of the front, that where the British had failed so spectacularly. Although on the southern sector the British and French corps had a brief window of opportunity to seize the German second position before the defence consolidated, lack of agreement between Haig and Joffre on how to proceed robbed them of the chance to push on rapidly, and the enemy were given vital days to reinforce their thinly held and vulnerable defensive positions. In fact so heated was the difference of views at this meeting that for some weeks Joffre had no contact with Haig, and left the running of the joint battle to Foch.[39]

In 1918, when appointed to the supreme allied command at the height of the crisis following the German March offensive, Foch was to remark, "you are handing me a lost battle, and expect me to win it." In 1916 he was faced with a similar dilemma, having been handed a broken battle, and being expected to fix it. Foch had never expected the rapid collapse of the German defence on the Somme. In his sober judgement the way to continue was steady pressure to complete the attrition of the German army, after which a further large-scale coordinated strike might smash the German defences once and for all. Thus the battle took on its character of a slow, steady push by the combined allied armies, in a succession of small operations against successive lines—the attritional attacks—punctuated by larger, better coordinated attempts to push forward under a massive curtain of artillery fire. The two were separate elements of a whole, the former being the means to secure an appropriate "jumping off" line for the latter. Both contributed to wearing out the German army.

Foch's battle had three distinct phases. The first, in July and August, was to take the high ground on either side of the river, pulverising the German defenders in the process. 1 July 1916 had certainly not been a victory for the German army, merely a reprieve. A large dent had been made in their forward system astride the river, although their defence had held, and the initial impetus had been taken out of the enemy's offensive. They retained the key high ground on which their second defensive position was sited, and, north of the river at least, had gained enough time to reinforce it before the allies could renew their attacks in strength. Over the ensuing weeks the British and French armies would push side-by-side along the northern ridge and master that second position, while the French enlarged their gains south of the river. By the second week in July the colonials had gained the Flaucourt plateau, in the bend of the river opposite Péronne, from which they could observe the German positions on the Hem plateau to the north, which the XX Corps wrestled from the enemy in the second half of July and early August. To the North the British took the Bazentin ridges and pushed on through the hellish Delville Wood to take the western edge of the ridge between Pozières and Ginchy. These battles were particularly costly for the British, who suffered some 126,000 casualties.[40]

But the strain was starting to tell on the enemy as well, whose divisions were being rotated through the firestorm. One participant wrote home to his family: "Those who experienced the Somme battle from the beginning, and unfortunately there are few of them still around, say that the [British] artillery fire of yesterday was worse than anything that has ever occurred before. Endless mines, grenades and shrapnel rained down on us so that getting to our forward position was a torment."[41] Ernst Jünger, in his well known novelization *Storm of Steel*, indicated how exposure to this excessive *Materialschlacht* would break the morale and fighting power of the hardiest of soldiers. "We felt no less aggressive than the troops which had marched over the border two years before" he recollected when his regiment left for the Somme in August, we were more experienced and therefore more dangerous. We were up for it, in the best and most cheerful conditions, and expressions like "avoid contact with the enemy" were not in our vocabulary. Anyone seeing the men round this jolly table would have to tell themselves that positions entrusted to them would only be lost when the last defender had fallen. . . . And that indeed proved to be the case.[42]

Jünger's company had only five men of its establishment from the start of the year left by the end of 1916.[43] Jünger himself wounded twice in the battle, and had several near misses.

Joffre, Foch, and Haig all believed that the war would be won by defeating the enemy's main army in the field: it was a principle they adhered too through all events and disappointments. They targeted its manpower, its material and, in Clausewitzian terms, its morale or "will to fight." In such a struggle the capture and holding of ground is important—it demonstrates moral and material superiority in practice, and obliges the enemy to fight—but it is probably the least important factor, although given excessive significance in the tactically focused studies of First World War operations. This was, to Jünger, a new and horrific sort of battle which replaced "the attempt to win a war by old-fashioned pitched battles, and the stalemating of the attempt in static warfare. What confronted us now was a war of *matériel* of the most gigantic proportions."[44]

The worst was still to come. The second phase of Foch's battle, in September, was designed to extend the battle, and to renew a large-scale coordinated advance. On 3 September nine Anglo-French divisions struck north of the river, and a whole new army, the French Tenth Army south of the existing battle front, struck with ten divisions on a hitherto quiet section of the German line a day later.[45] Less than a fortnight later 23 allied divisions delivered a succession of attacks north and south of the river (normally only considered worthy of note for the British army's first use of the tank on 15 September). The German army on the Somme was increasingly powerless against the renewed Anglo–French assault. Most of its limited but tactically significant objectives were captured with relative ease, as allied offensive tactics, particularly those of the British, had been refined with experience. On 15 September General Von Below, commander of the German defence, recorded "a very heavy day with serious losses, even by Somme standards."[46] The standard German counter-attacks were in vain. It appeared that the allies could effectively take what they wanted when they wanted. This was the crux of the battle, the point at which the allied pressure was really beginning to tell. Even Foch, always methodical and circumspect in practice despite his enthusiasm for the offensive in theory, put the cavalry on alert to exploit what he thought would be the imminent collapse of the German defence.[47] These successful blows were followed up in the last week of September. Combles and Rancourt on the eastern plateau of the ridge fell to the French, and Thiepval, a first-day objective and the defensive bastion on the western end of the ridge, finally fell to the British on 27 September. One German participant recorded this loss as "absolutely crushing . . . every German soldier from the highest general to the most lowly private had the feeling that now Germany had lost the first great battle."[48]

However, two unconnected factors now came to the assistance of the hard-pressed German defenders. Firstly, the French army itself was running out of fresh reserves to sustain its advance. Secondly, the weather, which had always been indifferent since August, broke, turning the battlefield into the quagmire for which it is notorious.[49] Moreover, the Germans, determined to hold on, had renewed their defending forces and adapted their defensive tactics in the face of the renewed allied thrust. As the Anglo-French push ran out of steam, so the defence stiffened once more. Thus the third—and grimmest—phase of the battle, the mud-covered slogging match of October and early November, ensued. Here the defenders reaped an advantage, for the preparatory routine of deploying men, manoeuvring guns into position and bringing up supplies for further attacks was rendered slow and exhausting. The allied advances continued for a further six weeks, but on a reduced scale. The British pushed on slowly towards Le Sars, and struck on the northern sector of the original line again, in the battle of the Ancre in the middle of November, but the ground won was insufficient to have any impact on the wider situation. South of the river the French attack stalled in mid-October, and to the north, hemmed in by the heavily defended mass of St. Pierre-Vaast Wood, it was focused into a narrow "arrow-head" which pushed slowly but inexorably towards the village of Sailly-Saillisel. The battle settled down for the winter in the second half of November. It was Joffre and Foch's intention to renew it at the start of February 1917, had politics not intervened, with both losing their commands.

IV

Henry Wilson, just returned to London from a corps command on the western front, summed up the strategic situation at the turn of 1917: "The last day of a year of indecisive fighting. Verdun, Somme, Greece and Rumania all indecisive, both sides claiming victory; on the whole victory inclining to us, and the final decision brought nearer." Although altogether "a very disappointing year," Wilson was fixed in his belief that the only way to win the war was to "beat the Bosches"; his method, he told Lloyd George, "two Sommes at once" in 1917.[50] There was no doubt in the eyes of contemporaries (or of the military at least) that the strategy of attrition was contributing to victory—"we and the French army have been steadily gaining a moral and material ascendancy over the enemy" Robertson advised the War Committee in November 1916[51]—and must be continued, although it would be a slow, drawn-out business, whose effects would take time to realise. Politicians, and Britain's new Prime Minister, Lloyd George, in particular, lacked that patience. Pessimism, as Brock Millman has identified, gripped Britain's war leaders, who looked for easier victories elsewhere.[52] While they did so the strategy of attrition continued, fitfully, to its denouement.

On the western front the most obvious strategic result of the battle of the Somme was the German withdrawal in spring 1917 from their now untenable positions in front of Bapaume and Péronne to the new Hindenburg line: these towns were, respectively, the objectives of the initial British and French thrusts, although it had taken a whole campaign to get close. By the end of 1916, after Verdun and the Somme (and an intensive campaign against Russia and Roumania on the eastern front), the German army had been mauled to such an extent that it needed to shorten its line to free up reserves for continuing the battle. Jünger later pinpointed the German army's main fear: "there were already rumours of some vast impending '*matériel* battle' in the spring, which would make last year's Battle of the Somme appear like a picnic."[53] In 1917 Germany adopted a strict defensive in the west, and looked to win the war by maritime means—the U-boat offensive against allied shipping—before the army was ground down to nothing in the attritional battle. Although Germany was to gain a reprieve with the temporary decline of French military morale after the over-ambitious aberration of General Nivelle's spring 1917 offensive, and the eclipse of Russian military effort following the February 1917 revolution, her army continued to suffer through 1917. In that year the British and French armies maintained their pressure on the German army in a series of "bite-and-hold" offensives which threw the German army off all the strategic high ground of the western front by the end of the year. Posterity tends to focus on Passchendaele for its Somme-like horror, but the battles of Arras and Bullecourt, Messines, second Verdun and Malmaison ought also to be identified as further nails in the coffin of the German army. The Somme strategy—attrition before collapse—maintained its inexorable progress.

V

It was the much-maligned Douglas Haig's view, putting the battle in context as he summed up his conduct of the British army's campaign between 1915 and 1918, that the Somme was an important moral victory for the allies. He contended that it was the attrition on the Somme which had underpinned the defeat of the German army in 1918, and that concentration on the western front had been the best policy, a point of view endorsed in General Ludendorff's own memoirs.[54] His detractors have accused him of post-facto self-justification, seeing in his approach to the Somme an old-fashioned purpose, to break the enemy's defensive front and defeat him in open battle.[55] Their tactical-operational, Anglo-centric approach which dominates the battle's historiography—a tendency to see the Somme as no more than a "bad day at the office" for Sir Douglas Haig—has stood in the way of any effective assessment of its importance as one element in a wider allied strategic plan, and of the campaign's significance in the Entente's defeat of Germany. While the campaign did not always go according to plan—Clausewitzian "friction," and that other unpredictable element, the enemy, saw to that—it fitted in with, and contributed to, the realisation of a broader strategic conception of how to win the war, formulated over the course of 1915 and early 1916, and adhered to by Haig and Foch despite the vicissitudes of domestic and alliance politics.

Although the Somme did not crack the German army, it certainly came close, in combination with the other allied offensives at Verdun, in Galicia and Italy, to doing so. Its objective was the enemy's manpower reserves, which would always have to be drawn in and defeated in an attritional battle before any decisive victory could be achieved. Breakthrough, still on the strategic agenda at the start of 1916, was no longer possible. The best that could be hoped for was "push-back," and the Germans were pushed back. September 1916 was the point of greatest strain for Germany, the point at which the defences on the Somme were most stretched. The battle forced the biggest gain of territory on the western front to date—to that wrested from the enemy at gunpoint must be added the large tract of ground voluntarily surrendered in March 1917—and put the enemy firmly on the defensive in 1917: although the gain of territory was more important for morale and propaganda purposes that strategically.

More significantly, however, in the context of an attritional strategy, the Somme was a chance to kill Germans, which was taken. Such a method—"*usure*" as the French termed it—is generally seen as representing a lack of ideas on the part of the allied leaders in this phase of the campaign. Being unable to break the German army's line owing to her ample manpower reserves, this costly "*grignotage*" (nibbling) was their default position, supposedly as costly, if not more so, to attacker as well as defender. More correctly, attrition should be seen as a strategic innovation of mass industrial warfare, rather than the result of a lack of imagination. In a war of mass armies, with millions of men on each side, a single decisive battle would never be possible. August to November 1914 had showed this using traditional "linear" methods of war; it ended with the mutual exhaustion of two manpower-intensive armies. The allied counter-offensive from July to November 1918 would show this again using what Jonathan Bailey has characterised as modern "three-dimensional deep battle" methods.[56] But this equally bloody struggle produced victory for the materially superior force. This victory was founded on the achievements of battle of the Somme.

General Debeney, himself a corps commander on the Somme and subsequently one of Foch's army commanders in the victorious 1918 offensive, summed up the Somme's importance succinctly in a speech he gave at Bouchvesnes in 1926, where he unveiled the statue of Foch which to this day adorns the easternmost village captured by French arms in the battle. The Somme was "the first of the great mass battles, in which we asserted our tactical superiority over the enemy. . . . After the Somme [Foch] began to abandon the simplistic idea of obtaining success by breaking a short section of the enemy's front, replacing it with the more fruitful idea, which was to give us victory, of progressively dislocating the various sectors of the front."[57]

From the Somme emerged the operational strategy, the so-called *Bataille Generale*, which Foch was to use in his victorious advance in the second half of 1918. Foch employed the methods of the Somme on a grand scale. Firstly, attrition: the enemy was to be constantly engaged to sap his morale and material powers of resistance. Secondly, overwhelming material preponderance: to save allied casualties by the use of machines rather than men, and to provide the ability to attack swiftly anywhere on the front. This is what the allies had lacked in 1916, and was the reason why Foch had argued for delaying the offensive. Finally, lateral rather than forward exploitation: this was also trialled on the Somme, in the French Tenth Army's attack in September, and the British Fifth Army's Ancre operation in November. Foch put all these strategic elements together to win in 1918.[58] If he had not been sacked at the end of the battle in favour of a untried fantasist, Robert Nivelle, he might have done so sooner.

Tactically the two allied armies performed very differently on the Somme, where the French army captured as much ground as the British for roughly half the casualties. The Somme took place on the cusp of what would nowadays be called a "Revolution in Military Affairs," and the contrast in tactics and achievements between the inexperienced and experienced allied armies on 1 July is testimony to this ongoing process. After their 1915 experience French tactical doctrine was considerably better formulated than that of the British. Their artillery intensive warfare paid off on 1 July, but it soon became clear to the high command that this was robbing the infantry of their élan and powers of initiative. What the French were able to do during the battle was to integrate their artillery and infantry far better, and restore some initiative to the latter, and so their confidence in their skill in the offensive battle developed, and their harrowing experiences in 1915 and at Verdun were put behind them. On the Somme French artillery techniques became much more professional, particularly in the areas of the rolling barrage and counter-battery fire which protected the infantry.[59] The infantry developed what would now be known as fire-and-movement "infiltration" tactics, based around small squads equipped with new offensive weapons—light-portable machine guns (*fusils-mitrailleur*), grenade launchers, 37mm trench guns and portable trench mortars—which gave them the firepower to take on an overcome the enemy's fixed defences.

The British army, although somewhat behind their allies, learned the methods of trench fighting on the Somme, which was a key phase in their now generally accepted tactical "learning curve." Contrast for example the successful 14 July surprise dawn attack on Longueval which captured all its objectives with 1 July 1916. It showed that Haig's "collection of divisions untrained for the field," as he characterised them before the battle, could improve rapidly once they were in it.[60] The British army's tactical changes introduced as the army gained more experience were codified at the end of the battle in new instructions for small and large unit attacks.[61] Moreover, the army's morale improved: in Charles Carrington's words, "though enthusiastic amateurs when the fighting began, the British were soldiers at the end . . . [they had] fought it out with the German army, and established their superiority, inflicting casualties which Germany could ill-afford. . . . The German army was never to fight so well again, but the British army went on to fight better."[62] Nevertheless, the process of defeating the enemy was difficult and not yet complete. As one Somme infantry officer who recognised the changing nature of battle commented astutely on Haig's despatch on the Somme, in which he reported the British army's mastery of their enemy: "The German is not what he was, but his falling off seems, on contact, to be no greater than ours. Without our superiority in guns where would we be? The French seem to be far ahead of us in recent attack technique, formation, and the co-ordination of rifle grenade and automatic fire."[63]

The process of finally defeating the enemy would still be long and costly, but the Somme had given the British and French armies the methods by which they could do so.

However, there is much more to the Somme than a tactical testing ground, despite the focus of the British historiography on the "operational level of war," the commanders and their decisions, and the men and their experience. At the strategic level the Somme was to be a prolonged trial of strength between two alliances organised for industrial war, and it is against this criterion that its true nature and impact should be judged.

Despite disagreements on its conduct, the battle represented a common effort, unprecedented in its intensity and duration. Such effective Anglo-French cooperation undoubtedly strengthened the alliance. Falkenhayn's strategy of splitting it by bleeding France white had rebounded upon him, although he was not around to see it, having been sacked during the course of the battle. The allied armies were finally imposing their will on the enemy. Attacked on all fronts, Germany was badly overstretched—the allied strategy of 1916 very nearly worked. But the downside was that it strained the allies themselves to breaking point. French and Russian failures in early 1917 meant that pressure was let up and it could not be immediately exploited.

While not decisive in itself, the Somme campaign can be seen as a success for the allied armies on all levels. The British learned the tactical lessons of modern industrial war, and the French learned the operational lessons, having already grasped the tactics. The strategy overall was sound. Being the battle that gave the allied armies tactical and operational superiority, it was the turning point of a four-year war of attrition. As Lord Esher, a close observer of allied strategy and strategists, wrote when reviewing the war at its end: "the battle of the Somme settled the inevitable issue of the war."[64] It was a fair verdict which deserves to be highlighted. While the battle of the Somme did not in itself win the war, without it the war would not have been won: an industrial mass war could not be won without such a battle to reverse the advantage between the belligerents. For these reasons the Somme, for all its blood and horror, was an Anglo-French victory, the decisive turning point of the war, although it would be two more years before the fruits of that victory were harvested.

NOTES

1. The casualties themselves remain controversial. Accurate figures for British and French losses are established in their respective official histories, although those for the German army were the subject of bitter dispute which has not been definitively settled. W. Miles, *Military Operations: France and Belgium, 1916*, vol. ii *2nd July to the End of the Battle of the Somme* (London: Macmillan, 1938), preface by Sir James Edmonds, pp. xii–xiv; *Les armées françaises dans la grande guerre*, tome iv *Verdun et La Somme* (3 vols., Paris: Imprimerie Nationale,1935) [hereafter *AFGG*], "Pertes françaises sur la Somme entre le 1er juillet et le 20 novembre," iii, appendix II, pp. 522–3.
2. In fact the Somme battlefield was far from small. From Beaumont Hamel at the northern extremity of the main British front, to Chaulnes at the southern extremity of the French front, is approximately 25 miles long, and including the rear areas of both armies the battlefield is about 15 miles deep, 375 square miles in all, roughly equivalent to Greater London south of the Thames.

3. Most recently in J. Sheldon, *The German Army on the Somme, 1914–1916* (Barnsley: Pen and Sword, 2005), pp. 396–9.

4. The British army's battlefield nomenclature committee subsequently identified 12 separate battles and 31 subsidiary actions comprising the Somme campaign. See G. Gliddon, *When the Barrage Lifts: A Topographical History of the Battle of the Somme* (Stroud: Alan Sutton Publishing, 1988), pp. 468–71. In contrast the French just call it the "Bataille de la Somme."

5. Typically their success on the first day is briefly remarked upon, and subsequently their commanders appear on and off as vexatious allies, interfering in Douglas Haig's conduct of the battle, and this has remained a constant over the years. See for example, A.H. Farrar-Hockley, *The Somme* (London: Batsford, 1964); R. Prior and T. Wilson, *The Somme* (New Haven, CT: Yale University Press, 2005), pp. 118–9.

6. A notable exception to this is Sheldon's recent *German Army on the Somme*, which looks at the German defence on both the British and French sectors of the front. This is however essentially a collation of translated German personal accounts rather than a balanced evaluation of the German army's conduct of the battle.

7. It is the principal matter of disagreement between this author and Elizabeth Greenhalgh in a debate which has been conducted in the pages of the journal *War in History*: E. Greenhalgh, "Why the British Were on the Somme in 1916," ibid. 6 (1999), pp. 147–73; W.J. Philpott, "Why the British Were Really on the Somme: A Reply to Elizabeth Greenhalgh," ibid. 9 (2002), pp. 446–71; E. Greenhalgh, "Flames over the Somme: A retort to William Philpott," ibid. 10 (2003), pp.335– 42. In attempting to put some context to the battle in their recent book, Robin Prior and Trevor Wilson confine themselves to the British War Council's deliberations, downplaying the crucial alliance dimension. Prior and Wilson, *Somme*, pp. 12–34 *passim*.

8. "The moral bankruptcy of attrition theory" as one recent analyst of the battle has dismissed it. Sheldon, *German Army on the Somme*, p. 398.

9. Appropriate comparisons can be made with the eastern front in the Second World War, where pre-Stalingrad the German army's operational expertise gave it many successes; whereas post-Stalingrad could only delay the inevitable as Soviet material-intensive warfare pushed it inexorably back to Berlin.

10. "Written Statement of the Conference Held at Chantilly, December 6th 1915," The National Archives (Public Record Office) [hereafter TNA(PRO)], War Office Papers [hereafter WO] 106/1454.

11. "Plan of Action Proposed by France to the Coalition," ibid., appendix 2.

12. Ibid.

13. Ibid.

14. For details of the negotiations see W. J. Philpott, *Anglo-French Relations and Strategy on the Western Front, 1914–1918* (Basingstoke: Macmillan, 1996), pp. 112–20.

15. Owing to the local geography, the British were attacking the hills on the northern bank of the river, which bent westwards at Péronne and cut through the middle of the allied front, and the French on the southern bank were attacking towards the river line itself, a major obstacle.

16. Haig diary, 14 Feb. 1916, in R. Blake (ed.), *The Private Papers of Sir Douglas Haig, 1914–1919* (London: Eyre and Spottiswoode, 1952), p. 129; J. Joffre, *The Memoirs of Marshal Joffre*, trans. T. Bentley Mott (2 vols., London: Geoffrey Bles, 1931) ii, pp. 417–9.

17. Philpott, *Anglo-French Relations and Strategy*, pp. 120–1.

18. *AFGG* iv/1, p. 633 and iv/2, p. 198.

19. Overall, including the allied strategic reserves, at the end of June there were 44 division, 26 British and 18 French, which might be drawn on to sustain the battle. Ibid., iv/2, p. 186.

20. Ibid., pp. 190–2.

21. Poincaré diary, 31 May 1916, in R. Poincaré, *Au Service de la France: Neuf Années des Souvenirs* (10 vols., Paris: Libraire Plon, 1931) viii, p. 251.

22. Ibid., 17 May 1916, pp. 223–6.

23. *AFGG* iv/2, pp. 395–401.

24. "Drawn out." Haig diary, 9 June 1916. Foch had indicated two months earlier that he envisaged a battle of several weeks against successive German positions to reach the Bapaume-Péronne road, note by Foch, 13 April 1916, *AFGG* iv/1, annexe 2015.

25. Prior and Wilson, *Somme*, pp. 49–51. Given the rapid and convoluted evolution of the operation there remained a certain ambiguity in Joffre's directions which probably contributed to Haig's error. On the eve of the operation, Joffre gave two hypothesis—a quick rupture of the enemy's front, or "a hard and long battle" on the Somme which might after wearing out the enemy eventually produce the desired breakthrough towards Bapaume and Cambrai. How hard and long he did not elaborate on. "Instruction personelle et secrète pour M. le général Haig et le général Foch," 21 June 1916, quoted *AFGG* iv/2, p. 207. Foch had certainly indicated to Haig in the earlier stages of the planning process that reaching this road was an essential precursor to any strategic result. Note by Foch, 13 April 1916, *AFGG* iv/1, annexe 2015.

26. J.M. Beach, "British Intelligence and the German Army, 1914–1918" (Ph.D. thesis, University of London, 2005), pp. 162–4.

27. See for example Fayolle diary, 12, 20 and 23 March 1916, Marechal Fayolle, *Cahiers Secrets de la Grande Guerre*, H. Contamine (Ed.) (Paris: Libraire Plon, 1964), pp. 150–1, 153 and 155.

28. Haig diary, 26 and 31 May 1916, in Blake (Ed.), *Private Papers of Sir Douglas Haig*, pp. 142–5.

29. War Committee minutes, 7 April and 30 May 1916, TNA(PRO), Cabinet Papers [hereafter CAB] 42/12/5 and 14/12.

30. Greenhalgh, "Why the British Were on the Somme."

31. *AFGG* iv/2, pp. 183–4.

32. "Instruction personnelle et secrète," 21 June 1916.

33. 30 June 1916, in Brig.-Gen. J. Charteris, *At GHQ* (London: Cassell, 1931), p. 151.

34. Excluding the separate subsidiary attack on Gommecourt by the British VII Corps of Third Army, which was itself partially successful on the first morning, but insufficiently to effect any permanent change in the front line.

35. On 2 July Joffre noted 4,000 French casualties, the majority lightly wounded. G. Pedroncini (Ed.), *Journal de Marche de Joffre* (Vincennes: Service historique de l'armée de terre, 1990), p. 33.

36. The most recent study by Prior and Wilson has indicated that the infantry attack formations on 1 July 1916 were flexible depending on circumstances, and that the real weakness in the British plan was the inadequate weight of supporting artillery fire, *Somme*, pp. 112–18.

37. C. E. Callwell, *Field Marshal Sir Henry Wilson: His Life and Diaries* (2 vols., London: Cassell & Co, 1927) i, p. 292.

38. Ibid., p. 287.

39. Joffre's war diary, 2–4 July 1916, in Pedroncini (Ed.), *Journal de Marche*, pp. 33–38.

40. Prior and Wilson, *Somme*, p. 186. In comparison, French losses for the first two months of the battle were 68,546. "Pertes françaises sur la Somme," *AFGG* iv/3, appendix II, pp. 522–3.

41. Quoted in L. V. Moyer, *Victory Must be Ours: Germany in the Great War, 1914–1918* (London: Leo Cooper, 1995), p. 156. Sheldon's *German Army on the Somme* contains many similar accounts of individual misery.

42. E. Jünger, *Storm of Steel*, trans. M. Hoffman (London: Allen Lane, 2003), p. 90.

43. Ibid., p. 119.

44. Ibid., p. 69.

45. *AFGG* iv/3, pp. 81–98.

46. Quoted in I. Passingham, *All the Kaiser's Men: The Life and Death of the German Army on the Western Front, 1914–1918* (Stroud: Sutton Publishing Ltd, 2003), p. 122.

47. *AFGG* iv/3, p. 129.

48. Quoted Passingham, *All the Kaiser's Men*, p. 123.

49. *AFGG* iv/3, pp. 152, 157–8.

50. Wilson diary, 31 December 1916, in Callwell, *Henry Wilson* i, p. 306.

51. War Committee minutes, 3 November 1916, quoted in Prior and Wilson, *Somme*, p. 311.

52. B. Millman, *Pessimism and British War Policy, 1916–18* (London: Frank Cass, 2001). See also Prior and Wilson, *Somme*, pp. 312–5.

53. Jünger, *Storm of Steel*, p, 124.

54. "Summary of Operations on the Western Front, 1916–1918," Haig Papers, National Library of Scotland, Edinburgh, file 213.

55. Most recently, Prior and Wilson, *Somme*. See also C. Malkassian, *A History of Modern Wars of Attrition* (Westport, Conn.: Praeger, 2002).

56. J. B. A. Bailey, "The First Word War and the Birth of Modern Warfare," in M. Knox and W. Murray (Eds.), *The Dynamics of Military Revolution, 1300–2050* (Cambridge: Cambridge University Press, 2001), pp. 132–153.

57. "Speech on the unveiling of the stature of General Foch," by Debeney, 1926, Foch papers (don Fournier-Foch), Service historique de l'armée de terre, Vincennes, 1K129/3.

58. W. J. Philpott, "Marshal Ferdinand Foch and Allied Victory," in M. Seligman and M. Hughes (Eds.), *Leadership in Conflict, 1914–1918* (Barnsley: Leo Cooper, 2000), pp. 38–53.

59. Such innovations as there were are customarily accredited to Pétain and Nivelle's successful counter-offensive at Verdun at the same time. Fayolle's Sixth Army on the Somme should be given the credit it deserves.

60. Haig diary, 29 March 1916, G. Sheffield and J. Bourne (Eds.), *Douglas Haig: War Diaries and Letters, 1914–1918* (London: Weidenfeld and Nicolson, 2005), p. 183.
61. P. Griffith, *Battle Tactics of the Western Front: The British Army's Art of Attack, 1916–18* (New Haven, CT: Yale University Press, 1994), pp. 76–9.
62. Quoted Passingham, *All the Kaiser's Men*, p. 125.
63. J. C. Dunn, *The War the Infantry Knew* (London: Abacus, 1991), p. 288.
64. Viscount Esher, *The Tragedy of Lord Kitchener* (London: Murray, 1921), p. 207.

AUSTEN CHAMBERLAIN AND BRITAIN'S RELATIONS WITH FRANCE, 1924–1929

Gaynor Johnson

Austen Chamberlain was one of the longest serving foreign secretaries of the twentieth century, remaining in office from October 1924 until the General Election in the early summer of 1929. His tenure coincided with the demise of the Geneva Protocol, the signature of the Treaty of Locarno, a major disarmament conference in Geneva, crisis in the Far East and a deterioration of Britain's relations with the United States.[1] By the time the second Baldwin government fell from office in the wake of the economic crisis caused by the Wall Street Crash, the diplomatic landscape was very different from that which had existed when Chamberlain had arrived at the Foreign Office. In particular, Britain had become party to two pacts that not only outlawed war but contained a commitment to use military might to enforce them. This was a remarkable departure from the more cautious approach of Chamberlain's predecessors, both before and after the First World War. They had been reluctant to allow Britain to offer concrete promises of assistance to her European neighbours in the event of invasion or war. Britain had, of course, been one of the founding members of the League of Nations, whose Covenant relied on the concept of collective security to operate effectively.[2] But by the mid 1920s, crises such as that caused by Benito Mussolini's annexation of Corfu in 1923, had demonstrated that this system for ensuring the satisfactory resolution of disputes between states could not be relied upon.[3]

At the heart of the discussion about the effectiveness of the League as a keeper of the peace during the 1920s and the wider diplomatic initiatives of Chamberlain's tenure as foreign secretary is Britain's relationship with France. Indeed, few would disagree that that relationship is central to understanding Chamberlain's own views on foreign policy between 1924 and 1929. A man often criticised for inconsistency in many of his policies, Chamberlain's Francophile inclinations were a unvarying feature of his diplomacy.[4] To his sister, Ida, he referred to "our pleasant relationship" with France.[5] To diplomats, he used stronger language. British foreign policy should be structured around the need to "remove the acute fears which distort French policy and reinforce French confidence in Britain."[6] Nevertheless, within this wide acceptance of Chamberlain's pro-French sympathies, there are differences of opinion and of emphasis. In the early 1960s, Douglas Johnson portrayed Chamberlain as being so fanatically pro-French that he was almost guilty of ignoring British relations with other key European powers.[7] A generation later, Chamberlain's biographer, David Dutton, suggested that his subject's French sympathies were more subtle and complex but that he also derived considerable moral support from the fundamentally pro-French Foreign Office of the time.[8] Dutton's portrayal of Chamberlain as a more moderate Francophile has, in turn been challenged in recent years by Richard Grayson. The latter's argument centres on the premise that hitherto, historians have placed far too much emphasis on Chamberlain's French sensibilities.[9] Grayson's Chamberlain is the quintessential "honest broker"—pro-European rather than specifically pro-French, whose diplomacy was rooted in the argument that the way to secure lasting peace in Europe was by according the same status to the diplomatic needs of the Germans as to those of France and Britain.[10] This is a point of view that the present author has taken some issue with, specifically in relation to Chamberlain's relationship with and attitude to the views of Lord D'Abernon, the British ambassador at Berlin between 1920 and 1926, during the negotiations of the Treaty of Locarno.[11] Viewed from this perspective, Chamberlain appears to be somewhere between the assessments of Dutton and Douglas Johnson.

This article broadens this analysis to examine Chamberlain's attitude towards France throughout the entire period as foreign secretary. It will focus on four key events. The first of these is the link between the Geneva Protocol of 1924 and the security negotiations of the following year.[12] The Protocol had been proposed by Chamberlain's predecessor at the Foreign Office, Ramsay MacDonald and his French opposite number, Edouard Herriot, to toughen up the wording of the League of Nations'

Covenant to include a more precise definition of what constituted an act of aggression and to introduce a compulsory system of diplomatic arbitration. The agreement also involved the British government in making more clearly defined commitments to maintain French security from aggression; a feature that contributed to the decision of the Baldwin government, which succeeded the MacDonald administration in October 1924, to abandon it. Or at least to seek an alternative way of achieving a similar effect but by commandeering support for a multi-lateral security pact that did not require the British to act as sole guarantors of French territorial integrity in the event of invasion or war. The result was the second, and in many respects, the most important area of Chamberlain's Anglo–French diplomacy—the negotiation of the Treaty of Locarno in October 1925. This pact guaranteed the German frontier with France and Belgium as it had been defined by the Treaty of Versailles six years earlier, contained a promise that the signatory powers would not go to war for ten years, secured German membership of the League of Nations and undertook to step up efforts for a workable international agreement on disarmament.

The first year of Chamberlain's period as foreign secretary represented the time when his pro-French sympathies are most evident and when his close rapport with his French opposite number, Aristide Briand, was at its height, and which observers were convinced was mutual.[13] Indeed, Chamberlain's views on the Geneva Protocol and on the Locarno treaty represent the time when he was most confident of the Anglo–French relationship. The second two examples—the diplomacy surrounding the so-called Anglo–French Compromise on disarmament in 1928 and the implications to Britain of the Kellogg-Briand Pact the same year—deal with an Anglo–French relationship that was undergoing a partial realignment. The difference between perceived and actual diplomatic influence is also at the heart of the discussion of Chamberlain's post-Locarno diplomacy towards France, especially in his reaction to Briand's decision to lead negotiations of a pact to outlaw war permanently with the American secretary of state, Frank Kellogg. The present author has written elsewhere that we still know disproportionately more about Chamberlain's first year as foreign secretary than we do about the remaining four.[14] While it is undoubtedly necessary to recognise the importance of his role in the negotiation of the Treaty of Locarno—and this article gives due credit to this—this still remains the case. This article attempts to continue the process of rebalance.

It is important to realise that Chamberlain's Francophile tendencies did not stem merely from the opportunities that presented themselves when he was foreign secretary, but from a life-long love affair with the country, its culture and its language.[15] As a young man, he had studied at the prestigious Ecole des Sciences Politiques in Paris, where he had listened to lectures given by Albert Sorel.[16] To Chamberlain, France was simply the most sophisticated country in Continental Europe; a much older country politically than Italy and Germany and in possession of a clearer national identity. As Lord Beaverbrook sarcastically noted, Chamberlain was "keener on the side of the French than the French premier."[17] France was, in short, the European power most like Britain; an association made all the more powerful by the relative geographical proximity of the two countries. Britain and France had a long tradition of democracy and had fought against autocracy during the First World War in a way that had forged an unprecedented degree of cooperation and understanding between the two countries. To Chamberlain, an Anglo–French diplomatic alliance as the basis of maintaining peace and the democratic tradition after the war was the logical extension of this.[18] The consequences of not doing so were, he argued, unimaginable. A memorandum about his grand vision for Britain's relations with France, written less than a month after his arrival at the Foreign Office, makes this clear.

> If the Geneva Protocol falls through, . . . the whole question of French security will be re-opened; and if we do not show the French that we are still prepared to consider it with every desire to reach a satisfactory conclusion, we may expect renewed accusations of bad faith from France, with a consequent deterioration of Anglo–French relations and a possible renewal of the nightmarish happenings of the past five years.[19]

Reflecting on this period twenty years later, Chamberlain identified an even greater bond between the British and the French: "The deeper Englishmen and Frenchmen penetrate into each other's nature," he argued, "the more they will find they have in common."[20] The aspirations of other European powers lacked the simple straightforwardness of the French. Chamberlain lacked the patience to penetrate the psychology behind Mussolini's foreign policy and the very different intellect of the German foreign minister, Gustav Stresemann.[21] Many discussions of Chamberlain's tenure as foreign secretary quote the observation that he loved France "like a woman"; that he remained pro-French despite recognising that French demands for additional protection from invasion were not always rational.[22] This article supports this point of view, although it also illustrates that Chamberlain himself would have preferred French policy to be less fickle and more consistently rooted in improving relations with Britain.

Traditionally, of course, consideration of foreign policy issues was not the province of the Cabinet. Since the First World War, this balance had been difficult to achieve, but both Chamberlain and Prime Minister

Stanley Baldwin were anxious that, where possible, this arrangement should be maintained. It would be wrong to claim that this meant that Chamberlain was allowed to develop a personal style of diplomacy unfettered by his colleagues in government. But he undoubtedly enjoyed greater freedom than other members of the Cabinet in placing his individual imprint on the priorities of his department. And unlike Lord Curzon, the last Conservative foreign secretary, Chamberlain did not have to endure the interventions of a prime minister with a strong interest in international diplomacy.[23] This was just as well, as Chamberlain's ideas were radically more pro-French than those of Curzon and his predecessors, and were often at odds with those of his Cabinet colleagues. On Chamberlain's arrival at the Foreign Office, the British government was wedded to the nineteenth century view that when it came to involvement in European diplomacy, Britain's interests were usually best served by a policy of studied, partial detachment.[24] This, Chamberlain argued, was fundamentally wrong-headed. In a speech in the House of Commons in March 1925, he stated:

> At periods in our history we have sought to withdraw ourselves from all European interests. No nation can live, as we live, within twenty miles of the shores of the Continent of Europe and remain indifferent to the peace and security of the Continent. It is more important today than ever before that we should regard ourselves as so protected and so separated from the rest of Europe and its misfortunes . . . as to remain indifferent to what happens, and callous and deaf to any appeal for help.[25]

Predictably, Chamberlain received little support for this line of argument within the Cabinet. During the debate about the workability of the Geneva Protocol, Chamberlain's proactive pro-French inclinations came under attack. Despite what has been claimed elsewhere, Chamberlain did not reject the agreement because it appeared insufficient to French security needs.[26] To him, by enhancing the power of the League, *ipso facto*, the Anglo–French relationship became strengthened because it was the working relationship between these countries that drove the diplomatic agenda of that organisation. At the same time, the Protocol offered the perfect reassurance to those wedded to a less proactive role in foreign affairs because it reinforced the idea of collective security and therefore collective (not exclusively British) action should war break out. But despite this, even the great League champion, Viscount Cecil of Chelwood, who was in favour of the Protocol, objected to the way in which Chamberlain was using the negotiations to place particular emphasis on French security. "[W]e hear a great deal about the necessity for

French security," he wrote, but "the necessity for security for some other nations in Europe seems no less essential to peace."[27] Their Cabinet colleague, the chancellor of the exchequer, Winston Churchill, also rejected the "axiom that our fate is invariably linked to that of France."[28] Even three years later, when Chamberlain's reputation as an international statesman was more assured, he felt compelled to lament: "I have been disappointed at receiving so little support from some of my colleagues and having my informed and considered opinions swept aside so lightly by them. . . . [They] don't know what I know of the state of Europe and how thin the crust is on which I have to tread."[29]

Nor could Baldwin's patronage entirely protect Chamberlain from other influential critics of his preferred policies. His instincts for a bilateral security agreement with France to build on the closer relationship proposed by the Geneva Protocol extended only later to include Germany, caused him to fall foul of the Committee of Imperial Defence (CID) during the early months of 1925.[30] This important group of predominantly Conservative grandees, which included the former foreign secretary, Curzon, raised different objections to Chamberlain's Cabinet colleagues. In particular, Chamberlain was accused of not paying sufficient heed to the text of the German note that had been dispatched to London and to Paris in February resurrecting an earlier plan for a security agreement between Britain, France and Germany—"a three-handed game," as he termed it—in which the signatory powers undertook not to wage war for a generation.[31] After this date, because of the intervention of the CID, Chamberlain was compelled to abandon his plans for a bilateral pact between Britain and France in favour of a multilateral agreement. But the disappointment does not appear to have had a devastating effect on Chamberlain, although he never accepted that it was the best course of action.[32] However, in 1925, his reaction was stoic and was founded in the reasoning that any security pact as long as it included Britain and France, would serve his purpose. In this respect, he was indeed, as Robert Self has argued, a *Realpolitiker*.[33]

Chamberlain's comments about the connection between the Geneva Protocol and what became the Locarno pact discussed above, also reveal another important point: that at the beginning of 1925, Chamberlain not only saw the Anglo–French relationship as being of great importance and potential but that he believed it to be weak not strong.[34] Furthermore, he was faced with a situation where one of the defeated powers at the end of the First World War, Germany, appeared to have a clearer and more coherent strategy for moving forward the European security agenda than Britain and France. But it is debatable whether Chamberlain's response to this was to step up his personal contact with Briand.[35] While it is true that he savoured the opportunity to talk to Briand at Geneva when they gathered for League Assembly and Council meetings, much of Chamberlain's communication with the French government concerning the negotiation of the security pact was done by conventional diplomatic channels, through the Marquess of Crewe, the British ambassador at Paris, and through Crewe's opposite number, Aimé de Fleuriau.[36] Indeed the impact that Chamberlain's relationship with these two men had on Anglo–French relations in the mid 1920s is an important gap in our knowledge of Locarno diplomacy. That said, it would be wrong to suggest that Chamberlain believed that Briand played an insignificant role in shaping French security policy during the Locarno negotiations. Chamberlain greeted every response by Briand as each round of the security negotiations progressed as the start of a "new chapter" in Anglo–French relations.[37] On conclusion of the Locarno treaty, Chamberlain generously celebrated the efforts of his friend. "No praise is too high for the part played by Briand . . . His courage, his statesmanship, and the generosity and liberality of his mind, made possible what with any lesser man might have seemed an impossibility."[38]

The Locarno agreements were intended to herald a new dawn in European diplomacy, not merely for supporters of an Anglo–French security entente. They were also intended to pave the way for further agreements that would reinforce the desire for peace and to lay the ghosts of the residual hostilities after the First World War further to rest. But as Jon Jacobson and others have demonstrated, that did not happen.[39] So what went wrong? The answer as far as Chamberlain was concerned is again related to the concepts of actual and perceived influence. Chamberlain believed that his role in the conclusion of the Locarno pact had secured his reputation not only as foreign secretary but as an international statesman. This was not an unreasonable assumption, especially as he was awarded the Nobel Prize for peace in 1925, with Stresemann and Briand being similarly honoured a year later in recognition of their part in securing the Locarno pact. Yet, despite this, neither his contemporaries nor subsequent generations of historians appear to have viewed Chamberlain as a significant player in European diplomacy for most of the rest of his time in office. It would be wrong, of course, to claim that before 1924 Chamberlain had lacked political presence and influence. But somehow, assessments of his period at the Foreign Office seem to have been tainted by the knowledge that had he not resigned the Conservative party leadership in 1922, he would have been premier not foreign secretary between 1924 and 1929. That said, Chamberlain himself undoubtedly viewed his years as foreign secretary as the high point of his career.[40] Nevertheless, both Briand and Stresemann had been the equivalent of prime minister before assuming the mantles of foreign minister, (although Stresemann has always been remembered more for his years at the *Auswärtiges Amt* than his period as chancellor). Unlike Chamberlain, neither came to Locarno with a reputation tainted by missed opportunity and misjudgement.

But there were also other factors at work. Another point that mitigated against Chamberlain's desire to keep alive a rapport with the French was that he failed to realize that his relationship with Briand during the Locarno negotiations was the exception rather than the rule when it came to Britain's relations with France. The concept of an *entente cordiale* was always perceived by the Foreign Office as an ironic term; that for the most part Britain's relationship with France was not close and harmonious.

In reality, during the Locarno negotiations, the relationship between Chamberlain and Briand flourished because it was in the interest of both parties and the diplomatic circumstances were auspicious. However, after 1925, other factors entered the equation that disrupted this equilibrium. The crisis affecting British interests in the opium trade in China and the Far East forced Chamberlain to give European affairs lower priority. But even then, Chamberlain did not lose sight of the British entente with France, as he feared that the two countries might be compelled to pursue separate policies that could undermine their relationship.[41] He also became increasingly overwhelmed by the proceedings of the Geneva Disarmament Conference in 1927 which threatened to impose more restrictions on the level of assistance that Britain could offer France in the event of an invasion of French territory. Locarno diplomacy was now fraught with tension. So much so that by 1927 Chamberlain was describing his meetings with Stresemann and Briand as "combats."[42]

Once again, we return to the concepts of perceived and actual influence. During his final years as foreign secretary, Chamberlain's principal interests in European diplomacy were disarmament and the quest to secure a permanent peace. For the most part, these were also the objectives of Briand and to a lesser extent, Stresemann. A further example of the difference between real and perceived influence in Chamberlain's diplomacy was his misjudgement concerning the so-called Anglo–French Compromise on Armaments in the spring of 1928. The origins of the compromise lay in the deadlock that had existed in the League's Preparatory Commission on Disarmament since the end of 1926. This hiatus was caused by a conflict between British desire to limit fleets on the basis of battleship size and French plans to calculate the reduction on the basis of tonnage.[43] There were also differences between the two powers on the issue of army conscription, with the French favouring its retention and the British favouring its abandonment. At Geneva in March 1928, Chamberlain had given Briand a clear indication that if France would give way on the naval question, Britain would agree to allow the French to retain conscription. This disastrous move immediately antagonised the Germans whose recent history with France had taught them that the French were willing to use their large conscript army to invade Germany in the event of German default of the terms of the Treaty of Versailles. And since the 1923 Ruhr crisis, the additional sanction of the Locarno treaty had been created. In the weeks that followed, Chamberlain displayed a remarkable degree of insensitivity to German concerns. In his mind, he was quite clear that it had been the Germans who were providing the obstacle to the success of the disarmament negotiations.[44] In words hardly resonating with the "spirit of Locarno," in June 1928 Chamberlain wrote: "Unless we make some progress in the question of disarmament we shall be faced inevitably by Germany's repudiation of the disarmament provisions of the Treaty of Versailles, with what consequences for the immediate or future peace of the world I cannot at this moment pretend to predict."[45]

The Americans were also annoyed by the foreign secretary's willingness to alter the outcome of the Washington Naval Conference, which had taken place seven years earlier, without reference to the other signatory powers.[46] Yet by the end of July 1928, despite Cabinet opposition, especially from Walter Bridgeman, first lord of the admiralty, which he eventually overcame through support from Baron Cushenden and the Marquess of Salisbury, Chamberlain was authorised to sign the compromise proposal document with Briand. Some have expressed surprise at the lack of Cabinet interest in what Chamberlain was trying to achieve, especially given the delicacy of the diplomatic situation, especially in regard to the United States.[47] And it would be tempting to view this situation as an example of Chamberlain imposing his personal authority on the development of the Anglo–French relationship. Chamberlain himself certainly wished that this had been the case. But as his comments discussed earlier suggest, despite his established reputation as an international statesman, after 1925 Chamberlain continued to fail to command the confidence of his Cabinet colleagues.

On 30 July 1928, Chamberlain announced the Anglo–French compromise in a speech in the House of Commons.[48] The agreement was immediately denounced in the press as a "betrayal" rather than a "concession" to the French.[49] For those who believe that Chamberlain's diplomacy was rooted in a desire to broker personal agreements with the French, the Anglo–French Compromise has been seen as an example of the continuation of this strategy after his Locarno success.[50] In contrast, scholars of the disarmament negotiations of the late 1920s are inclined to suggest that Chamberlain's relations with Briand were less convivial and that he concluded the Compromise to foster Anglo–French cooperation over the League's role in brokering a disarmament agreement.[51] It is claimed that this was because Chamberlain believed that in the summer of 1928, Anglo–French relations were at their lowest ebb since the Ruhr crisis.[52]

This latter view is too extreme. In 1923, the crisis surrounding the occupation of the Ruhr, in which the British and French had conspicuously failed to support each other, had brought Europe to the brink of potential war.[53] There was no situation of comparable severity between 1924 and 1929. What there was after 1925 was a gradual change of emphasis within the Entente, particularly in Paris; but never a major rift. Briand, in particular, wished to keep his diplomatic options as open and as varied as possible, to include negotiation with the United States as well as with the European powers. Indeed, the records of the British commissioners on disarmament in the mid 1920s suggest that the Anglo–French Compromise was concluded because Chamberlain was anxious to secure agreement with the French on disarmament since intelligence received from Sir Esme Howard, the British ambassador at Washington, suggested that the French and Americans were on the verge of signing a similar agreement themselves and that it would exclude Britain.[54]

Further evidence that the Anglo–French relationship underwent a process of realignment rather than radical deterioration can be seen through an examination of the extent to which Chamberlain was excluded from the wider debate about disarmament and security between 1925 and 1929. Chamberlain's correspondence with Howard makes it clear that the foreign secretary was concerned that Kellogg did not understand the 'special relationship' that existed between Britain and France.[55] During the negotiation of the second and more important diplomatic agreement of 1928, the Kellogg-Briand Pact—the Franco–American construct Chamberlain had been so concerned about during the Compromise negotiations—the authors made it clear that the Locarno powers would be asked to comment on drafts of the agreement before it was finally concluded. Chamberlain frequently received copies of the diplomatic correspondence that flew between Paris and Washington concerning the pact. Furthermore, he received excellent intelligence from Howard and from Crewe about the strategic thinking of the American and French governments on these issues. But what is important is how Chamberlain felt about Britain's new role of relative as opposed to central diplomatic importance. His policies did not contain the bitterness of a jilted lover, to extend the simile used earlier of Chamberlain loving France as a woman. Instead, he adopted a pragmatic approach that centred on ensuring that the interests of the other Locarno powers were adequately represented during the Kellogg-Briand negotiations. Consequently, it was at this time, and not during the preliminary negotiations of the Locarno Pact, that Chamberlain sought and found a *modus vivendi* with Stresemann.[56] The man who had expressed profound scepticism at the German role in the negotiation of the 1925 treaty was now describing his German opposite number as his "good friend" and the "strongest of allies."[57]

But too much should not be made of this warmer relationship with Stresemann. The highly successful loan system between Germany and the United States that had been established under the terms of the Dawes Plan of 1924, created a bond between the two countries that had the potential at least to extend into a wider system of commercial and fiscal agreements. While American financial aid was also offered to the French to help prop up their ailing currency in the late 1920s, the main economic axis nevertheless ran from Washington to the German capital. The recovery of reparations payments, which the Dawes Plan was supposed to ensure, was still of vital importance to the British and French economies. Nevertheless, the high-profile economic role of the United States in European affairs exposed another area of disagreement between the governments in London and in Paris. Throughout his period as foreign secretary, Chamberlain viewed the United States as the power that had let down the democratic alliance after the First World War by refusing to sign the Treaty of Versailles and join the League of Nations. The existence of such diplomatic selfishness was confirmed to him by the willingness of the American government to show much greater levels of economic benevolence to its former enemy after 1924 than it had to its allies concerning the repayment of war debts. The Kellogg-Briand Pact was therefore little more than an opportunity for the American government to reinforce those economic links politically and strategically.[58] Yet Briand believed that working with the Americans, rather than against them, could prove advantageous, especially if France's borders came under attack again. It was therefore Briand who was more inclined than Chamberlain to overlook previous American diplomatic transgressions. Different priorities thus made agreement between the British and French about the desirability of American involvement in matters relating to security unlikely. A detailed discussion of Briand's diplomatic priorities is beyond the remit of this article, but in emphasising his enthusiasm for American involvement in international diplomacy, it is important to note that the French foreign minister did not abandon his Locarno allies after 1925. His interest in and commitment to European integration is well known and his status as one of the founding fathers of the European Union is widely accepted.[59] As the present author has written elsewhere, in many respects, it is Briand who deserves to be seen as the quintessential Locarno statesmen; going further than Chamberlain, Stresemann or Mussolini to ensure a lasting legacy of European peace.[60]

It is ironic, given the importance that Chamberlain himself placed on his role in the conclusion of the Locarno Agreement, that it was his reaction to the negotiation of the Kellogg-Briand Pact that reveals more about his general diplomatic strategy concerning France on issues other than simply security. In particular, these negotiations revealed that, like his forebears at the Foreign Office, Chamberlain believed in balance of power diplomacy and in the creation of spheres of influence. In the summer of 1928, He demanded that as a condition of British signature of the pact to outlaw war, Briand and Kellogg should acknowledge the right of the British government to maintain special influence in areas of the world of strategic importance to Britain. He wanted a "British Monroe Doctrine."[61] In particular, he was anxious to guard British interests in Egypt and the Suez Canal region.[62] Thus we have a continuity with the rationale for the original *Entente Cordiale* agreement of 1904—an understanding concerning spheres of influence and one born more out of mutual diplomatic mistrust and jockeying for position than from a deep-rooted desire to work together. As in 1904, so in 1928, the British government was concerned about the impact of French foreign policy on British strategic interests. And as in 1904 also, it was speculation about German motives that coloured both British and French thinking.

Like most of his generation, Chamberlain's understanding of how to conduct diplomacy included the concept of the sphere of influence, especially the maintenance of British interests in this way. However, it is also possible to view Chamberlain's general approach to improving relations with France during his period at the helm of the Foreign Office as being partly concerned with a similar defensive phenomenon. Indeed, it is possible to see his Francophile tendencies as being fuelled partly by a desire to capitalise on French diplomatic associations with the successor states in Eastern Europe; a region not normally within the British sphere of influence. Through France the link would be created but one which Britain would not be directly tied to maintaining. When the Little Entente powers expressed concerns about the impact of the Kellogg-Briand Pact on their relationship with France, Chamberlain indicated that handling any diplomatic fallout would be French, not British responsibility. As he told Howard, it was not the British government's role to "defend or explain the French position."[63] When pressed by Viscount Chilton on the same issue a few months later, Chamberlain was even more direct: "it is true that we share certain obligations and rights under the Covenant of the League and Treaty of Locarno with France as also indeed with Germany but [the] policy of His Majesty's Government will be guided entirely by consideration for British and Imperial interests and obligations."[64]

The Locarno treaty five years earlier can also be seen as a statement of British and French balance of power diplomacy; linking as it did German signature of the treaty to membership of the British and French-dominated League of Nations.[65] At the same time, the French were not entirely to be trusted. The United States was also recognised by Chamberlain and Briand as a player of balance of power diplomacy through the development of the Dawes and Young Plan (1929) loans to Germany and the loans to the French to prop up the ailing franc prior to and during the Ruhr crisis. Chamberlain realized that British interests needed to be safeguarded should the French or Germans decide to offer an open door to greater American involvement in European affairs. Nor did this necessarily imply that the British government intended to pursue a policy of peace at all costs despite what compliance with the terms of the Kellogg-Briand Pact would entail. As Chamberlain told Howard: "our position in the world requires us, even in the altered circumstances in which modern warfare and modern commerce are conducted, to maintain as hithertofore belligerent rights at as high a level as possible."[66]

While Briand saw every advantage to concluding a pact to outlaw war with Kellogg, or the Pact of Paris as it became known, it was to be Chamberlain who was to have a clearer perception of how the pact would affect the conduct of European diplomacy.[67] By January 1928, it was also apparent that Chamberlain was concerned that sharing centre stage with the Americans during the Pact negotiations could go to Briand's head, leading to an increasingly bullish French foreign policy. The French foreign minister might be tempted to go down a path that played down the entente with Britain in a display of French diplomatic "independence" intended to impress the Americans. As Chamberlain told the Cabinet, the proposed pact could give France a "free hand to pursue in Europe policies appearing aggressive in American eyes."[68] The only way of preventing that was for the British government to ensure that the balance of power remained with all of the Locarno powers, not with France.

Nevertheless, Chamberlain did not simply intend the Locarno powers to act as one merely to protect the integrity of the 1925 treaty. His vision, as Howard told the new Foreign Office assistant under secretary, Robert Vansittart, extended beyond this. The Locarno powers were to form a single European bloc of diplomatic power—almost with the status of a mini state—with which to negotiate the pact to outlaw war with the Americans: to create "a bond of union between the United States and Europe."[69] In this process, Chamberlain saw little reason why he could not reprise his Locarno role of the "honest broker." That position had placed British interests at the heart of the negotiating process in 1925.[70] It was arguably even more vital that that should be the case in 1928 given Briand's propensity for negotiating with the Americans without Chamberlain at his side. Nor was Chamberlain prepared to allow the Americans to pursue a policy of divide and rule at the expense of Britain and France. No power should ever be in a position to set "France and England at loggerheads and destroying the basis of our common policy in Europe," he told Crewe.[71]

It is hardly original to claim that Chamberlain was a Francophile. What has perhaps been lost sight of, however, is that his love of France and the French was not unquestioning or two-dimensional but varied in degree and intensity while never entirely disappearing from view. Others have also claimed that his relationship with Briand is of central importance to understanding Chamberlain's European diplomacy in the mid 1920s. This is not disputed in this article, but attention has also been drawn to the foreign secretary's willingness to take a pragmatic and independent view of French foreign policy objectives if they were not entirely consistent with British interests. The first tests of the unity of the Locarno powers revealed a still fragile relationship between Britain and France that had not entirely overcome or forgiven the tensions of the first five years of peace. In that context, Chamberlain's efforts changed nothing. The Locarno Treaty was, of course, to be subjected to much sterner challenges in the decade that followed, but there was something incongruous about Chamberlain's belief that Briand's foreign policy should be rooted in European affairs, with French global interests forced into a secondary role, when he manifestly would not have argued for that for Britain. In 1904, it was acceptable for France to behave as a world power, provided that status was not greater than that of Britain or that it did not threaten British interests. By 1929, Britain was less certain that such a strategy would work but could not decide whether it was worth the effort to try. The price was a greater British commitment to maintain European security and, despite Chamberlain's rhetoric at Locarno, that was something even he shied away from after 1925. As to whether there was an *entente cordiale* between 1924 and 1928, the answer is that Chamberlain and Briand wanted it to exist, but for different reasons and on different terms, and it was for this reason that it was, in effect, unworkable.

NOTES

1. The wider context of these issues in European international history has been discussed by a large number of historians in the past. One of the best, and most recent, is Zara Steiner, *The Lights that Failed. European International History 1919–1933* (Oxford: Oxford University Press, 2005). The best study of the American dimension to Chamberlain's diplomacy remains Brian McKercher, *The Second Baldwin Government and the United States, 1924–1929* (Cambridge: Cambridge University Press, 1984).
2. George Egerton, "Conservative Internationalism: British Approaches to International Organization and the Creation of the League of Nations," *Diplomacy and Statecraft*, 5/1 (1994), pp. 1–20.
3. Peter Yearwood, "'Consistently with Honour': Great Britain, the League of Nations and the Corfu Crisis of 1923," *Journal of Contemporary History*, 21/4 (1986), pp. 559–79.
4. Leo Amery to Chamberlain, 20 Nov.1925, AC 37/12, University of Birmingham Library, Austen Chamberlain Papers.
5. Chamberlain to Ida Chamberlain, 22 Jan. 1927. Austen Chamberlain Papers, AC 5/1/46.

6. Chamberlain to D'Abernon, 18 March 1925. Austen Chamberlain Papers, AC 52/264.
7. Douglas Johnson, "Austen Chamberlain and the Locarno Agreements," *University of Birmingham Historical Journal*, 8/1 (1962), pp. 62–81.
8. David Dutton, *Austen Chamberlain: Gentleman in Politics* (Bolton: Ross Anderson, 1985), pp. 259–99.
9. Richard Grayson, *Austen Chamberlain and the Commitment to Europe: British Foreign Policy, 1924–1929* (London: Frank Cass, 1997).
10. Chamberlain to Crewe, 20 Jan. 1925. Austen Chamberlain Papers, AC 50/28.
11. Gaynor Johnson, "Lord D'Abernon, Sir Austen Chamberlain and the Origin of the Treaty of Locarno," *Electronic Journal of International History*, 1/1 (2000). Gaynor Johnson, *The Berlin Embassy of Lord D'Abernon, 1920–1926* (Basingstoke: Palgrave Macmillan, 2002).
12. Chamberlain's views on MacDonald's conduct of the negotiations of the Geneva Protocol can be found in Chamberlain to Mrs Carnegie, 11 Sept. 1924. Cited in Johnson, "Austen Chamberlain and the Locarno Agreements," p. 65.
13. Viscount D'Abernon, *An Ambassador of Peace Vol. III* (London: Hodder and Stoughton, 1931), p. 23.
14. Gaynor Johnson, "Austen Chamberlain and the Negotiation of the Kellogg-Briand Pact" in Gaynor Johnson (Ed.), *Locarno Revisited. European Diplomacy 1920–1929* (London: Routledge, 2004), p. 60.
15. See Chamberlain to Ida Chamberlain, 22 Jan. 1927. Austen Chamberlain Papers, AC 5/1/406.
16. Dutton, *Austen Chamberlain*, p. 16.
17. Beaverbrook to Borden, 29 April 1925. House of Lords Record Office, Beaverbrook Papers, C/51.
18. See his minutes on Memorandum by Tyrrell, 2 May 1928. *Documents on British Foreign Policy, 1919–1939*, series Ia, vol. V, no. 335. Hereafter *DBFP*.
19. Memorandum on the Necessity of the Early Consideration of the Question of French Security, 4 Nov.1924. Cited in Frederick George Stambrook, "'Das Kind"—Lord D'Abernon and the Origins of the Locarno Pact," *Central European History*, 1968, p. 236.
20. Austen Chamberlain, *Down the Years* (London: Cassell, 1935), p. 229.
21. See Jonathan Wright, *Gustav Stresemann: Weimar's Greatest Statesman* (Oxford: Oxford University Press, 2002).
22. Charles Petrie, *The Life and Times of the Right Hon. Sir Austen Chamberlain, Vol. II* (London: Cassell, 1940), p. 304.
23. Chamberlain to Mary Carnegie, 20 Sept. 1925. Austen Chamberlain Papers, AC 4/1/1264. Keith Middlemas and John Barnes, *Baldwin* (London: Weidenfeld and Nicolson, 1969), pp. 342–6.
24. Gordon Craig, "The British Foreign Office from Grey to Austen Chamberlain" in Gordon Craig and Felix Gilbert (Eds), *The Diplomats, 1919–1939 Vol. I* (Princeton: Princeton University Press, 1953), pp. 15–48
25. Speech by Chamberlain in the House of Commons, 5 March 1925, cited in Petrie, *The Life and Times II*, pp. 261–2. Chamberlain, *Down the Years*, pp. 165–6.
26. Robert Self (Ed.), *The Austen Chamberlain Diary Letters* (Cambridge: Royal Historical Society, 1995), p. 265.

27. Cecil to Chamberlain, 17 Nov. 1924. Cited in Johnson, "Austen Chamberlain and the Locarno Agreements," p. 72.
28. Churchill to Chamberlain, 1 Dec. 1924. Cited in ibid., p. 73.
29. Chamberlain to Ida Chamberlain, 20 Feb. 1927. Austen Chamberlain Papers, AC 5/1/410.
30. The impact of this was not lost on Baldwin. Baldwin to Chamberlain, 12 March 1925. Austen Chamberlain Papers, AC 52/80.
31. The Cuno Plan of 1923. For its details, see Gaynor Johnson, "'Das Kind' Revisited: Lord D'Abernon and German Security Policy, 1922–1925," *Contemporary European History*, 9/3 (2000), pp. 209–24. Chamberlain to Crewe, 16 Feb.1925. Austen Chamberlain Papers, AC 52/189.
32. Chamberlain, *Down the Years*, pp. 152–3, 166.
33. Self (Ed.), *Diary Letters*, p. 266.
34. In this Chamberlain was not alone. See Amery to Chamberlain, 6 Feb. 1925. Austen Chamberlain Papers, AC 52/25.
35. Dutton, in particular, has emphasized the importance that Chamberlain placed on his personal conversations with Briand. Dutton, *Austen Chamberlain*, p. 246.
36. Of the many examples, see Crewe to Chamberlain, 25 Jan. 1925. Austen Chamberlain Papers, AC 52/181. Fleuriau was French ambassador at London, 1924–1933.
37. For example, Chamberlain to D'Abernon, 2 April 1925. The National Archives (formerly the Public Record Office). Hereafter TNA (PRO). FO 800/127.
38. Chamberlain to Murray Butler, 2 No. 1925. Austen Chamberlain Papers, AC 37/60.
39. Jon Jacobson, *Locarno Diplomacy: Germany and the West, 1925–1929* (Princeton, NJ: Princeton University Press, 1972).
40. Chamberlain to Amery, 21 Nov. 1925. Austen Chamberlain Papers, AC 37/13.
41. Chamberlain to Briand, 29 Aug. 1925. Austen Chamberlain Papers, AC 52/110.
42. Chamberlain to Hilda Chamberlain, 14 March 1927. Austen Chamberlain Papers, AC 5/1/412.
43. Dick Richardson, *The Evolution of British Disarmament Policy in the 1920s* (London: Pinter, 1989), p. 177.
44. Chamberlain to Howard, 25 May 1928. *DBFP*, series Ia, vol. V, no. 358.
45. Memorandum by Chamberlain, 9 June 1928. CAB 24/ CP 183(28).
46. See Erik Goldstein and John Maurer (Eds.), *The Washington Conference, 1921–1922* (London: Frank Cass, 1994).
47. Richardson, *Evolution of British Disarmament Policy*, p. 179.
48. *Hansard Parliamentary Debates*, 5th series, HC, vol. 220, c. 1837.
49. *The Manchester Guardian*, 3 Aug. 1928, p.4.
50. Dutton, *Austen Chamberlain*, p. 279.
51. Richardson, *Evolution of British Disarmament Policy*, p. 180.
52. David Carlton, "The Anglo–French Compromise on Arms Limitation, 1928," *Journal of British Studies*, 8/2 (1969), p. 161.
53. Elspeth O'Riordan, *Britain and the Ruhr Crisis* (Basingstoke: Palgrave-Macmillan, 2001).
54. For example, Memorandum by Cushenden, 1 May 1928. Disarmament Policy Committee, Memoranda PRA (27) 45. TNA PRO), CAB 27/362.

55. For example, Chamberlain to Howard, 20 Jan. 1928; Howard to Chamberlain, 27 Jan. 1928. DBFP, series Ia, vol. IV, nos. 256, 263. Chamberlain to Howard, 13 Feb. 1928. Austen Chamberlain Papers, AC55/266.

56. See Grayson, *Austen Chamberlain and the Commitment to Europe*, pp. 121–2.

57. Chamberlain to Lindsay, 2 May 1928. Austen Chamberlain Papers, AC 55/312.

58. Johnson, "Lord D'Abernon, Sir Austen Chamberlain and the Origin of the Treaty of Locarno," p. 6.

59. For example, Robert Boyce, "Was there a 'British' alternative to the Briand Plan?" in Peter Catterall and C.J. Morris (Eds.), *Britain and the Threat to Stability in Europe 1918–1945* (London: Leicester University Press, 1993), pp. 17–34.

60. Johnson, "Austen Chamberlain and the Negotiation of the Kellogg-Briand Pact," p. 60.

61. Memorandum by Craigie, 31 May 1928. TNA (PRO), FO 371/12793, A3700/1/45.

62. Chamberlain to Howard, 25 May 1928. *DBFP*, series Ia, vol. V, no. 358.

63. Chamberlain to Howard, 22 May 1928. TNA (PRO), FO 371/12792, A3497/1/45.

64. Chamberlain to Chilton, 4 July 1928. TNA (PRO), FO 371/12794, A4480/1/45.

65. Chamberlain to Howard, 23 Jan. 1928. *DBFP*, series Ia, vol. IV, no. 261.

66. Chamberlain to Howard, 5 April 1928. TNA (PRO), FO 371/12823, A2280/133/45.

67. Crewe to Chamberlain, 9 Jan. 1928, *DBFP*, series Ia, vol. IV, no. 249.

68. Memorandum by Chamberlain, 24 Jan. 1928. *DBFP*, series Ia, vol. IV, no. 262,

69. Howard to Vansittart, 13 Jan. 1928. TNA (PRO), FO 371/12789, A290/1/45.

70. Chamberlain to Crewe, 27 April 1928, *DBFP*, series Ia, vol. V, no. 327.

71. Ibid.

ANGLO–FRENCH IMPERIAL RELATIONS IN THE ARAB WORLD: INTELLIGENCE LIAISON AND NATIONALIST DISORDER, 1920–1939

Martin Thomas

After the First World War the Entente partners regularly exchanged information about the populations of the Middle East under their nominal control. At local level, this material was relayed through five main channels, and was often passed on between them. These channels were the network of French and British Consulates in the Arab world; the military intelligence bureaux attached to garrison forces in Egypt, Palestine, Iraq, Lebanon and Syria; the police agencies in Cairo, Jerusalem, Baghdad, Beirut and Damascus; the tribal control officers policing the Southern Desert to the north of the Hijaz; and, finally, the security services monitoring the activities of Arab nationalist lobbyists in and around the League of Nations Assembly in Geneva.

The bulk of the information divulged was low-grade human intelligence, or HUMINT. Summaries of meetings between local politicians, urban notables or tribal sheikhs; the travel plans of nationalist dissidents; Arabic pamphlets, tracts, even billposters; and, above all, rumoured political activity—from insurrectionist plotting to imminent tribal raiding, were its staple fare.

The author wishes to thank the Leverhulme Trust for funding the research for this article.

Much of this information proved to be either baseless or, at best, insubstantial.[1] Ordinary correspondence, including telegrams sent between leading pan-Arabist organizers such as the executive committee of the Syrian-Palestine Congress, were, however, intercepted whenever possible.[2] Signals intelligence also figured larger in the 1930s, but was typically a matter of intercepted diplomatic ciphers relating to the intentions of other European powers in the Middle East rather than coded information sent among or between nationalist groups. Furthermore, if passed on at all, the information gathered by cryptanalysis was rarely acknowledged as such. Nor was it generally sent in full, but was instead referred to obliquely or buried in a situation report. At inter-governmental level, the two Foreign Ministries, the British Colonial Office, the Government of India, and the Service Ministries on both sides of the Channel were the principal recipients of intelligence reports about nationalist groups in Middle Eastern territories. After the reassignment of British administrative responsibilities in the Arab world imposed at Winston Churchill's behest at the Cairo conference in March 1921, the departments most engaged by this information were the Colonial Office Middle East Department, their clients at the Foreign Office Eastern Department, and the military intelligence directorates of the Air Ministry and the War Office.[3] The bureaucratic picture in Paris was rather simpler. The French Colonial Ministry had little involvement in Middle East affairs, and imperial policing in the Levant states of Syria and Lebanon was, by 1920, under the sole control of the War Ministry. The Interior Ministry handled incoming special branch (Sûreté Police spéciale) intelligence from Geneva, processed through the Sûreté offices at Annemasse near the Franco–Swiss border.[4] But it was the Levant section of the Quai d'Orsay's Africa-Levant department that amassed most information about the faces of Middle East nationalism after the Great War.

   The growing bureaucratic obsession with Muslim opinion was driven by two related factors. One was the gradual adoption by imperial governments of the covert surveillance techniques developed by the western democracies during the First World War. By 1918 the aggregation of information on the attitudes of a particular section of the community, whether it be factory workers, front-line troops or families awaiting loved ones, and the assessment of public opinion—always a more elusive and nebulous phenomenon—had become indispensable to policy formulation. Mass observation techniques already much in evidence in government policy before 1914, became instrumental to the governmental apparatus after the war.[5] The second factor was the emergence of mass political engagement in the imperial territories of North Africa and the Middle East. This helped ensure that from the outset the imperial authorities considered early indications of any shifts in public opinion fundamental to their capacity to maintain control.

Whatever its intrinsic value as evidence, French and British intelligence about Arab nationalism impacted on relations between the Entente partners in the Middle East throughout the inter-war period. This says as much about western threat perceptions of Arab nationalism as it does about the absence of trust in the Entente relationship in the Fertile Crescent. The enduring belief that most Arab nationalist organisations from the Muslim Brotherhood in Egypt to the People's Party in Syria shared common objectives, networks of political clientage, and the same sources of funding increased the temptation to see foreign hands at work in their operations. Germany, fascist Italy, the Soviet Union and Kemalist Turkey were the prime suspects variously accused of fomenting sedition in the Arab world.[6] But the Entente partners were key suspects too. Insults and accusations flew with such frequency between the imperial authorities in the Middle East that they became part of the background noise of day-to-day administration. Particularly commonplace were allegations of covert support for nationalist groups, sanctuary given to fugitive leaders, and Bedouin sheikhs bought off and diverted into neighbouring territory. Add to this recriminations about information withheld or deliberately distorted. The very regularity of such accusations makes it tempting to dismiss them as unimportant—indicative of blame shifted, steam blown off, spleen vented in what remained an unsettled political environment for more profound reasons than the inability of the British and French to cooperate without friction.

Yet to make light of intelligence breakdowns between the Entente partners in the Middle East is to overlook the very real political consequences that ensued. The impassioned belief shared by British and French Arab specialists that only they knew best how to govern Muslim societies had its comic side, and flew in the face of actual conditions on the imperial periphery. But between 1920 and 1923 alone, conflicting Franco-British readings of Arab and Turkish nationalism tested the Entente relationship to its limits in the Middle East on at least three separate occasions. Emir Feisal's eviction from Damascus in July 1920, his subsequent installation as ruler in Iraq in the following year, and the Chanak crisis in 1922–23 all caused short-term local breakdowns in Entente cooperation. By early 1923 Conservative premier Andrew Bonar Law was at the end of his diplomatic tether. A vocal supporter of the *Entente Cordiale*, he was exasperated by French occupation of the Ruhr, but more seriously concerned by Franco–British argument over Kemalist Turkey, demarcation of the Iraq-Syria frontier, and the danger of renewed political upheaval in Egypt.[7] Bonar Law's cherished ideal of *le parallélisme exacte*, whereby each Entente partner respected the integrity of the other's Arab mandates seemed to have disintegrated.[8] But this proved the high water mark of inter-governmental argument over the Middle East. With the exception of

Chanak, Entente disputes over the Middle East persisted below the horizon of Entente high policy. After Chanak, Franco–British arguments over security problems in the Middle East were bounded by two pivotal events: the Syrian uprising of 1925–26 and the Palestine Revolt of 1936–39. The recriminations that followed soured relations between the two imperial authorities long after the outbreak of war in 1939. But diplomatic waters in Paris and London were minimally disturbed by these storms of protest among Arab capitals. None the less, the unique and colourful culture of Entente partnership in the Middle East bore upon policy choices throughout the inter-war years, contributing in large part to the under-estimation of the intrinsic power and mass appeal of anti-colonial nationalism.

On several occasions during the inter-war years, intelligence liaison—or the withdrawal of it—shaped the course of Anglo-French imperial relations in the Arab world. In a sense, this was nothing new, just the continuation of longstanding rivalries. Well-founded British suspicions that France had sought to undermine Hashemite leadership of the Arab Revolt were nourished by the certainty that the French military mission to the Hijaz under Colonel Edouard Brémond had undercut the work of Britain's Arab Bureau in directing Hashemite operations against Turkish forces in Arabia.[9] These wartime disagreements persisted throughout the peace talks. Disputed interpretations of the conflicting wartime promises made by the western partners to Arab and Jewish leaders made fertile ground in which to sow Anglo–French discord. Writing his daily diary from Versailles on 6 October 1918, Sir Maurice Hankey, secretary to the Committee of Imperial Defence, recorded that day's discussions between prime minister David Lloyd George, chancellor of the exchequer Bonar Law and Lord Robert Cecil over Ottoman partition. The prime minister was determined to revoke the Sykes-Picot accords in order to secure an enlarged Palestine for Britain and the incorporation of the Mosul *vilayet* into a British-ruled Mesopotamia. He even had "a subtle dodge" to invite the United States to govern Palestine and Syria to make the French more amenable to a British-run Palestine in order to secure their own toehold in the Levant.[10] With convoluted scheming such as this, it was hardly surprising that in the unsettled Middle Eastern political climate after 1918, differing British and French calculations of the viability of a Hashemite regime informed the well-known rivalries between the two imperial powers over the future administration of Syria and Iraq.[11]

Since the legitimacy of Britain's claim to predominance in the Middle East rested in large part upon its sponsorship of the Arab Revolt, it was inevitable that the British relationship with Sharif Husayn, his sons and retainers would draw the interest of foreign intelligence services. At the French War Ministry the Deuxième Bureau's Eastern Section, for example, compiled detailed reports on Husayn's forces and his fraught relationship with his British patrons. They speculated about the solidity of the bond between British officials and Husayn's family long after Husayn's sons, Feisal and Abdullah, took office in Baghdad and Amman. During 1919 Franco-British tension in the Middle East became so severe that the mechanisms of inter-allied intelligence cooperation broke down. Attachés' visits, the pooling of HUMINT between regional military commands, and exchanges of information between Foreign Ministries, were all curtailed. French consular staff and commercial investors were variously suspected of looking on with ill-disguised glee as Egypt erupted into Wafdist revolution in the spring of 1919.[12] In their turn, British consular staff in the French zone of occupation centred on Beirut abandoned exploratory visits to the Lebanese interior after French accusations of collusion with Emir Feisal's Hashemite administration in Damascus.[13]

These allegations were not without substance. In February 1919 the War Office directorate of military intelligence admitted that British plans to equip a Sharifian army, ostensibly for self-defence against Wahhabite raiding from the Hijaz, actually amounted to arming an Arab force to fight a war with France over long-term control of Syria.[14] Clearly, the British were hardly innocent bystanders. By late October Field Marshal Lord Allenby, commander of the Egyptian expeditionary force and high commissioner in Cairo, had become convinced that the final evacuation of British forces from Syria would lead to a spate of inter-communal bloodletting and an inevitable showdown between French and Sharifian military forces.[15] Earlier that same month, Leo Amery, permanent under secretary at the Colonial Office and an ardent imperialistic voice on the right-wing of the Conservative Party, received Emir Amin Arslan, a leading Druze representative bitterly opposed to French installation in Syria. Amery shared Arslan's opinion that "the French are bringers of discord, always being violently partisan." He did not demur when Arslan told him he had advised Feisal to resist a French takeover of Syria and then pursue an Arab guerrilla war against occupying forces if evicted from Damascus.[16] The British were not alone in acting so openly at odds with the spirit of the Entente. On the strength of sigint intercepts, they levelled accusations of their own. Intercepts of Turkish military ciphers revealed the extent of secret Franco-Kemalist negotiations at variance with both Lloyd George's declared support for Greece and wider British efforts to restrict Kemalist irredentism in Cilicia and northern Iraq.[17]

Mutual observation of the Middle East occupation administrations, although severely restricted, lent further weight to the growing *mésentente*. French civil and military staff in Lebanon and Syria made much of their past administrative experience in the North African Maghreb. Their British counterparts dismissed "Moroccan style rule" as singularly inappropriate to the urban sophisticates of Syria.[18] For their part, French observers in Egypt found it hard to understand the British system of regimental rotation that saw occupation units come and go every two years—far too short a period to get to grips with Arab political culture in the French view.[19] Nowhere, it seemed, was there a meeting of minds. The flashpoints of inter-allied disagreement—adherence to the Sykes-Picot agreement, Feisal's Damascus government, possession of the Mosul *vilayet*, and relations with Kemalist Turkey—were all elements of a more fundamental difference of interpretation. Much of Britain's civil-military establishment in the Middle East calculated that British imperial interests were better served by sole control over the region, or, at minimum, complicated by the French presence in it. The force of British arms in Palestine and Mesopotamia as well as the Arab Bureau's shrewd gamble on the Hashemite cause in the Arab Revolt pointed to a single conclusion: to the victor the spoils. There was scant appreciation from the perspective of Cairo, Baghdad or Delhi for French claims to a share in this windfall consistent with France's sacrifices on the western front and its long-standing cultural influence in the Levant.[20]

Matters were slow to improve after the consolidation of French and British authority over Middle East mandates in 1920–21.[21] Whether or not, as was repeatedly alleged, British officers feigned ignorance of the jurisdictional boundaries laid down by Sykes-Picot and reassured prominent Syrian nationalists that French authority could be swiftly undermined, the Clemenceau government's fury at Britain's "self-righteous interference" in Syria was never entirely dispelled in later years. In 1920 Georges Clemenceau's successor as prime minister, Alexandre Millerand, was determined to press ahead with military action against Feisal whatever the British diplomatic alternatives offered.[22] And British recognition of the Emir as King of Iraq in 1921 was made with little concession to French pride.[23] This was marginally offset by assurances that, under British guidance, Feisal's brother, the Emir Abdullah, similarly installed as ruler in Transjordan, would contain opposition to French authority along Syria's south-eastern margins. But it was soon apparent that Abdullah's hostility to the French Mandate was not so readily placated.[24] His first government was dominated by Syrian members of the *Hizb al-Istiqlal al-'Arabi*, the Arab Independence Party, most of them exiles who had been prominent in Feisal's Damascus administration.[25] An assassination attempt against Levant high commissioner General Gouraud during a tour of inspection near the Transjordan frontier on 23 June 1921 was blamed upon Abdullah's supporters, antagonistic Druze chiefs who found shelter in Transjordan. Abdullah's British patrons in Amman drew French ire once it became clear that the would-be assassins were unlikely to be handed over.[26] Subsequent French efforts to buy off dissident tribal sheikhs commanding large bands of armed followers in Syria's borderlands reflected the knowledge that these influential leaders might seek alternative subsidy from neighbouring British-ruled territory, or even switch allegiance entirely by moving from Syria to Transjordan or Iraq.[27] Even Marshal Lyautey, then Resident-General in Morocco and the pre-eminent French imperial consul in the Arab world, advised French premier Raymond Poincaré in January 1922 to exploit gathering Muslim resentment at Britain's post-war repression of its Muslim subjects in Egypt, Iraq and elsewhere. According to Lyautey, Muslim allegiance was there for the taking. France could establish itself once and for all as the dominant partner in the Arab world by demonstrating greater sensitivity for Islamic cultural integrity.[28]

It seems that British officials across the Middle East had much the same idea. On 25 May 1922 French ambassador Paul Cambon had a fraught encounter with permanent under secretary Sir Eyre Crowe at the Foreign Office. The Quai d'Orsay instructed the ambassador to relay Gouraud's complaints about anti-French propaganda and intrigue variously sponsored by British officials in Egypt, Palestine, Tranjordan and Iraq, not to mention among the British diplomatic community in Syria. It was the last straw for Crowe. Brimming with righteous indignation he lambasted these "perpetual complaints" and "malicious inventions" always presented without a shred of evidence by French officials who were by no means innocent of just the kind of "disloyal manoeuvres" of which the British were accused. It was an impressive performance, and one that chimed with the gathering "Poincarophobia" in British diplomatic circles.[29] But it was also misplaced. Two months later Britain's chief military liaison officer in Damascus filed the last of his "Secret Syrian Reports" to Egyptian Expeditionary Force headquarters and the Palestine high commission. The report in question drew on intelligence gathered by a network of local informers in and around Aleppo and Alexandretta. Its purpose was to provide a detailed analysis of French prospects and profile leading Syrian political figures known to oppose the consolidation of the mandate.[30] This Syrian informer network may have been stood down over the summer of 1922 but elsewhere, covert intelligence gathering continued apace.

The French and British governments spied on one another with unprecedented vigour during the Chanak crisis and the brief Franco–Turkish war over Cilicia on the margins of Northern Syria in 1921–23.[31] Both sides used signals intelligence of intercepted diplomatic cipher telegrams to secure advantage in final negotiations. Curzon's Foreign Office was aware that successive Paris governments had concealed their efforts to conciliate Mustapha Kemal's regime from their British friends. Without consultation with London, during 1921 the French prime minister, Aristide Briand, pursued a separate peace with the Ankara government, conceding territorial and commercial privileges in Cilicia and Northern

Syria. Curzon was livid. Privy to key French and Turkish diplomatic tele-grams, deciphered by the Government Code and Cypher School newly attached to the Foreign Office, British officials dismissed the French pre-mier's denials that his envoy, senator Henri Franklin-Bouillon, was not conducting peace talks with Kemal.[32] Full details of the resultant Frank-lin-Bouillon Treaty duly reached Foreign Office staff thanks to the efforts of British army cryptographers working in the Middle East.[33] Not surpris-ingly, the conclusion of Franklin-Bouillon's treaty with the Ankara gov-ernment on 20 October 1921 caused outrage in Whitehall.

French actions over Cilicia in 1921 cast a long shadow over the Cha-nak crisis in the following year. The pull-out of French forces from the Chanak region on the Asiatic side of the Dardanelles in September 1922 made good strategic sense to a Poincaré government determined to avoid provoking renewed hostilities with the Kemalist regime. But it left the remaining British units more acutely exposed in the resultant military standoff with Turkish forces. Although the crisis was defused with the signature of an armistice agreement on 11 October, Chanak had by then unleashed a political storm in London that signalled the final collapse of the Lloyd George coalition eight days later. Curzon, who remained as for-eign secretary in the successor Unionist administration, immediately faced the prospect of treaty talks with Kemalist representatives at Lausanne, con-vinced that his ability to negotiate a compromise settlement had been undermined by a combination of Franco–Italian duplicity and Unionist divisions.[34]

The damage to the Entente stemmed primarily from conflicting Franco-British conceptions of policy toward Turkey, but covert intelli-gence gathering injected venom into the resultant disagreements between the former allies. As the Chanak crisis developed, the presence of British occupation forces and Secret Intelligence Service (SIS) station staff in Istanbul provided additional vantage points from which to collect regional military and diplomatic signals intelligence in addition to agents' reports and other local political intelligence. A sizeable proportion of this mate-rial dealt with the actions and intentions of other interested powers in addition to the likely course of Kemalist policy. In consequence, senior Foreign Office personnel received a stream of decoded diplomatic inter-cepts, including material from the competing Turkish governmental authorities in the Near East as well as diplomatic traffic between the Quai d'Orsay and French diplomats in London and Istanbul. As John Ferris has shown, the sheer volume of this material and the delays inherent in its transmission and assessment made intelligence evaluation problematic throughout the Chanak crisis in particular.[35]

But one thing was beyond dispute. Foreign Office sigint material on Near Eastern affairs in 1921–23 increased Curzon's exasperation with

French regional diplomacy. This culminated in the infamous encounters between Curzon and Poincaré on 22 September 1922, in which the trading of insults regarding underhand dealings and double-crossings signalled the emergence of a new *Entente Discordiale* in the Middle East.[36] Not surprisingly, French army intelligence staff in Paris remained intensely suspicious of the SIS station in Istanbul, and tried to keep abreast of its contacts with pan-Islamists and Syrian political exiles in particular.[37]

Only with the appointment of General Maxime Weygand as successor to Gouraud in April 1923 were British observers persuaded that French policy had changed for the better. Weygand cultivated a solid working relationship with Palestine high commissioner Sir Herbert Samuel, which culminated in the General's successful official tour of Palestine immediately prior to his recall from Beirut in November 1924.[38] In Switzerland, too, SIS staff and French Sûreté officers worked in parallel in their surveillance of Egyptian, Syrian and Palestinian nationalists and the contacts between them. In January 1924 SIS advised their Sûreté colleagues of the creation of a specialist unit in Geneva to monitor the activities of Egyptian supporters of Sa'd Zaghlul, leader of the 1919 uprising against British imperial control in Cairo. This complemented the work of the Annemasse Sûreté officers who tracked the efforts of the Syrian-Palestine Congress leadership to win support among League of Nations delegations for a challenge to the mandate system.[39] Here we see the emergence of what would become a common theme in the Entente intelligence relationship: the recognition of a community of interest in containing organized Arab nationalism regardless of the persistent imperial rivalries between France and Britain. Once the Syrian Revolt began in the summer of 1925, the Beirut High Commission acknowledged the cooperation of the Palestine Mandate authorities in monitoring and even suppressing Syrian emigré activity and those Arab organisations that lent material support to the neighbouring rebellion.[40] By contrast, French complaints about the presence of Druze fighters in Transjordan multiplied as the rebellion neared its end and large numbers of rebels sought refuge in and around Azrak near the Syria-Transjordan frontier.

The resultant squabbles between French and British police agencies about the presence of known rebels among the Azrak refugees dragged on throughout 1927, despite the signature of an extradition agreement between the two parties in October of that year.[41] However, these arguments were small beer next to the problem of pro-Syrian agitation in Egypt. French security agencies in Beirut were fixated with Syrian political activity in Cairo, a more important centre of Arab nationalist organization than Jerusalem, to which leading Syrian nationalists gravitated as French repression intensified. Armed with War Ministry Service de Renseignements (SR) intelligence, in early September 1925 the chief military secretary to high commissioner General Maurice Sarrail complained that, but for British obstructionism, the rebellion would have been crushed six months earlier (at which point it had not actually begun).[42] Whatever their liberties with the precise chronology of the revolt, the SR had a point. Whereas, for example, the British mandatory authorities warned the Palestine Arab Congress executive against raising funds or sending war materials and medicines to Syria (actions which the Congress pursued regardless), in Cairo the executive committee of the Syrian-Palestinian Congress operated without much restriction. Even British intelligence officers attached to the Air Staff in Baghdad acknowledged that the ability of Syrian rebel leaders to find sanctuary in British imperial territory undermined French efforts to re-impose order. Even this was eclipsed by the covert monetary aid, weapons trafficking and propagandist support for Syrian insurgents coordinated from British territories. Again, Cairo stood out in this respect. As the Baghdad air staff put it on 11 January 1926, 'It seems probable that the moral and financial support which the rebels are receiving from Egypt is doing as much as anything else to keep the rebellion alive.'[43]

French annoyance at British inactivity marred relations between the two western powers during the two years of the Syrian Revolt during 1925–26, and lingered on for years after the rebellion was suppressed. In July 1931, fully five years after the Levant army claimed to have suppressed the original Syrian Revolt, the War Ministry Deuxième Bureau was still adding agents' reports to its dossier on covert British support for the uprising. It was alleged that unnamed British officials employed Jordanian intermediaries to coax Syrian insurgents into fomenting disorder in Deraa, southern Syria. This would afford the pretext for a British military intervention, justified on the grounds of preventing the spread of violence into Transjordan, and prefiguring the annexation of the Deraa region to an enlarged Jordanian state.[44]

The link with Transjordan was a long-standing one. The Druze clan chiefs that rose against French mandatory rule in July 1925 ultimately found safe haven in Transjordan, only returning to Syria after the announcement of a general political amnesty in 1928.[45] Covert British contacts with other leading Syrian notables, including founder members of the country's two principal nationalist groups, the Syrian People's Party and the Syrian National Bloc, fuelled French accusations of ongoing British efforts to undermine the French presence in the Levant states. Dr. Abd al-Rahman Shahbander, leader of the Syrian People's Party, the principal nationalist group to capitalize on the revolt, lived in exile in Iraq and Egypt in the years immediately following the revolt. The fact that Shahbander apparently had no difficulty in obtaining a fraudulent Palestinian identity card from the Jerusalem High Commission in June 1926 came as no surprise to the Africa-Levant division in Paris, which had always suspected him of being a paid-up British agent.[46] In April 1926 the army intelligence office in Beirut confirmed its long held view that Palestine and Egypt ranked above Turkey and Germany as the two foremost organisational centres for Syrian nationalist groups implacably opposed to the French mandate.[47] Nationalist politicians, largely, though by no means exclusively, from the well-educated urban bourgeoisie of the Middle East had supplanted the Hashemites and their retainers as the foremost objects of French suspicion. (King Feisal even planned to take a cure at Vichy during the last stages of the Syrian Revolt in July 1926.)[48] British Middle Eastern consular staff nursed other grievances. The earlier French refusal to reveal their intelligence information regarding the location and strength of rebel forces, plus high commissioner Sarrail's failure to warn British residents of Damascus about imminent French plans to bombard the capital in October 1925, precipitated a renewed Anglo-French diplomatic crisis at the very moment that the two powers were celebrating the signature of the Locarno Treaty.[49]

Much to French consternation, in the decade after 1926, Syrian nationalists continued to find refuge in Palestine, and travelled back and forth to Cairo, headquarters of the leading pan-Arabist organization of the interwar years: the Syrian-Palestine Congress led by the Lebanese exile, Emir Shakib Arslan.[50] The War Ministry Deuxième Bureau maintained a list of Syrian political exiles in British Arab territories, regularly updated with intelligence supplied from the Beirut SR. Agents' reports enabled staff of the army staff's Muslim affairs section to follow the faction fighting endemic in exile politics.[51] This was not simply an academic exercise. French imperial security agencies were convinced that the cross-fertilization of political ideas and organisational methods between the opponents of the western presence in the Middle East was fundamental to the development of party political opposition in the Levant states. Egyptian nationalist groups such as the Young Men's Muslim Association inspired replica movements in Lebanon and Syria. In January 1926, for instance, Deuxième Bureau analysts described the Union Syrienne and the Union Syro-Palestinienne, two Cairo-based umbrella groups, as being committed to outright struggle against the western powers, and France in particular. Both were under the patronage of Lebanese émigré, Michel Lutfallah, a founder of the Syrian-Palestinian Congress and a major fundraiser for Shahbander's recently-founded Syrian People's Party. British officials in Cairo were accused at best of gross negligence and at worst of anti-French collusion.[52]

Not for the first time, security agencies rather than professional diplomats tried to ease the friction between the Entente partners. In this instance, there was an external catalyst to greater cooperation between western police services across the Middle East. Comintern support for Kuomintang uprisings in Shanghai in early 1927 occasioned the dispatch of a division of British troops to secure Britain's interests in the treaty port. Just as important, Soviet and Chinese Communist ability to exploit the political chaos in China, less than a year after a major Communist-led rebellion in the Netherlands East Indies, sent shock-waves through British and French imperial security agencies throughout Asia.[53] As a result, the heads of the Egyptian, Palestinian and Iraqi police forces convened in Cairo on 26 February 1927 to discuss improved intelligence liaison between them. Their anxiety to pre-empt the spread of Comintern influence in the Middle East met a sympathetic response from the Levant Sûreté, already in regular contact with the Palestine police over the policing of their shared frontiers.[54] Further results soon followed. In August 1927 the heads of the Palestinian and Egyptian Criminal Investigation Departments began exchanging information with Sûreté staff in the Levant states "about criminals in general and about Bolshevik movements in particular."[55] By October arrangements were in place for the pooling of information "about known suspects and fast-track extradition of Communist agitators wanted in neighbouring territories.[56] This low-level cooperation may not have dissipated the tensions between the mandate governments, but, once again, it sent a clear signal about the underlying community of interest between policing agencies throughout the mandated territories.

During the late 1920s the continuing presence in Transjordan of Druze refugee communities was another thorny issue in local relations between mandatory authorities. As the responsible Ministry, the Colonial Office felt hard done by. In January 1927 Gerard Clauson of the Middle East Department articulated the general frustration with French complaints "that it is shocking and horrible that the Transjordan Government with its small police force and the Trans-Jordan Frontier Force cannot stop rebels crossing the frontier into Transjordan while it is the most natural thing in the world for the French with their 50,000 troops in Syria to make no effort to prevent the same rebels from crossing exactly the same frontier out of Syria."[57] The flame of mutual incomprehension between the Entente partners flickered on. Yet this should not be exaggerated. Low-level intelligence liaison between British and French frontier police persisted, despite the competition for influence between them, and there was significantly less friction between the imperial police forces on either side of Syria's eastern frontier with Iraq.[58] The new Levant high commissioner, Henri Ponsot, was a genuine advocate of closer Franco–British liaison, a view shared by his opposite number Sir John Chancellor in Palestine.[59] More widespread disorder among desert tribes stemmed from other sources entirely. Between 1925–31 cross-border raiding by

Wahhabite clansmen from Saudi Arabia, by Syrian and Jordanian Bedouin, and by Iraqi tribesmen escalated beyond French or British control, causing a breakdown of civil order in much of the Syrian-Iraqi southern desert and the northern Hijaz.[60] Tension was most pronounced along the southern desert margins of Transjordan and Iraq where raiding escalated during the late 1920s. By 1919 Ibn Saud had already organized substantial levies of Najd Bedouin into cantonments that combined instruction in Wahhabism with rigid military discipline. These fighters, known as the Ikhwan, emerged as the most formidable fighting force in Arabia, and were in the vanguard of the northward progress of Saudi sovereignty.[61] As Ibn Saud extended Wahhabi control across the Hijaz, the Bedouin of the southern desert faced concerted pressure to acknowledge the house of Saud and submit to the Ikhwan's rigid codes of loyalty to Wahhabism.[62] Whereas the French military attaché at London, General Després, sent the War Ministry a reassuring series of intelligence assessments about likely British reaction to Ibn Saud's consolidation of Saudi dominance in the Arabian peninsula, there was less room for optimism about the destabilisation of mandate frontiers bound to follow extended Saudi control in the northern Hijaz.[63]

In September 1928 Captain John "Pasha" Glubb, then serving as a desert control officer in Iraq, expressed his frustration at the imperial authorities' failure to recognize the scale of the Ikhwan threat. British administrators tended to dismiss, even to romanticize, tribal raids as part of the eternal cycle of desert life. As Glubb warned, "The fallacy lies in the fact that there is little more similarity between the old-fashioned bedouin raid and modern Ikhwan methods of warfare, than between international rugby football and a European war."[64] French and British efforts to curb these attacks with tribal levies of their own were hampered by the limited exchanges of intelligence between border garrisons and police patrols. Aircraft and armoured car units reconnoitred the southern deserts in search of tribal insurgents often several thousand strong, but information gathered was never systematically shared between the two mandatory powers. Indeed, Glubb, Britain's outstanding tribal control expert in the inter-war period, was himself the subject of French security surveillance.[65]

Meanwhile, in 1931 the Jerusalem Congress of Arab nationalist representatives and Muslim religious leaders opened a new phase of multi-national contacts between groups at least nominally committed to pan-Arabism.[66] Although no Arab state was officially represented at the Congress, formally opened in the Al-Aqsa mosque on 6 December, Palestinian, Syrian and Iraqi delegates dominated the proceedings. The Congress, unsurprisingly, condemned French refusal to concede an Iraq-style treaty of independence to Syria. British failure to safeguard Muslim Holy Places in Palestine, and western capitalist infringement of the charitable status of the Hijaz pilgrimage railway also came in for criticism.[67] This, in turn, provoked a fresh round of mutual recrimination between the imperial powers over their respective failure either to conciliate or to suppress the forces of Arab nationalism. French resentment at Britain's reluctance to prohibit the Jerusalem Congress on the dubious grounds that it was a religious, rather than a political gathering was outstripped by Kemalist annoyance with France for permitting the deposed Ottoman caliph, Abdülmecid, then living in comfortable exile in Nice, to apply for a visa from the Palestine High Commission to attend the al-Aqsa gathering.[68] The Italian and Spanish governments were similarly offended at British failure to proscribe a meeting bound to criticise their repressive policies in Libya and Morocco.[69]

British security agencies in the Middle East remained deaf to these complaints. They were by this point less concerned than their European counterparts with pan-Arabism, and far more animated by the repercussions of the growing influx to Palestine of Jewish refugees from Europe. The growing Muslim fear of Zionist projects and Jewish immigration to Palestine were the subtext to the Jerusalem Congress proceedings. Persecution of Jewish populations in central and eastern Europe registered in heightened levels of immigration to Palestine in the mid-1920s, but immigrant numbers diminished in the depression years immediately after the Wailing Wall riots. Immigration took off once more as the impact of Nazi anti-Semitism stimulated a greater Jewish exodus from 1933 onward.[70]

Whereas British intelligence analysis initially viewed the issues of Jewish immigration to Palestine and pan-Arabism as quite distinct, their French equivalents were quicker to link the two together. Greater French sensitivity to these connections reflected the proliferation of Sûreté reportage on the network of international contacts between various pan-Arabist groups during the preceding decade. The centrality of the status of Palestine and the Muslim Holy Places in pan-Arabist propaganda was something with which the French security community in Geneva and the Levant were entirely familiar.[71] None the less, from 1931 onward French military intelligence analysts of the Beirut SR monitored political developments in Palestine and Transjordan more closely. They foresaw that the Jewish influx to Palestine was bound to provide a rallying point for otherwise disparate Arab nationalist groups, replacing the restoration of a Muslim Caliphate as a ready means to stir popular opposition to western imperialism.[72] The War Ministry Deuxième Bureau took this thinking one step further, concluding that antagonism to British policy in Palestine throughout the Muslim world would rekindle popular support for pan-Arabism.[73] It was only much later, faced with the prospect of general Arab revolt in early 1936 that British intelligence analysts and diplomatic observers arrived at a similar conclusion.[74] Echoing these earlier French warnings, the Chiefs of Staff Joint Intelligence Committee warned in February 1939 that the future of Palestine was the sole issue likely to unite Arab opposition to British imperial control.[75]

Jewish immigration had ramifications in French territory as well, creating additional pressures on agricultural land, urban housing and local administration in Lebanon and Syria. Long before the outbreak of the Palestine Revolt in early 1936, the Beirut High Commission complained about the destabilization of the Fertile Crescent region caused by the recurrent inter-communal clashes between Jewish settlers and Arab rural communities. By 1933 Zionist settlement extended into southern Lebanon and Syria where absentee Arab landlords faced with collapsing rental income in the depression years proved willing to sell agricultural land at a premium, much to the anger of their tenants. Nor was this the sole instance of communal violence in British territory to affect the stability of France's Levant states. In 1933 Assyrian Christian refugees began pouring across the northern Iraq frontier into the Syrian territory of Upper Jezirah to escape the murderous persecution of Iraqi army levies. Loathed in Iraq for their role in supplying trusted irregular forces to contain Arab and Kurdish dissent, the Assyrian refugee community was exposed to state retribution after the final conclusion of the Anglo-Iraqi treaty of independence.[76] The hapless Assyrians were never likely to be welcomed in the Jezirah, an area where separatist violence was already endemic. Here again French military intelligence staff blamed British failure to manage inter-communal relations, their haste in transferring power in Baghdad, and the eagerness of British officials to be rid of an embarrassing problem for the added difficulties that French officials now faced on the eastern margins of the Syrian mandate.[77]

By autumn 1933 French concerns about the confluence of pan-Arabism, Muslim hostility to Jewish immigration, and wider public opposition to the mandate regimes seemed justified. Anti-British demonstrations in the hitherto tranquil Transjordanian capital, Amman, in late October and early November, followed by a general strike in Palestine on 3 November, were both held up by the Beirut SR as evidence of a chronic political crisis in Britain's mandates born of the inter-communal friction between Arabs and Jews.[78] SR staff also felt vindicated in their hostility to the long-standing presence of Syrian and Iraqi nationalists in Amman as it became clearer that Syrian-born politicians in particular were prominent in the first party political groups to oppose Abdullah's continuing attachment to his British patrons.[79]

As soon as the Palestine Revolt began in April 1936, accusations began to fly once more between Jerusalem and Damascus, London and Paris. Riots in Jaffa and the emergence of several rebel bands, particularly in the "dangerous triangle" between Tulkarem, Nablus and Jenin, marked a major step forward in political cooperation between urban and rural Arabs. The new found unity of purpose among Palestinians was soon underlined by the protracted Arab general strike coordinated by the Arab Higher Committee comprised of Palestine's six major Arab political parties.[80] Thereafter, foreign volunteer fighters led by the Syrian Fawzi al-Din al-Qawuqji, and funds donated by sympathizers throughout the Arab world helped sustain the rebellion after the general strike collapsed in October.[81]

Franco-British relations in the Fertile Crescent were by this point strained by the earlier civil breakdown in Syria following a general strike there in January. Syrians extracted more immediate concessions from the French than their Palestinian brethren did from the British. The wave of mass protests, commercial boycotts and urban riots across Syria eventually compelled Albert Sarraut's government to concede the principle of inter-governmental negotiations over a long-delayed Franco-Syrian treaty of independence. Egyptian high commissioner Sir Miles Lampson acknowledged in February 1936 that French difficulties in Syria were part of a broader "Arab-Islamic unrest" systematically fomented by client nationalist groups whose organisational epicentre remained in Cairo.[82] Yet the official British line remained that renewed disorders in Syria were of purely local origin. Never slow to offer his expert opinion, Colonel Gilbert MacKereth, the influential British consul in Damascus, downplayed the importance of international contacts between Arab nationalists as a contributory factor to the irresistible pressure for treaty talks over Syrian independence.[83] But once the Palestine High Commission came face to face with Arab rebellion that, ironically, also originated in a Syrian-style general strike, the boot was firmly on the other foot.[84]

Exasperated by the persistence of diffuse rebel activity during 1937, British officials in Jerusalem and Damascus accused their French neighbours of revelling in Britain's difficulties in Palestine—a belated payback for British smugness during the Syrian Revolt ten years earlier.[85] It was now the semi-clandestine presence of Palestinian nationalist leaders in the French Levant as well as a pan-Arabist Congress in Syria, held at Bludan from 8 to 10 September 1937, that precipitated British complaints over French sluggishness in reacting to the threat of concerted Arab action against western imperial interests.[86] The Congress was convened by the Damascus Central Committee for the Defence of Palestine, which brought together leading political exiles, some of them former members of the Arab Higher Committee, still the principal political voice of the Palestinians. The Central Committee's key figure remained al-Hajj Amin al-Husayni, the Mufti of Jerusalem. Faced with arrest after the British outlawed the Arab Higher Committee in October 1937, he found refuge in French territory: first in Beirut and then in Damascus.[87] Predictably the 411 Bludan Congress delegates agreed to a series of resolutions condemning Zionist settlement in

Palestine and calling for an Arab boycott of Jewish goods.[88] After Bludan, numerous clandestine meetings between Syrian nationalists and Palestinian rebel leaders were reported in which arms deliveries, financial support and the recruitment of Syrian volunteer fighters were arranged.[89]

By the time the Bludan Congress opened there was a duality to the Entente relationship over Palestine and Syria. High policy-makers were still quick to find fault with one another's efforts to contain Arab protest. But security agencies were actually cooperating better and sharing intelligence more fully than ever before. There were, however, occasional, dramatic exceptions to this general rule. Foremost among these was the leakage of news that the Mufti had been allowed to slip his Sûreté minders after bribing the French director of the Syrian police with £500 to ensure his escape.[90] Inevitably, sensational incidents such as this grabbed more public and political attention than the improving Entente intelligence liaison conducted largely in the shadows.

Clearly, there remained room for improvement in Franco–British intelligence cooperation. According to the Palestine High Commission and the Colonial Office Middle East Department, French authorities did too little to prevent Syrian aid reaching Palestinian armed bands. These authorities, in turn, were criticised by the Beirut High Commission for failing to prevent displaced Palestinian peasants from crossing into southern Syria. Meanwhile, wealthier Palestinian bourgeois, increasingly targeted by band leaders for their failure to lend sufficient support to the rebel cause, flooded into Lebanon's summer resorts to escape the Revolt. Their arrival provided a welcome boost to the local tourist economy, but most outstayed their three-month visas and thus caused additional tensions between Entente diplomats on both sides of the Palestine-Lebanon frontier.[91] The Palestinian townspeople discussing the rebellion in the coffeehouses of Beirut posed less of a problem than the fighters that operated along Palestine's porous borders. By 1937 plans were even in hand to erect a wire fence along the length of Palestine's eastern frontier to keep out the arms and men allegedly infiltrated from Syria and Lebanon.[92]

All the while, the British continued their tacit support of Syrian nationalists emboldened by the conclusion of a draft Franco–Syrian treaty of independence in September 1936. Indeed, it was Jamil Mardam's Syrian government, far more than the French delegation in Damascus that held the key to the limitation of Syria's monetary, military and political support to the Arab uprising in Palestine.[93] Meanwhile, friction between security services continued to ebb. The Special Branch of the Palestine Police and its counterpart, the Damascus Sûreté Police spéciale, worked side by side to infiltrate informants into nationalist meetings, and regularly swapped intelligence about the movements and intentions of known organizers of Arab support for the Palestine Revolt. Hence, for example,

British consul MacKereth placed an informant inside the secret sessions of the Bludan Congress, quite a feat given the security provided by the Syrian Iron Shirts, or *Hadidi*, and the complete exclusion of journalists from conference proceedings.[94] Britain's ambassador at Paris, Sir Eric Phipps, also supplied the Quai d'Orsay Africa-Levant Department with detailed intelligence about Palestinian rebel activities in Syria, information that enabled Camille Chautemps' government to lever Jamil Mardam's Cabinet in Damascus into openly repudiating Syrian aid to Palestinian rebels.[95] Crucially, by February 1938 Beirut high commissioner Comte Damien de Martel agreed to make available to Britain's Damascus consulate SR intelligence on Palestinian sedition in Syria.[96]

British concerns regarding the limited intervention of the French security services in Syria against pro-Palestinian activity varied over the course of the Revolt. As we have seen, during 1936–37, Foreign and Colonial Office pressure centred on the expulsion of Palestinian rebel leaders from the Syrian capital. The evictions were deemed essential to stem the supply of guns and money to armed Palestinian bands, particularly those in and around the town of Nablus. French inability to expel known rebel activists linked to the rebellion's coordinatory authority, the Arab Higher Committee and its Damascus arm, the Central Committee for the Defence of Palestine, generated wave after wave of British protests. Dossiers of intelligence incriminating Damascus-based leaders such as such as Sheikh Attiyeh Ibrahim, Fakhri Abdel Hadi and Mu'in al Madi, were handed over to Count Ostrogog, French delegate in Damascus and his Sûreté chief Monsieur Périssé. Aside from pleading the necessity of Syrian governmental assent to any such expulsions, Sûreté staff were quick to remind the Jerusalem High Commission of past British refusal to hand over former leaders of the Syrian revolt. Admittedly, in 1934 the Foreign Office bowed to French diplomatic pressure and refused permission to Sultan al-Atrash, the Druze clan leader and foremost instigator of the 1925 uprising, to take up residence closer to Transjordan's Syrian frontier.[97] But in 1937 Muhammad al-Ashmar, another Syrian, who led rebel forces in Syria's Jabrun Mountains and was accused of the killings of two French officers and three NCOs in 1925, still enjoyed political refugee status in Palestine to the fury of the Damascus SR.[98] Once more, these resentments were soon reversed. In November 1937, al-Ashmar, like his fellow Syrian, Fawzi al-Din al-Qawuqji, an experienced insurgent commander, was asked by the Central Committee to assume the overall leadership of the rebel bands still operating in Palestine.[99]

Unable to prevent the movement of foreign fighters into Palestine, during 1938–39 the focal point of British security interest in Syria shifted to hostile press coverage and Arab propaganda in support of the Palestinian cause.[100] The presence in Damascus of rebel commanders and senior members of the Arab Higher Committee, still the political mouthpiece of the Palestine revolt, remained an issue. But it was one that both the British and French governments were anxious to contain.[101] Fears of another high-profile Congress, this time co-ordinated by Muslim Women's groups from Syria, Palestine and Egypt, prompted the British Consulate to warn Jamil Mardam in June 1938 against authorisation of any such political meetings with the potential to inflame anti-British feeling throughout the Middle East.[102] This article, much of the earlier heat in Franco-British exchanges over their respective security problems in Syria and Palestine had dissipated by the summer of 1938. Former resentments cooled as larger, more urgent crises loomed in Europe and the Mediterranean theatre. Mounting dissension between the Central Committee and rebel leaders in Palestine and a spate of fratricidal killings among rival bands also eased the pressure on British security forces.[103] In light of this, there was less point in arguing over the activities of Palestinians in Damascus. Such was the attitude of the ambassador at Paris, Sir Eric Phipps, who remained on excellent terms with the Africa-Levant division chief, Ernest Lagarde. Phipps became an important counterweight to the persistent moaning from Colonial Office officials about limited French collaboration over Palestine. He recognized the French predicament in Syria after the 1936 independence treaty fell foul of intractable Senate opposition, and convinced Foreign Office staff that the Levant authorities did all they could to assist British efforts to end the rebellion.[104]

The shared Entente interest in inhibiting Italian propaganda and covert funding of Arab nationalist groups in the Arab world was never in doubt. Whether in Syria or Yemen, Italian efforts to gain leverage with nationalist leaders hostile to the French and British presence provoked a common Entente reaction.[105] So, too, did German funding for nationalist groups in Palestine, Syria and, above all, Iraq.[106] From 1937 to 1939 counter-espionage services proliferated in France's Arab territories especially. Their primary targets were Italian agents agitating among European settler populations in North Africa, German agents and banking consortia with contacts among Arab nationalist milieux in Damascus and Beirut, and Comintern envoys linked to known Communist supporters in the Levant states. Counter-espionage officers attached to army corps commands took charge of the surveillance of known agents and were responsible for assuring the secrecy of military plans and movements, activities that were of direct benefit to their British partners.[107] As war neared, there was, if anything, less concern about independently organized Arab sedition. British and French service chiefs remained dubious that Arab nationalists would risk military confrontation with the mandatory powers, even with Axis support. But by 1938 there was broad agreement that Italian incursion into the Middle East was the most likely catalyst to more general disorder.[108]

It soon became a high priority for the British and French intelligence liaison officers posted with their partner counter-espionage services in Beirut and Jerusalem to ensure greater coordination of effort between the Entente partners in combating Italian subversion. Service attachés also relayed additional intelligence about Axis shipping movements in the eastern Mediterranean.[109] As the Czechoslovak crisis unfolded and Italian ambitions in the Mediterranean loomed larger, French and British strategic priorities cemented this cooperation as the two imperial powers strove to limit Axis influence in the Middle East while conciliating Turkey as the potential lynchpin of a Balkan Front.[110] Wireless communications between British and French colonial territories were also hurriedly upgraded on the eve of war, facilitating more rapid transmission of political intelligence between imperial administrations.[111]

Yet a quick glance behind the diplomatic curtain reveals that some of the old antagonisms endured. In May 1939 Zionist leaders took their complaints against Britain's 1939 Palestine White Paper to the French authorities in Beirut. They hoped to coax French officials into open criticism of British plans for partition with the promise of firm Jewish support in any war against Nazi Germany.[112] It was a mark of how far the Entente partners had come that such approaches got nowhere. Once war broke out, SR staff throughout French North Africa and the Levant states were advised to be alert to Axis attempts to drive a wedge between the British and French administrations in the Arab world.[113]

In French and British territories alike, the security services and irregular paramilitary forces played a central part in the outbreak of disorder and its subsequent vicious repression. During the 1920s the containment of disorder in Morocco and Syria, Egypt, northern Iraq and Palestine, confirmed the centrality of the security agencies to colonial control and mandatory authority. The interplay between repression of nationalist protest and the accretion of intelligence power in the French and British imperial regimes occurred in remarkably similar fashion. Yet collaboration between the French and British imperial intelligence communities was inhibited by their abiding mutual suspicions. In the Middle East, it seems, the French and British just could not get along. Yet both partners acted in similar ways. And both knew there were limits to their bickering. It remained an unspoken assumption—a genuine "entente" in the sense of a shared understanding—that ultimately the western powers stood shoulder to shoulder against external threats to their imperial position in the Middle East. It was also true that those most intimately involved in the day-to-day cycle of colonial policing recognized the benefits to information exchange and cross-border links with their Entente counterparts. But the diplomatic representatives and governments to which they reported were often unreceptive to this more pragmatic approach. Security agencies in French and British Arab territories were equally anxious to contain nationalist disorder, and each did so in comparable ways: the legal proscription of nationalist groups and the confinement of their leaders; the infiltration of nationalist organizations to gather intelligence; and the reliance on irregular paramilitary forces to conduct much of the routine work of imperial policing. Local collaboration between the imperial authorities and trusted indigenous intermediaries was therefore more common and more productive than inter-state cooperation between the imperial powers.

The irony here is obvious. The British and French authorities were quick to grasp that efficient policing of urban centres, tribal settlements, inter-communal violence and nationalist protest demanded good intelligence gathering. Neither power maintained sufficient standing forces, local levies or air force squadrons to deter challenges to European authority in any circumstance. Early detection of disorder was thus at a premium. But the consequences of French and British reluctance to share their intelligence systematically were considerable. By 1939 most Arab nationalist groups had built international links that thrived on their ability to operate outside the borders of their imperial overseers.

NOTES

1. See, for example, the following introductory statement to a report on Tunisian nationalism compiled in December 1934 by the Algiers military intelligence bureau: "The conclusions which follow constitute 'an impression' more than 'intelligence'; the brevity of our contact with the country in question prevent us from exploring the question more deeply. None the less, this impression was formed during the course of conversations with particularly well placed individuals, knowledgeable about native affairs, and inclined as a result of their positions or occupations to take close interest in Muslim opinion." See, Service Historique de l'Armée (SHA), Vincennes, Archives de Moscou (hereafter "Moscou"), C1109/D669, SEA Alger, "Note sur la question tunisienne," 29 December 1934.
2. See, for example, Deuxième Bureau telegram intercepts of Shakib Arslan's correspondence in SHA, 7N4173/D2. The contents of such intercepts were typically summarized in SR reports. See, for example: Beirut SR agent's report, "Voyage de Chekib Arslan en Palestine et Congrès Arabe improvisé à Jérusalem," n. d. July 1934.
3. The National Archives (formerly Public Record Office), London. Hereafter TNA (PRO). CO 730/13, Note by India Office Political Department, "Mesopotamia: Question of a Turkish ruler," 15 Feb. 1921. AIR 9/19, "Report on Middle East Conference held in Cairo and Jerusalem, March 12 to 30, 1921." See also John Darwin, *Britain, Egypt and the Middle East: Imperial Policy in the Aftermath of War, 1918–1922* (London: Macmillan, 1981), pp. 217–21.

4. Archives Nationales (hereafter AN) Paris, Ministry of Interior Police Générale files, F/7/13468, Commissariat spécial d'Annemasse (Haute-Savoie) Geneva surveillance reports, 1923–25.

5. Edward Higgs, *The Information State in England. The Central Collection of Information on Citizens since 1500* (London: Palgrave, 2004), pp.121–44.

6. See, for example, the Sûreté records in AN, F/7/13468: Moyen Orient, notes générales, 1921–25.

7. Sir Maurice Hankey Papers, Churchill College Archive, University of Cambridge. Hankey Diaries, HNKY 1/8, diary entry, 3 Feb. 1923.

8. The phrase was coined by Major Hubert Young of the Foreign Office. See Timothy Paris, *Britain, the Hashemites and Arab Rule, 1920–1925 The Sharifian Solution* (London: Frank Cass, 2003), p.72.

9. Paula Mohs, "British Intelligence and the Arab Revolt in the Hijaz, 1914–1917," University of Cambridge PhD, 2003, pp. 121–2. Regarding Brémond's mission and the Arab Bureau, see Bruce Westrate, *The Arab Bureau. British Policy in the Middle East, 1916–1920* (University Park: Pennsylvania State University Press, 1992), pp. 70–4.

10. Hankey Diaries: HNKY 1/6: 1918, diary entry, 6 Oct. 1918.

11. Paris, *Britain, the Hashemites and Arab Rule*, pp. 76–83.

12. TNA (PRO), FO 407/184, doc. 338, enclosure: General HQ Egypt telegram to DMI, 8 May 1919.

13. TNA (PRO), WO 106/196, Enclosure to Vice-Admiral J. de Robeck to Earl Curzon, 2 March 1920. Earl Curzon to Ambassador Cambon, 18 May 1920.

14. TNA (PRO), WO 32/5218, DMI to DMO, War Office, 20 Feb. 1919.

15. TNA (PRO), WO 32/5730, "War Office aide-mémoire in regard to the occupation of Syria, Palestine and Mesopotamia pending the decision in regard to mandates," 13 Sept. 1919. Lord Derby (Paris) record of conversation with Lord Allenby, 28 Oct. 1919.

16. Churchill College Archive, University of Cambridge, Leo Amery Papers, AMEL 7/15, diary entry, 13 Oct. 1919.

17. TNA (PRO), WO 106/64, no. 4578/16I, GHQ Constantinople intelligence report: "Negotiations between the French and the Ottoman nationalists," 7 December 1919. Report based on ten cipher telegrams detailing talks between Mustapha Kemal and Georges Picot at Sivas.

18. See, for example, the correspondence in TNA (PRO), WO 32/5757: War Cabinet, 1919—Middle East.

19. SHA, 7N4173/D1, Section d'Études Levant (SEL), "Note A/S de l'occupation militaire britannique en Egypte et l'armée egyptienne," 13 Feb. 1933.

20. As examples, TNA (PRO), FO 371/5032, E279/2/44, H. W. Young minute, 13 Feb. 1920; WO 106/196, EEF GHQ Intelligence Summary, 15 May 1920. Robert Blyth, *The Empire of the Raj: India, Eastern Africa and the Middle East, 1858–1947* (London: Palgrave, 2003), ch. 6.

21. For succinct analysis of the differing character of Middle East mandate systems, see Peter Sluglett, "Les Mandates/the Mandates: Some reflections on the Nature of the British Presence in Iraq (1914–1932) and the French Presence in Syria (1918–1946)," in Nadine Méouchy and Peter Sluglett (eds), *The British and French Mandates in Comparative Perspectives* (Leiden: Brill, 2004), pp. 103–27.

22. Millerand to Gouraud, 27 May and 13 June 1920. *Documents Diplomatiques Français*, 1920, vol. II, nos. 3 and 107. Dan Eldar, "France in Syria: The Abolition of the Sharifian Government, April–July 1920," *Middle Eastern Studies*, 29/3 (1993), pp. 487–504.

23. Paris, *Britain, the Hashemites and Arab Rule*, pp. 92–3, 126–7, 137, 143.

24. TNA (PRO), WO 32/5233, CM 14(21), 22 March 1921; draft conclusions of conference of ministers, 11 April 1921; CM 45(21), 31 May 1921.

25. Mary Wilson, *King Abdullah, Britain and the Making of Jordan* (Cambridge: Cambridge University Press, 1987), p. 62. Key figures in Abdullah's government included Rashid Tali'a, a Lebanese Druze under sentence of death in Syria, Mazhar Raslan from Homs, and Hasan al-Hakim, a Damascene.

26. Ibid., pp. 65–6. Ibrahim Hanunu, leader of anti-French resistance in the northern Syrian town of Aleppo, was also given refuge in Amman in September 1921 until he was duped into travelling on to Palestine where he was arrested and extradited to Syria.

27. Philip Khoury, "The Tribal Shaykh, French Tribal Policy, and the Nationalist Movement in Syria Between Two World Wars," *Middle Eastern Studies*, 18/2 (1982), pp. 184–6, 191 n. 34.

28. AN, Lyautey Papers, 475AP155D5, Lyautey private letter to Poincaré, 22 Jan. 1922. Ironically, at the height of the Rif war in northern Morocco three years later, Lyautey accused British sympathizers of providing arms and funds for Abd el-Krim's Riffian forces, an accusation foreign secretary Austen Chamberlain felt compelled to rebuff in the House of Commons. See TNA (PRO), FO 371/11083, W2646/2646/28, Consul R. H. Clive (Tangier) to Chamberlain, 12 March 1925.

29. TNA (PRO), FO 371/7847, E5461/274/89, Sir Lancelot Oliphant minute, 31 May 1922. On British diplomats' hostility to Poincaré, see John Keiger, 'Perfidious Albion?' French Perceptions of Britain as an Ally after the First World War,' in Martin Alexander (Ed.), *Knowing Your Friends. Intelligence inside Alliances and Coalitions from 1914 to the Cold War* (London: Frank Cass, 1998), pp. 48–50. Hostility to Poincaré among Foreign Office Arab specialists was also aroused by his attempt in March 1922 to bargain French acceptance of exclusive British strategic privileges in the Suez Canal zone with British surrender of capitulary rights in the international port of Tangier. The Army Council and Paris ambassador Lord Hardinge, a severe Poincaré critic, denied any equivalence between the two positions. This was not the end of the matter. In 1925 the French renewed their diplomatic pressure for more exclusive capitulary rights in Tangier. In response, the Government of India proposed French cession of its remaining Indian enclaves. See TNA (PRO), WO 32/5631, no. 793, Lord Hardinge (Paris) to Curzon, 29 March 1922, War Office MO2 note to FO, 13 April 1922; FO 371/11072, W6085/13/28, India Office letter to the Foreign Office permanent under secretary, 25 June 1925.

30. TNA (PRO), Damascus consular archives, FO 684/1, File: 1922 Secret Syrian Reports, Major McCallum to EEF HQ, 27 July 1922.

31. Robin Denniston, "Diplomatic Intercepts in Peace and War: Chanak 1922," *Diplomacy and Statecraft*, 11/1 (2000), pp. 244–54. John Ferris "'Far Too Dangerous a Gamble?' British Intelligence and Policy during the Chanak Crisis, September–October 1922," *Diplomacy and Statecraft*, 14/3 (2003), pp. 139–84.

32. Keith Jeffery and Alan Sharp, "Lord Curzon and Secret Intelligence," in Christopher Andrew and Jeremy Noakes (Eds.), *Intelligence and International Relations 1900–1945* (Exeter: University of Exeter Press, 1987), pp. 109–12. Christopher Andrew and Alexander Kanya-Forstner, *France Overseas. The Great War and the Climax of French Imperial Expansion* (London: Thames and Hudson, 1981), pp. 223–4.

33. Ferris "Far Too Dangerous a Gamble," p. 145.

34. George Henry Bennett, *British Foreign Policy during the Curzon Period, 1919–1924* (London: Macmillan, 1995), pp. 86–90.

35. Ferris, "Far Too Dangerous a Gamble," pp. 140–58.

36. Christopher Andrew, "Secret Intelligence and British Foreign Policy, 1900–1939," in Andrew and Noakes, *Intelligence and International Relations*, pp.15–17. Jeffery and Sharp, "Lord Curzon and Secret Intelligence," pp. 103–26.

37. Centre des Archives Diplomatiques, Nantes (hereafter CADN), Fonds Beyrouth, Cabinet Politique, vol. 894/D3, EMA-2, SR report, "A/S du Service Spécial britannique en Orient," 25 Feb. 1926.

38. TNA (PRO), FO 371/10165, E11337/10897/89, Samuel to Leo Amery, 21 Nov. 1924.

39. AN, F/7/13468, Commissariat spécial d'Evian, "SR anglo-égyptien à Genève," 24 January 1924; Commissariat spécial d'Annemasse, "Mouvement Syrio-Palestinien," 19 April 1924. Marie-Renée Mouton, "Le Congrès Syrio-Palestinien de Genève (1921)," *Relations Internationales*, 19 (1979), pp. 313–28.

40. TNA (PRO), CO 733/132/1, E. Stafford to Sir John Shuckburgh, "Activities in Transjordan taken on behalf of the French authorities during 1926," 11 Jan. 1927.

41. The Azrak refugee crisis is fully detailed in TNA (PRO), CO 733/132/1. On the extradition agreement, see TNA (PRO), CO 831/37/8, Lord Plumer to Levant high commissioner Ponsot, 4 Oct. 1927.

42. TNA (PRO), AIR 23/90, BL/S/10, British liaison officer Major Salisbury-Jones to GSHQ, Jerusalem, 8 Sept. 1925. For his part, Salisbury-Jones was no less condemnatory of the soon-to-be-replaced Sarrail, commenting, "It is not an exaggeration to say that 75% of the French troubles in Syria have been due to the appointment of politically-minded high commissioners, who have been too absorbed by politics to concentrate seriously upon the sound administration of the country." Quote from AIR 23/90, Salisbury Jones report to GSHQ, Jerusalem, 1 Sept. 1925.

43. TNA (PRO), CO 730/105/9, Iraq Air Staff Summary of Intelligence, no. 2, 11 Jan. 1926. In February 1926 alone the Deuxième Bureau reported that the Syrian-Palestine Congress executive relayed £50,000 in voluntary donations for Syrian insurgents from supporters in India, Egypt and Iraq. See CADN, Fonds Beyrouth, Cabinet Politique, vol. 894/D3, EMA-2, SR report, "A/S du Service Spécial britannique en Orient," 25 Feb. 1926.

44. SHA, 7N4171/D1, EMA-2, "Renseignements retrospectives sur les menées anglaises durant l'insurrection et les attachés de certains leaders nationalistes avec les Soviets," 17 July 1931.

45. The Druze leader, Sultan al-Atrash, also found refuge in Transjordan in the years preceding the Syrian revolt. See Wilson, *King Abdullah*, p. 74. An

important new account of the Syrian Revolt leadership is Michael Provence, *The Great Syrian Revolt and the Rise of Arab Nationalism* (Austin: University of Texas Press, 2005).

46. See the correspondence in TNA (PRO), CO 730/109/1: Dr Shahbander, 1926–7. Regarding the Quai d'Orsay accusation, see Philip Khoury, *Syria and the French Mandate. The Politics of Arab Nationalism, 1920–1945* (London: I. B. Taurus, 1987), p. 142.

47. SHA, 7N4171/D1, EMA-2, no. 1199, Service des renseignements du Levant, "Liste des associations, partis du comité de l'extérieur travaillant ou ayant travaillé contre le Mandat de la France en Syrie," 1 April 1926.

48. Ministère des Affaires Etrangères, Paris, Henry de Jouvenal papers, vol. 4: Syrie 1926, tel. 20, Maignet (Baghdad) to Foreign Ministry, 15 June 1926.

49. See Martin Thomas, "The Syrian Revolt and Anglo-French Imperial Relations, 1925–27," in Greg Kennedy and Keith Neilson (Eds.), *Incidents and International Relations. People, Power and Personalities* (Westport, Conn: Praeger, 2002), pp. 65–82.

50. SHA, Moscou, C286/D429, SCR Levant, "Renseignement—Chekib Arslan," 26 March 1934. The security services were more anxious about Arslan's activities in North Africa: Juliette Bessis, "Chekib Arslan et les mouvements nationalistes au Maghreb," *Revue Historique*, 259/2 (1978), pp. 467–89.

51. As an example: SHA, 7N4171/D1, EMA-2, Section de renseignements, Agent's field report: "Attitude des Syriens résidant en Transjordanie," 1 August 1931.

52. SHA, 7N4171/D1, EMA-2, SR "Renseignement d'Egypte—bonne source," 27 Jan. 1926.

53. Antony Best, *British Intelligence and the Japanese Challenge in Asia, 1914–1941* (London: Palgrave, 2002), pp. 63–8. S Smith, "The Comintern, the Chinese Communist Party and the Three Armed Uprisings in Shanghai, 1926–27," in Tim Rees and Andrew Thorpe (Eds.), *International Communism and the Communist International 1919–43* (Manchester: Manchester University Press, 1998), pp. 254–70.

54. CADN, Fonds Beyrouth, Cabinet Politique, vol. 842/D8, Beirut Inspector-General of Police annual report for 1927.

55. TNA (PRO), CO 732/28/13, Baghdad Council of Ministers to Iraq High Commission, 28 Aug. 1927.

56. Ibid.

57. TNA (PRO), CO 733/132/1, Minute by G. L. M. Clauson, 7 Jan. 1926 [sic—1927].

58. CADN, Fonds Beyrouth, Cabinet Politique, vol. 894/D3, BL/36, British Army Liaison officer to EMA-Levant, relays intelligence from Air Staff HQ, Baghdad, 21 Dec. 1923.

59. TNA (PRO), CO 732/41/19, Sir John Chancellor (Jerusalem) to Lord Passfield, 24 Oct. 1929.

60. SHA, 4H86/D1, SR Euphrate, Bulletin de renseignements no. 5, 25 Jan. 1930.

61. TNA (PRO), CO 732/34/9, F. G. Peake memorandum: "A Brief History of the Wahhabi Movement," 21 March 1928. John Habib, *Ibn Saud's Warriors of Islam: The Ikhwan of Najd and their Role in the Creation of the Saudi Kingdom, 1910–1930* (Leiden: Brill, 1978).

62. TNA, CO 831/1/2, C. H. F. Cox, Amman Residency quarterly reports on situation in Transjordan, 1928. The escalation of tribal raiding between Transjordan and Saudi Arabia in 1928–29 is also described in *British Documents on Foreign Affairs*, II: B, vol. 6, nos. 93, 305, 355.

63. SHA, 7N2797/D2, nos. 206, 211, 281, General Després reports to EMA-2, "Situation en Arabie et en Egypte," 10 and 14 March and 5 April 1928.

64. TNA (PRO) CO 730/137/9, Glubb memorandum: "Plans for forthcoming raiding season," 6 Sept. 1928.

65. SHA, 7N4171/D1, EMA-2, Agent's report ("très bonne source"), "Notice sur le Capitaine Glubb," 3 July 1931.

66. Martin Kramer, *Islam Assembled: The Advent of the Muslim Congresses* (New York: Columbia University Press, 1986), ch. 11.

67. TNA (PRO), CO 732/53/3: Report on General Islamic Congress held in Jerusalem, 7–16 Dec. 1931.

68. Kramer, *Islam Assembled*, pp.126–30. To Turkish relief, Palestine high commissioner Sir Arthur Wauchope refused the visa application.

69. TNA (PRO), CO 732/51/6, OGRW18/11, Secretary of state for colonies telegram to the officer administering the Government of Palestine, 18 Nov. 1931.

70. Jacob Metzer, *The Divided Economy of Mandatory Palestine* (Cambridge: Cambridge University Press, 1998), p. 217, table A.3.

71. As examples: AN, F/7/13468/D6, Commissaire spécial d'Annemasse memos., "Rapport su la situation en Palestine," 18 July 1924, and "Rapport sur le mouvement pan-Arabe," 1 Aug. 1924.

72. SHA, 7N4171/D1, EMA-2, Agent's report from "well-placed informant," "La situation en Palestine," 28 April 1931; SEL Beirut, "A/S Congrès Islamique de Jerusalem," 4 November 1931.

73. See, for example, SHA, 7N4171/D1, EMA-2, "Situation en Palestine et Transjordanie—le Sionisme," 7 Aug. 1931.

74. TNA (PRO), FO 371/20065, E1326/381/65, Sudan Agency (Cairo), "Report on the pan-Islamic Arab Movement," 14 Feb. 1936. For Arab and British perspectives on the Revolt, see Yoshua Porath, *The Palestinian Arab National Movement, 1929–1939. From Riots to Rebellion* (London: Frank Cass, 1977); Michael Cohen, *Palestine: Retreat from the Mandate. The Making of British Policy, 1936–1945* (London: Frank Cass, 1978); Ylana Miller, *Government and Politics in Rural Palestine, 1920–1948* (Austin: University of Texas Press, 1985), pp. 121–38; Tom Bowden, "The Politics of Arab Rebellion in Palestine 1936–39," *Middle Eastern Studies*, 11/2 (1975), pp. 147–74; Charles Townshend, "The Defence of Palestine: Insurrection and Public Security, 1936–1939," *English Historical Review*, 103 (1988), pp. 919–48.

75. TNA (PRO), WO 106/2018B, COS 847(JIC), "Attitude of the 'Arab World' to Great Britain with particular reference to the Palestine Conference," 20 Feb. 1939.

76. For background to the Assyrian crisis, see David Omissi, "Britain, the Assyrians and the Iraq Levies, 1919–1932," *Journal of Imperial and Commonwealth History*, 17/3 (1989), pp. 301–22; Sami Zubaida, "Contested Nations: Iraq and the Assyrians," *Nations and Nationalism*, 6/3 (2000), pp. 363–82.

77. SHA, 7N4173/D1, EMA-2, SEL Beirut, report, "Situation des minorities en Djezireh sous Mandat Français," 3 Oct. 1933.

78. SHA, 7N4173/D1, EMA-2, SEL Beirut agent report, "Situation en Palestine et Transjordanie," 8 November 1933.

79. SHA, 7N4173/D1, EMA-2, SEL Beirut agent report ("Well-placed source"), "Situation politique en Transjordanie," 28 Nov. 1933.

80. Yuval Arnon-Ohanna, "The Bands in the Palestinian Arab Revolt, 1936–1939: Structure and Organization," *Asian and African Studies*, 15/2 (1981), pp. 229–36.

81. W Abboushi, "The Road to Rebellion: Arab Palestine in the 1930s," *Journal of Palestine Studies*, 6/3 (1977), pp. 33–42. Arnon-Ohanna, "The Bands in the Palestinian Arab Revolt," pp. 237–8.

82. TNA (PRO), FO 371/20065, E1326/381/65, "Report on the Pan-Islamic Arab Movement," Enclosure to Lampson telegram to foreign secretary Anthony Eden, 24 Feb. 1936.

83. TNA (PRO), FO 684/9, E1147/563/8, MacKereth memorandum: "Pan-Arabism," 15 May 1936.

84. TNA (PRO), FO 684/9, E1957/1956/2, "Memorandum on the reactions in the Damascus district to the Palestine disturbances," Enclosure to Foreign Office dispatch, 21 August 1936. Townshend, "The Defence of Palestine," p. 921.

85. Michael Cohen, *Palestine: Retreat from the Mandate* (London: Paul Elek, 1978), pp. 54–6.

86. For details of the Congress, see Elie Kedourie, "The Bludan Congress on Palestine, September 1937," *Middle Eastern Studies*, 17/1 (1980), pp. 107–25.

87. Abboushi, "The Road to Rebellion," p. 40. Arnon-Ohanna, "The Bands," pp. 237–8.

88. TNA (PRO), FO 684/10, E1980/1692/2, MacKereth (Damascus) memorandum to Foreign Office: "Bludan Congress," 15 Sept. 1937.

89. TNA (PRO), FO 684/10, MacKereth (Damascus) to Eden, 19 Oct. 1937.

90. Cohen, *Palestine: Retreat from the Mandate*, p. 62.

91. TNA (PRO), CO 733/368/1, no. 65/2/15/3, G. W. Furlonge (Beirut) to Palestine High Commission, 27 Oct. 1938. Abboushi, "The Road to Rebellion," pp. 42–4.

92. Townshend, "The Defence of Palestine," p. 943.

93. For an analysis of the Syria-Palestine relationship in longer-term perspective, see Philip Khoury, "Divided Loyalties? Syria and the Question of Palestine, 1919–39," *Middle Eastern Studies*, 21/3 (1985), pp. 324–48.

94. TNA (PRO), FO 684/10, E1980/1692/2, MacKereth (Damascus) memorandum to the Foreign Office, "Bludan Congress," 15 Sept. 1937.

95. TNA (PRO), CO 733/368/4, Foreign Office copy telegram E7601/22/31, Sir Eric Phipps (Paris) to Eden, 29 Dec. 1937.

96. TNA (PRO), CO 733/368/4, 15/2207/2, Damascus dispatch no. 7: MacKereth (Damascus) to Palestine High Commission, 5 Feb. 1938.

97. TNA (PRO), CO 733/368/4, E7601/22/31, copy telegram, Phipps (Paris) to Eden, 29 Dec. 1937.

98. TNA (PRO), FO 684/10, MacKereth (Damascus) to Eden, 19 Oct. 1937.

99. Arnon-Ohanna, "The Bands," pp. 237–8. Aware of the worsening factionalism among the rebel groups, al-Ashmar refused the offer.

100. TNA (PRO), WO 32/4562, Lieutenant-General R. H. Haining, HQ British Forces Palestine, memorandum, "British propaganda in Palestine. Its origin and progress in 1938," 1 Dec. 1938.
101. TNA (PRO), CO 733/386/4, E279/10/31, MacKereth (Damascus) to Eden, 7 Jan. 1938.
102. TNA (PRO), CO 733/368/1, E3591/10/31, MacKereth (Damascus) to foreign secretary Lord Halifax, 8 June 1938; E3862/10/31, Charles Baxter (FO) to G. T. Havard (Beirut), 7 July 1938.
103. Arnon-Ohanna, "The Bands," pp. 238–41.
104. TNA (PRO), FO 406/77, E622/284/65, Phipps (Paris) to Viscount Halifax, 23 January 1939.
105. TNA (PRO) CO 732/81/3, War Office Military Intelligence directorate report by Major W. J. Cawthorn, "Notes on the possibility of concerted military opposition from the Arab peoples to H. M. Government's policy in Palestine," 2 Feb. 1938.
106. TNA (PRO), FO 371/23201, telegram 133, Houstoun-Boswell (Baghdad) to the Foreign Office, 10 April 1939.
107. SHA, Moscou, C464/D174, Rapport du mission du Commandant Schlesser, "Le problème du contre-espionnage en Afrique du Nord," March–April 1938; Service Historique de l'Armée d'Air, 2B43, EMA-5ᵉ Bureau, "Note au sujet de l'instruction en matière de contre-espionnage aux Armées," 16 Nov. 1939.
108. See, for instance, TNA (PRO), CAB 104/6, CID 462-C, COS committee report, "Strategical aspect of the partition of Palestine," 14 Feb. 1938; SHA, 7N4190/D1, Commission d'études de la défense des états du mandat, rapport, 28 December 1938.
109. SHA, Moscou, C623/D1419, SEL Beirut, "TSMF—liaisons entre les services anglais et français," 17 Feb. 1939.
110. Martin Thomas, "Imperial Defence or Diversionary Attack? Anglo-French Strategic Planning in the Near East, 1936–40," in Martin Alexander and William Philpott (Eds.), *Anglo-French Defence Relations between the Wars* (London: Palgrave-Macmillan, 2002), pp. 168–78.
111. See, for example, the correspondence in TNA (PRO), FO 371/23361: Wireless communications between the Sudan and French Equatorial Africa, 1939.
112. SHA, 7N4190/D7, Conseil Supérieur de la Guerre, Note of conversation between General Huntziger and Dr Hayyim Weizmann, 31 May 1939.
113. SHA, Moscou, C194/D134, SR report, "Propagande italienne: Les agissements italiens en AFN," n.d. April 1940.

YVON DELBOS AND ANTHONY EDEN: ANGLO–FRENCH COOPERATION, 1936–1938

Glyn Stone

Anthony Eden was appointed foreign secretary at the end of 1935 following the dismissal of Sir Samuel Hoare for his part in the infamous Hoare-Laval Pact. Yvon Delbos, a member of the Radical party, became French foreign minister six months later as a result of the victory of the Popular Front in the May 1936 elections. Eden resigned as foreign secretary on 20 February 1938. Delbos followed suit less than four weeks later on 14 March 1938. When he became foreign secretary at the age of thirty-eight, Eden was already the ambitious, rising star of the Conservative party and had accumulated an impressive degree of experience in foreign affairs having been parliamentary private secretary to foreign secretary Austen Chamberlain between 1926 and 1929, under secretary of state for foreign affairs from September 1931 until January 1934 when he became lord privy seal, and then in June 1935 minister of league of nations affairs (without portfolio). In comparison, Delbos was far less experienced, as Robert Young has observed:

Yvon Delbos went to the Quai d'Orsay in his early fifties, equipped with a respectable if unspectacular reputation as a competent member of the Chamber and as a journalist with special interest in foreign affairs. A quiet, moderate man of modest political ambitions . . . Significantly, in a political world renowned for its gastronomic and alcaholic excesses, here was one, a curiosity, who did not suffer from liver complaints. But he was not the sort of man from whom one could expect either brilliance or novelty in foreign policy.[1]

Yet, the two foreign ministers developed a good working relationship and contributed much to the improvement in Anglo–French relations after the Abyssinian débâcle and the mutual recrimination of the Rhineland crisis. In his memoirs Eden recollected on this relationship: "For me a new and much happier era of relations with France now opened up. From this moment [the victory of the French Popular Front Government] until my resignation in February 1938, French Ministers and I worked together without even a momentary breach of an understanding which grew increasingly confident."[2] His first impression of Delbos, having met him at Geneva on 25 June 1936, was that he was "rather voluble, and not very sure of his facts."[3] But he soon came to respect the French foreign minister and in his memoirs praised Delbos specifically for his "many acts of friendship"; not least in using his influence to restrain the French press at the time of the Abdication Crisis in late 1936.[4]

The feeling was certainly mutual. Delbos made the revival of a close diplomatic relationship with the British the centrepiece of his foreign policy which accorded with the aims of his prime ministers, the Socialist Léon Blum and the Radical Camille Chautemps. Blum, for example, told the Chamber on 5 December 1936 that: "Yvon Delbos has given first priority to the close cordiality of our relations with England, and he is right. For our other friends are unanimous in recognizing and declaring that the Franco-English accord affects the whole realm of international affairs."[5] So close had the relationship become between the two foreign ministers that when Eden resigned in February 1938 Delbos was so personally affected that, according to Phipps, he offered his resignation to Chautemps several times.[6] John Dreifort has noted in this context:

> Eden's resignation came as a shocking personal blow to Delbos. His relationship with the pro-French Eden had become quite cordial during the previous twenty months. Their frequent correspondence, their meetings, and their common recognition of the need for a revitalized *Entente Cordiale* had led to an increased understanding between the two men.[7]

The question for the historian is to ask whether this mutual admiration actually translated itself into close cooperation in the diplomatic field.

How far, in other words, did British and French foreign policy converge in the period when Eden and Delbos were responsible for the conduct of foreign affairs in their respective countries? To answer this question it is intended to focus on four key issues which impacted on the relationship: French discussions with the Soviets respecting a military convention in the aftermath of the Franco–Soviet Pact which was ratified by the French Senate at the end of February 1936; the outbreak and development of the Spanish Civil War from July 1936 onwards; the respective attitudes of Delbos and Eden towards the appeasement of fascist Italy; and the respective attitudes of both towards the appeasement of Nazi Germany.

Prior to the making of the Franco–Soviet Pact in 1933, Delbos published a book, *L'Expérience Rouge*, in which he predicted that "the progress of the fascist leprosy" would bring France and Soviet Russia together. He had welcomed Soviet Russia's entry into the League of Nations in 1934 and was a firm supporter of Edouard Herriot and Louis Barthou and eventually Pierre Laval in their efforts to conclude the Franco–Soviet Pact.[8] Eden, meanwhile, had visited Moscow, as lord privy seal, in late March 1935 and had spoken personally with the Soviet dictator, Joseph Stalin, his foreign minister, Maxim Litvinov, and Vyacheslav Molotov, chairman of the Council of Commisars. The Soviet dictator had stressed the need for strong collective security by "some scheme of pacts" to counter German aggression while Eden had emphasized Britain's world wide interests which would have to be considered before she came to any decision on European policy. Stalin had agreed and he left an impression on Eden and his officials, the British ambassador at Moscow, Viscount Chilston, and William Strang, Foreign Office adviser on League of Nations affairs, who had accompanied him, of "a man of strong oriental traits of character with unshakeable assurance and control whose courtesy in no way hid from us an implacable ruthlessness."[9] While, according to Robert Manne, the Eden-Stalin talks had marked "the moment of greatest cordiality since the October Revolution," there was no substantive improvement in Anglo–Soviet relations.[10] Indeed, the Foreign Office rejected the case for providing a loan to the Soviets in February 1936 following the intervention of the Soviet ambassador, Ivan Maiskii, who had proposed the idea. Eden, now foreign secretary, having initially favoured the idea of a loan, agreed with his officials. While "I want good relations with the bear," he wrote, "I don't want to hug him too close. I don't trust him, and am sure there is hatred in his heart for all we stand for."[11] His disdain for the Franco–Soviet Pact was revealed at a meeting of the Cabinet on 12 February 1936 when he informed his colleagues that according to Sir George Clerk, the British ambassador at Paris, the French ambassador at London, Charles Corbin, would probably call to consult him as to the desirability of French ratification of the pact. He proposed "to express no opinion. We had not been consulted before the signature of the pact and there appeared no reason why we should express any opinion now, although unfortunately it might be impossible for us to remain outside the consequences of the pact." Following a brief discussion, in which it was suggested that "it would be a distinct advantage to be able to tell Germany that we had nothing to do with the matter," the Cabinet approved Eden's proposed approach to the French ambassador.[12]

Although the Pact had become a reality by the time Delbos became foreign minister in May, having been ratified by the French Senate on 28 February 1936 and having provided Hitler with a pretext to remilitarize the Rhineland, the Soviets were anxious to strengthen it with the signing of a military convention and, accordingly, discussions took place between the Popular Front government and the Soviets during 1936 and 1937. However, there was no question of the French engaging in close military cooperation with Soviet Russia, not only because of ideological hostility on the part of the French general staff which Delbos and other ministers shared—the French generals genuinely feared, and the Spanish Civil War accentuated that fear,[13] that too close contact with the Soviets could encourage subversion in the army and the spread of communism in France—but also because of reservations about the quality of the Soviet armed forces whose military capacity was, in the words of General Victor-Henri Schweisguth who had attended Soviet manoeuvres in September 1936, "a great sham."[14] These reservations were shared to some extent by the British military authorities.[15]

On the political side, both the Quai d'Orsay and the Foreign Office were increasingly anxious and critical of Soviet intervention in the Spanish Civil War which gathered momentum in the autumn of 1936 with the despatch of large consignments of weapons for the Spanish Republican forces and the arrival of Soviet technical staff and the tens of thousands of volunteers of the international brigades organized by the Comintern.[16] Prompted by Delbos, the secretary general of the Quai d'Orsay, Alexis Léger, went so far as to advise Moscow in October 1936 that relations would suffer if the Soviet Union did not pursue a less aggressive policy in Spain. In London, Eden and his permanent under secretary at the Foreign Office, Sir Robert Vansittart, remained wedded to their policy of non-intervention in the civil war in Spain and deplored Soviet intervention.[17] On 19 November Eden went so far as to accuse the Soviets in the House of Commons of being more to blame than the Germans and Italians of breaches of the Non-Intervention Agreement to which all of the European great powers had adhered in August 1936.[18] In the longer term, the commitment to non-intervention in both countries undermined Soviet attempts to use the Spanish conflict as a means of achieving collective security against German and Italian fascism and instead enhanced the suspicion of Soviet motives.

For Delbos and his officials at the Quai d'Orsay the value of the Franco–Soviet Pact lay in the fact that its existence made a Soviet–German rapprochement much less likely. As Phipps noted while still ambassador at Berlin on 7 April 1937, shortly before he became ambassador at Paris: "If Russia after copiously watering her red wine were ready to abandon France and wished to fall into the German arms, those arms would probably be very willing to receive her."[19] Eden and his officials took the same view but believed that was no reason to turn the Pact into a military alliance. He need not have worried. On 15 May 1937, when he told Delbos personally that he regarded any improvement in Franco–Soviet solidarity as inopportune at that time, the foreign minister clarified his position on the issue and confided that the French had no intention of entering into any military agreement with Soviet Russia. The most the French intended to do, when confronted by further Soviet pressure, was to permit the exchange of information between French and Soviet military attachés. However, even this limited development worried Eden. He told Delbos that he much regretted this decision because "he foresaw that such collaboration between the French and Russian governments would be bound to become public" and might easily have the "most serious psychological effects both in England and in the lesser countries of Europe."[20]

The whole question of military concessions to the Soviets was rendered academic, however, when, at the end of May 1937, Stalin commenced his purge of the Red Army high command and provided a clear reason for ending negotiations, so that even the proposed exchange of information by the French and Soviet military attachés was abandoned. In any case, even without the purges, the question mark over Soviet military credibility, the ideological concerns of the French governing elite and British opposition, the prospects for concluding a Franco–Soviet military alliance were never high because as in August 1939 so in the spring of 1937 the Russians made it clear that their assistance was contingent on the full cooperation of France's eastern allies, Poland and Romania, which was extremely unlikely.[21]

The alienation of France from Soviet Russia was complete when in December 1937 Moscow was deliberately excluded from Delbos' itinerary of his tour of eastern European capitals. Moreover, at the end of January 1938 the foreign minister, in terms which would have been understood and appreciated by Eden and prime minister Neville Chamberlain, expressed his suspicion that the Soviets were determined to undermine French efforts, and those of their "friends and allies," to achieve a détente with Germany and reach a general European settlement by perpetuating Franco–German tension.[22] In addition, a few days before Eden's resignation, Delbos told Phipps that "Chautemps and he would far sooner resign than consent to serve in the same Cabinet as a Communist, excepting in a War Cabinet" and he added, in confidence, that "even Blum, who had tried to form a Cabinet of this kind, had confessed to him great relief at that attempt having failed."[23]

Just as Delbos and Eden and their respective governments were largely in accord in their relations with Soviet Russia, there was a considerable degree of agreement with regard to their respective responses to the Spanish Civil War. Throughout the conflict, which began in July 1936 and lasted until the end of March 1939, the British government adhered to a policy of strict non-intervention in the political and military spheres, though not the economic. The French government for the most part maintained non-intervention while selling a number of largely obsolete aircraft to the Spanish Republicans, occasionally opening the Pyrenees frontier to enable the transit of Soviet and Czech arms to their forces and facilitating a number of financial transactions on their behalf, including the export of gold from the Bank of Madrid.[24] The British and French responses contrasted starkly with Germany, Italy and Soviet Russia who intervened on a substantial scale, the first two on the side of the rebellious Spanish Nationalists, led by General Francisco Franco, the latter on the side of the democratically elected Spanish Popular Front Republican Government.

Eden and Delbos viewed the civil war in Spain and the prospects of foreign intervention in it, as threatening to European peace and both were appalled by the thought that the Spanish conflict might provoke a European conflagration, possibly along ideological lines.[25] Delbos also shared the fears of his ministerial colleagues, including Blum, that by intervening in the war in Spain in support of the Spanish Popular Front Government they would provoke a civil war or alternatively a military coup in France and also jeopardize the social reform programme of the Popular Front.[26] As a result, having agreed initially to provide support for the Spanish Republicans, the French government on 25 July decided not to intervene in Spain.[27] Delbos was a leading advocate of non-intervention partly because he had been persuaded that Britain had no intention of intervening in the civil war in Spain. Eden, taking his cue from Prime Minister Stanley Baldwin's stricture that "on no account, French or other, must he bring them into the fight on the side of the Russians,"[28] was resolved to ensure British neutrality in the Spanish conflict. Delbos and his officials at the Quai d'Orsay were equally determined not to get involved but they were concerned at reports that both Germany and Italy intended to intervene. As a result, Delbos backed the secretary general of the Quai d'Orsay, Alexis Léger, when he proposed a non-intervention agreement by which all the European powers would desist from intervening in the Spanish struggle.[29]

During the next few weeks Delbos worked closely with Lord Halifax, lord president of the council, who during the first fortnight of August acted as foreign secretary, and then with Eden on his return from a short break in Yorkshire, to make the Non-Intervention Agreement a reality.[30] By the end of August 1936 all the European powers had adhered to this agreement though Germany, Italy, Portugal and later Soviet Russia consistently undermined its intention to prohibit intervention of any kind in Spain. Within France there was strong opposition to non-intervention within the Popular Front, which demanded arms for Republican Spain, and it was only with British support, which he and his officials consistently solicited and which was readily reciprocated, that Delbos was able to establish the non-intervention policy and persuade a reluctant Blum to go along with it.[31]

Delbos also succeeded in persuading Eden to agree to the establishment of a non-intervention committee to supervise the Non-Intervention Agreement and to locate it in London rather than Paris.[32] In this connection, Delbos told the British ambassador, Sir George Clerk, that his government were most grateful for Eden's agreement to hold the meetings of the Committee in London.[33] This was a perceptive move on the part of Delbos and his colleagues because by locating the Committee in London rather than Paris it enabled them to avoid inevitable protests and recrimination from those elements within the broader Popular Front movement who were opposed to non-intervention and who were agitating for armed intervention on the side of the Spanish Republic. Moreover, in accepting the Committee's location in London, Eden saddled the British government before history with the burden of its failures and enabled the French to escape this fate.

Within the Non-Intervention Committee Britain and France sought to make the Non-Intervention Agreement more effective in containing foreign intervention in the civil war. To this end, Delbos and Eden cooperated closely in making a number of proposals in the late autumn of 1936 and the winter of 1936–1937, including attempts to curtail the passage of arms and "foreign volunteers" into the Spanish arena and also to mediate between the two belligerents—Nationalist and Republican Spain. Delbos succeeded in convincing Eden not to grant belligerent rights to General Franco's forces or to grant *de facto* recognition to his regime, though most of the British cabinet would have done so had Madrid fallen to the Nationalists as expected in November 1936.[34] After several months of diplomatic interchange Delbos and Eden succeeded in March 1937 in establishing a naval patrol scheme—involving the British, French, German and Italian navies—around the coast of Spain to prevent illegal arms deliveries to the Republican and Nationalist forces and also a land observation scheme on the Franco–Spanish and Portuguese–Spanish frontiers.[35] Unfortunately, the naval patrol scheme broke down three months later as a result of the *Deutschland* and *Leipzig* incidents—the first a real attack by Spanish Republican aircraft on the German battleship *Deut-schland* engaged in the naval patrol, and the second, a supposed tor-pedo attack by a Republican submarine on the German cruiser *Leipzig*, also engaged in the naval patrol, but which was never properly verified.[36]

The subsequent withdrawal of the German and Italian navies from the patrol and the suspension of international observation on the Portuguese-Spanish frontier threatened to undermine the whole non-intervention pol-icy of Britain and France. In these circumstances, Eden and his officials proposed a revised "British Plan" which aimed to explicitly link the con-trol scheme with plans to remove foreign "volunteers" from both sides in Spain and the grant of belligerent rights to Franco's forces as well as the Republicans.[37] Delbos was not enthusiastic but his opposition to the "British Plan" was soon overshadowed by events in the Mediterranean in the summer of 1937, namely the sinking of Russian, Spanish and other merchant ships bound for Republican Spain by Italian submarines[38] which eventually led the French foreign minister to urge a conference to deal with these "acts of piracy." He was convinced that only common action by France and Britain would "serve to bring about a modification in the Italian attitude."[39] Eden agreed immediately and succeeded in per-suading the British Cabinet, including Chamberlain, that such a confer-ence was necessary, though with Italy included.[40] As a result of the Nyon Conference, a full naval patrol was re-established, consisting almost entirely of French and British ships patrolling the Atlantic coastline of Spain, the western Mediterranean and the Aegean. The Soviet navy was excluded from the naval patrol in the Aegean in deference to the wishes of Greece and Turkey while the Germans and Italians refused to participate at Nyon though Mussolini eventually accepted an Italian zone in the Tyr-rhenian Sea.[41] The French Pyrenees frontier was closed once more.

The Nyon Conference has been referred to as one of the few occasions during the inter-war period when the western powers made a firm and res-olute stand against totalitarian aggression. According to AJP Taylor, "here was a demonstration, never repeated, that Mussolini would respect a show of strength." The American foreign correspondent, Louis Fischer, put it another way: "Mussolini understood the smoke of British cruisers better than the perfumed notes of the British Foreign Office. Mussolini saw that the British meant business and that the French, at last, were play-ing ball with the British."[42] These glowing testimonials are a little wide of the mark. Unfortunately for Delbos and Eden, the impact of Nyon was lessened by the British Admiralty's categorical rejection of the French suggestion that the Mediterranean patrol should be extended to hostile surface ships and aircraft threatening merchant ships as well as taking action against submerged submarines.[43] Moreover, after Nyon the Italians changed their tactics and Italian submarines were handed over to Franco's forces and Italian aircraft on Majorca flew with Spanish markings. As a result, the bombing of all Republican ports and cargo ships bound for them could be carried out with virtual impunity for the rest of the civil war.[44]

For Eden and Vansittart, Nyon, and the cooperation they shared throughout with their French counterparts, brought a change in their view of the Spanish Civil War. Henceforth, both wished for a Republican victory, not for ideological reasons, but because it would be a considerable setback to the ambitions of the Axis powers.[45] Accordingly, when in late September and early October 1937 Delbos insisted on French participation in tripartite talks relating to Spain with Italy and Britain instead of simple Anglo-Italian bilateral talks, Eden gave his full support and persuaded a reluctant Chamberlain to agree.[46] Previously, the French foreign minister had gone so far as to call for the abandonment of non-intervention by Britain and France, including the reopening of the French Pyrenees frontier for the transit of arms to the Spanish Republic, unless the Italians ceased to send "volunteers" to Spain and cooperate with Britain and France in the Non-Intervention Committee in progressing the "British Plan" of the summer. Eden and his senior advisers, and even more so Chamberlain and the rest of the British Cabinet, were not prepared to go so far and in the face of opposition to such action by his own officials, including Léger and René Massigli, and also of prime minister Camille Chautemps, Delbos retreated.[47]

In the event, Mussolini rejected the tripartite talks and the "British Plan" became stalled in the Non-Intervention Committee and it remained more or less in this condition when Eden resigned in February 1938 and Delbos followed suit in March; at which point the new second short lived Blum Ministry reopened the French frontier for the transit of arms to the Spanish Republic, which remained open until the summer of 1938. In view of all the difficulties confronting the British and French governments with regard to the Spanish Civil War since its outbreak, the degree of cooperation between Delbos and Eden was quite remarkable. Moreover, in terms of their original fears and concerns in the summer of 1936 about a European war based on ideological divisions, Delbos and Eden had succeeded in their aim of containing the Spanish Civil War. Indeed, at a meeting of British and French ministers in London in late November 1937, Chautemps insisted that their two countries "could congratulate themselves that the Spanish [non-intervention] policy had undoubtedly helped them to pass a very difficult year without a breach of the peace."[48] An uneasy peace in Europe was maintained but ultimately at the price of Spanish democracy and strategic dangers for both countries as the shared experience in Spain of Germany and Italy gradually consolidated the Rome-Berlin Axis.

It is somewhat surprising that Britain should seek to appease Mussolini's Italy during most of Eden's tenure at the Foreign Office. Even Chamberlain was moved to remark in July 1937 that "if only we could get on terms with the Germans I would not care a rap for Musso."[49] Eden may have set out with some hopes that appeasing the Italian dictator would prove beneficial to British interests but the abortive Gentleman's Agreement of January 1937 soon disillusioned him. Delbos had absolutely no time for Mussolini. He told the American ambassador at Paris, William Bullitt, in August 1937 that while "every effort should be made to reach conciliation with Germany" Italy "should be treated with contempt and disdain as a relatively unimportant jackal."[50] While they ended sanctions against Italy in July 1936, following Britain's lead, there is no doubt that Mussolini's continuing disregard of the Spanish Non-Intervention Agreement, despite Italy's adhesion in August 1936, made Delbos and Blum less and less inclined to pursue an Italian rapprochement. Delbos shared Eden's grave concern at the growth of Italian influence in the Balearic Islands from the last months of 1936 onwards. Eden had presented a memorandum to his Cabinet colleagues in mid December 1936 drawing attention to the extent of Italian activities in the Balearics, notably on Majorca.[51] The French were even more concerned because it was clearly understood that the establishment of permanent Italian air bases on the islands, particularly Majorca, would seriously threaten French lines of communication with their North African empire.[52] In this connection, Eden and Vansittart returned from talks with Delbos and Chautemps at Geneva and Paris (20–21 September 1937), convinced that all classes of Frenchmen, including the General Staff, were united in holding that "the Italians must be got out of Spain at once and especially out of the Balearic Islands."[53] The Quai d'Orsay was apparently prepared to contemplate the occupation of Minorca as a *gage*.[54] To the surprise and dismay of Vansittart and Eden, the British Chiefs of Staff were less concerned about Italian activities in the Balearics, including their use of Majorca as an air base to attack the cities and towns of Republican Spain.[55]

As part of their growing animosity towards Italy, Delbos and Blum took the decision in October 1936 not to replace the retiring French ambassador at Rome, Count Charles de Chambrun, with René Doynel de Saint-Quentin because Mussolini had decided that his credentials must be addressed to Victor Emmanuel III not only as "King of Italy" but also as "Emperor of Ethiopia" which would imply French recognition of the Italian annexation of Ethiopia. For the remainder of Delbos' tenure at the Quai d'Orsay France was represented at Rome by the chargé d'affaires, Jules Blondel.[56] The issue was symbolic of the poor relations which existed between Rome and Paris and those relations continued to deteriorate as Italy intervened further in Spain, did nothing about preventing the annexation of Austria and drew closer and closer to Hitler's Germany. When Mussolini sent Delbos a special message in January 1937 hinting at rapprochement Delbos backed Blum when he replied that the best way for Italy to improve Franco–Italian relations would be to honour the Non-Intervention Agreement.[57] The French government continued to oppose *de jure* recognition of the Italian conquest of Abyssinia and Delbos' attitude in this matter hardened considerably during the summer of 1937.[58] The Nyon conference and its aftermath further highlighted his animosity towards Italy and it was hardly surprising that anti-French feeling should grow in Italy. The British ambassador at Rome, Lord Perth, was moved to observe in October 1937 that "mutual distrust and dislike are an almost constant factor in Franco-Italian relations."[59] When Delbos and Chautemps visited London at the end of November 1937 they showed, according to Eden, "more signs of irritation" over Italy "than on any other subject."[60]

Eden's perception of Mussolini's Italy was no less critical than Delbos'. At the beginning of the negotiations for what became the Gentlemen's Agreement between Britain and Italy Eden asked a pertinent question: "Does anyone in the Foreign Office really believe that Italy's foreign policy will at any time be other than opportunist? Any agreement with Italy will be kept as long as it suits Italy. Surely nobody can now place any faith in her promise." However, at this stage, the foreign secretary believed it was still worth pursuing an improvement in Anglo-Italian relations but he counselled against "placing an exaggerated valuation on any such improvement if and when we get it."[61] This was wise advice and Italy's further intervention in Spain—in contravention of the Non-Intervention Agreement 15,000 Italian troops were sent to assist Franco in late December 1936 and early January 1937 and by the end of February there were some 50,000 in Spain[62]—put the Gentleman's Agreement, signed on 2 January 1937, into perspective. In contrast to Italian perfidy, the French government, according to Eden, had "behaved very well, and I have been repaid for keeping Delbos informed . . . by an excellent message of goodwill which Delbos gave the French Press."[63]

Henceforth, Eden demonstrated no particular hurry to improve Anglo–Italian relations to the chagrin of Chamberlain who within two months of becoming prime minister in May 1937 took the extraordinary step of writing to Mussolini without first consulting his foreign secretary and using his sister-in-law, Austen Chamberlain's widow, as an intermediary in Rome.[64] Unfortunately for Chamberlain, Italy's actions in the Mediterranean in the summer of 1937 and the resulting Nyon Conference set back his initiative and made starting conversations between London and Rome much more problematic for several months. By the autumn of 1937, Eden was openly disagreeing with the prime minister and other senior colleagues, including his predecessor as foreign secretary, Sir Samuel Hoare, who were prepared to turn a blind eye to Italy's activities in the Mediterranean and Spain, so anxious were they to get conversations started.[65] Eden was clearly bemused by this attitude. He told his private secretary, Oliver Harvey, that he believed Chamberlain "*au fond* had a certain sympathy for dictators whose efficiency appealed to him" and that the prime minister "really believed it would be possible to get an agreement with Muss[olini] by running after him."[66]

Italy's adhesion to the Anti-Comintern Pact and her exit from the League of Nations in late 1937 reinforced Eden's scepticism. He continued to maintain his view of the limited value of an Anglo–Italian rapprochement into the New Year and it was only reinforced when Chamberlain finally lost patience in February 1938 and insisted on opening conversations with the Italians, accusing Eden and the Foreign Office along the way of missing chance after chance to secure an agreement with Italy. Eden believed that the timing was wrong and countered that the Italians had to make prior concessions as an act of good faith, such as the withdrawal of Italian "volunteers" from Spain and clarifying their passive attitude with regard to events developing in Austria, before conceding conversations, which everyone involved knew would inevitably result in an agreement under which Britain would have to recognize the Italian annexation of Ethiopia. Chamberlain was not prepared to ask for prior concessions and wanted conversations to begin immediately. As a result, Eden resigned.[67]

Delbos, as noted previously, was shocked by the foreign secretary's exit. While he did not wish to take the initiative for a rapprochement with Italy he did not oppose Chamberlain's efforts or those of Eden's successor, Lord Halifax. On 25 February 1938, five days after Eden's resignation, he told the Chamber of Deputies that he agreed with Chamberlain's approach but he also declared, echoing Eden, that a final liquidation of the Abyssinian question would be possible only if an end was put to the despatch of Italian men and arms to Spain and anti-French propaganda ceased.[68] The French foreign minister clearly had not altered his position which was in tune with Eden's thinking prior to his resignation. The congruence of Delbos' and Eden's views on Mussolini's Italy did not, of course, result in a convergence of French and British policy. France showed no inclination to follow the British lead after the Anglo–Italian Agreement was signed in April 1938. Indeed, when Alfred Duff Cooper, the British first lord of the admiralty, visited Paris during Easter he found great scepticism among French ministers as to the value of the agreement in view of Italy's past betrayal of agreements and allies. Edouard Daladier, who had just become prime minister, went so far as to argue that the British government had saved Mussolini from disaster following his passive response to the German annexation of Austria in March.[69] As predicted by Eden, the Anglo–Italian Agreement proved of little value to British interests. Italy's Pact of Steel with Germany of May 1939 meant far more to Mussolini than did the Anglo–Italian Agreement.

Both Delbos and Eden viewed the appeasement of Germany far more seriously than they did the appeasement of Italy. Chautemps told Eden at Geneva in January 1938 that while the one question mark with regard to the European situation generally was Mussolini, Germany was the real problem and he and Delbos both stressed that no effort "should be spared to improve relations with Berlin."[70] In their respective foreign policy statements on 23 June 1936 Delbos told the Chamber and Blum told the Senate that "the *Rassemblement populaire* have always fought for a Franco–German entente."[71] Eden had been more than ready to make the concession of recognizing Hitler's "illegal" rearmament and of permitting the remilitarization of the Rhineland prior to the Führer's decision to pre-empt the latter on 7 March 1936.[72] From the inception of the Popular Front government, Delbos and Eden worked closely to persuade Germany and Italy to enter a five power pact (to also include Belgium) to replace the Rhineland pact of Locarno; unfortunately with no success.[73] At the same time, Blum and Delbos readily entered talks with the German economics minister, Hjalmar Schacht, in August 1936 and, assured that he was acting with Hitler's authority, conceded further talks on the subject of colonial restitution to the Third Reich provided colonial concessions were part of a wider European settlement.[74] Eden, who had publicly disclaimed in the House of Commons in late July 1936 any intention to discuss the colonial question, was not best pleased.[75] He told Blum on 20 September that Britain's position on colonial appeasement remained as stated in his July speech and he reiterated his belief to Delbos on 23 September that a five power conference was the most suitable instrument for achieving a European settlement.[76] Confronted with this British reluctance to disturb the diplomatic process surrounding the five power initiative and disturbed by increasing German intervention in Spain, Delbos and Blum decided not to pursue discussions on the Schacht initiative. Indeed, when he saw Eden in Paris on 9 October, Delbos concurred in his view that "there were moments when to show a certain stiffness was the best way to promote agreement."[77]

The Foreign Office remained ambivalent about colonial appeasement but by February 1937, with discussions on the five power conference permanently stalled, Eden wished to pursue the alternative of negotiations for a general settlement based on the Schacht initiative. Moreover, he was anxious to forestall a French suggestion for a Franco–British–American initiative, which included colonial restitution, to meet Germany's economic difficulties.[78] For the next four months Eden and the Cabinet Foreign

Policy Committee discussed at great length how they might appease Germany by means of colonial concessions.[79] Eventually, they concluded that colonial revision was possible provided Britain herself and her Dominions were not required to make any territorial sacrifices. They did not expect Belgium or Portugal to make any either, only France. Unsurprisingly, Delbos and Blum were less than keen to consider the cession of the French colonial mandates (Cameroons and Togoland) because, as Delbos surmised, it would "raise a storm in French public opinion and cause an outburst against Great Britain." He was also opposed to the transfer on strategic grounds as it would place "French North Africa, from the air, between Germany and the Cameroons." Delbos and Blum were only willing to consider the cession of the Cameroons and Togoland to Germany as part of a final general settlement, but they would only do so if the British made at least as great a territorial sacrifice.[80] As this was not possible the prospects for colonial appeasement on the basis of the Schacht initiative were eventually extinguished.

None the less, colonial restitution remained the best means of reaching a general settlement with Germany, particularly after Lord Halifax's visit to Berlin in November 1937. When Delbos and Chautemps met Eden and Chamberlain in London at the end of the month it was clear that the British ministers saw colonies as the way forward. Eden and Chamberlain agreed with Delbos that no negotiations on colonies would take place before a discussion of the other elements of a general settlement—disarmament, Germany's return to the League of Nations and the conclusion of a western pact. Directly following the conversations it was announced publicly for the first time that the British and French governments were prepared to study the colonial question.[81]

By the end of 1937, in contrast to Delbos and the Quai d'Orsay, Eden and his officials had developed a sense of urgency. The foreign secretary stressed to the Foreign Policy Committee on 1 January 1938 that a long delay should be avoided "to prevent the hopes created by the recent conversations from evaporating."[82] Chamberlain was in complete agreement with Eden and both recognized the importance of connecting colonial revision to general appeasement in Europe. They also agreed that exploratory talks with the German government should precede concrete proposals. Eden and the Foreign Office prepared instructions for the British ambassador at Berlin, Sir Nevile Henderson.[83] Delbos was informed on 17 February of the British intention to begin exploratory talks with Hitler and Eden reassured him that no proposals would be put forward which did not involve an equivalent contribution from Britain to any made by the French. In view of the developing crisis in Austria, Delbos was unimpressed and warned that by merely taking soundings on the colonial question Germany would be given the impression that "Great Britain and

France were unduly weak and unduly impressed by German violence."[84] Three days later, Eden resigned as foreign secretary and when Henderson saw Hitler two weeks after on 3 March 1938 the Führer explicitly expressed his disinterest in colonial appeasement in the short term.[85] Hitler's attitude came as no surprise to Delbos who by the end of 1937, unlike Eden, had reached the conclusion that Germany had no intention of agreeing to a general settlement. He had been helped in reaching this conclusion by a conversation he had had with the German foreign minister, Constantin von Neurath, while travelling through Berlin by train as part of his eastern tour. Delbos asked a pertinent question. Why did Germany always seem to resent any suggestion of a general settlement? Neurath's reply that "the right method was to settle matters bit by bit" confirmed the French foreign minister in his belief that a general settlement with Germany was unattainable. As a result, he also concluded that faced with the threat of Germany's increasing power it was essential for France to revitalize its security system in eastern Europe.[86] The annexation of Austria just days before Delbos' own resignation and the subsequent crises over Czechoslovakia made that task virtually impossible.

The Anglo–French search for a general European settlement with Germany was, of course, doomed to fail because of Hitler's hegemonic ambitions. As Delbos recognized, there was a risk in entering conversations with Hitler without close cooperation between London and Paris and he warned Phipps in late April 1937 that even with such cooperation "any far reaching tête-à-tête with Berlin would be certainly dangerous and might be fatal."[87] In view of the growing fascist challenge, it was fortunate that there was much improvement in Anglo–French relations during the Delbos-Eden period despite British concerns about domestic developments within France, the weakness of the French economy, as shown by the flight of capital and the devaluation of the franc, and the retardation of French rearmament.[88] In July 1937, for example, Eden was moved to declare in the House of Commons that "one of the facts which have enabled us to pass through the last twelve months without the major disaster of a European War has been the steadily growing confidence and intimacy of the relations between our two countries."[89] Yet, there remained no prospect of the Anglo–French entente becoming a fully developed alliance. The British defence review completed during the last three months of 1937 placed the continental commitment last in order of priority, well behind the defence of the United Kingdom, defence of trade routes and imperial lines of communication and defence of the British empire. While Delbos would not have disputed these priorities, he still expected British support for French security. In December 1936 in a speech to the Chamber of Deputies he had declared that France would come to the assistance of Britain and Belgium if they were the victims of unprovoked aggression.[90]

But there was an expectation of reciprocity so that in January 1937 at Geneva he told Eden that what France looked for from Great Britain, apart from the Navy, was a large and imposing air force as a deterrent and that as far as the army was concerned the contribution that would be most useful would be a "small but powerful and highly mechanised force, even if there were only two divisions of it." What was required was "concentrated striking power rather than mass."[91] For his part, Eden agreed with Vansittart in December 1937 that while the air defence of the United Kingdom was the first priority, if France (and the Low Countries) were overrun Britain's position would be impossible "no matter how densely we had packed this country with anti-aircraft guns and no matter how many Fighter Squadrons we had constructed."[92] The prospects of a British expeditionary force, no matter how small, were extremely unlikely during the period that Eden and Delbos remained at their posts. By the time the British alliance was secured by France in February-March 1939 with its promise of an expeditionary force, Eden and Delbos no longer wielded influence on the respective policies of their governments.

NOTES

1. Robert Young, *In Command of France: French Foreign Policy and Military Planning, 1933–1940* (Cambridge MA: Harvard University Press, 1978), p. 132. Both Delbos and Eden served in the First World War when the former was wounded twice and the latter won the Military Cross.
2. Lord Avon, *The Eden Memoirs: Facing the Dictators* (London: Cassell, 1962), p. 372.
3. Eden to the Foreign Office, 26 June 1936. Avon Papers, FO 954 (located at the Library of the University of Birmingham), FR/36/13.
4. Avon, *Facing the Dictators*, p. 430.
5. John Dreifort, *Yvon Delbos and the Quai d'Orsay: French Foreign Policy during the Popular Front, 1936–1938* (Lawrence KS: University Press of Kansas, 1973), p. 84.
6. Ibid., p. 187.
7. Ibid., p. 101.
8. Ibid., pp. 105–7. See also Nicole Jordan, *The Popular Front and Central Europe: The Dilemmas of French Impotence, 1918–1940* (Cambridge: Cambridge University Press, 1992), pp. 29–31, 36–40.
9. Viscount Chilston, British ambassador at Moscow, to Sir John Simon, secretary of state for foreign affairs, 30 March 1935. *Documents on British Foreign Policy, 1919–1939*, 2nd series, vol. XII, nos. 669, 670, pp. 766–9. Hereafter DBFP. See also Avon, *Facing the Dictators*, pp. 152–3.
10. Robert Manne, "The Foreign Office and the Failure of Anglo-Soviet Rapprochement," *Journal of Contemporary History*, 16/4 (1981), p. 743.

11. Ibid., p. 749. See also Michael Roi, *Alternative to Appeasement: Sir Robert Vansittart and Alliance Diplomacy, 1934–1937* (Westport, Conn: Praeger, 1997), pp. 105–7.

12. The National Archives, Kew, London (formerly the Public Record Office). Hereafter TNA (PRO). CAB 23/83 CM 6(36). Eden told his Cabinet colleagues that during his recent visit to attend King George V's funeral the French Prime Minister, Pierre Etienne Flandin, had informed him of the French intention to ratify the Franco–Soviet Pact and he had declined to give an opinion.

13. See Peter Jackson, "French Strategy and the Spanish Civil War" in Christian Leitz and David Dunthorn (Eds.), *Spain in an International Context, 1936–1959* (Oxford: Berghahn, 1999), pp. 60–1 and Jordan, *The Popular Front and Central Europe*, pp. 208–9.

14. Young, *In Command of France*, pp. 145–7. Martin Alexander, *The Republic in Danger: General Maurice Gamelin and the Politics of French Defence, 1933–1940* (Cambridge: Cambridge University Press, 1992), pp. 292–3. Anthony Adamthwaite, *Grandeur and Misery: France's Bid for Power in Europe, 1914–1940* (London: Arnold, 1995), p. 208. Patrice Buffotot, "The French High Command and the Franco–Soviet Alliance, 1933–1939," *Journal of Strategic Studies*, 5/4 (1982), pp. 549–51. Michael Carley, "Prelude to Defeat: Franco–Soviet Relations, 1919–1939" in Joel Blatt (ed.), *The French Defeat of 1940: Reassessments* (Oxford: Berghahn, 1998), p. 193.

15. James Herndon, "British Perceptions of Soviet Military Capability, 1935–1939" in Wolfgang Mommsen and Lothar Kettenacker (Eds.), *The Fascist Challenge and the Policy of Appeasement* (London: Allen and Unwin, 1983), p. 302.

16. For details of Soviet intervention in the Spanish Civil War see Glyn Stone, *Spain, Portugal and the Great Powers, 1931–1941* (Basingstoke: Palgrave Macmillan, 2005), pp. 40–50.

17. Carley, "Prelude to Defeat," p. 95. Glyn Stone, "Sir Robert Vansittart and Spain, 1931–1941" in Thomas Otte and Constantine Pagedas (Eds.), *Personalities, War and Diplomacy: Essays in International History* (London: Frank Cass, 1997), pp. 137–8.

18. *Hansard Parliamentary Debates*, 5th series, HC, vol. 317, c. 1923.

19. Foreign Office Memorandum: Summary of Recent Correspondence on the Value of the Franco–Soviet Pact, 27 May 1937. TNA (PRO), FO 371/21095, N3129/45/38.

20. Conclusions of an exchange of views between Delbos and Eden, 15 May 1937. *Documents Diplomatiques Français, 1932–1939*, 2nd series, vol. V, no. 429, p. 427. Hereafter DDF. "Extract from a record of conversation at a lunch given by the Secretary of State to M.M. Delbos and Léger, 15 May 1937." TNA (PRO) FO 371/20702, C3685/532/62. Incomplete memorandum relating to a discussion between Eden and Delbos with regard to the Franco–Soviet Pact, n..d. The Avon Papers, FO 954 FR/37/23. See also John Dreifort, "The French Popular Front and the Franco–Soviet Pact," *Journal of Contemporary History*, 11/2 and 3 (1976), pp. 222–5.

21. René Girault and Robert Frank, *Turbulente Europe et Nouveaux Mondes: Histoire des Relations Internationales Contemporaines Vol. II: 1914–1941* (Paris: Masson, 1988), pp. 214–15.

22. Delbos to Robert Coulondre, French Ambassador at Moscow, 22 Jan. 1938. DDF, 2nd series, vol. VIII, no. 19, pp. 38–9. See also, John Herman, *The Paris Embassy of Sir Eric Phipps: Anglo–French Relations and the Foreign Office, 1937–1939* (Brighton: Sussex Academic Press, 1998), p. 67. In addition, see Chamberlain's admonishment to his sister on 20 March 1938 of "the Russians [who were] stealthily and cunningly pulling all the strings behind the scenes to get us involved in war with Germany (our Secret Service doesn't spend all its time looking out of windows)." Chamberlain to Ida Chamberlain, 20 March 1938. Neville Chamberlain Papers (located at Birmingham University Library), NC18/1/1042.

23. Phipps to Eden, 16 Feb. 1938. Avon Papers, FO 954 FR/38/5.

24. Stone, *Spain, Portugal and the Great Powers*, pp. 51–2.

25. Glyn Stone, "Britain, France and the Spanish Problem, 1936–1939" in Dick Richardson and Glyn Stone (Eds.), *Decisions and Diplomacy: Essays in Twentieth Century International History* (London: Routledge, 1995), p. 131.

26. For a discussion see Jordan, *The Popular Front and Central Europe*, pp. 208–9; Young, *In Command of France*, pp. 139–41; Dreifort, *Yvon Delbos*, pp. 38–43; David Carlton, "Eden, Blum and the Origins of Non-Intervention," *Journal of Contemporary History*, 6/3 (1971), pp. 46–7; and Haywood Hunt, "The French Radicals, Spain and the Emergence of Appeasement" in Martin Alexander and Helen Graham (Eds.), *The French and Spanish Popular Fronts: Comparative Perspectives*, Cambridge: Cambridge University Press, 1989, pp. 38–49.

27. Dreifort, *Yvon Delbos*, pp. 40–1. Jean Baptiste Duroselle, *La Décadence, 1932–1939: Politique Etrangère de la France* (Paris: Imprimerie Nationale, 1979), pp. 302, 304.

28. Thomas Jones, *A Diary with Letters, 1931–1950* (London: Oxford University Press, 1954), diary entry, 27 July 1936, p. 231. Jones was a former high civil servant and close confidant of leading politicians including four prime ministers: David Lloyd George, Andrew Bonar Law, Stanley Baldwin, and Ramsay MacDonald.

29. Delbos to Diplomatic Representatives in London, Rome and Brussels, 2 Aug. 1936. DDF, 2nd series, vol. III, no. 59, pp. 100–1. Elizabeth Cameron, "Alexis Saint-Léger Léger" in Gordon Craig and Felix Gilbert (Eds.), *The Diplomats, 1919–1939: Volume 2: The Thirties* (New York: Atheneum, 1974), p. 391.

30. See Glyn Stone, "Britain. Non-Intervention and the Spanish Civil War," *European Studies Review*, 9/1 (1979), pp. 138–41. Before departing for Yorkshire Eden arranged for all important papers on Spain to be sent to him and he kept in touch with the Foreign Office by telephone while away. Avon, *Facing the Dictators*, p. 401.

31. Stone, "Britain, Non-Intervention and the Spanish Civil War," pp. 139–41.

32. Charles Corbin, French ambassador at London, to Delbos, 24 August 1936. DDF, 2nd series, vol. III, no. 197, p. 276. Eden to Sir George Clerk, British Ambassador at Paris, 24 Aug. 1936. DBFP, 2nd series, vol. XVII, no. 128, p. 161. According to Eden, the French government attached great importance to the Committee's location in London because "to be frank, they felt that our capital was more neutral than the capitals of any of the other great Powers in this difficult business."

33. Clerk to the Foreign Office, 28 Aug. 1936. TNA (PRO), FO 371/20573 W9986/9549/41.

34. Jill Edwards, *The British Government and the Spanish Civil War, 1936–1939* (London: Macmillan, 1979), pp. 184–6. Duroselle, *La Décadence*, pp. 318–20.

35. See Stone, *Spain, Portugal and the Great Powers*, pp. 78–9.

36. Hugh Thomas, *The Spanish Civil War* (London: Penguin, 3rd edition, 1977), p. 685. Baron Constantin von Neurath, German foreign minister, to the German embassies at London, Paris and Rome, 19 June 1937. *Documents on German Foreign Policy, 1918–1945*, series D, vol. III, no. 339, pp. 354–6. Hereafter DGFP. The permanent under secretary at the Foreign Office, Sir Robert Vansittart, told the Labour MP, Hugh Dalton, on 24 June that he was extremely doubtful whether any torpedo had been fired at the *Leipzig* and the Admiralty shared his opinion. Dalton Diaries (located at the Library of the London School of Economics and Political Science), 1.18, diary entry, 24 June 1937.

37. Stone, *Spain, Portugal and the Great Powers*, pp. 81–3.

38. For details of the Italian submarine attacks see John Coverdale, *Italian Intervention in the Spanish Civil War* (Princeton, NJ: Princeton University Press, 1975), pp. 306–8, 311–13 and Reynolds Salerno, "Britain, France and the Emerging Italian Threat" in Martin Alexander and William Philpott (Eds.), *Anglo–French Defence Relations between the Wars* (Basingstoke: Palgrave Macmillan, 2002), pp. 79–81. See also Malcolm Muggeridge (Ed.), *Ciano's Hidden Diary, 1937–1938* (New York: Dutton, 1953), diary entries 23 and 31 Aug., 2 and 4 Sept. 1937, pp. 3, 6–9.

39. Note communicated by the French chargé d'affaires [Roger Cambon] at London, 30 Aug. 1937. TNA (PRO), CAB 24/271 CP 208(37).

40. "Comments made by Eden on the Note communicated by the French chargé d'affaires on 30 August 1937," 1 Sept. 1937. "Record by Eden of a [telephone] conversation with Chamberlain," 1 Sept. 1937. "Extracts from draft notes of a meeting of Ministers," 2 Sept. 1937. DBFP, 2nd series, vol. XIX, nos. 110, 111, 114, pp. 203–6, 211–18. See also TNA (PRO) CAB 24/271 CP 208(37).

41. The Italian foreign minister, Galeazzo Ciano, was jubilant at the eventual outcome of the conference: "From suspected pirates to policemen of the Mediterranean and the Russians whose ships we were sinking, excluded." Muggeridge (ed.), *Ciano's Hidden Diary, 1937–1938*, diary entry, 21 Sept. 1937, p. 17.

42. Alan John Patrick Taylor, *The Origins of the Second World War* (London: Penguin, 2nd edition, 1963), p. 163. Louis Fischer, *Men and Politics: An Autobiography* (London: Jonathan Cape, 1941), p. 421.

43. Reynolds Salerno, *Vital Crossroads: Mediterranean Origins of the Second World War, 1935–1940* (Ithaca, NY: Cornell University Press, 2002) pp. 28–9.

44. Michael Alpert, *A New International History of the Spanish Civil War* (London: Macmillan, 1994), p. 145.

45. See Stone, "Sir Robert Vansittart and Spain," pp. 144–5.

46. TNA (PRO) CAB 23/89 CM 35(37), 29 Sept. 1937.

47. TNA (PRO), CAB23/89 CM 37(37), 13 Oct. 1937. Unpublished [Sir Alexander] Cadogan Diaries (located at the Churchill College Archive Centre, Cambridge), entries 22 and 28 Sept. 1937. Minute by Sir Orme Sargent, 12 Oct. 1937 and

Phipps to Eden, 20 Oct. 1937, Phipps Papers (located at the Churchill College Archive Centre, Cambridge), PHPP 1/19. John Harvey (Ed.), *The Diplomatic Diaries of Oliver Harvey, 1937–1940* (London: Collins, 1970), diary entry, 5 Oct. 1937, pp. 49–50. Oliver Harvey was private secretary to Eden and his successor, Lord Halifax.

48. Record of conversations between British and French Ministers, 29–30 Nov. 1937. DBFP, 2nd series, vol. XIX, no. 354, p. 614.

49. Chamberlain to Ida Chamberlain, 4 July 1937. Neville Chamberlain Papers, NC 18/1/1010.

50. William Bullitt to Secretary of State Cordell Hull, 26 Aug. 1937. *Foreign Relations of the United States*, 1937, vol. I, p. 118.

51. Memorandum by Eden on Spain and the Balearic Islands, 14 Dec. 1936. DBFP, 2nd series, vol. XVII, no. 471, pp. 677–84.

52. Young, *In Command of France*, pp. 137–8. Young also stresses that Italian and German air bases on the Balearics and Canaries respectively would severely impair "the ease with which Britain and France could coordinate the operations of the Mediterranean and Atlantic fleets."

53. Sir Orme Sargent, assistant under secretary at the Foreign Office, to Phipps, 15 Oct. 1937. Phipps Papers, PHPP II 2/1. See also Martin Thomas, *Britain, France and Appeasement: Anglo–French Relations in the Popular Front Era* (Oxford: Berg, 1996), p. 218.

54. Minute by Orme Sargent of his meeting with Roger Cambon, French chargé d'affaires at London, 12 October 1937. Phipps Papers, PHPP 1/19. According to Oliver Harvey, the "idea of a temporary occupation of Minorca in conjunction with the French coupled with an offer of international neutralisation" appealed to Eden. Harvey (Ed.), *Diplomatic Diaries*, diary entry, 15 Oct. 1937, p. 51.

55. In early October 1937 Vansittart commented on a report by the Chiefs of Staff Sub-Committee on Anglo–Italian Relations, 29 Sept. 1937 that: "I have always regarded it as a minimum that we should get the Italians out of the Balearic Islands. The Chiefs of Staff dismiss the necessity. I stand corrected but unrepentant. It is the Chiefs of Staff who will one day be repentant if we don't . . . If we are ever engaged in a struggle for existence, it will almost certainly be on the same side as France. What weakens France therefore impairs our own chances of survival. . . . If therefore France's position is endangered by our failure to get the Italians out of the Balearic Islands or the Spanish mainland, we stand to lose." DBFP, 2nd series, vol. XIX, no. 209, pp. 350–1.

56. Dreifort, *Yvon Delbos*, pp. 154–5.

57. Ibid., pp. 155–6.

58. Thomas, *Britain, France and Appeasement*, p. 214.

59. Perth to Eden, 22 Oct. 1937. TNA (PRO), FO 371/21182, R7066/2143/22.

60. TNA (PRO), CAB 23/90A CM 45(37), 1 Dec. 1937.

61. Minute by Eden, 5 Nov. 1936. DBFP, 2nd series, vol. XVII, no. 352, pp. 513–14.

62. Stone, *Spain, Portugal and the Great Powers*, p. 39.

63. Avon Papers, diary entry, 4 Jan. 1937, AP20/1/1–17.

64. Chamberlain to Mussolini, 27 July 1937. DBFP, 2nd series, vol. XIX, no. 65, pp. 119–20. The prime minister's letter was a response to a message from

Mussolini, conveyed by the Italian ambassador at London, Dino Grandi, the same day. See DBFP, 2nd series, vol. XIX, no. 64, pp. 118–19.

65. See, for example, TNA (PRO), CAB 23/89 CM 37(37), 13 Oct. 1937.

66. Harvey (ed.), *Diplomatic Diaries*, diary entry, 22 Sept. 1937, p. 48.

67. See Avon Papers, AP 20/1/18 diary entry, 17 Feb. 1938; Harvey (Ed.), *Diplomatic Diaries*, diary entries, 17–20 Febraury 1938, pp. 92–7; TNA (PRO), CAB 23/92 CM 6–7(38), 19–20 Feb. 1938.

68. Dreifort, *Yvon Delbos*, p. 158.

69. Alfred Duff Cooper, *Old Men Forget* (London: Hart Davis, 1953), p. 219.

70. Mr Edmond, Geneva, to the Foreign Office, 26 Jan. 1938. DBFP, 2nd series, vol. XIX, no. 473, p. 819.

71. Dreifort, *Yvon Delbos*, pp. 159–60.

72. Anthony Peters, *Anthony Eden and the Foreign Office, 1931–1938* (Aldershot: Gower, 1986), pp. 173–7.

73. See William Norton Medlicott, *Britain and Germany: The Search for Agreement, 1931–1937* (London: Athlone Press, 1969), pp. 25–32.

74. André François-Poncet, French ambassador at Berlin, to Delbos, 24 August 1936. Meeting between Léon Blum and Hjalmar Schacht at the Hotel Matignon, 28 August 1936. DDF, 2nd series, vol. III, nos. 196, 213, pp. 275, 307–11.

75. *Hansard Parliamentary Debates*, 5th series, HC, vol. 315, cc. 1131–2.

76. Sir George Clerk, British ambassador at Paris, to the Foreign Office, 20 Sept. 1936. DBFP, 2nd series, vol. XVII, nos. 210, 211, pp. 286–90. Eden to Delbos, 23 Sept. 1936. Avon Papers, FO 954, FR/36/25.

77. Minute by Eden, 10 Oct. 1936. Avon Papers FO 954 FR/36/34. See also Dreifort, *Yvon Delbos*, pp. 168–9.

78. Record by Orme Sargent of a Meeting on 18 Jan. 1937. DBFP, 2nd series, vol. XVIII, no. 86, pp. 112–14. See also Andrew Crozier, "Prelude to Munich: British Foreign Policy and Germany, 1935–1938," *European Studies Review*, 6/3 (1976), p. 366.

79. See the 7th, 8th, 10th and 11th meetings of the Foreign Policy Committee, 18 March 1937, 6 April 1937, 10 May 1937, 19 May 1937. TNA (PRO), CAB 27/622.

80. Phipps to Eden, 4 May 1937. DBFP, 2nd series, vol. XVIII, no. 462, pp. 701–3. See also Phipps to Orme Sargent, 6 May 1937. TNA (PRO), FO 800/274.

81. "Visit of the French Ministers to London, 29–30 Nov.1937: Memorandum by Eden," 6 Dec. 1937. TNA (PRO), CAB 27/626 FP (36) 40. DDF, 2nd series, vol. VII, nos. 287, 291, 297, pp. 518–45, 554, 573–4. See also Andrew Crozier, "Imperial Decline and the Colonial Question in Anglo-German Relations, 1919–1939," *European Studies Review*, 11/2 (1981), pp. 231–2.

82. "The Next Steps towards a General Settlement with Germany: Memorandum by the Secretary of State for Foreign Affairs," 1 Jan. 1938. TNA (PRO), CAB 27/626 FP (36)41.

83. TNA (PRO), CAB 27/623 FP (36) 21st meeting, 24 Jan. 1938 and 22nd meeting, 3 Feb. 1938. CAB 23/92 CM 4 (38), 9 Feb. 1938. Eden to Henderson, 12 Feb. 1938. DBFP 2nd series, vol. XIX, no. 512, pp. 890–2.

84. Eden to Phipps, 14 Feb. 1938 and Phipps to Eden, 17 Feb. 1938. DBFP, 2nd series, vol. XIX, nos. 515, 541, pp. 894, 914–15.

85. Joachim von Ribbentrop, German foreign minister, to Nevile Henderson, 4 March 1938. DGFP, series D, vol. I, no. 138, pp. 240–9.
86. Phipps to Eden, 20 December 1937. Phipps Papers, PHPP 1/19. See also Drei-fort, *Yvon Delbos*, pp. 141–2. According to Georges Bonnet, writing in retro-spect, Delbos, contrary to his intentions, was not prepared to make any firm commitments to Czechoslovakia during his last weeks as foreign minister. Indeed, following a hearing of the Senate Foreign Affairs Committee of 2 March 1938, Delbos refused to include in his communiqué a reaffirmation that France would be loyal to its commitments. See Georges Bonnet, *Quai d'Orsay* (Isle of Man: Times Press, 1965), p. 159. See also Girault and Frank, *Turbulente Europe II*, p. 231.
87. Phipps to Eden, 2 May 1937. Phipps Papers, PHPP 1/19.
88. See Michael Dockrill, *British Establishment Perspectives on France, 1936–1940* (Basingstoke: Macmillan, 1999) pp. 69–76.
89. *Hansard Parliamentary Debates*, 5th series, HC, vol. 326, c. 1805.
90. Dockrill, *British Establishment Perspectives*, p. 49.
91. Eden to the Foreign Office, 22 Jan. 1937. Avon Papers, FO 954 FR/37/3. See also Dockrill, *British Establishment Perspectives*, p. 58.
92. Vansittart to Eden, 17 Dec. 1937. Avon Papers, FO 954 FP/37/20.

"A VERY GREAT CLERK": SIR RONALD CAMPBELL AND THE FALL OF FRANCE, MAY–JUNE 1940[1]

Christopher Baxter

During an attack on Britain's European policy in 1994, Alan Clark, the former British defence minister, claimed that any attempt to describe twentieth-century Franco-British relations as cordial was "wholly invalid." As part of his case he focused on the fall of France in 1940, claiming that the French Army "ran away at Sedan" while its government made a separate peace with Germany, "in breach of solemn and repeated undertakings" to the British.[2] In early 2003, during the lead up to the Iraq War, sections of the British press largely condemned the French stance towards the crisis, invoking once more images of their treachery, the defeat of 1940 and Vichy.[3] Are such outbursts justified? One person who was able to assess the traumatic events of 1940 at first hand while also providing advice to London was the British ambassador to France, Sir Ronald Campbell. Campbell was a career diplomat: he had entered the Foreign Office in 1907, and was well equipped to assess the French political scene, having attended the Paris Peace Conference in 1919 while subsequently serving as minister to the British Embassy in Paris between 1929 and 1935. Campbell, having served as legation head at Belgrade, returned to France as ambassador at the age of 57, replacing Sir Eric Phipps, who retired in October 1939.

Phipps had lost the confidence of many in the Foreign Office after his poor performance during the Munich crisis. As early as November 1938, both Sir Alexander Cadogan, the permanent under secretary at the Foreign Office, and Oliver Harvey, private secretary to foreign secretary Lord Halifax, argued that Campbell should replace Phipps.[4] However, Halifax postponed the early appointment of Campbell until the autumn of 1939, and was ready to defer his posting once more when war was declared. It was understandable that Halifax considered it unwise to change ambassadors at the outbreak of war but there is a suspicion that other factors played a part in his decision-making. In May 1939, responding to Phipps's decision to retire later that September, Halifax conceded that Campbell was "a very suitable successor," but the foreign secretary confessed he would miss the current ambassador's "unique knowledge of France." Halifax was confident that Campbell would "adequately" fill his place but such anodyne language did not confer a ringing endorsement upon Phipps's successor.[5] There was no doubt that Campbell was a hard working and determined man but his persona was not particularly notable. He had an unfortunate reputation of being "diffident," "dull," and "outwardly stiff," which tended to hamper his ability to mix well in social circles. For a man who could at best be described as "a very great clerk," and one readily unsuited to the challenge of total war, Campbell's arrival in Paris was worrying.[6]

When Campbell arrived in France he had been away from the French political scene for four years and unlike his American counterpart, William Bullitt, did not have the time to nurture a close relationship with the French premier, Edouard Daladier, who resigned in March 1940. Sir Ronald therefore failed to realise that Daladier had become worn and discouraged. Bullitt's anti-British bias and passionate Francophilia could not have helped the ambassador's cause either.[7] Campbell, as well as senior Foreign Office officials, did not particularly welcome Daladier's successor, Paul Reynaud. Although, as Campbell remarked, Reynaud was sharp-witted and "brilliantly clever," he was also "superficial" while Halifax thought him "a light-weight."[8] Reynaud had a majority of just one vote, with the Right and Centre firmly ranged against him, forcing the new French premier to give posts to many whose commitment to the war was lukewarm.[9] As a consequence, Campbell told Halifax, Reynaud was impulsive due to a constant desire to protect his own position.[10]

The cracks quickly became apparent just days after German forces invaded France on 10 May, leading Reynaud to reshuffle his Cabinet. In a despatch to London, Campbell reported that most French ministers were "suffering under the unexpectedness of the blow" in the same way as French troops went down under the first shock of the German onslaught.

Campbell concluded, "Alas, there is no [Georges] Clemenceau."[11] However, Campbell welcomed the appointment of Marshal Philippe Pétain as vice president of the council and the announcement of General Maxime Weygand as the new commander-in-chief of the French Army. The arrival of these respected First World War figures on 18–19 May, heralded a surge of enthusiasm in France.[12] But the alarm bells had rung in the Embassy with the arrival of François Charles-Roux as secretary general to the Quai d'Orsay; "a wild appeaser" according to Oliver Harvey, who was now British minister at Paris. There were suggestions that less savoury elements, such as Reynaud's mistress, Hélène, Comtesse de Portes, and his *Chef de Cabinet*, Paul Baudouin, had lobbied for Charles-Roux's appointment.[13] Both Harvey and Campbell were aware of the defeatist de Portes and her connection with Baudouin and anti-war circles.[14] And, within ten days of Reynaud's reshuffle, Campbell quickly reassessed his opinion of Pétain and Weygand, informing London that both men offered little but the impression that the situation was "hopeless." Campbell's reports alerted the British government to a growing defeatist element while the latter was already considering possible courses in the event of France's collapse.[15]

The disorder that Winston Churchill, the recently appointed British prime minister, found in the capital during his urgent visit to Paris on 15 May, had led him to approve Campbell's plans to evacuate the female members of the Embassy. But, the prime minister's attempt to console Lady Campbell by suggesting that, "This place will shortly become a charnel house," was hardly calculated to cheer Sir Ronald's wife as they said goodbye to each other.[16] Churchill was also about to introduce a potentially troublesome figure on to the scene. He had asked his old friend, Major General Sir Edward Spears, who had served as liaison officer between the French and British armies during the First World War, to become his personal representative to Reynaud.[17] Spears had a short temper and was touchy about any assumptions of French superiority. His appointment caused disquiet in the Embassy.[18] Aware that he was encroaching on Campbell's responsibilities, when he arrived in France on 25 May, Spears set out at once to see the ambassador to explain that he was concerned only with Reynaud in the latter's new capacity as minister of defence. Spears initially found Campbell "wizened up," apparently not understanding military messages from Churchill and "brow-beaten" by Reynaud, but "genuinely glad" at his arrival. Spears had felt it wrong to expect an ambassador to deal suddenly with unfamiliar military problems expressed in a language of their own. Immediately upon Spears's arrival, the ambassador warned him that Reynaud's theme of the moment was that of British generals always making for the harbours, a reference to the British decision to fall back to Dunkirk.[19]

These had been particularly difficult days for Campbell as rumours also spread that senior officials in London had been floating the idea of sending some "super Englishmen to reside in Paris in addition to the Ambassador."[20] Baudouin, who had been appointed as under secretary of state for foreign affairs on 5 June, was often found approaching Spears rather than Campbell in his efforts to obtain British help.[21] It was no doubt something in the nature of Campbell's personality and his less than flamboyant air that explains why he did not vociferously object to Spears's appointment or attempt to combat rumours about his position more vigorously. As it turned out Spears's bluster worked well with Campbell's reserve and they formed a good working relationship together. Harvey would soon note that the General was 'being very useful after all', not only as a direct link to Churchill but in his capacity as a military expert.[22]

Although Dunkirk helped to fuel French suspicions that the British were deserting the battlefield, political-military links between the French and the British continued, and the latter sent two fresh divisions back to France.[23] The insoluble problem for the British government was that it could not simultaneously prepare to defend the homeland *and* send all possible help to France, especially precious fighter squadrons to challenge German command of the air. Campbell forcefully told Reynaud that Britain would continue to give as much as it could and was not prepared to denude Britain of all its air defences on the eve of invasion, "an unforgivable responsibility."[24] But Campbell had not lost all sympathy with the French. Although he described the sometimes-violent appeals for more fighters as "deplorable," Campbell understood that, "The argument that the invasion of the British Isles is clearly the next German objective cannot be expected in the circumstances to appeal to the French with quite the same force as it does to us."[25] With Spears's concurrence, Campbell therefore urged Churchill on 7 June, to send the maximum amount of air power that was possible, asking: "Is it fair to suggest that every German pilot and machine destroyed in France means one each less for use against the British Isles later?"[26] In a separate letter to Halifax that same day, Campbell stressed that Reynaud, even if he stood firm, "could hardly play a lone hand if Pétain and possibly Weygand abandoned him." The ambassador had little doubt that Pétain *would* abandon the French premier and stressed "the importance of giving the French all the help we *possibly* can, *now*."[27] These appeals seem to have worked. Campbell was given a message from the British prime minister for Reynaud and Weygand, which spoke of plans to send two more squadrons to be based in France and four squadrons to be based in Britain to operate daily from advanced fuelling grounds south of the Somme. When Campbell saw Reynaud the next day, the French premier showed his gratitude for the extra fighter support, but Campbell found that he was still inclined "to press for more and more."

By now Churchill had become exasperated with Reynaud's persistent requests and stated categorically to the French leader late on 8 June, that Britain would not ruin its capacity to continue the struggle.[28]

In early June Campbell forewarned London that Weygand's attitude remained downcast and although Reynaud continued to preach that France would never make terms, even if the Government had to move to North Africa, he tended to qualify his statements by adding, "so long as I am in control." This led Campbell to warn the Foreign Office that if the Government moved to Bordeaux, amidst panic and confusion, those forces in favour of surrender might overwhelm Reynaud. The chances of the French government then moving to North Africa would be slim. Campbell therefore concluded that it was necessary to prepare for the worst, and to be ready for the worst "to come more quickly than we expect."[29] Working conditions in the Embassy remained, in the ambassador's words, "frightful," forcing Campbell to reduce telegrams to a minimum of length that included "only the bare essentials." On 6 June, Campbell told London that he continued "to put on an appearance of being calm and confident in our ultimate victory" but could not pretend that his continual efforts to stiffen the French were proving successful.[30] Four days later the French were on the move. Harvey recorded that many French Ministries had been slipping away to the Touraine "without a word to anyone."[31] Campbell's final interviews with Reynaud and Weygand before they left Paris on 10 June were positive, although Baudouin wrote privately that the General was "depressed." Both Baudouin and Weygand had also been pressing the French premier to take up the issue of a separate peace with the British.[32] At a time when the opinions of senior French leaders were so mercurial, the ambassador's assessments should not be criticised too heavily.

On 11 June, when Campbell reached his new abode in the Touraine, the Château de Champchévrier, London had lost all contact with their ambassador.[33] On the ground, French ministries were spread over a wide area of the Touraine and the telephone system was completely inadequate. The only means of communication was by car over roads which, Campbell recounted, were "thronged with refugee traffic of every description."[34] During the morning, Campbell and Hal Mack, the urbane and cheerful Embassy first secretary, succeeded in finding Charles-Roux and Baudouin. Campbell recalled that "they were in complete ignorance of what was going on," having had no news since they left Paris the previous day.[35] Indeed, Campbell remained in the dark about Churchill's meeting with Reynaud and Weygand at Briare on 11–12 June, until Spears arrived at the Château de Champchévrier late on the evening of 12 June. It demonstrated how easy it was to cut the ambassador out of the dialogue. Spears gave a most gloomy account of the conference at Briare and

Harvey recorded: "French completely exhausted, no reserves, not even a battalion left."[36] The British party was more optimistic when they saw Reynaud at the Château de Chissay the following morning. Reynaud felt he had thwarted Weygand's and Pétain's push for an armistice during the last Cabinet meeting and would fight on in North Africa.[37] As the British party broke up and left, they were all about to receive some astonishing news. Churchill was due to arrive in Tours that afternoon. The first indication that the Embassy had received of Churchill's visit was when Hal Mack received a telephone call from Commander Thompson, Churchill's aide-de-camp, exclaiming, "We're here." "Where?" the astonished Mack asked. Left once more out of the diplomatic loop, Sir Ronald had fortunately bumped into Reynaud and been told by him that Churchill had arrived but it was extraordinary that Churchill's visit had not come up in conversation that morning.[38]

Campbell played only a small part in the meeting at Tours, supplying information to British Ministers and officials when asked. Both the ambassador and Spears were initially horrified at the alteration in Reynaud and stressed to Cadogan that he had been far more upbeat that morning.[39] The meeting has been surrounded in controversy as to whether Reynaud's decision to ask Britain to release France from its obligation not to conclude a separate peace was hypothetical or not.[40] In essence the problem remained the same but what made Campbell's role more difficult during his final days in France was Churchill's heartfelt refusal.[41] Baudouin deliberately interpreted Churchill's use of "je comprends" to mean that he would understand if France signed a separate peace.[42] By late evening, Baudouin's rumour mongering was in full swing and in his final despatches from Tours before he left for Bordeaux, Campbell noted that there were now only a handful of ministers "who showed any backbone," while Reynaud himself was "in a mood of indecision."[43] It was not surprising that just a few days later Campbell telephoned London to state that the question put by Reynaud at Tours had now been put again in "brutal form."[44]

When the British government returned its initial answers on 16 June, Campbell and Spears were disappointed. The first telegram, a clear infringement of French sovereignty, stated that France was released from its obligation not to enter into negotiations with Germany, "provided, but only provided, that the French fleet is sailed forthwith for British harbours pending negotiations."[45] A second telegram stressed that the British government expected "to be consulted as soon as any armistice terms are received."[46] When Campbell delivered the two telegrams, Reynaud did not take them well and had been hoping for a blank refusal to use in Cabinet as an argument for continuing the struggle. However, Campbell was about to receive some startling new instructions: his Government now asked him to delay action on the first telegram and suspend action on the second. Churchill, with the approval of the War Cabinet, had decided to offer Reynaud a Franco–British Union. Campbell, who according to Spears was "beaming," reported that the proposal had "acted like a tonic" on Reynaud who said that for a document like that he would fight to the last.[47] But Campbell, in his enthusiasm to keep France in the war, told Reynaud that he should consider both the previous telegrams "cancelled."[48]

Although the Ambassador botched his instructions, he was not alone in interpreting them in this way. Spears agreed with him while Harvey thought the telegram meant cancel not suspend.[49] As a result, when the French Cabinet met, Reynaud made only a passing reference to the two telegrams answering the French request for an armistice, saying, "the British Government had given its conditional assent and then withdrawn it." As Baudouin's version of events at Tours had gained wide currency, to the French it appeared that the British stance had changed from assent to a firm rejection. In fact, Britain's position had swung from refusal to conditional assent. To Reynaud's utter dismay as he laid a Franco-British Union before Ministers, his words were greeted with a strong, hostile silence. The episode finally overwhelmed Reynaud and he resigned that evening, giving way to Pétain, who immediately sought an armistice.[50]

When Campbell arrived in Bordeaux he found an atmosphere of rout, panic and moral decomposition. Campbell had intended to set up the Chancery in the Consulate, but as this was being besieged with British refugees demanding to be evacuated, he used a lumber-room where telegrams were enciphered and deciphered. As messages took two to three hours to transmit in cipher, and at least another hour to deliver, the Ambassador freely used the telephone. Campbell once found four decipherers slumped over their work and until his departure on 17 June, Spears had agreed with Campbell to send reports jointly to ease the strain.[51] Meanwhile, French ministers were dotted about in different parts of the town and frequently changed their habitat. The physical conditions, in which Embassy staff moved and lived, constituted, in Campbell's words, "a serious handicap to our activities."[52] Campbell also found communication with the Pétain government extremely frustrating, if not hostile. It is clear that Baudouin, now the new foreign minister, and Campbell loathed each other. Baudouin wrote in his diary that:

> I have never on any day or at any moment felt that behind the icy manner of Sir Ronald Campbell there beat the heart of a friend. I have always had before me the faultless representative of England, the very aloof high official who was opposed to any display of personal feeling and who was devoid of any real initiative. . . . [H]is cold looks hardly

concealed his extreme caution. . . . What hope is there that in the days to come this ambassador will help me to save what is left of Franco-British friendship?[53]

For his part, Campbell wrote in his final despatch that Baudouin, "either withheld information or gave it belatedly," while interviews with him were brief and "wholly unsatisfactory."

Baudouin failed to convince Campbell that France would sign honourable terms and that the fleet would not be allowed to fall into German hands.[54] However, Campbell, unsure of London's intentions after the confusion of 16 June, had initially failed to mention the two telegrams requesting that the French fleet sail for British harbours once negotiations had opened with Germany. Campbell had always disliked the wording of these telegrams and it is possible that he may have deliberately avoided mentioning them, as implicit in their wording was an air of distrust and infringement of French sovereignty. The ambassador may have thought it wiser not to refer to them specifically and proceed on a more cautious basis. As Campbell told Halifax on 17 June, in all his conversations he had spoken "*in the terms* [author's italics] contained in your telegrams" about bringing the French fleet within British control.[55] Whatever Campbell's reasons, which are not documented, Baudouin naturally used the confusion to good effect. When London asked Campbell to resubmit the telegrams, Baudouin noted in his diary, "What is the significance of these telegrams 'taken back,' and communicated afresh?"[56] In retrospect, it is difficult to criticise Campbell too sharply who, throughout this period, constantly tried to elicit a straight answer from French ministers about the fate of the fleet. Even stern messages from Churchill and several visits by British ministers to Bordeaux failed to achieve any greater assurances than Campbell had already obtained.[57]

The ambassador's interviews with Pétain were equally discouraging. The Marshal, according to Campbell, "seemed quite unable to grasp the necessity either of not succumbing so long as any resistance, however feeble, could be offered, or of sending the Government overseas to keep the flag flying." "He was entirely absorbed," Campbell recorded, "with one thought and one only—that of putting an end to further bloodshed and of remaining himself in France in the hope of mitigating the sufferings of the people under German occupation." Sir Ronald recalled that he was often "driven to the undignified expedient" of waiting about in darkened halls, "thronged with little groups of whispering secretaries," in the hope of forcing an interview either with Pétain or Baudouin as they went into or came out from a meeting of ministers.[58]

When the German armistice terms were finally telephoned to Bordeaux on 21 June—the naval clauses of the Treaty demanded the recall of the fleet to French ports to be disarmed under German control—Campbell was hardly reassured. The ambassador had to endure a painful and acrimonious encounter with Baudouin to ascertain how the French would respond. Baudouin told him that it had been decided to make a counter-proposal by which the fleet would be sent to French North African ports where it would be dismantled. Campbell emphasised strongly that it ought to be sent further away. If sent to a Mediterranean port, it would risk falling into Italian hands. Baudouin replied that in that case it would be scuttled in accordance with the decision already taken. When pressed by Campbell the French foreign minister insisted that he did not have a spare copy of the German conditions but on the ambassador's continued insistence he eventually provided a copy. This 'shameful scene' sufficed to show Campbell that the French had "completely lost their heads" and were now "totally unmanageable."[59] Sir Ronald did 'not believe for a moment' that the French would hold out against the original German condition to recall the fleet to French ports, which they eventually didn't, and might even reverse scuttling orders.

Seldom has a British mission in a major allied country changed so completely or so quickly. In late June, an editorial in *The Times* neatly summed up the intrigue that Campbell faced at Bordeaux:

> Little more than a fortnight ago he [Campbell] was seeing members of the French Government almost hourly, entirely trusted himself and passing on to them with the utmost frankness all the military news and views of an Ally. [In] Bordeaux he could only with the greatest difficulty see any of the new Ministers—and when he did see them there was little to be said. They were in no mood to hear either reminders of solemn pledges or warnings of what capitulation to tyranny would mean.[60]

When, on the evening of 22 June, the Germans rejected French proposals to amend the naval clauses of the armistice, Charles-Roux secretly informed Campbell that Admiral François Darlan, the Anglophobic minister of marine, had made sure that all ships would be made safe from German interference. The ambassador was dismayed. Charles-Roux argued that these decisions gave Britain complete satisfaction. Naturally, Campbell disagreed and had already dismissed Darlan's assurances as "pathetic."[61] Campbell expressed his profound regret to Charles-Roux that the Franco-British alliance, on which such confident hopes had been founded, should have dissolved in such circumstances. At the close of this interview, Campbell told Charles-Roux that he intended to leave with his staff as soon as the armistice had been signed. Charles-Roux "affected surprise" and asked for Campbell's reasons. Campbell said that he had been accredited to a free and allied government. He did not think that his Government would wish him to stay with a French government which within a few hours would be under the control of the enemy. Furthermore, the ambassador argued, it would be futile to suppose that in these circumstances the Germans would allow him to communicate with the French government. Since he could be of no further use in France, Campbell told Charles-Roux that he ought to return to London for consultation and report. He added this "rider" in order to avoid giving the impression that Britain might abandon France altogether and to discourage the French government from thinking that they were now free from further obligation to Britain, particularly with regard to scuttling their fleet.[62]

The omens were not good. During the evening of 22 June, the French signed the armistice and as Harvey noted, "did not even bother" to tell Campbell. The British ambassador only learned of the signature when he called on Weygand to take his leave.[63] As Campbell made his final call on Baudouin, he was struck by the general surprise evinced at his decision to leave. The ambassador offered two explanations. The first was that his interlocutors had "so deluded themselves into believing that a French Government would be allowed to function freely" that they presumed he could render further service. The other, much more likely, was that the French government hoped by detaining Campbell, it would "give the French public and outside world the impression that His Majesty's Government had condoned their actions."[64] Campbell took his decision to leave on his own initiative. He did not wish to become an embarrassment to his own Government, presumably by being captured. Given the distrust of the French government, which he had developed, it would be difficult to argue that Campbell should have stayed in Bordeaux. But it has been argued that he should have left someone behind from the diplomatic staff, both as a channel of information and as service to British subjects. His departure gave the French the chance to claim that Britain had taken the initiative towards breaking off diplomatic relations.[65] However, Halifax remained "satisfied" that Campbell did all that was "humanely possible" to prevent the final French surrender and that his decision to withdraw the Embassy was, in the circumstances, "entirely justified." The foreign secretary warmly concluded that the Government owed a great debt to Campbell and to all the members of his staff for their devoted services during such a critical period of the war.[66]

To conclude, the evidence suggests that Campbell worked extremely hard to keep the French in the war. The difficulty for Campbell, unlike Phipps, was that upon his arrival in France, he had to cope with a plethora of problems arising from the transformation of a diplomatic alliance into a military alliance. In Campbell's defence, he had been schooled in the best traditions of the British Diplomatic Service and, unsurprisingly, was not comfortable when it came to dealing with military matters. Sir Ronald, therefore, was no doubt relieved to some extent to see the arrival of Spears, whatever that meant for his position as ambassador. In the end, however hard he worked for the cause of Franco–British relations, Campbell was unable to sustain his authority in the overall management of the relationship. The unfolding events of the summer of 1940 indicated that the role of an ambassador in a major allied Embassy was changing. An ambassador could no longer be just a "very great clerk" sending out polished diplomatic despatches: he now needed the requisite management skills to maintain a firm controlling hand over a multitude of competing political, military and economic demands.

NOTES

1. The author would like to thank Patrick Salmon and Keith Hamilton for their helpful suggestions on this paper.
2. Alan Clark, "Why we need a strategy, not platitudes," *The Times*, 1 Jan. 1994.
3. Boris Johnson, "Would you share your currency with this lot?," *The Daily Telegraph*, 13 Feb. 2003.
4. John Harvey (Ed.), *The Diplomatic Diaries of Oliver Harvey, 1937–1940* (London: Collins, 1970), diary entry, 17 Nov. 1938, pp. 220–1.
5. John Herman, *The Paris Embassy of Sir Eric Phipps: Anglo-French Relations and the Foreign Office, 1937–1939* (Brighton: Sussex Academic Press, 1998), pp. 137–8, 175–6.
6. Cynthia Gladwyn, *The Paris Embassy* (London: Collins, 1976), pp. 224, 231. Roderick Barclay, *Ernest Bevin and the Foreign Office 1932–69* (London: Private Publication, 1975), p. 125. Edward Spears, *Assignment to Catastrophe, Vol. I: Prelude to Dunkirk, July 1939–May 1940* (London: Heinemann, 1954), p. 178. "Sir Ronald H. Campbell: The Quest for Accuracy," *The Times*, 24 Nov. 1953.
7. The French premier had drawn close to Bullitt, for example, over the issue of purchasing American military aircraft and parts. See *Foreign Relations of the United States, 1939, Vol. II* (Washington, 1956), pp. 520–8. Hereafter FRUS. See also Julian Jackson, *The Fall of France: the Nazi Invasion of 1940* (Oxford: Oxford University Press, 2003), p. 70; John Cairns, "Reflections on France, Britain and the Winter War Prodrome, 1939–1940" in Joel Blatt (Ed.), *The French Defeat of 1940: Reassessments* (Oxford: Berghahn, 1998), pp. 284–85; Philip Bell, *A Certain Eventuality: Britain and the Fall of France* (Farnborough: Saxon House, 1974), p. 8 and William Shirer, *The Collapse of the Third Republic: An Inquiry into the Fall of France in 1940* (London: Heinemann, 1970), pp. 509–10, 525–26.
8. Llewellyn Woodward, *British Foreign Policy in the Second World War, I* (London: HMSO, 1974), pp. 189–90. Sir Ronald Campbell to the Foreign Office, 22 Mar. 1940 and Campbell to the Foreign Office, 29 Mar. 1940. The National Archives (formerly the Public Record Office), Kew, London. Hereafter TNA (PRO). FO 371/24309, C4383/C4658/65/17. Lord Halifax to Campbell, 30 Apr.1940, FO 800/312.
9. Julian Jackson, *France: The Dark Years 1940–1944* (Oxford: Oxford University Press, 2001), pp. 117–18.

10. Halifax to Campbell, 30 Apr. 1940 and Campbell to Halifax, 1 May 1940. TNA (PRO) FO 800/312. Bell, *A Certain Eventuality*, p. 10.

11. Woodward, *British Foreign Policy in the Second World War I*, p. 195.

12. Ibid., pp. 209–210. Richard Griffiths, *Marshal Pétain* (2nd ed., London: Constable?, 1994), p. 226. Spears, *Assignment to Catastrophe, I*, p. 20. Harvey (Ed.), *Diplomatic Diaries of Oliver Harvey*, diary entry, 20 May 1940, p. 363.

13. Harvey, *Diplomatic Diaries of Oliver Harvey*, diary entry, 28 May 1940, p. 371. Eleanor Gates, *The End of the Affair: The Collapse of the Anglo-French Alliance, 1939–40* (Berkeley and Los Angeles: University of California Press, 1981), pp. 131–2. Jackson, *The Fall of France*, p. 126.

14. Harvey (Ed.), *Diplomatic Diaries of Oliver Harvey*, diary entry, 30 May 1940, p. 373. Shirer, *The Collapse of the Third Republic*, pp. 534–35. Jackson, *The Fall of France*, p. 126. Campbell's Final Despatch to Lord Halifax, 27 Jun. 1940. TNA (PRO), FO 371/24311, C7541/65/17.

15. Harvey (Ed.), *Diplomatic Diaries of Oliver Harvey*, diary entry, 29 May 1940, p. 372. Campbell to Halifax, 30 May 1940. TNA (PRO), FO 800/312.

16. Harvey (Ed.), *Diplomatic Diaries of Oliver Harvey*, diary entry, 16 May 1940, p. 359.

17. Max Egremont, *Under Two Flags: The Life of Major-General Sir Edward Spears* (London: Weidenfeld and Nicolson, 1997), p. 162. Spears, *Assignment to Catastrophe, I*, pp. 235, 238, 245.

18. Winston Churchill, *The Second World War, Vol.II: The Finest Hour* (London: Cassell, 1949), p. 97. Jackson, *The Fall of France*, p. 99. Gladwyn, *The Paris Embassy*, p. 226. Brian Bond, "The British View" in Brian Bond and Michael Taylor (Eds.), *The Battle of France and Flanders 1940: Sixty Years On* (Barnsley: Leo Cooper, 2001), p. 228.

19. Egremont, *Under Two Flags*, pp. 164–5. Spears, *Assignment to Catastrophe, I*, pp. 178–9. 199, 201, 273, 280. Gladwyn, *The Paris Embassy*, p. 226. Campbell to Halifax, 27 May 1940. TNA (PRO), FO 800/312. Harvey (Ed.), *Diplomatic Diaries of Oliver Harvey*, diary entry, 30 May 1940, p. 372.

20. Harvey (Ed.), *Diplomatic Diaries of Oliver Harvey*, diary entries, 2 and 6 June 1940, pp. 377, 380.

21. Paul Baudouin, *The Private Diaries: March 1940 to January 1941* (London: Eyre and Spottiswode, 1948), diary entry, 6 June 1940, p. 82.

22. Spears, *Assignment to Catastrophe, I*, pp. 273, 280. Harvey (Ed.), *Diplomatic Diaries of Oliver Harvey*, diary entry 30 May 1940, p. 372.

23. Baudouin, *The Private Diaries*, diary entries 26 May 1940 and 3 June 1940, pp. 56–8, 76.

24. Campbell to the Foreign Office, 5 June 1940 in Annex III to WM(49)156, 6 June 1940. TNA (PRO), CAB 65/3.

25. Campbell to Halifax, 7 June 1940. TNA (PRO), FO 800/312.

26. Woodward, *British Foreign Policy in the Second World War, I*, pp. 220–1.

27. Campbell to Halifax, 7 June 1940. TNA (PRO), FO 800/312.

28. Woodward, *British Foreign Policy in the Second World War, I*, pp. 222–3 and Bell, *A Certain Eventuality*, p. 26.

29. Campbell to Halifax, 4 June 1940. TNA (PRO), FO 371/24383, C7074/5/18. Woodward, *British Foreign Policy in the Second World War, I*, pp. 217–19.

30. Campbell to Cadogan, 6 June 1940. TNA (PRO), FO 371/24383, C7121/5/18.

31. Harvey (Ed.), *Diplomatic Diaries of Oliver Harvey*, diary entry, 10 June 1940, pp. 383–4.

32. Baudouin, *The Private Diaries*, diary entry, 10 June 1940, pp. 93–4.

33. Gladwyn, *The Paris Embassy*, p. 228. Churchill, minute, 11 June 1940. TNA (PRO), FO 371/24383, C7074/5/18.

34. The Quai d'Orsay was at Langeais, 18km from the Château in Cleré. The Ministry of Finance was at Chinon, about 50 km distant. The Ministry of Interior was at Tours, 28 km away. The Air Ministry was at Amboise and the Ministry of War was still further, while the Ministry of Supply was established somewhere in the Massif Central, 200 km away. Campbell's Final Despatch to Lord Halifax, 27 Jun. 1940. TNA (PRO), FO 371/24311, C7541/65/17.

35. Baudouin, *The Private Diaries*, diary entry, 11 June 1940, p. 95. Campbell's Final Despatch to Lord Halifax, 27 June 1940. TNA (PRO), FO 371/24311, C7541/65/17.

36. Woodward, *British Foreign Policy in the Second World War*, I, p. 252, n.1. Harvey (Ed.), *Diplomatic Diaries of Oliver Harvey*, diary entry, 12 June 1940, p. 386.

37. Edward Spears, *Assignment to Catastrophe, Vol.II: The Fall of France, June 1940* (London: Heinemann, 1954), pp. 191, 193. Egremont, *Under Two Flags*, pp. 183–4. Campbell's Final Despatch to Lord Halifax, 27 June 1940. TNA (PRO), FO 371/24311, C7541/65/17.

38. Spears, *Assignment to Catastrophe, II*, pp. 196–7, 199, 230–1. Harvey (Ed.), *Diplomatic Diaries of Oliver Harvey*, diary entry, 13 June 1940, p. 388.

39. Spears, *Assignment to Catastrophe, II*, p. 200. David Dilks (Ed.), *The Diaries of Sir Alexander Cadogan, 1938–1945* (London: Cassell, 1971), diary entry, 13 June 1940, p. 298.

40. Campbell's Final Despatch to Lord Halifax, 27 June 1940. TNA (PRO), FO 371/24311, C7541/65/17. Woodward, *British Foreign Policy in the Second World War*, I, p. 257. Baudouin, *The Private Diaries*, diary entry, 13 June 1940, p. 102.

41. Churchill, minute, WM(40)165, 10.15 p.m., 13 June 1940. TNA (PRO), CAB 65/13.

42. Egremont, *Under Two Flags*, p. 185.

43. Campbell's Final Despatch to Lord Halifax, 27 June 1940. TNA (PRO), FO 371/24311, C7541/65/17. Woodward, *British Foreign Policy in the Second World War*, I, p. 263. Geoffrey Warner, *Pierre Laval and the Eclipse of France* (London: Eyre and Spottiswoode, 1968), p. 169.

44. Woodward, *British Foreign Policy in the Second World War*, I, pp. 272–73.

45. Ibid., p. 275. Appendix I, WM(40)168, 16 June 1940. TNA (PRO), CAB 65/13.

46. The Foreign Office to Campbell, telegram 3.10 p.m., 16 June 1940. TNA (PRO), FO 371/24310, C7263/65/17. Spears, *Assignment to Catastrophe, II*, pp. 282–5.

47. The Foreign Office to Campbell, telegrams 3.10 p.m. and 4.45 p.m., 16 June 1940. TNA (PRO), FO 371/24310, C7263/65/17. Woodward, *British Foreign Policy in the Second World War*, I, pp. 276–77, 279–80. Campbell to the Foreign Office, telegram 7 p.m., 16 June 1940. FO 371/24311, C7294/65/17. Spears, *Assignment to Catastrophe, II*, p. 293. Paul Reynaud, *In the Thick of the Fight* (London: Cassell, 1955), pp. 529–30, 536.

48. Campbell's Final Despatch to Lord Halifax, 27 June 1940. TNA (PRO), FO 371/24311, C7541/65/17. Warner, *Pierre Laval and the Eclipse of France*, p. 175. Reynaud, *In the Thick of the Fight, 1930–1945*, p. 536.

49. Harvey (Ed.), *The Diplomatic Diaries of Oliver Harvey*, diary entry, 16 June 1940, p. 391. Spears, *Assignment to Catastrophe, II*, p. 293.

50. Shirer, *The Collapse of the Third Republic*, pp. 802–6. John Sherwood, *Georges Mandel and the Third Republic* (Stanford, CA.: Stanford University Press, 1970), pp. 247–9.

51. Egremont, *Under Two Flags*, pp. 191–2.

52. Campbell's Final Despatch to Lord Halifax, 27 June 1940. TNA (PRO), FO 371/24311, C7541/65/17.

53. Baudouin, *The Private Diaries*, diary entry, 16 June 1940, p. 119.

54. Campbell's Final Despatch to Lord Halifax, 27 June 1940. TNA (PRO), FO 371/24311, C7541/65/17.

55. Campbell to the Foreign Office, telegram 8.10 p.m., 17 June 1940. TNA (PRO), FO 371/24311, C7301/65/17.

56. Baudouin, *The Private Diaries*, diary entry, 17 June 1940, p. 123.

57. Campbell's Final Despatch to Lord Halifax, 27 June 1940. TNA (PRO), FO 371/24311, C7541/65/17. See also Campbell to the Foreign Office, telegram 3.45 p.m., 18 June 1940, and Campbell to the Foreign Office, telegram 6.50 a.m, 20 June 1940. FO 371/24311, C7301/65/17. In addition, see Harvey (Ed.), *Diplomatic Diaries of Oliver Harvey*, diary entries, 15 and 18 June 1940, pp. 389–90, 394; Shirer, *The Collapse of the Third Republic*, p. 826; Gladwyn, *The Paris Embassy*, pp. 228–30; Spears, *Assignment to Catastrophe, II*, p. 240; Woodward, *British Foreign Policy in the Second World War, I*, pp. 296–7; Gates, *End of the Affair*, p. 271; Colin Forbes Adam, *Life of Lord Lloyd* (London, 1948), pp. 299–300.

58. Campbell's Final Despatch to Lord Halifax, 27 June 1940. TNA (PRO), FO 371/24311, C7541/65/17.

59. Campbell to the Foreign Office, 22 June 1940. TNA (PRO), FO 371/24348, C7375/7362/17. Campbell's Final Despatch to Lord Halifax, 27 June 1940, TNA (PRO), FO 371/24311, C7541/65/17. Woodward, *British Foreign Policy in the Second World War, I*, p. 307. Diary entry for 21 June 1940 in Baudouin, *The Private Diaries*, diary entry, 21 June 1940, p. 134. Baudouin's account does not differ in substance, though he does not mention any unwillingness to hand over a copy of the terms.

60. "Intriguers active in Bordeaux: Sir Ronald Campbell's Return," *The Times*, 26 June 1940.

61. Woodward, *British Foreign Policy in the Second World War, I*, pp. 289–90, 308. TNA (PRO), Campbell's Final Despatch to Lord Halifax, 27 June 1940. FO 371/24311, C7541/65/17.

62. Campbell's Final Despatch to Lord Halifax, 27 June 1940. TNA (PRO), FO 371/24311, C7541/65/17.

63. Harvey (Ed.), *Diplomatic Diaries of Oliver Harvey*, diary entry, 22 June 1940, p. 400.

64. Campbell's Final Despatch to Lord Halifax, 27 June 1940, TNA (PRO), FO 371/24311, C7541/65/17.

65. Bell, *A Certain Eventuality*, pp. 100–1.

66. Halifax to Campbell, draft letter, 17 July 1940. TNA (PRO), FO 371/24311, C7352/65/17.

ENTENTE NEO-COLONIALE?: ERNEST BEVIN AND THE PROPOSALS FOR AN ANGLO–FRENCH THIRD WORLD POWER, 1945–1949

Anne Deighton

The British and French empires were quite different in character: they were won in different ways; conceptualized and run in different ways; and their endings were differently managed. Yet in the years immediately following the Second World War it seemed for a while that the two, old European powers would find a way of cooperating through a new *"entente néo-coloniale."* Such an Anglo-French-led entente might be used to manage economic development, postpone the inevitable loss of empire, or perhaps even reinvent empire to confront the emerging bipolarity of the postwar world.[1] This article will look at the British input into the project: sometimes called its quest to be a Third World Power, and will examine in particular, the role of Ernest Bevin. Bevin, a former trades union leader, wartime minister of Labour, and then foreign secretary between 1945 and 1951, took the Third World Power project as his own.

A preliminary word of description is needed. The definition which gives the project the greatest clarity comes, ironically, from those in the British Foreign Office who had largely buried the project by mid 1949. It was that there "should be the eventual creation of a system which would enable Western Europe, plus the bulk of the African continent, and in some form of loose association with other members of the Commonwealth, to run an independent policy in world affairs which would not necessarily coincide with either Soviet or American wishes."[2] Association was assumed to include economic, political and defence components.

In reality, the project was less clear, even in Bevin's own speech launching the project in the House of Commons in January 1948. It was not always assumed that the Commonwealth should have a role; nor was it clear which Western European countries would participate, although Britain and France, as the leading imperial powers, were obviously the key players.[3] It was not clear whether this was primarily a functional project that related to demands for colonial development through the exploitation of colonial resources; some kind of neo-colonial customs union designed to give Europe access to raw materials; or whether it was a grander ideological, political and defence project that would seek global strategic space between the Soviet Union and the United States. However, Europe's relationship with its colonies was a live one in the early postwar years. Colonial offices in both London and Paris were already working on development issues; further, how to manage declining imperial power was a major policy issue in both capitals, although it was being addressed in different ways.

Perhaps the most confusing definitional question is the relationship of Bevin's project to other Third Force projects that emerged within the Labour Party after 1945. These, especially from the self-appointed "Keep Left" group, had a more specifically ideological stance. Ironically, they defined themselves by their vociferous opposition to the apparent hostility to the Soviet Union and subservience to the U.S. that they saw in Bevin's own foreign policy.[4] As we shall see, by the early months of 1948—the high point of Bevin's Third World Power project—Bevin managed to lance the boil of this left wing opposition and to proceed with his own project, without incurring the wrath of the majority of the left wingers. He also managed to enlist the backing of those who thought that a global anti-communist propaganda crusade should be the first priority of the government; the Colonial Office which had been working since the end of the war on colonial development issues; as well as those who favoured ever closer relations with France and other West European countries.

The Third World Power idea had its roots in the pre-war years, and a number of plans and proposals relating to the "middle of the planet" or "*Eurafrique,*" circulated before the Second World War. Euro-African dreams were not the prerogative of either the left or the right.[5] Most British proposals that related to sub-tropical Africa were dominated by the perception of Britain as a continuing imperial power, whose assets should be managed in the interests of Britain.[6] Ideas relating to federation or joint action in Europe itself also appeared in many forms from the 1920s. In France, for example, Popular Front leaders hoped that the common exploitation of imperial territories (not North Africa) might deter the German führer, Adolf Hitler.[7] The role of Britain within a European federation was also discussed as a European war became more likely, and as France's weaknesses became more apparent. However, whether such federation implied integration or simply cooperation was often unclear; for example, Bevin's remark that "if Europe were a commonwealth with a unified economy, how much better it would be for the world" was actually a plea for cooperation.[8]

As a trades union leader in the 1920s and 1930s, Bevin took a great interest in these ideas. He was, in this sense, an exceptional trades unionist, as the international dimension of the movement was not a notable feature of interwar unionism. He was coopted onto a number of national committees, including the Colonial Development Advisory Committee that assessed funding under the 1929 Colonial Development Act. The Trades Union Council (TUC), of which he was a leading member, also began to hold regular meetings to discuss Commonwealth trade and development. Bevin was not wedded to free trade, arguing that he had never accepted "as a Socialist, that an inflexible free trade attitude is synonymous with Socialism": in his view, protection would not stop economic rationalisation, but it would give inefficient industries—in the metropole at least—time to put their houses in order.[9] His thinking was driven by two ideas which never left him: a desire to improve employment and trading conditions for working people in the UK; and a growing sense that international economic development could, by stimulating trade, be the key to preventing war.[10] In 1937, he addressed the TUC conference as its president, and this speech led to the establishment of a TUC Colonial Advisory Committee to investigate overseas living conditions. It then persuaded the Colonial Office to set up a Labour Department, and in 1940, the Colonial Development Act was passed.[11]

In 1938, Bevin spent four months in Canada, New Zealand, and then Australia, and he returned with an even stronger commitment to shared international action, and an admiration for federalists, principally Lionel Curtis, but also Lord Lothian (Philip Kerr).[12] In an address to the Royal Institute of International Affairs, he argued that the Ottawa system offered "a road along which we in the British Empire—possibly in common with the great colonial powers . . . could use . . . for collective economic rights and collective defence," as long as the aim was to raise the standard of life and not be used for aggression. He was deeply concerned by what he saw as the obvious weakness of France in the international system. So, if we invite countries like Scandinavia, Holland, Belgium, Russia, France and the USA . . . to come within our preference system, would that not for the first time result in a real pooling of the whole of the colonial empires of the world and their resources? It would bring the Haves together as they would in fact control 92% of the essential raw material of the world . . . . and so equip ourselves in a Peace Bloc with a far greater weapon than arms can give. . . . Is it too much to dream that we might yet change the name of the British Commonwealth to one of European Commonwealth, and open up avenues without destroying political institutions at all?[13]

This was, he argued, an economic equivalent of a defence pact, which might even appeal to aggressors, as, in time, it would improve the living standards of all, give them a chance to have a place in the sun, and reduce the desire for war.

He also wondered, in the *Spectator* magazine, not only if Europe would not be better off with a unified economy, but also whether there should not be an Assembly of the British Commonwealth, which might be "tantamount to a nucleus for the establishment of a World Order" in the future.[14] This assembly might also consider admitting more states, thus "creating an economic attraction for the development of Commonwealth cooperation and adhesion, instead of the present clamour for colonies." Whilst the argument of much of the article is not very clear, it does seem that in the desperate months leading up to war, Bevin was exploring the extent to which Commonwealth-style cooperation and the resources of the Empire-Commonwealth, might be used as bait to preserve peace.

Bevin's early biographer, Francis Williams, makes it very clear that the development of Africa was a question of great importance to Bevin in the months leading up to the war. Bevin

envisaged a great United Africa Authority to which all the Colonial Powers in Africa together with the United States should be invited to belong and membership in which should also be offered to Germany and Italy if they would alter their politics of international aggression. British, French and Belgian knowledge of Colonial administration, allied to American capital and the American genius for large scale development plus the technical and research skill of the Germans and the emigrants Italy desperately needed to send abroad could, he argued, turn the undeveloped areas of Africa into one of the great treasure houses of the world.[15]

These ideas were those of a man who, in 1938, thought that he was about to retire from national life, and was therefore liberated to speak without any institutional constraint. He admired the British Commonwealth concept as a source of economic stability and growth for all its members, and had seen the potential of closer collaboration in Africa between the European colonial powers—especially France.[16]

However, Bevin was not to retire yet, and in 1940 he was appointed minister of labour in the coalition government under the leadership of Winston Churchill. During the war, the strategic and economic value of the empire became evident to British decision-makers, fuelling the already settled notions in Bevin's mind about the potential of imperial cooperation. Indeed, after the fall of France, and especially during the latter stages of the war, Anglo–French cooperation in the colonies was considerable. This cooperation tended to be at the official, rather than the ministerial level,

> Franco-British collaboration was conceived and led by a small group of senior officials who knew each other well. They had convinced each other that the war had brought such an upheaval to international relations, that, where this was possible, a joint revision of colonial conduct was now called for.[17]

However, there remained substantial differences of opinion between the French and the British about the purpose of reform. Or, as one cynic reflected, "the established French policy of turning the African native into a good Frenchman . . . compared with the British policy of helping the native to become a good African."[18]

Although primarily concerned with the home front during the war, Bevin was a member of the War Cabinet, and learnt much about the workings of foreign policy and postwar planning. He was increasingly trusted by Churchill, (and, as it was to turn out, also by Clement Attlee, the leader of the Labour Party). Bevin also had close relations with the foreign secretary of the Coalition Government, Anthony Eden. He adhered to the Eden view that France would be the essential ally and the necessary partner in the post war period, despite the wartime problems that Anglo–French relations had encountered.

Bevin hoped to become chancellor of the exchequer if the Labour party won the general election after the war. (If Labour did not win, he was being approached, for the second time, to lead the International Labour Organisation.) Much is known about the circumstances in which Attlee decided to make him foreign secretary.[19] What is less generally appreciated is that Bevin's views about the strategic importance of France; his belief that prosperity was a route to the avoidance of war; his aspiration to use economics as a way of defending the West against communism; and his acceptance of economic blocs as the route to economic improvement for workers in the metropole and in the colonies all clearly derived from the experience he had gained since the 1930s, although colonial matters were not included in Labour's election manifesto. In one of his first speeches in the House of Commons as foreign secretary, he condemned "the vicious circle whereby between the wars, trade could not flourish because of lack of security, while security was endangered through lack of trade."[20] These beliefs help to explain his thinking about the potential of a global Third World Power.

When Bevin became foreign secretary, the Foreign Office had already begun to think about future strategy, Orme Sargent's celebrated July 1945 *tour d'horizon*, "Stocktaking on VE Day," argued that the UK should secure leadership of Western Europe and the Empire/Commonwealth, despite, or indeed, because of its own economic and military weakness. Britain had to enrol

> the Dominions and especially France, not to mention the lesser Western European Powers, as collaborators with us in this tripartite system [with the US and the Soviet Union]. Only so, shall we be able, in the long run, to compel our two big partners to treat us as an equal. . . . For the same reason we shall probably find it useful to organize under our leadership the lesser colonial Powers who have a stake in the Far East; in other words, France, the Netherlands and Australia.

A European base of countries with global dependencies carried with it the possibility of unrivalled access to much-needed raw materials and strategic bases in the postwar world. The obligations of the government in this one world policy were now to reinforce British leadership, to ensure rising welfare provision for the population, and to bring security.[21]

Bevin's early notion of the third great power centre (U.K., France, Italy, Greece, Turkey, Dominions, India, and the U.K. colonial empire in Africa) was similar, but was conceived as a fallback position if international collaboration through the United Nations Organisation and other multilateral institutions that favoured British interests could not in fact be achieved. In 1945 and 1946, Bevin nevertheless worked to consolidate Britain's empire, and to extend it if possible in North Africa, as well as to sustain the close relations with the Commonwealth, while opposing withdrawal from India.[22]

The starting point for Britain's leading role in a global third force had to be France, a natural imperial as well as continental European partner for the postwar period. However, Franco–British relations were bad in the aftermath of the war, with disagreements over policy in the Levant and over Germany, as well as ongoing concern in London about political instability and the presence of communists in the French government. It was a highly significant gesture, then, that Bevin kept the Conservative Duff Cooper on as the British ambassador to France after 1945. Indeed, it was a decision of Bevin's which surprised even Duff Cooper himself. Part of the reason for Bevin's decision was Duff Cooper's good relations with French elites, and his determination to secure an Anglo–French treaty.[23] The ambassador was delighted by Bevin's attitude to France, noting in his diary that, "Bevin's policy and sentiments towards France could not be better. . . . There should now be no difficulty about the Levant and little, I hope, about Germany." Duff Cooper had also worked on colonial issues in the war, and was soon to suggest to Bevin that it might actually be easier for Britain to build links with France in Africa than in Europe itself, given the specific difficulties in Anglo–French relations.[24] But bad bilateral relations, not least over what to do with Germany, did not immediately ease, despite Duff Cooper's optimism, although Bevin did explore the possibility of an Anglo–French, and European customs union.

The most intense phase on Anglo–French discussion on joint imperial ventures took place during 1947, although Bevin had been in general discussions with successive French leaders about imperial cooperation since mid 1946.[25] Both Paris and London had already agreed that American notions about a trusteeship over colonial territories under the emerging United Nations Organisation could not be encouraged, and between them, were to successfully manage to contain this idea.[26] In January 1947, as the Treaty of Dunkirk was finally being negotiated by Duff Cooper, Bevin proposed to the Cabinet a study on some kind of Anglo–French customs union, especially if multilateralism and the proposed International Trade Organisation broke down. He argued that his study should include the possibility of a special regime with colonial dependencies and the Dominions.[27]

Then, only six months later, and in the context of the Marshall Plan, in bilateral discussions with French premier Paul Ramadier, Bevin also discussed the possibilities of a wider, Anglo–French colonial dimension to the Plan. Philip Bell argues that the Marshall Plan negotiations were straining Anglo–French relations, and that perhaps Bevin saw the prospect of an Anglo–French led imperial Third Force as easing this.[28] The sterling crisis of the summer of 1947 proved to be another reason for Britain to try, with France, to exploit colonies more effectively as a way of easing the U.K.'s own financial burden. In September, Bevin asked for studies on an imperial customs union; a commonwealth customs union; a combination of the two; a European customs union, and on the relationship between the imperial and commonwealth customs union, and a customs union in Europe.[29] The main areas of interest were West Africa, where the Colonial Office had already established close working relationships with their counterparts in Paris. However, as his request to the Foreign Office shows, his thinking was not at all clearly articulated, although he was already prepared to air this idea publicly at the TUC annual meeting in the same month, when he explained that a European Customs union was not "a panacea for our difficulties," and that the Empire and Commonwealth should be joined with the European powers in this customs union.[30]

The high point of the Third World Power debate in the U.K. came during the early months of 1948. The idea of a Western European Union with a sub-Saharan dimension came to Cabinet on 8 January 1948, although the specifics of economic relations in Europe, or, indeed with Africa, do not appear to have been spelt out. This discussion took place at a critical moment in the Cold War. The Council of Foreign Ministers, in which Britain, the U.S., the Soviet Union, and France had tried to work for a peace treaty, had collapsed over the issue of Germany; and Marshall Aid was not yet confirmed. The French government was in crisis once again and was receiving emergency funds from the U.S., while Bevin was also trying to persuade French Foreign Minister Georges Bidault that the two had to work together to create "some sort of federation in Western Europe, whether of a formal or informal character," and to keep the Americans with them.[31]

Bevin also secured the backing of the colonial secretary, Arthur Creech Jones, who now gave Bevin powerful and informed support. Creech Jones was a long standing ally of Bevin, had been the deputy secretary of the TGWU, and was one of the few people who, through the Fabian Colonial Research Bureau, had specialised in colonial development issues from the 1930s onwards. It is clear from the record that, in early 1948, he backed Bevin's initiative, although Bevin's tone was far more strategic—if not apocalyptic—than the development plans that Creech Jones had himself been working on with Colonial Office officials.

At home, Bevin had at least temporarily dealt with the "Keep Left" members of the Labour Party with a dramatic and effective speech at the Margate Labour Party conference. He was now able to steal their clothing by using the phrase Third Force, and to consolidate quickly his dominance over them.[32] So for both foreign policy and domestic reasons, Bevin injected a predictable note of urgency both into the Cabinet meeting, and then into the House of Commons debate that followed two weeks later.

As Bevin told the Cabinet, his aim since 1945 had been to save the outer crust of Europe and to keep it clear of dependence on the U.S.A. Now,

> it would be necessary to mobilize the resources of Africa in support of a Western European union; and if some such union could be created, including not only the countries of Western Europe but also their Colonial possessions in Africa and the East, this would form a bloc which, both in populations and productive capacity, could stand on an equality with the western hemisphere and the Soviet blocs.

The cabinet paper talked of the union of West European countries (including Portugal), and the potential for British leadership of such a European third force, agreeing that "[m]aterial aid will have to come principally from the United States, but the countries of Western Europe which despite the spiritual values of America will look to us for political and moral guidance and for assistance for building up a counter attraction to the baleful tenets of communism." Beginning with Anglo–French economic cooperation, Western Union could proceed, quietly, onto the development of Africa—the last hope of the old imperial powers—from which the U.S. would eventually be left out.[33] Indeed, according to the official historian's reading of the Cabinet secretary's notebook, he said that, "as soon as we can afford to develop Africa, we can cut loose from US." But time was now running out, and he told his colleagues that he feared that the Russians were responding to the Marshall Aid proposal by attempting to "smash western Europe" before a Western Union could be brought into existence, which meant that a far-reaching propaganda and information programme for Britain, its European partners, and colonial dependencies, was essential.[34] Bevin knew from his September talks with Ramadier that such thinking resonated well in Paris, not least given the fear in France that the U.S. might make a bid for American control of French imperial interests in Africa. Such talk would also have resonated well with those who harboured sympathy for Keep Left thinking.[35]

In retrospect, such self-confidence about Britain's capacity to survive, lead and influence seems Churchillian in tone. Bevin confronted the Cabinet with the prospect of a potential Soviet assault upon Western civilisation, for which the response could not be military, but had to be political, economic, and psychological. He sought to create a bloc based upon Britain's imperial "capital," which would, in the longer term, both provide Britain with the base from which to lead and give moral guidance to the European continent, while at the same time becoming economically powerful enough to exclude the influence of the U.S.

Two weeks later, in the House of Commons, Bevin returned to this theme in the context of a more general account of the breakdown of the postwar consensus on peacemaking. While proposing the extension of the 1947 Dunkirk Treaty to the Benelux countries, Bevin also emphasized the clauses relating to economic cooperation, raw materials and the need to develop Africa to strengthen Europe, which would generate a win-win situation for both. He argued to MPs that,

> [t]he organisation of Western Europe must be economically supported. That involves the closest possible collaboration with the commonwealth and with overseas territories, not only British but French, Dutch, Belgian and Portuguese. These overseas territories are

large primary producers and their standard of life is evolving rapidly and is capable of great development. They have raw materials, food and resources which can be turned to very great advantage, both to the people of the territories themselves, and to the world as a whole. The other two great world powers, the United States and Russia, have tremendous resources. There is no need of conflict with them in this matter at all. If western Europe is to achieve its balance of payments and to get a world equilibrium, it is essential that those resources should be developed and made available, and the exchange between them is carried out in a correct and proper manner. There is no conflict between the social and economic development of those overseas territories to the advantage of their people, and their development as a source of supplies for Western Europe, as a contributor, as I have indicated, [that is] so essential to the balance of payments . . . we intend to develop the economic cooperation between Western European countries step by step, to develop the resources of the territories with which we are associated, to build them up a system of priorities which will produce the quickest, most effective and most lasting results for the whole world. We hope that other countries with dependent territories will do this with us.

We shall thus bring together resources, manpower, organisation and opportunity for millions of people. I would like to depict what it really involves in terms of population whose standard of life can be lifted. We are bringing together these tremendous resources which stretch through Europe, the Middle East and Africa, to the Far East. In no case would it be an exclusive effort. It would be done with the object of making the whole world richer and safer.[36]

This speech, and the debate, relating to it, was considered to be critically important. Richard Crossman, leading member of the "Keep Left" group, admitted in the House of Commons that his views about the U.S. in world politics had changed since the Marshall Plan proposals, and the foreign secretary received warm support from both sides of the House, with copies of his speech then being widely requested.[37] An agenda that Bevin had been contemplating since the 1930s, and working towards for nearly a year, was at last out in the open.

The problem for Bevin was how to transform such a dramatic declaration of an alternative vision of British foreign policy into practical action.[38] As his colleague Hugh Dalton remarked towards the end of 1948, Bevin was still trying to "reorganise the middle of the planet" using Western Europe, the Mediterranean, the Middle East, and the Commonwealth. He thought that, "if we only pushed on and developed Africa, we could have the US dependent on us and eating out of our hands in four or five years . . . [the] US is barren of essential material and in Africa we have them all."[39] Yet, after mid 1948, the sub-Saharan dimension of the Brussels Treaty, signed in March 1948, evaporated, as Colonial Office officials took charge of what was, after all, their area of government policy, based on the premises that an Africa-up approach would be more useful than a centralised imperial top-down plan. Creech Jones' support was also to fall away over time.[40] John Kent has described the ways in which Anglo–French colonial cooperation developed after this, and shows that the projects did not in practice extend to any economic developments such as a customs union on the grandiose scale that Bevin had envisaged, but were restricted to constitutional and social questions.[41] In the Foreign Office, individual officials worked hard to support Bevin's thinking, but there had been constant resistance for both bureaucratic and ideational reasons from the Colonial Office, as well as the Board of Trade. (It was, for example, argued by the Colonial Office that the Colonial Governors would not accept any ideas of wide-ranging customs unions). It was significant that Kenneth Robinson, a senior Colonial Office official who had been a passionate advocate of a close "imperial" partnership between Britain and France, left the Colonial Office in 1948. It is probably fair to say that Colonial Office officials, and, indeed Foreign Office officials were prepared to give the Bevin scheme the benefit of the doubt, but that, over time, the institutional expertise of the Colonial Office brought a reversion to functional cooperation between British and French colonial departments.

Neither was there substantial scope for a strategic-military development of his ideas through 1948. Bevin's thinking about the "middle of the planet" had always had a military dimension, and here also, he felt that the way forward was in cooperation with France. Field Marshal Bernard Montgomery had also become involved in this debate at the end of 1947. Montgomery had gone out to Africa, and had sent Bevin a long report about his visit and the prospects that Africa offered to British global strategic thinking, and the scope for its development by Britain, and then also with other continental European powers. This letter gave rise to an interdepartmental and extremely hostile discussion within Whitehall, which was led by Creech Jones himself, who argued that a centralized blueprint, or any idea of federation for Africa was simply unworkable, and would encourage both local opposition, and with it, communist penetration.[42] Nevertheless, military talks were restarted with France in early 1948 in the wake of the Brussels Treaty, but these talks were not easy—either with the French, or indeed, within the U.K. itself.[43] The Chiefs of Staff had established very early on that the new key threat was the Soviet Union, and France offered little prospect as a military ally. Moreover, compared to the importance of the Middle East, strategic planning for Africa was seen as a peripheral exercise.[44]

In 1949, as we have seen, the Foreign Office formally buried the Third World Power project, as the North Atlantic treaty which seemed to characterize the emergence of a bipolar system, was finally signed. As Kent eloquently phrases it, if "Empire had initially been seen as a form of economic salvation that would produce independence from the Americans, by 1949 dependence on the Americans was seen as necessary if the Empire was to be saved."[45]

Why was the Third World Power project dropped by 1949? It is clear that, from the start, it suffered from a number of basic problems. The first was that it was vague: this was no formal joint strategy built upon a firm Anglo–French alliance, and it lacked a real policy edge, as it depended upon the hope of bilateral and then, hopefully, multilateral cooperation between European powers, cooperation perhaps with the Commonwealth, as well as cooperation with the colonial powers, and with those ruling them on the ground. It has not, for example, proved possible to identify one key planning document that encapsulates both the principles and the practicalities of such a scheme, beyond a wish to develop the resources of Africa for the benefit of France and Britain, which would, in time, it was considered, also bring benefits to Africa. Western Union soon lost any potential it might have had as a vehicle for an Anglo–French-led imperial project. Neither was the Marshall Plan a suitable vehicle. For neither Britain nor France had spare capital to invest even if the long term benefits were intended to be for Britain and France; and Marshall Aid was intended to be targeted towards the European recipients, not their overseas peoples. One has to ask how seriously the project was conceived and followed through, and how far it was based upon a personal initiative of Bevin.

The scheme did not meet the demands of the international system as it was developing by mid 1948. The emergence of the two bloc world was a far more powerful and dynamic process than European schemes to develop sub-Saharan Africa as a resource for Europe's benefit. The rising fear of communism, which preoccupied Bevin so intensely was, as he himself admitted, best dealt with alongside the U.S., with its far greater power capabilities. It is clear that Bevin took this view. Alan Milward also argues that, even in early 1948, "the USA, if it could be made to see Britain's point of view, was still in any case the preferred choice of Bevin and the Foreign Office." Indeed, it might well have been the case that in his heart, Bevin would have liked to imagine a genuine third force that could say No to both the U.S. and the Soviet Union, and which would realize his own long-held views about the relationship between economic development and peace, as well as the intrinsic merits of the Commonwealth as a model for global organization. However, his head clearly told him otherwise, and it is likely that his remarks about autonomy from the U.S. were as much to satisfy the left wing of his own party, as they were a realistic policy assessment.

The project however, tells much about the problems of policy development. It was not well executed by London. The idea of the Third World Power cut across the accepted delineations of foreign policy-making in the U.K., as it embraced political, economic and military dimensions (the Foreign Office, Treasury, Board of Trade, Ministry of Defence, Chiefs of Staff), as well as Europe and the Dominions/Colonies (Foreign Office, Dominions and Colonial Offices). It derived very largely from a grafting of Bevin's own ideas that had been formulated before the war on to the development work that was already under way between the colonial departments of Paris and London. In an act typical of the "imperialist Foreign Office" Bevin thus appears to have taken over and run with an expanded version of the Colonial Office's functional cooperation schemes for Africa development, backed by his former trades union subordinate, Creech Jones.[46] But this was still an intractable policy area, and Bevin had only partial authority over policy, as decisions required close cooperation between Whitehall departments. It is arguable that Foreign Office officials allowed Bevin to run with a personal idea, as had also been the case with his proposed Anglo–Soviet Treaty of 1947, without really prioritising it as a primary governmental project. The position was then further complicated by disagreements between Whitehall and the Quai d'Orsay over any of the specific planning for schemes, and the growing apprehension that this was exploitation that amounted to old-fashioned "imperialism."[47]

However, it is also possible that the Third World Power proposal was seen to be as much a way of encouraging the French to hold firm during the winter of 1947–8, as a serious neo-colonial proposal in itself. That is to say, Bevin and his officials very much wanted France as a strong post-war ally after 1945. However, the French did not make easy partners. Communists within the government; chronic political instability; an obstructive German policy; as well as real problems over Indo-China and the Levant all militated against a close relationship.[48] This is not to say that the Third World Power concept was a chimera, for it represented a genuine if conservative dimension of Bevin's thinking at a time when he had great personal influence within the government; but it also had an instrumental value that was as much to do with European politics as any *entente néo-coloniale*. When it proved complicated, and when the demands of cold war politics loomed even more strongly, then it evaporated. By 1949 France was once again finding its confidence, and was able to play the delicate balancing game between the U.S., the Soviet Union, a new Germany, as well as its old partner Britain. Even as France became more significant to the U.S. as a potential leader in Europe, the prospects of a bilaterally-led global Third World Power declined.[49]

What was the effect of all this upon Anglo-French relations? Bevin never had a particularly high reputation in France, and if he and his officials feared the antagonism of France on European issues, they were entirely correct, as relations between the two countries deteriorated after 1949—particularly on European questions—and remained tense. At least the failure of the Third World Power concept did not have the same disastrous effect as the next Anglo–French imperial scheme: Suez.

Yet, while Third World Power thinking fizzled out in Britain, the French took a different and tougher policy line.[50] Links with sub-Saharan Africa were more effectively promoted by France and its continental partners through the institutions that were created in the 1950s: the Schuman Declaration of 9 May 1950, for example, included a reference to the development of Africa as one of Europe's essential tasks. When he accepted the Charlemagne prize in Aachen in 1950 in the same month, Coudenhove-Kalergi argued that the Carolingian empire could be revived through a united Europe, creating "a great new empire . . . whose territory, stretching from the Baltic to Katanga, would be second only to the Soviet Union in vastness . . . (and would) cause economic prosperity to blossom as never before in Europe."[51] France was able to set a post-colonial economic agenda that was dynamic, and which was managed through the EEC Treaty of Rome, (articles 131–136), which also embedded features that were beneficial to France's own imperial interests, especially in North Africa. Some advocated Eurafrican communities for petrol, gas and iron ore, to mimic Europe's coal and steel community and Euratom.[52] The Yaoundé (1963, 1969) and the Lomé agreements (1975) institutionalized new, neo-colonial relationships between EEC powers and the developing world.

Meanwhile, the British focused upon imperial cooperation with the US in the global fight against communism. The first wave of postwar decolonisation was over by 1948, and the Colombo Plan of 1950 was to be Bevin's last attempt to build security upon international economic cooperation, and this did not involve cooperation with France. Between 1950 and 1973 British non-participation in the continental European ideas of federation and the multilateral colonial and post-colonial relationships that the EEC spawned, meant that, after 1949, it was left on the sidelines of collective West European thinking about sub-tropical Africa.[53]

NOTES

1. The phrase in the title of this article, "*entente néo-coloniale*," is taken from Marc Michel, "La cooperation intercoloniale en Afrique noire, 1942–1950: néocolonialisme éclairé?," *Relations Internationales*, 34 (1983), pp. 155–171.

2. "A Third World Power or Western Consolidation," The National Archives (formerly the Public Record Office), Kew, London. Hereafter TNA (PRO). CAB129, CP (49) 208, 18 October, 1949. This also appears as a UK Delegation brief, ZP2/58, of 19 April 1950, *Documents of British Policy Overseas*, series II, vol. II, no. 20. Hereafter DBPO.

3. See generally, John Kent, *The Internationalization of Colonialism: Britain, France and Black Africa, 1939–1956* (Oxford: Clarendon Press, 1992), and his *British Imperial Strategy and the Origins of the Cold War, 1944–49* (Leicester: Leicester University Press, 1993); Marc Michel, "The End of Empire, 1945–97" in Richard Mayne, Douglas Johnson, Robert Tombs (Eds.), *Cross Channel Currents: 100 years of the Entente Cordiale* (London: Routledge, 2004), pp. 143–53.

4. Jonathan Schneer, *Labour's Conscience: The Labour Left, 1945–51* (Boston: Unwin Hyman, 1988), ch. 3. There is a succinct summary of debates in Rhiannon Vickers, *The Labour Party and the World, Vol I: The Evolution of Labour's Foreign Policy, 1900–1951* (Manchester: Manchester University Press, 2003), especially pp. 159–62, 168–73. Alexandre Solioz, "La Grande-Bretagne de 1945 à 1948 et le concept de Troisième Force: un Projet et une Politique Etrangère," (Geneva: IHEI, 2004).

5. Marie-Thérèse Bitsch and Gérard Bossuat (Eds.), *L'Europe Unie et l'Afrique: De l'Idée d'Eurafrique à la Convention de Lomé*, (Brussels: Bruylant, Baden-Baden : Nomos, Paris: LGDJ, 2006). Count Coudenhove-Kalergi, *Europe must Unite* (Switzerland: Paneuropa, 1924 ed.). C-R Ageron, "L'Idée d'Euro-Afrique et le Débat Colonial Franco-Allemand dans l'Entre-Deux-Guerres," *Revue d'Histoire Moderne et Contemporaine*, 22 (1975), pp. 446–75. Roger Griffin, "Europe for the Europeans: Fascist Myths of the European New Order, 1922–1992," Humanities Research Centre Occasional paper, no. 1 (Oxford: Oxford Brookes University, 1994).

6. See, generally, William Roger Louis, *Imperialism at Bay, 1941–1945* (Oxford: Clarendon Press 1977); Nicholas Owen, "Critics of Empire in Britain," in Judith Brown and William Roger Louis (Eds.), *The Oxford History of the British Empire: The Twentieth Century* (Oxford: Oxford University Press, 1999), pp. 188–212; Partha Gupta, *Imperialism and the British Labour Movement, 1914–1964* (London: Macmillan, 1975).

7. Anthony Adamthwaite, *France and the Coming of the Second World War*, (London: Frank Cass, 1977), p. 55.

8. *The Spectator*, February 1939.

9. Alan Bullock, *The Life and Times of Ernest Bevin: Trade Union Leader, 1880-1940, Vol. I* (London: William Heinemann, 1960), p. 446. Alan Milward, *The Rise and Fall of a National Strategy, 1945–1963* (London: Frank Cass, 2002), p. 19.

10. Trades Union Congress Conference Proceedings, 1930.

11. Marjorie Nicholson, *The TUC Overseas: The Roots of Policy*, (London: Allen and Unwin, 1986), p. 191.

12. Martin Ceadel, *Semi-Detached Idealists: The British Peace Movement and International Relations, 1854–1945* (Oxford: Oxford University Press, 2000), p. 417. Deborah Lavin, *From Empire to International Commonwealth: A Biography of Lionel Curtis* (Oxford: Clarendon Press, 1995), p. 282. Curtis thought that, under

Bevin's influence, an organic union of the Commonwealth could become Labour Party policy.

13. Ernest Bevin, "Impressions of the British Commonwealth Relations Conference, 1938," *International Affairs*, 18 (1938), pp. 56–76.

14. *The Spectator*, February 1939.

15. Francis Williams, *Ernest Bevin: Portrait of a Great Englishman*, (London: Hutchinson, 1952), p. 209.

16. Nicholson, *TUC Overseas*, p. 262. See also, Anne Deighton, "Ernest Bevin and the Idea of Euro-Africa from the Interwar to the Postwar Period," in Bitsch and Bossuat (Eds.), *L'Europe Unie et l'Afrique*.

17. Michel, "Coopération Intercoloniale," p. 157.

18. Ronald Hyam, *The Labour Government and the End of Empire, 1945–1951, Part I, High Policy and Administration* (London: HMSO, 1992), introduction, p. xxxi.

19. Ben Pimlott, *Hugh Dalton* (London: Jonathan Cape, 1985), pp. 410–17.

20. *Hansard Parliamentary Debates*, 5th series, HC, vol. 413, 23 August 1945.

21. DBPO, series I, vol. I, no.102. Or, as Hall-Patch in the Treasury put it, "if we became the recognised and vigorous leader of a group of Western powers with large dependent territories we would gain that weight in counsels of the Big Three the need of which has been stressed." TNA (PRO), T 235/779, July 1945.

22. Saul Kelly, *Cold War in the Desert: Britain, the United States and the Italian Colonies, 1945–1952* (Basingstoke: Macmillan, 2000). Kenneth O Morgan, *Labour in Power, 1945–1951* (Oxford: Clarendon Press, 1984), pp. 190–5.

23. John Charmley, *Duff Cooper* (London: Wiedenfeld and Nicolson, 1986), p. 204. Duff Cooper saw this as a way of recovering from his less than successful wartime career, and was more consistently in favour of an Anglo-French alliance than was Bevin himself.

24. John Julius Norwich (Ed.), *The Duff Cooper Diaries*, (London: Weidenfeld and Nicolson, 2005), p. 382. Kent, *British Imperial Strategy*, p. 30. It was also argued that it might be easier to create an African Union under European guidance rather than unify in Europe itself. TNA (PRO), FO 371/67697, Parr memorandum, January 1947.

25. TNA (PRO), T236/1975, 5 September 1946. FO 371/49069, FO 371/67673 and T 236/1975 for talks with successive French leaders on this theme.

26. Anthony Adamthwaite, "Britain, France, the United States and Euro-Africa, 1945–1949," in Bitsch and Bossuat (Eds.), *L'Europe Unie et l'Afrique*.

27. TNA (PRO), CAB 129/16 CP (47) 35, January 1947. Hoyar-Miller minute, 15 March 1947. FO 371/67696.

28. Philip Bell, *France and Britain, 1940–1994: The Long Separation* (London: Longman, 1997), pp. 88–9. Sean Greenwood, *The Alternative Alliance: Anglo–French Relations Before the Coming of NATO, 1944–1948* (London: Minerva, 1996), p. 252ff.

29. Bevin to Attlee, 5 September 1947. TNA (PRO), FO 371/62553.

30. *Report of Proceedings of the 97 Annual Trades Union Congress, 1–4 September, 1947* (London: Cooperative Printing Society Ltd (TU), 1947), pp. 415ff.

31. Anne Deighton, *The Impossible Peace: Britain, the Division of Germany and the Origins of the Cold War, 1945–1947* (Oxford: Clarendon Press, 1990), pp. 218–20.

32. Weiler calls it "appropriation" of their term Third Force. Peter Weiler, *British Labour and the Cold War* (Stanford, CA: Stanford University Press, 1988), p. 205.
33. TNA (PRO), CAB 129/23 CP (48) 6, 5 January 1948. CAB 128/12, CM (48) 2, 8 January 1948,
34. Milward, *National Strategy*, p. 32. The Cabinet had three major papers to deal with in the meeting. TNA (PRO), CAB 129 /23, CP (48) 6, 4 January 1948; CP (48) 7, 5 January 1948,; and CP (48) 8, 5 January 1948. The meeting is minuted at CAB 128 /12, CM (48) 2, 8 January 1948.
35. Milward, *National Strategy*, p. 32. Milward, as an Official Historian employed by the U.K. Cabinet Office, had privileged access to the notebooks of the Cabinet Secretary from which this quotation is taken. However, U.S. interest in Africa did not in fact start until the mid 1950s. Ironically, in 1948 American policy-makers were just beginning to see the value of the European empires as a strategic asset against worldwide communism. Irwin Wall, "Les États-Unis et la Décolonisation de l'Afrique. Le Mythe de l'Eurafrique," Bitsch and Bossuat (Eds.), *L'Europe Unie et l'Afrique*.
36. *Hansard Parliamentary Debates*, 5th series, HC, vol. 446, cc. 383–409. The debate ran from 22–23 January 1948.
37. Christopher Mayhew, *A War of Words: A Cold War Witness* (London: IB Tauris, 1998), p. 30. Mayhew claims that it was he who largely wrote Bevin's speech.
38. TNA (PRO), PREM 8/1146; EPC (47) 6th; CAB 134 /217, memorandum of Chancellor of the Exchequer, January 1948.
39. 15 October, 1948. Hugh Dalton, *High Tide and After: Memoirs 1945–1960*, London: 1962.
40. Arthur Creech Jones was Colonial Secretary from 1947. Nicholas Owen, "Decolonisation and Postwar Consensus," in Harriet Jones and Michael Kandiah, (Eds.), *The Myth of Consensus: New Views on British History, 1945–1964*, (Basingstoke: Macmillan, 1996), pp. 157–180.
41. Kent, *British Imperial Strategy*, gives a comprehensive account of these bilateral ventures.
42. TNA (PRO), FO 800/435. Montgomery to Bevin. See FO800/ 435 for Creech Jones' response, January 1948. Ronald Hyam, "Africa and the Labour Government, 1945–1951," *Journal of Imperial and Commonwealth History*, 16/3 (1988), pp. 148–72.
43. John Young, "The Failure of the New Entente Cordiale, 1947–50" in Alan Sharp and Glyn Stone (Eds.), *Anglo-French Relations in the Twentieth Century: Rivalry and Cooperation* (London: Routledge, 2000), pp. 264–7.
44. TNA (PRO), FO 800/452, 4 February 1948.
45. Kent, *British Imperial Strategy*, p. 216.
46. Stephen Howe, *Anticolonialism in British Politics: The Left and the End of Empire, 1918–1964* (Oxford: Clarendon Press, 1993), p. 146.
47. On the Anglo-Soviet treaty proposals of 1947 see Deighton, *Impossible Peace*, p. 161. Cabinet Secretary Brook warned Attlee of the danger of following a traditional imperial policy. Brook to Attlee, 14 January 1948. TNA (PRO), PREM 8/923. David Fieldhouse suggests that the economic exploitation of the colonies was "benevolent intentions vitiated by ignorance and . . . a simplistic

belief that what might constitute economic exploitation if undertaken by capitalist agencies became development if done by socialists," David Fieldhouse, "Labour Governments and the Empire-Commonwealth," in Ritchie Ovendale, (Ed.), *The Foreign Policy of the British Labour Governments, 1945–1951* (Leicester: Leicester University Press, 1984), pp. 83–121, quotation at p. 101.

48. Milward, *National Strategy*, pp. 16, 31.

49. William Hitchcock, *France Restored: Cold War Diplomacy and the Quest for Leadership in Europe, 1944–1954* (Chapel Hill: University of North Carolina Press, 1998), p. 208.

50. See, for example, Combaux, "Nécessité d'une Eurafrique," *Revue de Défense Nationale*, 13 (November 1957), pp. 1816–26. The French government under the premiership of Guy Mollet proposed French membership of the British Commonwealth in 1955, but this was turned down by the Conservative government of the day, and the phrase *Eurafrique* fell into disuse by the late 1950s, in favour of "association."

51. Karis Muller, "The Birth and Death of Eurafrica," *International Journal of Francophone Studies*, 3/1 (2000), pp. 4–17, quotation at p. 5. She argues that the spirit of Eurafrica ran through all French projects for European integration like a cultural thread, culminating in *Francophonie*, which still manifests anti-Americanism.

52. Quoted in Muller, "The Birth and Death of Eurafrica," p. 9.

53. Except for moments when Commonwealth agricultural policies were discussed in the context of Britain's possible accession to the EEC.

SEPARATED BY THE ATLANTIC: THE BRITISH AND DE GAULLE, 1958–1967

James Ellison

On 18 June 1964, the British ambassador at Paris, Sir Pierson Dixon, was received by the president of France, General Charles de Gaulle, for an interview. After discussing the German question, the war in Vietnam and China, de Gaulle turned to Anglo–French relations. The exchange that followed reveals much about that which divided Britain and France during de Gaulle's presidency, and beyond.

> [T]he General said that he would now like to say something not as President of the French Republic but as a "philosopher." In his opinion we had had a rough deal after the war and not obtained rewards commensurate with our tremendous achievements. Faced by the emergence of the Soviet Union and the United States as major nations, we had rather been left behind. If he might permit himself a critical judgment, it was that we had not been sufficiently "ourselves"; we had been too prone after the war to lean on the Americans.[1]

The author would like to express his gratitude to the Arts and Humanities Research Council and the British Academy for their generosity in supporting the research upon which this article is based.

Dixon's record does not indicate that a pause in the conversation occurred once de Gaulle had completed these few sentences, but given that the British ambassador had frequently and forcefully reported to London his view that de Gaulle had become "actively hostile to the Anglo-Americans," it is not difficult to imagine that one took place.[2] What we can say with certainty is that Dixon was moved to reply in kind:

> I felt that I should not let these remarks pass without comment and, saying that I too was speaking as a philosopher, agreed that World War II had certainly been a crucial event in the history of nations. At the outbreak of the Second World War we had instinctively joined with the French as our principal allies, as we had done in World War I. However, despite all our efforts France had collapsed. When we were left alone we had naturally tried to obtain all the help we could from the Americans and eventually, when the Americans came in to the war, we found ourselves working with them in the most intimate relationship. This comradeship in war had been projected into the period of peace and still persisted, to our mutual advantage.[3]

According to Dixon, de Gaulle "took this well, admitting that the fall of France had played a highly significant part in the present relationships between nations." Yet in making this admission de Gaulle had conceded nothing to Dixon. In fact, he had implicitly reaffirmed the profound criticism that he had just made of post-war British foreign policy. For de Gaulle, a vital lesson drawn from 1940 was that greatness could only be restored if France rejected reliance on other states and pursued an independent foreign policy. Such principles were born in part from de Gaulle's wartime dependence on Britain, a dishonourable necessity in his view, and his conclusion, described to Jean Monnet in June 1943, that "Anglo-Saxon domination in Europe was a growing threat and if it continued after the war France would have to turn to Germany or Russia."[4] In the mid-1960s, de Gaulle remained convinced of this threat and his ensuing foreign policies brought France into direct confrontation with Britain.

De Gaulle's foreign policies had many facets, but his search for French independence began with France's leadership of the European Economic Community (EEC). It was this institution which gave France its economic security, a method of containing the Federal Republic of Germany, and the potential to create a power-base free of American control. Hence, when in 1961 and 1967 successive British governments attempted to gain membership of the Community, de Gaulle unilaterally vetoed both applications. He did so to prevent any loss of French leadership in the EEC and to defend the institution from exposure to American influence via the British. This area of the Anglo–French conflict is increasingly well understood, but there is a parallel area which is less so and is explored here.[5] The most dramatic act of independence during de Gaulle's presidency was his withdrawal of France from the integrated military command structures of the North Atlantic Treaty Organisation (NATO) in 1966. By this move, de Gaulle sought to free France from what he described as "subordination" and thereafter strike an independent course in the pursuit of Cold War détente.[6] Ultimately, de Gaulle failed, and by 1967, NATO was strengthened and its members, apart from France, remained firm supporters of the organisation and of a multilateral approach to détente.[7] The significance of this subject for the development of Anglo–French relations is that while de Gaulle proved an obstacle to Britain's membership of the EEC in 1967, the British were able to use the NATO crisis to outmanoeuvre him and work towards their foreign policy aims. De Gaulle's attempts to reform NATO personally were a tactical error in contrast with his vetoes of Britain's EEC applications. In NATO, the British could act with greater freedom of movement and authority and, unlike in the realm of the EEC, they could do so with American support and cooperation. Hence, the central argument of this article is that the crisis in the Atlantic Alliance over NATO in the 1960s enabled the British, with American encouragement, to isolate de Gaulle and contemporaneously strengthen transatlantic relations and improve the prospects of achieving EEC membership. The analysis will begin with a brief description of how the British and French found themselves largely at odds in the post-war world over the Atlantic Alliance and European integration. It will then describe how Anglo–French relations were strained in both areas after de Gaulle's return to power. Thereafter, it will concentrate on the evolution of the NATO crisis and its solution before reaching conclusions about its importance for the Anglo–French relationship.

The divergence between Britain and France that reached its peak during de Gaulle's presidency had its origins in the separate paths taken by the two countries in the aftermath of the Second World War. The British and the French were confronted with similar problems and both shared the same primary aims: national rejuvenation, economic reconstruction, colonial adjustment and security in the emerging Cold War. Nonetheless, during the period 1948–50, they reached fundamentally different conclusions about how to solve those problems. Their resulting foreign policies are epitomized, if in caricature, by Winston Churchill's sponsorship of the "fraternal association of the English-speaking peoples" and de Gaulle's description of Europe as "the chance for France to become what she [had] ceased to be since Waterloo: the first in the world."[8] Although Anglo-French relations were always subject to dispute after 1945, they faced their most fundamental discord over the future of European integration and Western Europe's relationship with the United States.[9]

From the end of the 1940s, Britain's foreign policy had a global horizon, reflecting the country's assets and objectives, and was based on sterling,
free trade and strong relations with the Commonwealth and the United
States.[10] Cooperation with Western Europe received lower status in Britain's international priorities, both economic and political, and as stated in
a Foreign Office memorandum for the Permanent Under-Secretary's
Committee on 9 June 1951, the aim of British policy was "to try to lead
the integration movement away from exclusively European ideas towards
an Atlantic community."[11] The French thought differently. Europe was
not a function of France's global policy, it was the basis of it. French governments chose and fashioned European economic integration as the
instrument of their own national revival. Parallel to France's economic
revival would be its political ascendancy to the leadership of Western
Europe and, in particular, predominance over the Federal Republic of
Germany. With economic and political strength achieved, so France
would be able to secure independence in the Cold War. The logic of this
process overcame instinctive opposition to supranational integration in de
Gaulle's mind when he returned to power in June 1958. In the decade that
followed, France's foreign policy saw its most potent evolution as de
Gaulle aspired to create an independent France within a European Europe
which was free from American influence.[12]

British and French foreign policy strategies began to clash in the mid-
to late 1950s as Britain realized that it would have to find some means of
coming to terms with the EEC and as de Gaulle attempted to break what
he saw as the Anglo-Saxon monopoly of the Atlantic Alliance and
NATO. The first quarrel came over economic integration. As the six
European Coal and Steel Community (ECSC) powers negotiated their
way towards treaties establishing the EEC after their meeting in Messina
in June 1955, the British government recognised that it would have to
adapt to this new development.[13] It was not so much that the British had
enthusiasm for it but, rather, that they feared isolation from this American-
sponsored enterprise at a time when the Commonwealth and Empire
increasingly failed to offer distinct sources of power. The British thus
sought to draw strength from the developing integration of western European economies by proposing in 1956–7 a European Free Trade Area
(FTA) to encompass the EEC.[14] The problem was that the French were
protective of the opportunities offered by this new European economic
cooperation and did not wish to share it, for numerous reasons, with Britain.
Consequently, the French parried the British proposal and stalled the
negotiations. Despite British hopes that de Gaulle's patent anti-suprana-
tionality would ensure his support of Britain's looser, confederal plan, the
new French president only continued his predecessors' policy of prevari-
cation while he developed enough support to intervene against the FTA.

There was painful recognition of this in London; on 26 October 1958 Harold Macmillan noted in his diary that "De Gaulle is bidding high for the hegemony of Europe" and the prime minister subsequently made desperate, empty threats to reappraise Britain's role in European institutions, including the Western European Union (WEU) and NATO if the FTA failed.[15] De Gaulle was indeed "bidding" for "the hegemony of Europe," having recognized the significance of the EEC for French power. He also believed, not entirely inaccurately, that the FTA was a British attempt to wrest the leadership of Europe from France and dilute the EEC within an Atlantic-Commonwealth arrangement. Hence, in December 1958 he unanimously rejected the FTA, the first of what would be a hat trick of vetoes of British European initiatives.[16]

Whereas the quarrel over the FTA had been essentially economic with political overtones, the second dispute was set squarely in the geopolitical realm of the Atlantic Alliance. It began on 17 September 1958 when de Gaulle attempted to break what he perceived as Anglo-Saxon control of the Atlantic Alliance by suggesting a tripartite directorate for the defence of the free world.[17] In a memorandum sent to President Dwight D. Eisenhower and Macmillan, de Gaulle contended that the "Atlantic Alliance was conceived and its functioning is prepared with a view to an eventual zone of action which no longer corresponds to political and strategic realities." De Gaulle had in mind events in the Middle East and Africa and stated that "France could, therefore, no longer consider that NATO in its present form meets the conditions of security of the free world and notably its own." His answer was to advocate "on the level of world policy and strategy" the establishment of "an organization composed of: the United States, Great Britain and France."[18] This organization would not only deal in matters of diplomacy but also defence; de Gaulle was clearly signalling his conviction that France's forthcoming national nuclear deterrent qualified the French to join with the Americans and the British in a nuclear directorate.[19] Lacking no ambition, de Gaulle's proposal ran against the policies of the United States towards leadership of the Alliance and was contrary to the exclusive Anglo–American nuclear arrangements recently agreed in 1957.[20] The offer of tripartitism was thus politely declined, perhaps as de Gaulle had hoped it would be in order to give him opportunity to begin slow withdrawal of France from military integration in NATO. In any case, the failure of any high level and meaningful Anglo–American–French consultation into the 1960s only served to strengthen de Gaulle's view that France would have to stand alone.[21]

In these disagreements between the British and the French early in de Gaulle's presidency, it is possible to see the connection between colliding ambitions over the future of Europe and the association between Europe and the United States. For de Gaulle, European integration paved the way for independence and the rejection of his tripartite proposal served to clarify his preconceptions about the exclusivity of the Anglo–American relationship. For the British, European cooperation became an ever-increasing necessity for national strength but integration amongst Western European powers was not an end in itself and was only ever conceived of as an integral part of interdependent Atlantic partnership with the U.K. and the U.S. taking a leading role. The clashes of 1958 caused by these opposing positions were, however, relatively small in scale in comparison with the diplomatic dissent following de Gaulle's infamous press conference of 14 January 1963. On that day, the French president activated his policy of French independence in an unprecedented manner by issuing a double *non* to Britain's first EEC application and to president John F. Kennedy's Grand Design for an Atlantic Community.[22] These vetoes reveal how the issues of Europe and the Atlantic Alliance were linked in de Gaulle's view of France and its place in the world. The veto of Britain's membership bid had the same motive that produced the rejection of the FTA in 1958: to sustain French leadership of the EEC and protect that institution from American influence. The veto of Kennedy's Grand Design, including its proposal for multilateral nuclear collaboration, rested on the criticisms de Gaulle had made of NATO in his tripartite memorandum of 1958: the organization was outdated and its Anglo-Saxon monopoly was unacceptable to France. The French president had thus, in one press conference, activated the challenge that would extend throughout the 1960s. In 1963, he had out-manoeuvred the Americans and the British but as the decade progressed, they adapted their tactics to deal with him.

There were initial calls in Britain and the United States for retribution against de Gaulle. The atmosphere in London included both exasperation—embodied in the view of the permanent under secretary at the Foreign Office, Sir Harold Caccia, "The Cross of Lorraine we can bear without too much burden, the double cross I find less tolerable"—and defeat, as revealed in Harold Macmillan's often-quoted diary entry of 28 January 1963, "All our policies at home and abroad are in ruins."[23] In Washington, president Kennedy exposed his anger at a meeting of the National Security Council's Executive Committee 11 days after the vetoes when he said that the United States "should look now at the possibility that de Gaulle had concluded that he would make a deal with the Russians, break up NATO and push the U.S. out of Europe."[24] Once tempers had cooled, however, a consensus emerged between the Americans and the British on how best to prevent de Gaulle from causing further damage to their interests. Indeed, one consequence of de Gaulle's actions was to encourage Anglo–American cooperation in the pursuit of those interests.

Although the Americans and the British, under Kennedy and Macmillan and thereafter Lyndon B. Johnson and Sir Alec Douglas Home and

Harold Wilson, continued to uphold the goals of Atlantic partnership and European integration, cooperation between them to achieve advances in these arenas did not emerge immediately. There was little progress to be made in terms of Britain's relationship with the EEC as enthusiasm for any new attempt to gain EEC entry had been dampened in January 1963 and dissuaded thereafter by de Gaulle's continued resistance. It was also the case that when the new Labour government of Harold Wilson assumed power in 1964, it did so with no initial desire to reinvigorate Britain's policies to achieve EEC membership.[25] There was also little progress to be made on the primary focus of diplomacy within the Atlantic Alliance and NATO, the American proposals for a Multilateral Force (MLF). This idea for a military atomic authority in which NATO member states would have some control over a NATO nuclear force had been championed by the Kennedy administration in 1961. The MLF had numerous aims, but its foremost purpose was to give the West Germans a legitimate but restricted role in the multilateral nuclear defence of the West. Such multilateralism implied, however, that existing nuclear member states, namely the British and the French, would commit their nuclear forces to NATO, thus surrendering their national deterrents. So controversial and divisive was this idea that it went nowhere fast until the incoming Wilson government proposed in December 1964 an alternative idea, the Atlantic Nuclear Force (ANF).[26] In contrast to the MLF, the ANF would allow the British to retain their nuclear independence, yet while the British did their best to portray the ANF as a positive contribution to rectify the impasse over the MLF, it did little to improve the situation. Instead, the nuclear sharing question beleaguered the Alliance as the Americans continued to back the MLF, the West Germans maintained their demands for involvement in the control of NATO nuclear hardware, the British remained intransigent on their independent deterrent and the French openly criticised the whole concept. In fact, it was de Gaulle's continued criticisms of the MLF and what he saw as the shortcomings of NATO which gave the Americans and the British some common ground on which to cooperate in defence of the Atlantic Alliance when otherwise they found themselves divided over the question of nuclear sharing. The same effect would occur when de Gaulle's NATO policies reached their height in 1966.

In spring 1964, the Foreign Office in London began to contemplate diplomatic action to counter the ill effects of de Gaulle's foreign policies on British interests. One of the spurs to do so was Britain's ambassador at Paris, Sir Pierson Dixon, who reported throughout the year of de Gaulle's hostility towards British and Western interests. On 12 March, for example, he warned that it ought to be "anticipated that France in the coming period will be found to be moving in the opposite direction to that which her Western Allies wish to take" and recommended full cooperation between Britain, the United States and European allies to prevent de Gaulle blocking progress in NATO and the Kennedy Round trade negotiations.[27] On 22 April, he urged London to inform France's EEC partners and the Americans of French duplicity, especially in their policy towards the United States, a recommendation which by early summer became policy.[28] The British government would seek to avoid giving the impression that it was "conducting a vendetta against de Gaulle or the French" but the Foreign Office noted that there was no reason why diplomats "should be too mealy-mouthed about saying what we think to our friends about French policy whenever we find it, or its manner, objectionable"; indeed, Britain's ambassadors in the EEC capitals and in Washington were instructed to "take suitable opportunities when discussing specific issues . . . to point to those negative or disruptive aspects of French policy which are harmful to the interests of the Western Alliance as a whole."[29] The fact was, however, that making Britain's allies more aware of de Gaulle's mischief making, as seen from London, did little to prevent the persistence of the problem.

By spring 1965, one year on from Dixon's attempts to invigorate British policy towards de Gaulle, the Atlantic Alliance and Europe, the head of the Foreign Office Planning Staff, Michael Palliser, took up the task. In a bleak assessment which spoke of de Gaulle's successful exploitation of the crisis in leadership of the Atlantic Alliance, Palliser warned of the immediate danger of Britain's "growing irrelevance" to American and European allies. His conclusions, as he admitted, were unoriginal and reminiscent of those reached in papers on British foreign policy since 1956: "unless [the British government] can soon evolve a more effective relationship with Western Europe and the United States within the Atlantic framework Britain will cease to be a world power." The difference in 1965, however, was that this increasingly long-held conviction had been "obscured by our own economic difficulties and our commitments east of Suez." Palliser thus urged a "genuine reappraisal" of "Britain's role within Europe and the Atlantic Alliance" which would be seen as such by the outside world. If the government embraced this idea, "the current reluctance of the United States to take the lead in Western affairs could give Britain the opportunity to reassert both her own importance in the Atlantic field and the sort of policies which are at present going by default and being undermined by General de Gaulle." This did not mean that Britain could "lead the Atlantic world" (Palliser added that "Only the United States can do this"), it meant Britain indicating by its actions "the kind of Atlantic association the Americans will want to lead." In essence, Palliser was urging "a more robust approach to de Gaulle."[30]

Where Dixon had failed, Palliser succeeded. The Foreign Office was increasingly concerned about Britain's "growing isolation from Europe" and on 3 March 1965, in a memorandum to the prime minister which went to Cabinet later that month, the foreign secretary, Michael Stewart, made the case for an invigorated policy towards "the right sort of Europe" within an Atlantic framework.[31] Harold Wilson's own priorities did not, however, chime with those of his foreign policy advisers. The prime minister's commitment to the commercial revival of the Commonwealth and his instinctive caution towards the EEC led him to reject a new European policy and instead continue to improve links between the EEC and the European Free Trade Association (EFTA).[32] While the Foreign Office had recommended the building up of EFTA as part of a reinvigorated European policy, this course could not singly halt Britain's isolation and de Gaulle's progress.

Although the prime minister did not embrace a more far-reaching policy towards the EEC, neither did he prevent the Foreign Office from active diplomacy in the Atlantic Alliance, especially alongside the United States, when in the second half of 1965 de Gaulle's challenge escalated. On 1 July, France began a six month boycott of the EEC which threw its future into question, and on 9 September de Gaulle announced that by 1969 "at the latest" France would free itself from the "subordination called 'integration'" in NATO.[33] This statement of intent left the exact moment of withdrawal open for speculation but the distinct possibility of action prior to 1969 led the Johnson administration to start the process of protecting NATO from de Gaulle. From June 1965, the Americans and the British instituted contingency planning and diplomacy to hold France's fourteen NATO partners together.[34] Long-standing Anglo-American cooperation in NATO led to an easy exchange between London and Washington on how to deal with de Gaulle, although from the American standpoint the British remained part of Europe's problems given their objections to the MLF and their continued financial weakness. Hence, the Johnson administration encouraged the Wilson government to agree to Anglo–American–West German talks and establish a tripartite exchange as a way of resolving the nuclear and financial ills of the Atlantic Alliance.[35] The British welcomed cooperation with the United States, although they were wary of a possible dilution of their relationship with the Americans through the inclusion of the West Germans.[36] The only answer to this predicament was, as Palliser had suggested in February 1965, for Britain to "reassert . . . her own importance in the Atlantic field" and in 1966, de Gaulle gave the British reason and opportunity to do so.[37]

There was recognition on both sides of the Atlantic that de Gaulle's agreement to the Luxembourg compromise in January 1966 which ended the EEC's empty chair crisis indicated that the French president would now turn his attention to NATO.[38] It was widely accepted that there was an interrelationship between de Gaulle's EEC and NATO policies and that his intent, through withdrawal from NATO, was to achieve real and symbolic independence for France ahead of his planned visit to Moscow in June 1966 where he would try to play the role of arbiter between East and West. Supposition that de Gaulle would act on his criticisms of NATO was confirmed on 21 February 1966 when in a press conference he gave notice that France would seek to restore her sovereignty "as regards soil, sky, sea and forces, and any foreign element that would be in France, will in the future be under French command alone."[39] This speech was the prelude to de Gaulle's letter to Johnson on 7 March confirming, as Dean Acheson put it, "The indisputable fact . . . that France want[ed] everything French out of NATO and everything NATO—especially everything American—out of France."[40] The ensuing crisis, the greatest in NATO's history, produced a disquieting degree of instability which, it was feared, would be exploited in de Gaulle's dealings with the Soviets. Despite the attempts of Maurice Couve de Murville, de Gaulle's foreign minister, to dismiss the links between NATO withdrawal and de Gaulle's Moscow visit as "infantile," those links did exist.[41] And the potential for Cold War disunity in the West that they created heightened the NATO crisis above that of January 1963 in its possible impact on the Atlantic Alliance and U.S.–European relations. It also offered the Wilson government the opening to meet the challenge de Gaulle had posed to British interests since his return to power in 1958.

De Gaulle's letter of 7 March to Johnson was accompanied by similar letters to the leaders of Britain, the Federal Republic of Germany and Italy. A State Department comparison of all four messages pointed out that "Great Britain receives the most fulsome praise both as a tested and traditional ally and as a great and wise European power." US officials also speculated that de Gaulle's "effusive tone . . . may reflect [his] hopes that, in due course, Britain will cast in its lot with French schemes for reorganizing the continent."[42] A more likely explanation is that de Gaulle expected a robust response from the British to his NATO actions and thus indulged in a little timely flattery; his description of Britain as a "great European state which is, *par excellence*, aware of the world situation" was in direct contrast to comments made in 1963 and those which would be made in 1967.[43] It is also no coincidence that on 15 March 1966, the French state secretary for foreign affairs, Jean de Broglie, "intervened unexpectedly" in a Western European Union (WEU) debate on the NATO crisis "to say that France was involved in the construction of the Common Market which she earnestly hoped that Britain would join."[44] This enigmatic invitation to the British was quickly dampened by the French government which depicted it as nothing more than a restatement of policy and in doing so strengthened suggestions that it had been made to deflect attention from events in NATO.[45] Although it was kept afloat

briefly for electoral reasons by Stewart ("to take the European wind out of
Tory sails"), the British had been distrustful of a French "policy of
smiles" for some time.[46]

De Gaulle was right to be wary of the British reaction. He had created
just the conditions for the Wilson government to initiate the reinvigora-
tion of Britain's policies towards the Gaullist challenge that had been
wanting since 1963. The NATO crisis produced the chance for the British
to take a lead in the Atlantic Alliance, enhance Britain's status in
Washington and Western European capitals and, for the first time since
January 1963, take on de Gaulle from a position of relative authority.
These had been objectives that the Foreign Office had pressed the prime
minister to focus upon from spring 1965 but slow progress on the nuclear
sharing issue in the Alliance and Wilson's own indifference to a renewed
British EEC policy had prevented activity. That indifference remained in
March 1966 but the prime minister recognised that this was a moment
when he could endorse and act upon Foreign Office recommendations to
influence the resolution of NATO's problems, not least because they did
not demand an immediate decision on the question of Britain and the
EEC. Indeed, the NATO crisis, if handled well, could see de Gaulle and
his foreign policy agendas sidelined and Britain's own agendas elevated.
Hence in his communications to Johnson about France and NATO in
March 1966, or "The General's rogue elephant tactics" as he put it, Wilson emphasized that he saw them "both as a threat and as an opportunity"
and outlined Britain's own conception of Atlantic relations. This included
a "radical examination of [NATO's] structure, force levels and financial
arrangements"; a solution to the nuclear sharing question with an eye on
German reunification; and forward-looking policies towards détente
with the East. And to achieve these aims, Wilson urged Anglo–American
cooperation.[47]

Although the Johnson administration had worked closely with the
British on the France–NATO question during the second half of 1965, it
remained cautious about giving the appearance of exclusive U.S.–U.K.
cooperation and kept other senior allies, especially the West Germans, in
touch.[48] In light of de Gaulle's actions in March, however, the Johnson
administration recognised the value of collaboration with Britain and
combined its diplomatic forces with those of the British to hold NATO
together against the French assault. Foreign policy advisers in Washington
concluded that the British could champion NATO and rally France's fourteen partners in a way the Americans could not. They knew that they
would play into de Gaulle's hands if they led the NATO response as he
would transform it into a public bilateral Franco–American struggle.
There would be no such struggle if the British government helped lead the
fourteen. Moreover, by taking a prominent role in NATO, the British

could give succour to France's allies in the EEC, especially the troubled West Germans, by acting as an Atlantic-European minded potential EEC member-state.[49] What de Gaulle had done by pursuing his foreign policies to the point when they destabilised the Atlantic Alliance was to create the conditions which had always produced Anglo–American cooperation: a shared interest in defeating a common enemy. And by focussing his attention on NATO, he had done so in an arena where France was not dominant. The EEC could not exist without France, NATO could. What is more, in relation to the EEC, Anglo–American diplomacy could have little effect, but over NATO the Americans and the British could call on established modes of cooperation and work efficiently together. Mutual objectives—protecting NATO from the Gaullist challenge and solving NATO's problems and reforming it for the future—produced congruity between the Americans and the British on the tactics to neutralize de Gaulle and on the strategy of turning the NATO crisis into an opportunity for renewal. Those tactics were based on the premise, shared by London and Washington, that the best way to deal with de Gaulle was not to retaliate but to treat him as an ally, avoid direct confrontation and isolate him by holding his allies together in opposition.[50] In the days after the January 1963 vetoes, Arthur Schlesinger Jr. had encapsulated this approach in one line—"recrimination does no good: de Gaulle is a natural force, and there is no point in reviling a tornado"—and it was implemented with accomplishment over 1966–7.[51]

The NATO crisis was quietened as the organization united in the face of French withdrawal. This achievement was due in part to the energetic role played by the British in the diplomacy within NATO to hold the fourteen allies together and set the agenda for renewal. The British were given the lead by the Americans to organize the fourteen's official response to France in the form of the declaration of 18 March 1966, they played a significant role in the crucial June 1966 Ministerial Meeting and continued to work actively towards the settling of the crisis by December 1966.[52] Thereafter, throughout 1967, NATO underwent a full review in the Harmel Exercise, an initiative of the Belgian Foreign Minister, and in December the Harmel Report signalled the defeat of the Gaullist challenge.[53] The British were only one of a number of key allies who ensured the success of the Harmel Exercise but in their defence of NATO multilateralism and the U.S.–European defence relationship that underpinned it, they secured their goal of taking a leading role in the Alliance. The Wilson government had presented Britain as the senior European ally in NATO and saw Britain's diplomatic stock among Western Europeans rise in contrast to the fall in French fortunes. In turn, this created improved conditions for the receipt of Britain's second application for EEC membership in May 1967.[54] From October 1966 Wilson had led his Cabinet and the country towards another bid after continued economic problems had revealed that the Labour government's failed National Plan offered no hope for future economic stability and growth. The uncomplicated, one-line EEC application (which distinguished itself from its predecessor by attaching no conditions in advance), in combination with the active loyalty exhibited by the British in NATO, ensured that despite de Gaulle's veto in November 1967, Britain's position in Europe, and in the Atlantic Alliance, was stronger by the end of the 1960s than it had been at the start.

This description of events reads like the successful execution by the British of a well-designed plan which set out to use the NATO crisis of 1966 as an opportunity to achieve interrelated objectives. A note of caution must be added to this analysis. Britain did achieve diplomatic successes, but there are other factors which help explain why by the end of the 1960s de Gaulle's policies had failed to achieve the greatness for him and France that he aspired to, and why Britain was on the verge of entry into the EEC whilst playing a leading role amongst Europeans in NATO. The first is the failure of de Gaulle to secure the position of European arbiter in East-West relations. Prior to the French president's June 1966 Moscow visit, there had been concerns that the Soviets would enter into "dialogue [with de Gaulle] in order to exploit to the hilt de Gaulle's disruptive value."[55] These fears proved to be over-stated and while de Gaulle continued to seek a role in the pursuit of détente, such as his trip to Poland in September 1967, he did not secure the influence that he desired.[56] Accordingly, his status within the Atlantic Alliance and the EEC declined. The second factor is that while the British contributed to the survival of NATO after March 1966, they were not alone. Multilateralism overwhelmed de Gaulle's unilateralism, especially in relation to the future role of NATO in moves towards détente, and the solution to the 1966 crisis was a multilateral affair. Britain was a leading actor but it was the statesmanlike diplomacy of Lyndon Johnson which has received particular praise recently.[57] Without American cooperation, the Wilson government would not have been able to take such a prominent role. Similarly, the solution to many of the specific problems of the Alliance would not have been achieved without flexibility from the Federal Republic of Germany. The third factor centres on the development of the EEC as an institution and on the maturity of France's five partners in pressing for enlargement. The Gaullist challenge and its promotion of the nation-state over the Community, at its height during the empty chair crisis, strengthened the ambition of France's partners to protect EEC institutions and to extend the Community programme further. British entry was supported as a means of diluting French influence and became embroiled in the wider revival of integration that would be heralded by The Hague summit of December 1969.[58]

Thus, a composite of Britain's diplomacy during the NATO crisis, the form of its application for EEC membership in 1967, de Gaulle's failed ambitions, the assistance of NATO allies and the desire for enlargement within the EEC explain why the British were in a relatively strong position in Europe by 1969. There is also one last factor which needs to be mentioned. As a result of the paradigmatic changes in Britain's international policy brought by the 1967 decisions to devalue and hasten the withdrawal from East of Suez, Britain had prioritised Europe in its foreign policy agenda in an unprecedented manner in the post-war era. The evidence of Britain's second application and its promotion of multilateralism in the Atlantic Alliance and continued interest in European cooperation corroborated statements of Europeanism from British ministers which had in the past rung hollow. This may have been achieved less by design than by decline, but it was nevertheless a reality that Britain's foreign policy had undergone an evolution; Europe was no longer a part of wider policy but had instead become the centre of it.

There was an irony about the Anglo–French disputes over the Atlantic Alliance and Europe during de Gaulle's presidency. Britain and France had become closer than they had been since the end of the Second World War. In 1967 Britain took decisions that gave Europe unprecedented importance in its future order of foreign policy priorities as a critical mass inside the government built up behind entry into the EEC. Britain agreed with much of what de Gaulle had said about NATO (sharing his opposition to the MLF and to West Germany receiving equal nuclear status in the Alliance, and his belief in NATO reform). The British also shared some of de Gaulle's basic principles regarding the EEC, such as his opposition to supranationalism. And they agreed with the General's reservations about the growing power of the Federal Republic. Yet ultimately what separated the British and the French by the close of the 1960s was what had separated them in the late 1940s: a fundamental difference of opinion about their relative positions of power in the world and about the relationship between Europe and the United States. This had been at the base of decisions to take separate paths at the end of the 1940s and lay at the heart of de Gaulle's dissatisfaction and his attempts to reform Atlantic relations after 1958. The British and the French agreed that the United States should not dominate the Atlantic Alliance, but where they disagreed was on how to respond to American power. The British thought it best to work with the Americans; the French did not. These were irreconcilable positions, rooted in national histories and attitudes.

Up until the mid-1960s, the British had made no headway in overcoming French opposition to their desire for an enhanced role—economic and political—in Europe. As it had done since the inception of the EEC and Britain's decision to try to come to terms with it, French foreign policy priorities prevented the achievement of British foreign policy priorities. This dynamic changed in the second half of the 1960s. While de Gaulle moved rapidly to achieve his ambitions for France, from the empty chair crisis, to withdrawal from NATO, to his Moscow visit and to his veto of Britain's second application, he antagonised his allies in the EEC and in the Atlantic Alliance and he worked against the prevailing political atmosphere in the West. That atmosphere was the product of changes in the Cold War, in the Atlantic Alliance and in the EEC. What it comprised of was a general belief in interdependence and integration and their achievement through a reformed NATO and Atlantic Alliance and an advancing EEC. During the second half of the 1960s, independence and national sovereignty became outmoded and it was amid de Gaulle's pursuit of them that this became clear. Britain's post-1966 role in NATO and its post-1967 approach to the EEC—its new Euro-centred foreign policy—whilst not the antithesis of de Gaulle's approach in its motivation, was effectively presented as such by the British whose diplomacy in dealing with European allies had progressed significantly since de Gaulle's return to power in 1958. It was a new look British foreign policy which placed Britain in a role that all its partners, including the U.S.A, wished it to play. It found a welcome audience everywhere, except, of course, in the Elysée Palace.

NOTES

1. Dixon to Caccia, 19 Jun. 1964. The National Archives (formerly Public Record Office), Kew, London. (Hereafter TNA (PRO)). FO 371/177865, RF1022/57.
2. For example, Dixon to Caccia, 7 Feb. 1964. TNA (PRO), FO 371/177864, RF1022/21G; Dixon to Butler, 12 Mar. 1964. TNA (PRO) FO371/177865, RF1022/31; Mason, "Policy Towards France," 30 Apr. 1964. TNA (PRO) FO 371/177865, RF1022/44.
3. Dixon to Caccia, 19 Jun. 1964.TNA (PRO), FO 371/177865, RF1022/57.
4. Quoted in Julian Jackson, *The Fall of France: The Nazi Invasion of 1940* (Oxford: Oxford University Press, 2003), p. 241.
5. On the 1961 application see Alan Milward, *The UK and the European Community Volume I: The Rise and Fall of a National Strategy 1945–1963* (London: Frank Cass, 2002), pp. 463–83. On the 1967 application see Helen Parr, *Britain's Policy Towards the European Community: Harold Wilson and Britain's World Role, 1964–1967* (London: Routledge, 2006), in general.
6. Charles de Gaulle, *Discours et Messages: Août 1962-Décembre 1965* (Paris: Plon, 1970), p. 372ff.
7. On de Gaulle, France and the NATO crisis, see Frédéric Bozo, *Two Strategies for Europe: De Gaulle, the United States and the Atlantic Alliance* (Oxford: Rowman and Littlefield, 2001), pp. 143–85.
8. For the Churchill quotation see John Baylis, *Anglo-American Relations since 1939: The Enduring Alliance* (Manchester: Manchester University Press, 1997),

p. 42. For the de Gaulle quotation see Julian Jackson, *De Gaulle* (London: Haus Publishing, 2003), p. 99.

9. On Anglo-French differences over Europe see Clemens Wurm "Two Paths to Europe: Great Britain and France from a Comparative Perspective" in Clemens Wurm (ed.), *Western Europe and Germany: The Beginnings of European Integration 1945–1960* (Oxford: Berg, 1995), pp. 175–200.

10. For example, Milward, *The UK and the European Community, I*, in general.

11. Wurm, "Two Paths to Europe," p. 191.

12. Georges-Henri Soutou, "French Policy towards European Integration, 1950–1966" in Michael Dockrill (Ed.), *Europe within the Global System, 1938–1960: Great Britain, France, Italy and Germany: from Great Powers to Regional Powers* (Bochum: Universitätsverlag Brockmeyer, 1995), pp. 119–133, specifically pp. 126–7. See also Maurice Vaïsse, *La Grandeur: Politique Etrangère du Général de Gaulle, 1958–1969* (Paris: Fayard, 1997), in general.

13. On Messina, see Hanns Jürgen Küsters, "The Origins of the EEC Treaty" in Enrico Serra (ed.), *Il Rilancio dell'Europa e i Trattati di Roma* (Brussels: Bruylant, 1989), pp. 211–38.

14. James Ellison, *Threatening Europe: Britain and the Creation of the European Community, 1955–58* (Basingstoke: Macmillan, 2000), in general.

15. Macmillan Papers, Bodleian Library, Oxford, MS Macmillan dep.d.33*, diary, 26 Oct. 1958. See also, Harold Macmillan, *Riding the Storm, 1956–1959* (London: Macmillan, 1971), p. 455. For Macmillan's threats see Ellison, *Threatening Europe*, pp. 200–3, 209–14.

16. Ellison, *Threatening Europe*, pp. 198–220. Francis Lynch, "De Gaulle's First Veto: France, the Rueff Plan and the Free Trade Area," *Contemporary European History*, 9/1 (2000), pp. 111–35.

17. Charles de Gaulle, *Memoirs of Hope: Renewal and Endeavour* (New York: Simon and Schuster, 1971), pp. 202–3.

18. De Gaulle to Eisenhower, 17 Sep. 1958. *Foreign Relations of the United States, Hereafter FRUS, 1958–1960, Volume VII, Western Europe*, no. 45.

19. Bozo, *Two Strategies*, pp. 18–19.

20. Michael Dockrill, "Restoring the 'Special Relationship': The Bermuda and Washington Conferences, 1957" in Dick Richardson and Glyn Stone (eds.), *Decisions and Diplomacy: Essays in Twentieth-Century International History* (London: Routledge, 1995), pp. 205–23.

21. De Gaulle, *Memoirs*, pp. 202–3. Bozo, *Two Strategies*, pp. 19–23.

22. Jeffrey Glen Giauque, *Grand Designs and Visions of Unity: The Atlantic Powers and the Reorganization of Western Europe, 1955–63* (Chapel Hill: University of North Carolina Press, 2002), in general.

23. Caccia quoted in Giauque, *Grand Designs*, p. 158. Alistair Horne, *Macmillan 1957–1986* (London: Macmillan, 1989), p. 447.

24. John F. Kennedy Library, Boston, Massachusetts, Papers of President Kennedy (hereafter JFKL, Kennedy Papers), National Security Files, Meetings and Memoranda, Box 316, Bromley Smith, Summary Record of NSC Executive Committee Meeting No. 38 (Part II), 25 Jan. 1963.

25. Parr, *Britain's Policy*, pp. 15–69.

26. John Young, "Killing the MLF? The Wilson Government and Nuclear Sharing in Europe 1964–66" in Erik Goldstein and Brian McKercher (Eds.), *Power and Stability: British Foreign Policy 1865–1965* (London: Frank Cass, 2003), pp. 295–324.

27. Dixon to Butler, 12 Mar. 1964. TNA (PRO), FO 371/177865, RF1022/31.

28. Mason, "Policy Towards France," 30 Apr. 1964. TNA (PRO), FO 371/177865, RF1022/44.

29. Hood to Ambassadors, 2 June 1964. TNA (PRO), FO 371/177865, RF1022/44. Foreign Office to Certain of Her Majesty's Representatives, 3 Jul. 1964. FO 371/177867, RF1022/115.

30. Palliser to Nicholls, 9 Feb. 1965. TNA (PRO), FO 371/184288, W6/12.

31. Nicholls to Caccia and Caccia minute, both 26 Feb. 1965. TNA (PRO), FO 371/184288, W6/13. Stewart to Wilson, 3 Mar. 1965. TNA (PRO), PREM13/306. C (65)51, 26 Mar. 1965, TNA (PRO), CAB 129/121.

32. Parr, *Britain's Policy*, pp. 46–53.

33. On the empty chair crisis see N. Piers Ludlow, "Challenging French Leadership in Europe: Germany, Italy, The Netherlands and the Outbreak of the Empty Chair Crisis of 1965–1966," *Contemporary European History*, 8/2 (1999), pp. 240–4. On the September press conference see Bozo, *Two Strategies*, p. 155.

34. Memorandum of Conversation, 16 Jun. 1965. *Foreign Relations of the United States, 1964–1968, Volume XIII, Western Europe Region* (Washington: United States Government Printing Office, 1995).

35. Leddy to Ball, 23 Sep. 1965. FRUS, 1964–68, vol. XIII, no. 103.

36. C (65)119, 5 Aug. 1965, TNA (PRO), CAB 129/122.

37. Palliser to Nicholls, 9 Feb. 1965. TNA (PRO), FO 371/184288, W6/12.

38. State to Brussels 948, 28 Jan. 1966. FRUS, 1964–68, vol. XIII, no. 127. C (66)16, 28 Jan. 1966, TNA (PRO), CAB 129/124.

39. Charles de Gaulle, *Discours et Messages: Janvier 1966–Avril 1969* (Paris: Plon, 1970), p. 19.

40. Lyndon Baines Johnson Library, Austin, Texas (hereafter LBJL), Papers of Francis M. Bator (hereafter Bator Papers), Subject File, Box 27, Acheson, Memorandum for the Secretary, 10 May 1966.

41. Dean to Foreign Office 806, 7 Mar. 1966. TNA (PRO), PREM 13/1042.

42. National Archives and Records Administration, College Park, Maryland, USA (Hereafter NARA). RG59 Lot File 67D516 NATO-French Relations Box 6, REU-19, 11 Mar. 1966.

43. Le Cheminant to PM, 9 Mar. 1966, TNA (PRO), PREM 13/1042.

44. Foreign Office to Paris 695, 15 Mar. 1966. TNA (PRO), PREM 13/1043,

45. LBJL, Papers of Lyndon Baines Johnson, National Security Files (hereafter Johnson Papers, NSF), Country File, Europe and USSR, UK, Box 209, Intelligence Note 173, 19 Mar. 1966.

46. NARA RG59 DoS CF EEC 3 Meetings, Sessions, Box 3292, London to State 4408, 18 Mar. 1966. Dixon to Butler, 2 Oct. 1964. TNA (PRO), FO 371/177866, RF1022/81.

47. Wilson to Johnson, 21 Mar. 1966. TNA (PRO), PREM 13/1043. LBJL, Johnson Papers, NSF, Head of State Correspondence, Box 9, Wilson to Johnson, 29 Mar. 1966.

48. Memorandum of Conversation, 27 Jan. 1966. FRUS, 1964–68, vol. XIII, no.126.
49. State Circular 1646, 8 Mar. 1966 and Solomon and Stoessel to Ball, 19 July 1966. FRUS, 1964–68, vol. XIII, nos. 139, 188.
50. The Foreign Office to UKDNATO 355, 8 Mar. 1966. TNA (PRO), PREM 13/ 1042. LBJL, Bator Papers, Subject File, Box 27, Bator, Memorandum for the President, 8 Mar. 1966. For Foreign Office-State Department exchanges see Dean to the Foreign Office 780 and 781, 4 Mar. 1966. PREM 13/1042.
51. JFKL, Kennedy Papers, President's Office Files, Countries, Box 116A, Schlesinger Memorandum for the President, 29 Jan. 1966.
52. See James Ellison, "Defeating the General: Anglo-American Relations, Europe and the NATO Crisis of 1966," *Cold War History*, 6/1 (2006), pp. 85–111.
53. Andreas Wenger, "Crisis and Opportunity: NATO's Transformation and the Multilateralization of Détente, 1966–1968," *Journal of Cold War Studies*, 6/1 (2004), pp. 22–74.
54. On the second application see Parr, *Britain's Policy*, pp. 129–84.
55. LBJL, Johnson Papers, NS File, Country File, France, Box 177, Bromley Smith to Johnson, 10 Mar. 1966.
56. On de Gaulle's Cold War policies, see Garret Martin, "Untying the Gaullian Knot: France and the Struggle to Overcome the Cold War Order, 1963–1968" (unpublished Ph.D. thesis, London School of Economics, 2006). The author is grateful to Dr. Martin for allowing him to read drafts of his thesis.
57. Thomas Alan Schwartz, *Lyndon Johnson and Europe: In the Shadow of Vietnam* (Cambridge, MA: Harvard University Press, 2003), in general.
58. Piers Ludlow, *The European Community and the Crises of the 1960s: Negotiating the Gaullist Challenge* (London: Routledge, 2006), pp. 174–98.

BRITAIN, FRANCE, AND AMERICA'S YEAR OF EUROPE, 1973

Keith Hamilton

President Pompidou said that to be European, if one expressed the idea with nuances, meant to be on good terms with both Washington and Moscow. . . . But if one had a good relationship with one and a bad one with the other, then it led to "subjection"—though he perfectly accepted that there was a difference between an ally and the "merchants of détente."[1]

Britain's admission to the European Community (EC) in January 1973 required a new *Entente Cordiale*. Agreement between Britain and France was vital to the success of the entry negotiations and that, in the words of

This article is based very largely upon documents reproduced on CR-ROM in *Documents on British Policy Overseas, Series III*, Vol. IV, *The Year of Europe: America, Europe and the Energy Crisis, 1972–1974* (London: Whitehall History Publishing/Routledge, 2006). The relevant documents are footnoted as DBPO3, iv. The opinions expressed in the article are the author's own and should not be taken as an expression of official Government policy.

Christopher Soames, the British ambassador at Paris, had to form part of a "broader reconciliation of the two countries, based on the mutual acknowledgement that [their] future interests lay in working together both in the fields covered by the enlarged Community and in those where broader co-operation on a European scale [was] still in the future."[2] As French president, Charles de Gaulle had twice vetoed British applications for Community membership. Evidently perturbed about the possible impact of Britain's joining upon France's own position within the Community, he shared with many of his fellow-countrymen the fear that a Britain, still clinging to its "special relationship" with the United States, might reinforce America's influence over Western Europe, and he openly questioned Britain's European "vocation."[3] Moreover, by the time of Britain's signing of the EC accession treaty on 22 January 1972 the French, having achieved most of their immediate objectives within the Community, were in a very strong diplomatic position. No wonder then that Edward Heath's Conservative government wished to demonstrate its commitment to working with France in an *esprit communautaire*. British diplomats were anxious that their country should not be perceived as an American Trojan horse in Europe. Yet, they and their political masters also hoped that a European union could be forged in cooperation, rather than competition, with the United States. Heath informed the American president, Richard Nixon, in a personal message of 30 October 1972 that he was determined to ensure that the Community's long-term relationship with the United States would be "constructed so as to correspond with our real interest in maintaining the closest possible ties."[4] He could hardly, however, have anticipated the degree to which both transatlantic and cross-channel diplomacy would be tested by the Nixon administration's attempt to redefine that relationship through the launch in the following spring of its "Year of Europe" initiative.

The year in question was 1973. But the initiative, like the Europe it addressed, was some time in the making. Already, prior to Nixon's re-election, Henry Kissinger, his national security adviser, had indicated that the president was contemplating a tour of European capitals. Kissinger told a press conference on 16 September 1972 that Nixon was hoping to resume "most intense consultations . . . on how to put relationships between Europe and the United States on a new even more dynamic and constructive basis, consistent with the change in the international situation."[5] This was reassuring from a British point of view. Heath may have preferred to speak of a "natural," rather than a "special," relationship with the United States, but there was still a feeling amongst senior Whitehall officials that of late Britain's particular interests had too frequently been ignored in Washington. They had been irritated by the failure of the Americans to take full account of their concerns at the time of Nixon's visit to Beijing[6] and they, like other Western Europeans, were disturbed by Kissinger's courtship of the Soviet Union and the emergence in the name of détente of what some perceived as a potential superpower condominium. In the wake of dollar devaluation and defeat in Vietnam, there also remained the danger that Congress might heed calls for cuts in defence spending and the withdrawal of U.S. forces from abroad, and let America drift towards protectionism and isolation, leaving Western Europe to face the Soviet bloc alone and under the threat of "Finlandisation." The British and their continental allies and partners, nonetheless, viewed with considerable scepticism the emergence, in parallel with the idea of a "Year of Europe," of the concept of treating future transatlantic negotiations on commercial, monetary and security issues as "one ball of wax."[7]

The Americans had good reason to emphasize the interdependence of the several aspects of their relations with Europe. As Lord Cromer, Britain's ambassador at Washington, reasoned in a despatch of 15 November 1972, the recently re-installed Nixon administration had "the political objective of a strong Western Alliance and a balanced relationship between the US and the enlarged European Community," but "the economic objective of reversing a vast trade deficit." Washington desired compensation for the losses Americans assumed they would incur as a result of the extension of the EC's tariff regime to Britain, Denmark and Ireland, and hoped that this could be achieved during the forthcoming round of GATT (General Agreement on Tariffs and Trade) talks. The U.S. government was also looking for a constructive European response to the international monetary problems resulting from the 1971 suspension of dollar convertibility and the consequent collapse of the Bretton Woods system. Europe's increasing prosperity seemed to add substance to the American case for greater burden-sharing within the Atlantic alliance.[8] There was, however, little institutional logic in the notion of a transatlantic negotiating process embracing defence as well as economic matters. EC membership was not synonymous with European membership of NATO. And while the EC might have collective responsibility for settling terms of trade, the nine member states were far from united on how international monetary reform could best be achieved, and political cooperation amongst the Nine in the sphere of foreign relations was still only in its infancy. If indeed the Nine were agreed on anything, insofar as their dialogue with the United States was concerned, it was that there should be no "globalisation of issues."[9]

Whitehall officials gave a good deal of thought to the future management of relations between the United States and the enlarged Community. They were well aware that their commitment to the framing of a common European foreign policy could conflict with their desire to maintain close bilateral relations with the United States. There was, for instance, the problem of how to handle with Washington those issues on which an agreed position amongst the Nine was still in evolution. One idea, backed by Jean Monnet, the longstanding protagonist of European union, was for the establishment of some kind of transatlantic consultative machinery. Member states and the EC Commission might then be better able to speak with one voice, and there would be less opportunities for the Americans to divide and rule. Yet such an arrangement could also facilitate Washington's efforts to establish linkage between trade, money and defence. Moreover, given French aversion to the creation of special mechanisms for the conduct of EC/U.S. relations, the Foreign and Commonwealth Office (FCO) was reluctant to recommend more than periodic informal meetings of the foreign ministers of the Nine with the U.S. secretary of state and a representative of the Commission. British diplomats were equally cautious about an American proposal that Nixon might use a European tour to participate in a multilateral summit with EC heads of state or government. Such a meeting seemed unlikely to produce any substantive results unless well-prepared over many months, and could prove a "somewhat rigid affair" if the Community were to decide to speak from a common position.[10] Probably of greater concern to Sir Alec Douglas-Home, the foreign and commonwealth secretary, was, however, the determination of the French that any EC/US summitry should be conducted through the presidents of the Commission and the Council of Ministers.[11] Georges Pompidou, de Gaulle's successor as president of France, had earlier indicated that he favoured consultations "at the highest level to clarify economic and above all political relations amongst the democracies."[12] Nonetheless, in conversation with Heath in Paris on 22 May, he was emphatic in his opposition to involving himself in a "kind of "court circle"" with the U.S. president. "Even the Emperor Nero," he added, "only summoned Ambassadors to his presence and not Kings."[13]

This was not simply a matter of procedural pedantry. A multilateral gathering such as the Americans envisaged could have the appearance of introducing Nixon into the internal workings of the Nine—an economic community in being and a political union still in the early stages of formation. And Gaullist doctrine, enunciated by Pompidou in his speech to the EC summit in the previous October, insisted "that Europe affirm its individual personality with regard to the United States."[14] The French were in any case, as Christopher Ewart-Biggs, the British minister in Paris, averred, "pathologically sensitive about any implication that Europe [was] in any sense subordinate to or dependent upon the United States."[15] The danger from the FCO's point of view was that the administration in Washington evidently hoped that the British would be able to persuade their Community partners, and especially the French, to assume a more cooperative attitude towards the Americans. "Indeed," Cromer observed, "such is the trust of President Nixon [in the British government], that therein lie the seeds of disillusion in the future, on occasions when Community policy, which will of course embrace British policy, is at variance with American thinking."[16] When Heath visited Washington in early February 1973 he tried to explain the new situation to Nixon. He pointed out that while the British government would continue to take account of U.S. views in deciding its contributions to the foreign relations of the EC, it would nonetheless be bound by such policies as the Community decided upon. But Nixon's remark that Britain and the U.S. must "must do some really hard thinking together—without necessarily informing the rest of the Alliance at any particular stage but keeping privately in step and moving publicly, if not together, at least in parallel," hardly suggests any readiness on his or Kissinger's part to abandon their penchant for bilateral and secret diplomacy.[17]

The British government was better placed than most to appreciate the methods of the Nixon administration. Sir Burke Trend, the Cabinet secretary, was already involved in intermittent bilateral talks with Kissinger on sensitive matters of security, and as the result of one such meeting, in Washington in July 1972, British officials became party to one of the most occult of Nixon's diplomatic ventures. Sir Thomas Brimelow, then deputy under-secretary in the FCO, was thus invited through Trend by Kissinger, without the knowledge of the State Department or for that matter any other body outside the White House, to assist in drafting what eventually emerged on 22 June 1973 as the US/Soviet agreement on the prevention of nuclear war. In effect, Brimelow became Kissinger's secret desk officer for the Soviet Union in an operation which those in the know in London code-named "Hullabaloo." This helped ensure that the resulting accord left the U.S. commitment to NATO, and particularly its nuclear umbrella, largely unimpaired. British officials nonetheless doubted the merits of Nixon's decision to respond positively to this Soviet proposal, and they were fully alive to the fact that disclosure of their role in the negotiation, whose outcome was interpreted in France as a fresh manifestation of superpower condominium, could leave Britain vulnerable to charges of duplicity from other European members of the alliance.[18] Albion would surely be confirmed in French eyes as perfidious as ever. That said, visits by Brimelow and Trend to Washington in the context of "Hullabaloo" kept the British appraised of Kissinger's thinking on world affairs. They also had the opportunity to influence his future conduct, and it was during discussions of a conceptual framework paper on East-West and transatlantic relations, prepared by Brimelow at Kissinger's request, that on 19 April 1973 Kissinger revealed to Trend the purport of the "Year of Europe" address he was due to deliver four days later at the annual luncheon of Associated Press in New York.[19]

The notion of a "Year of Europe" owed much to Kissinger's belief that U.S. foreign policy had for so long been focused upon ending the war in Vietnam and improving relations with the Soviet Union and communist China, that America's allies must be feeling neglected. He told Trend that he wished to give "symbolic impetus" to the transatlantic relationship and to find some way of making it "an 'emotional necessity' to United States public opinion": "It was necessary," Kissinger explained, "to try to stimulate the same degree of public interest and pride in Atlantic relations as in the President's initiatives towards Peking and Moscow." To this end he wanted to secure agreement on a broad statement of principles which should guide Atlantic relations and extend beyond a mere "reaffirmation of traditional liturgies." And in his speech in New York on 23 April he endeavoured to define and give philosophical content to these ideas. He spoke of a world in transition, of the movement of Europe towards economic unification, of the shift in the East-West relationship from American preponderance to near equality, of the relaxation of tensions, of the emergence of Japan as a major power centre, and of whether an Atlantic unity "forged by a common perception of danger [could] draw new purpose from shared positive aspirations." Nixon, he indicated, would travel to Europe towards the end of the year, and Kissinger proposed that by then the United States and its European partners should have worked out the basis of a "new Atlantic Charter setting the goals for the future" — a relationship in whose progress he hoped Japan might participate.

In addition, Kissinger spoke of the linkage between various policy issues, of the need for mutual concessions in the economic sphere, of the administration's desire for a "new consensus on security", and of maintaining the "momentum of détente . . . by common objectives rather than by, drift, escapism or complacency." The United States, he asserted, "has global responsibilities. Our European allies have regional interests. These are not necessarily in conflict, but in the new era neither are they automatically identical." If the Atlantic nations wanted to foster unity, they must, he maintained, "find a solution for the management of their diversity," and identify "interests and positive values beyond security in order to engage once again the commitment of peoples and parliaments."[20]

The speech was in many respects a counterblast to those in Congress pressing for more protectionist measures and cuts in U.S. forces in Europe. But, as Trend knew from his talks in Washington, Kissinger was looking for an early and favourable reaction from Europe. Indeed, in Cromer's opinion, if this were forthcoming it "could have a similar influence in terms of its effect on the detailed development of U.S. policy to the constructive British response to Marshall's historic offer in 1948." On the other hand, in the event of a "crabbed" European reaction the initiative could well fall flat.[21] The FCO was quick off the mark, and on 24

April its News Department released a statement welcoming Kissinger's acknowledgement of the concept of a unified Europe working cooperatively with the United States.[22] There was, however, also some uncertainty in London over what exactly Kissinger had in mind when he spoke of a new Atlantic Charter, and very little enthusiasm for the implied assumption that a package solution could be found to outstanding differences over defence, trade and monetary matters. In a speech at Dunblane on 27 April Douglas-Home, while endorsing Kissinger's language as "realistic and timely," said that he would have preferred the EC to have had more time in which to "find its way to common positions with greater deliberation."[23] Moreover, although most of Britain's EC partners agreed that a common European approach should be adopted to relations with America, the French predictably had the gravest reservations about Kissinger's pronouncement.[24] Sir Edward Tomkins, Soames's successor as British ambassador at Paris, reported that there was a feeling in the Quai d'Orsay that the Kissinger proposal was "mainly a tactical ploy, designed to put American demands on the table in advance of the forthcoming negotiations and to put Europe on the defensive." French officials likewise dismissed Kissinger's reference to the United States having a "world role" compared with the "regional responsibilities of Europe" as patronising, and his presentation likely to make the task of reaching an agreement on political and economic questions more difficult.[25]

Michel Jobert, France's newly appointed foreign minister, was certainly in no mood to applaud a gesture which he would later, with due exaggeration, characterise as "consecrating American hegemony over the western world."[26] This posed an obvious dilemma for the British. "[W]e," Trend reminded Heath in a minute of 2 May, "must be wary of any United States attempt to drive a political wedge between ourselves and our European allies or to use us as a stalking horse for Washington's purposes in Europe." Thus, while he thought that Britain must respond to the speech in as "positive and constructive a manner as possible," he considered it preferable that the United States "having launched the project, should also be responsible for following it up and making the running for the next round or two."[27] Talks between Kissinger and Jobert on 17 May seemed to suggest that there was some scope for a Franco–American understanding. Jobert had, according to Helmut Sonnenfeldt of the National Security Council (NSC), appeared receptive to the idea of the establishment of a four-power steering group composed of representatives of the U.S., Britain, France, and West Germany, with a view to creating some new form of transatlantic superstructure.[28] Yet, French insistence that the political machinery of the Nine remain completely separate from the economic functions of the EC Council of Ministers and the Commission, made it difficult to see how the Europeans could agree upon any coordinated response to the American initiative. During his meeting with Heath on 22 May, Pompidou declared that an EC/US declaration "could only be made within the field of the Community's competence. Its scope was therefore limited. It could be clear cut and firm, but it could not have the general content of declarations dealing with bilateral state-to-state relationships since many of these general responsibilities were not yet within the sphere of the Community."[29] Two days later, at a dinner with his opposite numbers amongst the Nine in Brussels, François Puaux, Jobert's political director, made it plain that, despite the desire of others to proceed with the preparation of an analysis of EC/US relations, his government could not even contemplate engaging in this task. It would, the French claimed, "amount to putting a finger into the cogwheels of a process that would lead to some kind of collective high-level response to the Kissinger speech . . . and would thus amount to playing the American game of 'globalisation.'"[30]

This was doubly frustrating for a British government wedded to the idea of a constructive dialogue with Washington and eager to pursue the further integration of Western Europe. It was especially so at a time when Europe's bargaining position was perceived by some in the FCO as having improved as the result of the Watergate affair and the Nixon administration's need of a foreign policy success. This last contention Kissinger denied: though he later conceded in his memoirs that "Watergate made us more persistent than prudent."[31] He also rejected French claims that the United States was, by emphasizing the inter-relationship of various transatlantic issues, seeking to blackmail the Europeans in the economic field. But Jobert still chose to believe otherwise. During a Franco/U.S. summit in Reykjavik on 30 May–1 June he suggested that the Americans were trying to create a new Atlantic organization to force France back into full participation in NATO, to "abridge French autonomy," to seek to force decisions that would split the EC, and to organize a U.S./Soviet condominium. And whilst Pompidou was apparently more accommodating, conflicting reports of what the two presidents had actually said to each other resulted in further misunderstanding. The American account asserted that Nixon and Pompidou had agreed that the study and development of the concept of the "Year of Europe" should be pursued "through both bilateral and multilateral exchanges, carried out simultaneously and at high levels"; that discussions should be held in the NATO context in the forthcoming ministerial meeting in Copenhagen; and that a meeting at deputy foreign minister-level might be desirable to evaluate the result of consultations "with a view to the possible formulation of a Declaration of Principles."[32] It subsequently emerged, however, that Pompidou did not feel himself committed to such a detailed programme, and at a political cooperation meeting of EC foreign ministers on 5 June Jobert, despite his protestations to the contrary, showed no desire to begin work on preparing a common European position.[33]

On this issue the French were in a minority and, as Douglas-Home observed, Jobert displayed particular sensitivity about "appearing isolated in a position which could be represented as not being 'European.'"[34] Indeed, if, as Kissinger later contended, Jobert was set upon using the American initiative "to pursue the old Gaullist dream of building Europe on an anti-American basis,"[35] he was remarkably inept in his choice of tactics. Puaux was even less inhibited than Jobert when two days later he took up the subject with Ewart-Biggs. He told the British minister that he "thought that Europe should not let itself be eaten by the United States and saw the whole operation as designed by Kissinger to get them to 'rentrer dans la discipline atlantique.'" The British, though doubtful about the timing of Kissinger's initiative, harboured no such fears. They simply wanted to find a practical way by which the Nine could agree on a common response even if that meant a blurring of the distinction between economic and political cooperation. This, as Ewart-Biggs contended, was quite different from "'globalising' the negotiation itself." Puaux, nonetheless, insisted there was no common European position. "If," he continued, "all France's partners shared her desire to distinguish Europe from the United States then she would lose her inhibitions about political cooperation and the machinery of the Community. But they did not. Some of them seemed to want to start the negotiation with the United States from the premise that Europe must make concessions." Some of this, Tomkins admitted, "was pumped . . . straight out of Puaux's personal bilges." Yet it expressed the "present tone of French prejudice and pessimism on this crucial issue." It meant that France would almost certainly impede progress towards formulating a common European response to Kissinger. It also implied that the future of political cooperation amongst the Nine and their eventual achievement of a joint foreign policy must depend on France's partners adopting a similarly negative attitude towards the United States.[36]

While Tomkins and his staff were confronted with a sullen Puaux, who proclaimed the French in a "mood of withdrawal" on political cooperation,[37] Cromer and Trend had to assuage a petulant Kissinger who, on 4 June, threatened that unless the Europeans did something quickly Congress would legislate for the withdrawal of some 75–90,000 U.S. troops from Europe. Kissinger also rejected a suggestion from Cromer that the French should be inspired to draft a transatlantic declaration of principles. He was, he said, opposed to giving them a "veto over what might be the last chance (as far as the US was concerned) to anchor the Atlantic relationship."[38] Yet, following talks with Jobert on 8 June, Kissinger reported that the latter had agreed to consider an *ad hoc* multilateral meeting of deputy foreign ministers, and had offered to draft a section of the projected declaration. Neither of these assurances was ever confirmed by the French.[39] Nor was a French draft forthcoming. True, by mid-June the EC was ready to address Washington's commercial grievances and there remained a possibility that something might emerge from NATO. The White House also supplied Cromer "in strictest confidence" with a brief but all-embracing list of subject headings for a projected declaration: it covered the nature and goals of the Atlantic community and the problems of reconciling unity and diversity.[40] Nevertheless, French intransigence, Western Europe's institutional deficit, and a general reluctance amongst EC member-states to enter upon negotiations which might link defence and economics, meant that there was little prospect of any broad based draft declaration emerging from the deliberations of the Nine. The problems facing the adoption of a single declaration were, the FCO concluded in a paper of 18 June, "insuperable," and they would have to "think in terms of more than one Declaration, with a different pattern of European countries subscribing to them."[41] To this end officials prepared the bases of two draft declarations, one intended to address specifically NATO issues and another which sought to define the future relationship between the EC and the United States.[42]

The notion of two separate transatlantic declarations was endorsed by a Cabinet meeting on 20 June. Heath then informed colleagues that he was convinced that the American initiative could not be ignored. It was, he thought, essential that the United States should continue to share in the defence of Western Europe, and if Nixon needed help to contain domestic pressures to reduce American commitments, the Europeans must do their best to respond. But if, as the prime minister saw it, the Americans were "finding it difficult to adjust themselves to the loss of their pre-eminence in military, economic and monetary affairs," it was equally apparent to ministers that the French were bent on retaining the net advantage they derived from Community membership and on using their growing economic strength to establish themselves as the "dominant force in Europe." Moreover, while the maintenance Atlantic alliance was judged vital to Britain's security, Anglo-French cooperation was considered "basic to the success of the Community." And in French eyes the US military presence in Europe served American as well as European interests, and Washington was in no position to demand diplomatic recompense from Brussels. Ministers nevertheless felt that in encouraging a Community approach to America they "should not be inhibited by a wish to avoid difficulties with the French" and, though there was no desire to precipitate a "major confrontation," there was equally "no disposition to appease them." "In our own interests," Cabinet ministers suggested, "we might take a tougher line with the French and this might be welcomed by other members of the

Community."[43] The problem was how to translate such sentiments into diplomatic action, especially when the FCO remained far from certain as to what exactly the French position was. Reports from Washington at the end of June indicated that, in recent talks with Kissinger at San Clemente, Jobert had reaffirmed his intention of drafting a section of the projected draft declaration. When, however, Douglas-Home subsequently put to Jobert the British idea for two declarations, the latter replied that the French government "were not at all sure that they wanted a document or documents."[44]

There was little in anything Heath said to his Cabinet colleagues to support Kissinger's contention that the prime minister was striking the "pose of a pained bystander at an incipient family quarrel."[45] British statesmen and diplomats had to reckon with the simple fact that the fate of America's "Year of Europe" must depend on the achievement of a consensus amongst the Europeans and that without France that was impossible. They hoped that a meeting on 23 July, under the EC's current Danish presidency, of the foreign ministers of the Nine in Copenhagen would break the existing procedural impasse, and that it would then be possible to inform Washington that they had embarked on a process which "should enable them to make a coherent and positive response" when Nixon visited Europe in the autumn.[46] But again the French proved reluctant to sanction more than minimal progress. The most Jobert was ready to concede was that work might begin on a paper establishing Europe's "identity" *vis-à-vis* the United States and on the preparation of a report dealing with subjects which could be taken up in a Euro-American dialogue. And in a brief exchange with Sir Michael Palliser, Britain's permanent representative to the EC, he went on to accuse the British government of failing to keep its partners fully informed of its own dealings with the United States. He had apparently learnt that Cromer had been supplied with two American draft declarations, one prepared by the NSC and another by the State Department, both of which he himself had earlier received from Kissinger at San Clemente.[47] This was particularly galling since a week later, on 30 July, Trend and Brimelow were taken to task by Kissinger over both the tardiness of the European response to his proposals, and the fact the Nine seemed determined to exclude the Americans from their own discussion of what a transatlantic declaration might contain. "It was," Kissinger objected, "a new development in US relations with Britain. Never before had there been a failure at the beginning of a major negotiation to keep each other informed of their thinking."[48]

Heath attributed Kissinger's rancour to his failure to make more progress with the "Year of Europe" and the domestic difficulties faced by the Nixon administration. There had been insufficient consultation with the Europeans before the New York speech, and Kissinger's understanding of the mechanics of the Community was imperfect and his diplomacy too obscure. Yet, there appears to have been no doubt in the prime minister's mind that if the Community were to be galvanised into action and Kissinger provided with the response he wanted, the French must be brought into line. With this in view, he sought to enlist West German support, urging the federal chancellor, Willy Brandt, to meet with him and Pompidou in Paris at the end of August or in early September for informal discussions ahead of the next meeting of EC foreign ministers in Copenhagen.[49] Meanwhile, the FCO persisted with the preparation of a draft declaration for submission to representatives in Brussels of NATO's EC member-states, and on 8 August two texts were despatched to Brussels: a draft EC/US communiqué or declaration, for issue at the end of an American presidential visit; and a paper on how Europe's identity might be defined in relation to the United States. All three documents asserted, in one form or another, Europe's independence and the value of transatlantic cooperation, be it in the defence or economic spheres.[50] British diplomats doubted whether such texts would win French approval. Ewart-Biggs feared that they would regard the projected EC/US communiqué as "too much directed to common purposes and values" and "too much like what the Americans want[ed]."[51] Nevertheless, under pressure from the British embassy in Paris, and evidently perturbed by the readiness of the West Germans to pursue a more independent course in their relations with both Washington and Moscow, the Quai d'Orsay appeared to soften its stance.[52] On 28 August Puaux indicated to Ewart-Biggs that an EC/US declaration on the lines proposed by the British might provide a basis for discussion, and that the French could contemplate a NATO declaration at the conclusion of Nixon's projected European visit.[53]

Subsequent progress towards achieving agreement amongst the Nine on the drafting of an EC/US declaration was by Community standards fairly rapid. A meeting of EC political directors on 9 September settled on a text that might be recommended to foreign ministers, and two days later, the latter decided that a draft should be ready for delivery to the Americans on 19 September.[54] The resulting paper almost inevitably placed more emphasis on reaffirming the *status quo* rather than on breaking new ground, and it was therefore rather less than what the Americans might have hoped for. But, as Douglas-Home explained to Cromer, it represented a considerable achievement on Britain's part in persuading its EC partners, "particularly the French," to accept the "principle that there should be a collective response to the Americans and that declarations should be produced."[55] Unfortunately, from the British point of view, Kissinger was far from pleased with EC procedures which had seemed to deny him any part in the initial drafting of the text. During a conversation with Douglas-Home in New York on 24 September, Kissinger, who had recently succeeded William Rogers as U.S. secretary of state, again complained of Britain's role in the affair. "Britain," he said, "had never been treated as a foreign government," Washington "had not expected to have to take so literally the concept that Europe as a unit should respond" to the US initiative, but now found itself confronted with a *fait accompli* and the prospect of having to negotiate with the Danish foreign minister in his capacity as spokesman for the Nine.[56] Kissinger's impatience with the workings (and unworkings) of the Community was understandable: Douglas-Home was similarly irritated by the manner in which the French frequently insisted on putting matters of form before ministerial convenience. Yet, as one schooled in the history of diplomacy, Kissinger might have been expected to show more sensitivity towards Europe's evolving institutions. Diplomats were, after all, seeking to define a relationship in which the two parties involved were at very different stages of development. "It is," Ewart-Biggs opined, "a question of trying to relate what America is to what Europe is hoping to be—a relationship between a society of aspiration and evolution with a society of actuality and even of decay, or between a partly-formed phoenix and a complete but groggy Leviathan."[57]

The British could, however, draw some consolation from an unexpected source. On 8 October Puaux remarked to Oliver Wright, the FCO deputy under-secretary responsible for representing Britain at EC political directors' meetings, that the French "had been pleasantly surprised to find that, far from being a Trojan Horse, British views had proved [that] summer to be very 'European.'"[58] The tabling of a French draft NATO declaration in Brussels, and its acceptance by the Americans as a basis for negotiation, also suggested that there was scope for transatlantic compromise.[59] Meanwhile, talks in New York between U.S. officials and the political committee of the Nine on the terms of an EC/US declaration were friendly and non-adversarial.[60] The Americans found the EC draft "thin," and they wanted more emphasis to be given to the changes they perceived in the nature of the transatlantic relationship and a firmer commitment to "partnership" and consultation. And the French, unsurprisingly, were opposed to any formalisation of such a concept and they remained unreconciled to anything that implied the further institutionalisation of the transatlantic relationship.[61] Meetings in Copenhagen on 18–19 October of the political directors of the Nine, and between these and representatives of the EC Commission and the United States, nevertheless, went better than expected. Both Sonnenfeldt and Walter Stoessel, assistant secretary for European affairs in the State Department, were clearly impressed by the unity of the Nine, and the French appeared ready to adopt a more conciliatory approach. Puaux emerged as a convert to European political cooperation, and there seemed reason to hope that the exercise might proceed to an eventual success.[62] Two developments suggested it would not. The continuing Watergate saga, compounded with the opening of a criminal investigation into the affairs of Vice-President Spiro Agnew, made it unlikely that Nixon would wish to visit Europe before the end of the year; and the attacks launched on 6 October by Egyptian and Syrian forces against Israeli positions in the Sinai and on the Golan relegated the "Year of Europe" to the periphery of international diplomacy.

The outbreak of the fourth Arab–Israeli war revealed profound differences between the United States and Western Europe and amongst the Nine themselves in their approach to the Middle East. From the start Kissinger appeared to see the conflict very largely in terms of East-West relations, whilst at a government level both the British and the French were inclined to blame the Americans for their previous lack of urgency in persuading the Israelis to make concessions to their neighbours, and were increasingly alarmed by the prospect of the Arabs seeking to exploit Europe's economic dependence on their oil for diplomatic ends.[63] Kissinger was in his turn dismissive of such fears and highly critical of British conduct when, on 13 October, Douglas-Home refused to sponsor an American draft United Nations Security Council resolution calling for a ceasefire *in situ*. Neither of the two superpowers intended to participate in the vote on the draft, and the British government had good reason to question Kissinger's claim that the Egyptians would acquiesce in such a move.[64] Meanwhile, the refusal of the Europeans to assist the United States in the re-supply of arms to a temporarily beleaguered Israel seemed only to confirm Kissinger in his view that the Atlantic alliance "never cohered on anything except the one thing least likely to arise: a military attack on Western Europe."[65] However, far more disconcerting was Washington's announcement on 25 October that U.S. forces were being placed on a "low level of military alert" in response to reports that the Soviet Union was planning to send contingents to Egypt in order to enforce a three-day-old ceasefire. Although Cromer had prior knowledge of the American decision, other European ambassadors did not, and its formal communication to the North Atlantic Council hours after the press had learned of the story was hardly calculated to inspire confidence within the alliance.[66]

Developments related to the Middle Eastern conflict, and more particularly the escalation of an already nascent energy crisis, continued to exercise an adverse influence on transatlantic relations throughout the remainder of 1973. Kissinger may have been determined not to give way to Arab "blackmail,"[67] but no Western European government could ignore producer-country demands for the effective doubling of posted oil prices. They were certainly more vulnerable than the United States to the announcement on 17 October by the Organisation of Arab Petroleum Exporting Countries (OAPEC) that member-states would be reducing oil production by 5% per month until the Israelis had withdrawn from the territories occupied in 1967.[68] Nevertheless, in the aftermath of the ceasefire, the British were not unsympathetic to Kissinger's efforts to reserve peacemaking in the region to the United States, the Soviet Union and the principal belligerents. It had, after all, long been accepted in London that the Americans alone were capable of persuading the Israelis to make the concessions judged necessary for the achievement of a lasting settlement. With this in mind, British diplomats urged the French to "accept the realities of the situation," and to desist from pressing for the inclusion in a declaration then being drafted by the Nine of an appeal for the UN Security Council to have a greater role in the negotiations. But Douglas-Home was also keen to remind the Americans that the Nine had every right to take an interest in, and express a view on, developments in the Middle East. "Europe," he protested, "is too large and its vital interests too closely involved for it to be silent while great events take place over their [sic] heads."[69]

The declaration agreed by EC ministers on 6 November was in part intended to shield those member-states, such as the Netherlands, whose position the Arabs considered too sympathetic to Israel, against the rigours of a reinforced oil embargo. It was meant to demonstrate the unity of the Nine in their approach to the Middle East and, as such, simply called for a return of Egyptian and Israeli forces to the armistice lines agreed on 22 October and looked forward to negotiations taking place "in the framework of the United Nations" and Israel's withdrawal from occupied Arab land.[70] Even this, however, was too much for an American administration reluctant to brook any interference in what it understood to be its own diplomatic domain.[71] On 7 November Nixon's secretary of defense, James Schlesinger, protested to his British opposite number, Lord Carrington, over Britain's tendency to work in "close collusion" with the French and of the adoption of policies which were "taking on the quality of 'decayed Gaullism.'"[72] A week later, when challenged by Cromer on these remarks, Schlesinger further explained that the British had continually to prove to the "doubters," particularly the French, that they were "good Europeans." "To the US," he continued, "French policy . . . appeared to be to clear the US out of Europe so that the resulting vacuum could be filled by French leadership. From the standpoint of the Alliance this was a very unproductive role."[73] Such criticism contained an element of truth. But in this, as in other instances Anglo–French "collusion," was of limited consequence. Reluctant to expend accrued political credit on behalf of other Community member states, the French were slow to endorse a British proposal to combine the declaration with a joint EC démarche to Arab capitals aimed at ensuring the continued supply of oil on a non-discrimi-natory basis.[74] Indeed, as James Cable, the head of the FCO's planning staff, argued, there was a danger that, with transatlantic relations already under strain, Britain might "find that the European alternative [had] crumbled when confronted with the first major challenge."[75]

This point seemed to be borne out when on 24 November Kissinger engaged in a fresh bout of Euro-bashing. Then, after expressing to Cromer his indignation over reports of a proposed EC/Japanese declaration, he claimed that the "special relationship was collapsing," and that while Britain's entry into the EC should have raised Europe to the level of Britain, it had in fact reduced Britain to the level of Europe. It was "tragic," Kissinger said, that the EC/US declaration, which he had conceived as a cooperative gesture, should have "led to the establishment of an adversary relationship": the British were no longer acting as a counterweight to the French, who were "being allowed to dominate European thinking on the Atlantic relationship . . . and were seeking to build up Europe on an anti-American basis." This, he characterised, as "the worst decision since the Greek city states confronted Alexander."[76] Douglas-Home's response was frank and robust. In a personal message to Kissinger of 29 November, he reminded the Americans that, while Britain remained firmly alongside them on East-West issues, they must take their allies more into their confidence in the build-up to crises and confrontation.[77] Meanwhile, however, his support for an idea, initially floated by Washington, for discussions between Kissinger and the foreign ministers of the Nine in the margin of a forthcoming NATO ministerial meeting soon landed him in trouble with the French.[78] During a conversation with the British ambassador in Paris, which ranged over such topics as the projected EC/US declaration, the European identity paper and transatlantic relations, Geoffroy de Courcel, the secretary-general at the Quai d'Orsay, accused the British of returning to their "old ways" in their dealings with Washington. "In short," Tomkins observed in a letter to Brimelow of 30 November, "we are both agreed that there should be a distinct European personality vis-à-vis the Americans, but we want this personality to have a close and satisfactory dialogue, and they want it to behave like a young woman anxious to preserve her virginity from the GIs."[79] It was unlikely that Sir Alec, for all his tact and honesty of purpose, would be able to achieve a compromise between the new Alexander and this coy virgin without offending susceptibilities on one or both sides of the Atlantic.

Kissinger seemed inclined to regard all the Nine did independently of the United States as evidence of a potentially adversarial relationship: Jobert viewed almost anything agreed by the Nine in consultation with the United States as a denial of Europe's independence. Meetings between Kissinger and NATO and EC foreign ministers on 10 and 11 December were, nevertheless, far from unproductive. Kissinger gained broad assent for the idea of substituting a "shorter and more eloquent [EC/US] declaration" for the current draft, which he appeared to consider "too legalistic and journalistic." And, Douglas-Home's suggestion to a private gathering of NATO ministers that they should use the alliance's 25th anniversary to restate old truths might well be considered the most positive contribution to the continuing "Year of Europe" debate.[80] From it there eventually emerged the NATO summit of June 1974 and the Ottawa declaration reaffirming the fundamental principles of the alliance.[81] Yet of more immediate consequence for transatlantic relations and for Anglo–French cooperation in Europe was the emphasis placed by Kissinger in Brussels upon the need for a common effort to solve the energy crisis. "The United States," he said, "could solve its energy problems only with great difficulty, Europe could not solve them at all."[82] His audience was, however, still very much divided amongst themselves on how to cope with cuts in oil production and selective restrictions on its export, and the Community was far from devising an agreed energy policy. Britain and France were at one in their reluctance to jeopardize their own supplies, on which they had received assurances from Arab governments, by adopting too confrontational an approach towards producer states. Any attempt openly to frustrate the Arab oil embargo appeared likely to provoke further restrictive actions, and British and French diplomats were sceptical about the value of the EC adopting concrete measures to deal with the embargo which went beyond cooperation on energy conservation and further coordinated démarches towards the Arabs and, possibly, the Israelis. An FCO telegram to Bonn of 10 December argued that the EC should focus on the "development of new relationships between the Community and oil-producing states which alone [could] ensure security of oil supplies to the consumers and technological and industrial development to the producers."[83] As for Jobert, he was ready to work for consumer-producer cooperation, but was resolutely opposed to associating France with any declaration on the energy problem restricted to the consumer nations alone.[84]

Their stance endeared neither the British nor the French to their Dutch and German neighbours, both of whom were trying to cope with severely reduced supplies. It also proved unsustainable in the wake of Kissinger's call on 12 December, in an address to the Pilgrims' Society of Great Britain, for Europe, North America and Japan to join in the formation of an Energy Action Group of senior and distinguished individuals to initiate a programme for dealing with the crisis.[85] This appeal was followed, on 9 January 1974, by Nixon's despatch of invitations to the governments of industrially developed oil-consuming nations to a foreign ministers' conference in Washington with a view to establishing a task force to formulate a consumer action programme.[86] The American move was evidently conceived primarily as a catalyst for mobilising the resources of oil consumer countries. British diplomats nevertheless felt that in the medium and longer terms it offered scope for consumer-producer cooperation of the kind they wanted to promote. It might also stave off the threat of an unseemly scramble amongst the industrially developed nations for oil, and help safeguard Kissinger's efforts to achieve a Middle Eastern settlement. The FCO was in any case concerned lest the Nine once more appear unduly cautious in responding to an American initiative. This appeared only too likely when during a European summit on 14–15 December Heath failed to persuade Pompidou to agree to the EC's welcoming Kissinger's action group proposal. The French considered it too confrontational, and insisted that the Europeans must first elaborate their own energy programme.[87] Likewise, they objected to the American idea for an international energy conference. It would, Quai d'Orsay officials contended, look too much like a front of rich nations lined up against the producer states; and they could see no reason why it should be held in Washington or at foreign minister level.[88] The British were not wholly unsympathetic to the French case.[89] But by January the energy situation appeared to require urgent international action. A meeting of the Organisation of Petroleum Exporting Countries (OPEC) in Tehran had just announced a further doubling in the posted price of oil, thereby effectively quadrupling oil prices since October. This constituted more than just a threat to the balance of payments of individual oil-importing countries: it endangered the global economic system. Britain may have enjoyed better relations with the Arab oil producers than some of its EC partners, and it could look forward to deriving a regular supply of oil and revenue from its unexploited North Sea reserves. Faced, however, by the rising cost of fuel imports, mounting industrial unrest, and more particularly the effects on domestic energy supplies of a miners' overtime ban, Heath's government was persuaded of the need to ensure American cooperation in coping with the broader international crisis.[90]

The previous twelve months had indeed seen a considerable shift in the transatlantic balance of power. At the time of Kissinger's "Year of Europe" speech the United States was having to cope with a serious balance of payments problem and with the consequences of dollar devaluation. Yet, by January 1974, in the eyes of some, only America seemed capable of saving the European economies from the hike in the price of Gulf crude.[91] The American economy had been relatively strengthened by the energy crisis: it stood to attract the surplus funds of oil-producing states and was bound to play a major role in recycling them. And any relaxation in the Arab use of their oil weapon must ultimately depend on some progress towards a Middle Eastern peace settlement and that was inconceivable without American pressure on Israel.[92] These developments were hardly congenial to the French and, although they were eventually persuaded by their Community partners to agree to a positive response to Nixon's conference invitation, the EC mandate, approved at a European Council meeting on 5 February, was far from unambiguous. It declared, as the French insisted, that the Washington conference should not become a permanent body or lead to the institutionalisation of a new forum of international cooperation restricted to the most industrialised countries. None the less, it left open the possibility of establishing a framework of international cooperation. In addition, it reserved for the Community freedom of action to define its own energy policies and its own relations with producer states, but endorsed continuing cooperation with other consumer countries.[93] Jobert continued to voice his doubts about the conference, acting, Tomkins observed, according to French conventional wisdom, which made distrust of the Americans a measure of European cohesion. Yet French behaviour also seemed likely to be determined by Pompidou's wish not to alienate the Americans altogether and his attachment to the Western alliance. Tomkins in any event thought the French would be manageable at Washington, and that it should be possible to achieve this without alienating the Americans or letting the French involve Britain and other EC states in a European failure. "We diverge," he wrote on 9 February, "only where French prejudices take them away from reality. It is thus in a sense an exercise . . . in trying to save them from themselves."[94]

Britain's ambassador to France was far too optimistic. The conference, which opened on 11 February and continued until the 13th, soon ran into difficulties over machinery to coordinate follow-up work. Kissinger proposed a programme for negotiations which would begin with the formation of a coordinating group to carry out consultations, leading via another foreign ministers' meeting to a conference of oil consumers and producers. But this vision was rejected by Jobert. After what Douglas-Home described as a "notably graceless intervention," he and his colleagues put up a staunch resistance to any agreement on continuing consultations, and it was this issue which came to dominate the entire conference.[95] There was, however, a strong feeling amongst other Europeans that on this occasion the French "should not be allowed to get away with it this time," especially when the issues were "too big and their procedural objections too petty." In consequence, during the drafting of a conference communiqué Douglas-Home intervened to give full support to an American text which spelt out in fairly precise terms the concept of continuing consultations. This proved a turning point in the conference. It also placed Britain in direct confrontation with France, though on this occasion Douglas-Home was able to rely on the support of seven other

EC heads of delegation. Jobert continued to fight a tedious rearguard action over a reference in the draft to future consultations on follow-up within the Organisation for Economic Cooperation and Development (OECD). But left isolated at Washington, he was unable to do anything more than express France's dissent from communiqué paragraphs he had earlier endeavoured to emasculate. Even at the cost of France's dissociation, other EC members thus endorsed the force of Kissinger's arguments and agreed to the concept of progress in the energy crisis through joint action with America as distinct from separate and private bargains.[96]

The French were naturally aggrieved at the outcome of the conference. In their view they had been betrayed by partners who had failed to respect either the Community mandate or Europe's independence. Kissinger had, according to their analysis, wanted to reduce the EC to an "American poodle":[97] he had lured European foreign ministers to Washington, and he had there exposed their disarray. Admittedly, French anger was not directed solely against Britain. It extended to other partners who had also deserted them, particularly the West Germans, who held the EC presidency and whose foreign minister, Walter Scheel, represented the Community at the conference.[98] None the less, the gathering had, as Tomkins had earlier predicted, brought "to a point of uncomfortable focus the central problem of our convergences and divergences with the French over the position of Europe vis-à-vis the United States and over the balance of our European and Atlantic connections."[99] British diplomats had once hoped that Community membership would enhance their influence in Washington, and they had long since recognised that little could be achieved with, or within, the Community in opposition to France. They had also been fully alive to the dangers of Britain, through its close ties with the United States, appearing to act as an agent of Washington in Brussels. It was unfortunate that during their first full year in the EC they had to deal with an American administration that evidently expected more from them in Europe than they could possibly deliver, and a French government which set its Gaullist face steadfastly against any transatlantic gesture which might appear to formalise Western Europe's subordination to America. Had there been no Arab–Israeli war, and no subsequent oil embargo and rise in fuel prices, the British would probably have been able eventually to coax the French into subscribing to an EC/US declaration, less substantial than that originally desired by Washington, yet nonetheless acceptable to Nixon and Kissinger.[100] But when, at the energy conference, the British were forced to choose between what they perceived as the "economic realities" of the situation and respect for the political susceptibilities of the French, they chose the former. French obduracy seemed to stand in the way of the adoption of practical solutions to handling a global crisis.

The disappointment felt by British diplomats over the failure of the Nine to maintain any semblance of unity at Washington was but one manifestation of a growing sense of disaffection with the broader European project.[101] In conversation with Philippe Cuvillier, counsellor at the French embassy in London, on 15 February, Oliver Wright, who had himself been a participant in the conference, admitted that there was no denying the Community had been damaged. "Those," he said, "who argued in Whitehall that British interests were best pursued through the Community would now find their position significantly weakened." In reply, Cuvillier simply remarked that "the European identity had been a dream with a short life."[102] Within a fortnight a general election, itself in part a by-product of the energy crisis, deprived Heath's government of its majority in parliament and Douglas-Home was replaced at the FCO by James Callaghan, a secretary of state with distinctly eurosceptic inclinations. By then America's "Year of Europe" was over;[103] so too in some respects was Britain's. Political cooperation amongst the Nine continued and proved highly successful in the context of the ongoing Conference on Security and Cooperation in Europe,[104] and Callaghan, though determined to give priority to the "special relationship," appears to have found it easier to collaborate with Britain's European partners than with the United States when it came to responding to the challenges posed by political change in Spain and Portugal.[105] None the less, since 1974 no British prime minister has been so committed, either to European integration or to the maintenance of Anglo–French understanding, as was Edward Heath. The *entente cordiale* he had helped revive differed in form and purpose from its Edwardian predecessor. The latter had in the first instance been about managing extra-European rivalries and only later did it evolve into a *quasi* continental alliance. That of the early 1970s was intended to facilitate Britain's accession to the European Community: its development was constrained by differing perceptions of the transatlantic relationship and Europe's future role upon the world stage. On 12 December 1973 Douglas-Home publicly assured Kissinger that the Nine were not seeking a position half-way between the Communist powers and the United States. "We are," he declared, "not a Third Force. We are a second force at your side." As Michael Palliser subsequently commented, it was questionable whether that view was shared by the French.[106]

NOTES

1. Record of conversation between Edward Heath and Georges Pompidou, 22 May 1973. DBPO3, iv, no. 98.
2. Cited in David Hannay (Ed.), *Britain's Entry into the European Community: Report by Sir Con O'Neill on the Negotiations of 1970–1972* (London: Whitehall History Publishing/Frank Cass, 2000), p. 402.

3. See Joanne Wright, "The Cold War, European Community and Anglo-French Relations, 1958–1998" in Alan Sharp and Glyn Stone (Eds.), *Anglo-French Relations in the Twentieth Century. Rivalry and Cooperation* (London: Routledge, 2000), p.325; and Alan Milward, *The United Kingdom and the European Community, Vol. I: The Rise and Fall of a National Strategy, 1945–1963* (Whitehall History Publishing/Frank Cass, 2002), pp. 463–83.

4. DBPO3, iv, no. 1.

5. The National Archives (formerly the Public Record Office) at Kew, London. CAB 164/1235, GEN 161, FCO Planning Staff draft paper enclosed in N.P. Bayne to B.M. Webster, 20 Aug. 1973.

6. K. A. Hamilton, "A 'Week that changed the World': Britain and Nixon's China Visit of 21–22 Feb. 1972," *Diplomacy and Statecraft*, 15/1 (2004), pp. 117–135.

7. See note 5 above. DBPO3, iv, no. 14.

8. Ibid., no. 2.

9. Ibid., no. 12.

10. Ibid., nos. 4, 8 and 12.

11. Ibid., nos. 97 and 101.

12. Pompidou made this remark in an interview with James Reston, published in the *New York Times* of 14 December 1972. Henry Kissinger, *Years of Upheaval* (London: Phoenix Press paperback edition, 2000), pp. 130–1.

13. DBPO3, iv, no. 98.

14. See note 5 above.

15. DBPO3, iv, no. 210.

16. Ibid., no. 29.

17. Ibid., no. 20.

18. Ibid., nos. 15, 17, 32, 44, 59–61, 95 and 131. The text of the agreement is printed in *Weekly Compilation of Presidential Documents* (Washington: NARA, 1973), vol. ix, p. 822. See also for a French view of the agreement: Michel Jobert, *Mémoires d'Avenir* (Paris: Bernard Grasset, 1974), p. 241.

19. DBPO3, iv, nos. 62, 65, 69, 70, 75 and 95.

20. Ibid., no. 70.

21. Ibid., no. 71.

22. Ibid., no. 77.

23. Ibid., no. 79. Heath later commented on the exercise: "For Henry Kissinger to announce a Year of Europe without consulting any of us was rather like my standing between the lions in Trafalgar Square and announcing that we were embarking on a year to save America!." Edward Heath, *The Course of My Life: My Autobiography* (London: Hodder and Stoughton, 1999), p. 493. This, however, overlooked the fact that, according to Kissinger, even if the European powers had not been consulted, the French, the Italians and the West Germans, had, like the British, all been informed of the speech's content prior to its delivery. Kissinger, *Years of Upheaval*, pp. 147–50.

24. DBPO3, iv, no. 78.

25. Ibid., no. 75.

26. Jobert, *Mémoires d'Avenir*, p. 232.

27. DBPO3, iv, no. 81.

28. Indeed, according to Kissinger, on this occasion Jobert left him under the impression "that in the end he would not only go along but take the lead in shaping an outcome consonant with our objectives," provided he was "permitted to play the leading role and that we not use the Year of Europe to isolate France within the Community." Kissinger, *Years of Upheaval*, pp. 164–5.
29. DBPO3, iv, no. 98.
30. Ibid., nos. 102–04.
31. Kissinger, *Years of Upheaval*, p. 162.
32. DBPO3, iv, no. 106.
33. Kissinger, *Years of Upheaval*, p. 180. DBPO, e-vol. I, nos. 110 and 115.
34. Ibid.
35. Kissinger, *Years of Upheaval*, p. 165.
36. DBPO3, iv, no. 114.
37. Ibid.
38. Ibid., no. 108.
39. Ibid., nos. 117 and 135.
40. Ibid., nos. 123–4.
41. Ibid., no. 130.
42. Ibid., no. 144.
43. Ibid., no. 137.
44. Ibid., nos. 145–6.
45. Kissinger, *Years of Upheaval*, p. 171.
46. DBPO3, iv, no. 164.
47. Ibid., nos. 167–71. Kissinger, *Years of Upheaval*, p. 181.
48. DBPO3, iv, no. 179.
49. Ibid., nos. 181–2.
50. Ibid., nos. 192–3.
51. Ibid., no. 201.
52. At the beginning of July the West German Foreign Ministry had supplied Washington with its own substantial draft of a transatlantic declaration. Kissinger, *Years of Upheaval*, p. 186.
53. DBPO3, iv, nos. 209–11.
54. Ibid., nos. 219–22 and 226–7.
55. Ibid., no. 221.
56. Ibid., no. 232.
57. Ibid., no. 201.
58. Ibid., no. 254.
59. Ibid. no. 257. Kissinger, *Years of Upheaval*, pp. 705–6.
60. DBPO3, IV, nos. 307–8.
61. Ibid., nos. 240–1.
62. Ibid., nos. 307–8.
63. Ibid., nos. 57, 63 and 109.
64. Ibid., nos. 267, 269–70, 274–8 and 280–2.
65. Ibid., no. 328.
66. Ibid., nos. 329, 332 and 371.
67. Ibid., nos. 396–7.

68. On the background to the 1973–74 energy crisis and its diplomatic conse-quences see: Fiona Venn, "International Co-operation versus National Self-Interest: the United States and Europe during the 1973–1974 Oil Crisis" in Kathleen Burke and Melvyn Stokes (Eds.), *The United States and the European Alliance since 1945* (Oxford: Berg Press, 1999), pp. 71–97.
69. DBPO3, iv, nos. 362 and 365.
70. Ibid., no. 383.
71. Kissinger, *Years of Upheaval*, p. 718.
72. DBPO, e-vol. I, no. 379.
73. Ibid., no. 394.
74. Ibid., nos. 385–6, 393, 400–03, and 424.
75. Ibid., no. 360.
76. Ibid., no. 412.
77. Ibid., nos. 420–1.
78. Ibid., nos. 405 and 416.
79. Ibid., nos. 425–6.
80. Ibid., nos. 449–50.
81. Cmnd 6932, *Selected Documents Relating to Problems of Security and Cooperation in Europe, 1954–77* (London: HMSO, 1977), pp. 184–6.
82. DBPO3, iv, no. 447.
83. Ibid., nos. 445–6.
84. Ibid., no. 448.
85. Kissinger, *Years of Upheaval*, pp. 725–6.
86. DBPO3, iv, nos. 493–5.
87. Ibid., no. 489.
88. Ibid., nos. 499, 501, and 505.
89. Douglas-Home argued that a favourable EC response to Nixon's invitation would not "preclude any or all of us from making the point that producers and other developing countries ought to be brought in virtually from the beginning." Ibid., no. 502.
90. John Campbell, *Edward Heath. A Biography* (London: Jonathan Cape, 1993), pp. 561–97. DBPO3, iv, no. 516.
91. "Our overriding objective," noted Douglas-Home in a telegram of 25 January 1974, "is to seize the opportunity afforded by the Washington Conference to engage the co-operation of the Americans in the solution to the world's energy problems." Ibid.
92. Ibid., no. 539.
93. Ibid., nos. 534–5 and 543.
94. Ibid., nos. 544 and 547.
95. Ibid., nos. 548–9.
96. Ibid., nos. 550–1, 553 and 562. One result of the Washington energy conference was the creation in November 1974 of the International Energy Agency (IEA) as an adjunct to the OECD. France was not a member. Venn, "International Co-operation versus National Self-Interest," pp. 86–8.
97. DBPO3, iv, no. 552.
98. Ibid., no. 559.
99. Ibid., no. 547.

100. Nixon suspended further work on an EC/U.S. declaration following the Nine's decision on 4 March 1974 to proceed with a Euro-Arab dialogue culminating with a meeting of Arab foreign ministers. Kissinger, *Years of Upheaval*, pp. 929–34.

101. Rising food prices during 1973 were widely, though wrongly, perceived by the British public as resulting from Community membership. But at a diplomatic level there was disappointment over the EC's failure to agree on the establishment of a regional development fund and the lack of progress towards economic and monetary union.

102. DBPO3, iv, no. 554.

103. For a useful summary of subsequent developments in relations between the US and the Europeans in both the EC and NATO contexts, see: Eugène Berg, *La Politique Internationale depuis 1955* (Paris: Economica, 1989), pp. 452–55.

104. Keith Hamilton, *The Last Cold Warriors: Britain, Détente and the CSCE, 1972–1975* (Oxford: European Interdependence Research Unit, 1999).

105. British policy towards Spain and Portugal during 1974–76 is documented in *Documents on British Policy Overseas*, Series III, Vol. IV, *The Southern Flank in Crisis, 1973–76* (London: Whitehall History Publishing/Routledge, 2006) See also on the foreign relations of the incoming Labour government: Ann Lane, "Foreign and Defence Policy," in Anthony Seldon and Kevin Hickson (Eds.), *New Labour, Old Labour. The Wilson and Callaghan Governments, 1974–79* (London: Routledge, 2004), pp. 154–69.

106. DBPO3, iv, no. 517.

NOTES ON CONTRIBUTORS

Christopher Baxter is currently a Research Fellow at Queen's University Belfast, having previously worked for the Foreign and Commonwealth Office as one of their resident historians. He has worked for Professor Sir Lawrence Freedman as the principal researcher on the Official History of the Falklands Campaign and has published "In Pursuit of a Pacific Strategy: British Planning for the Defeat of Japan, 1943–45," *Diplomacy and Statecraft*, 15/2 (2004).

Philip Bell, formerly of the University of Liverpool and now retired, is widely considered to be the leading authority on the history of Anglo-French relations in the twentieth century. He has published numerous works on this and other subjects, including *France and Britain, 1900–1940: Entente and Estrangement* (1996), *France and Britain, 1940–1994: The Long Separation* (1997), and *The World since 1945: An International History* (2001).

David Brown is a Lecturer in Modern British History at the University of Strathclyde. His principal research interests lie in the field of nineteenth century British political history, including foreign policy. Among his publications are *Palmerston and the Politics of Foreign Policy, 1846–1855* (2002) and (co-ed.), *Palmerston Studies* (2 vols., 2005). He is currently writing a biography of Lord Palmerston.

John Charmley is Professor of Modern History at the University of East Anglia. He is the biographer of Duff Cooper, Lord Lloyd and Winston Churchill. Among his publications are *Churchill's Grand Alliance* (1995), *Splendid Isolation?: Britain and the Balance of Power, 1874–1914* (1999), and *Princess Lieven and the Politicians* (2005).

Anne Deighton is a lecturer in European International Politics in the Department of Politics and International Relations at the University of Oxford, and is a fellow of Wolfson College. She is currently on leave at the Geneva Centre for Security Policy, Switzerland. She has published extensively on British foreign policy; the Cold War; and contemporary European security. She is currently working on a study of the international career of Ernest Bevin.

James Ellison is Senior Lecturer in Modern and Contemporary History at Queen Mary, University of London. He is a specialist on Anglo–American and Anglo–European relations after 1945 and has a specific interest in the history of the Cold War and European integration. Anglo–French relations are a particular theme in his research as can be seen in his first book, *Threatening Europe: Britain and the Creation of the European Community, 1955–1958*. They are also an important feature of his next book on Anglo–American relations and the Gaullist challenge of the 1960s.

Keith Hamilton is a retired civil servant, having worked previously as a historian for the Foreign and Commonwealth Office. He co-edits with Professor Patrick Salmon the series *Documents on British Policy Overseas*, the latest volumes of which, *The Year of Europe: America, Europe and the Energy Crisis, 1972–1974*, and *The Southern Flank in Crisis, 1973–1976*, are currently awaiting publication.

Gaynor Johnson is Senior Lecturer in History at the University of Bolton. She is the author of *The Berlin Embassy of Lord D'Abernon, 1920–1926* (2002) and is the editor of *Locano Revisited: European Diplomacy, 1920–1929* (2004) as well as a number of other books on British foreign policy in the twentieth century. She is currently writing a biography of Viscount Cecil of Chelwood.

T. G. Otte is Lecturer in Diplomatic History at the University of East Anglia. He specialises in nineteenth century Great Power relations and has published or edited five books, the most recent being (co-ed.), *The Path of Empire: Railways in International Politics, 1848–1945* (2006). A monograph on the Permanent Under-Secretaries of the Foreign Office is forthcoming (2007). He is currently working on a study of the "Foreign Office Mind, 1856–1914."

William Philpott is Lecturer in War Studies at King's College London, specialising in twentieth century military history, particularly Anglo-French military relations. Among his many publications are *Anglo-French Relations and Strategy on the Western Front* (1996) and (co-ed), *Anglo-French Defence Relations between the Wars* (2002).

Alan Sked is Senior Lecturer in International History at the London School of Economics. His expertise lies especially in the field of Austro-Hungarian history. Among his numerous publications are *The Survival of the Habsburg Empire: Radetzky, the Imperial Army and the Class War* (1979), *The Decline and Fall of the Habsburg Empire, 1815-1918* (1989), *Post-war Britain* (1993) and *An Intelligent Person's*

Guide to Post-War Britain (1997). He is currently writing a study on Prince Metternich.

Glyn Stone is Professor of International History, University of the West of England, Bristol. His research focuses on Anglo–French and Anglo–Portuguese relations before, during and after the Second World War and he has a particular interest in the international politics of the Spanish Civil War (1936–39). His publications include *The Oldest Ally: Britain and the Portuguese Connection, 1936–1941* (1994), *Spain, Portugal and the Great Powers, 1931–1941* (2005) and *Anglo-French Relations in the Twentieth Century: Rivalry and Cooperation* (2000) (co-edited with Professor Alan Sharp). He is Secretary of the British International History Group.

Martin Thomas is Reader in Colonial History at the University of Exeter. He is the author of numerous works, including *The French Empire at War, 1940–1945* (1998) and *The French Empire between the Wars: Imperialism, Politics and Society* (2005). His latest book *Empires of Intelligence: Security Services and Colonial Disorder* is forthcoming with the University of California Press.

David R. Watson, formerly of the University of Dundee and now retired, is Georges Clemenceau's leading English-language biographer (1974). He is the author of numerous publications on nineteenth and twentieth century French history and Anglo–French relations.

INDEX

Printed in Poland
by Amazon Fulfillment
Poland Sp. z o.o., Wrocław

53983112R00161